SARAH BROWN

Behind the Black Door

EBURY
PRESS

KT-573-284

1 3 5 7 9 10 8 6 4 2

This edition published 2012
First published in 2011 by Ebury Press, an imprint of Ebury Publishing
A Random House Group company

The Random House Group Limited Reg. No. 954009

Addresses for companies within the Random House Group can be found at
www.randomhouse.co.uk

A CIP catalogue record for this book is available from the British Library

The Random House Group Limited supports The Forest Stewardship Council
(FSC®), the leading international forest certification organisation. Our books
carrying the FSC label are printed on FSC® certified paper. FSC is the only forest
certification scheme endorsed by the leading environmental organisations, including
Greenpeace. Our paper procurement policy can be found at
www.randomhouse.co.uk/environment

Printed and bound by CPI Group (UK) Ltd, Croydon, CR0 4YY

ISBN 9780091940584

To buy books by your favourite authors and register for offers visit
www.randomhouse.co.uk

For Gordon, John and Fraser
And remembering Jennifer,
always

Contents

Preface

In writing this book, I hope to cast a light on the role of the Prime Minister's spouse and all that it entails. As the wife of Gordon Brown, I spent three years living and working at Number 10 Downing Street. It was a time of immense change and upheaval, a time that included the global financial crisis, the MPs' expenses scandal and great public disaffection with politicians, along with much hard-earned progress and reform for our schools, hospitals, families and communities.

This book is not the autobiography of my whole life, but an attempt to open up the day-to-day business behind the scenes of ongoing politics, and to share what that looked like and felt like – to share what made me laugh and cry the most.

I was advised before I started at Number 10 that there is no guidebook for what to do, only a big rulebook of what not to do. The 'not to' bit seemed to be just commonsense, but the blank page of what a PM's spouse can do, and perhaps even should do, was a welcome opportunity to start from scratch. There is no formal spouse job to step into, no permanent office, no salary, no allowance, no pre-set duties or official role, not even an official title, but I did have ten years' experience in hosting receptions and dinners as first the girlfriend, then the wife, of the Chancellor of the Exchequer to stand me in good stead.

Before Downing Street, I had worked all my life, starting as a Saturday girl in a gift shop in North London, followed by three years at university at Bristol, then working my way up to running my own business. Nonetheless, it seemed right to do justice to the huge privilege of my new role, and set aside my formal career for a while, while I supported Gordon and the kids and focused completely on the causes and campaigns closest to my heart.

We live in a time of rapid change thanks partly to the internet; of rising national insecurity, terrorism and environmental catastrophe. We also live in a world where one billion people don't get enough to eat every day, and half of them are in Africa; where we don't value girls enough, protect families sufficiently well and need to solve the problem of global poverty. However, we also live in a time where being in public office offers a real chance to do some good, which is as it should be.

I was able to get behind some powerful issues and use every ounce of my thinking, writing, and (over time) public-speaking skills as well as some gentle diplomacy of my own. With only a small team, our efforts required my own brand of leadership and organisational dexterity. The catchphrase of my office was pretty much 'we know how to make a little go a long way'. We supported and promoted British interests and causes all around the world, from taking the chair at the United Nations in New York to the British handover at the end of the Beijing Olympics.

We opened up the doors of Number 10 to as many VIP visits, charities and inspiring individuals as we could accommodate. Plus we greeted and received all the visitors from around the globe and down the road who came to experience Number 10 firsthand – an extraordinary historic building that started life as an unfinished property development.

I am fortunate to have a circle of good friends and family members who stepped up to help out in all kinds of ways, from being on hand to greet guests to just sitting me down with a cup of tea or glass of wine to unwind. I also met many new people and formed new friendships from SureStart centre managers to CEOs of great businesses, from super-models to super-nurses. I suspect I made the odd enemy, too, but I hope only because I was loyal and determined to be the best I could.

I discovered that every day out in public as the Prime Minister's spouse meant a day of great scrutiny of what I was wearing. This could become a chore, but I was delighted to wear clothes and accessories from some of Britain's established and emerging designers. And while I've never pretended to be a fashion model myself, I have certainly taken my turn standing next to some of the world's most beautiful women and I have learnt to enjoy looking good in my own way next to them, too!

To get the most out of my time at Number 10 I knew I needed to just put my all into it. I know I was a frenetically busy person during my time there (as friends and family will attest), and thankfully may never need to be quite so busy again. I could land back from a trip representing Britain on the far side of the world, and then slip back into the kitchen to make a family meal, and by the evening find myself struggling for recognition on a guest list to enter a trendy Soho club to attend a friend's book launch. I could step out of our flat some mornings to meet a visiting President or a Hollywood movie star, and then within hours be on the school run chatting to other mums and dads in the playground about afterschool clubs and the end-of-term play.

Our own children were kept well away from the forefront of our public life, but in attending local schools were still able to experience many memorable moments. Without intruding on their own privacy, I have attempted to share what our family life was like when one floor below great matters of state were being discussed and international crises resolved. John and Fraser arrived as very tiny people but walked out with us for the last time, fully aware that as a family we were all very proud of each other — and relishing the time we could now spend together (book writing not withstanding).

But I have no regrets. I take a great deal of pride in our many achievements and can't wait to share the story of one of the most daunting and exciting times of my life.

Here is my version of what life is like – from the inside.

CHAPTER 1

Taking Office

2007

Wednesday 27th June

Gordon and I are standing in his office in the Treasury building, where he has served as Chancellor of the Exchequer for the past ten years. Three days ago, he was voted the leader of the Labour Party and is now about to go to Buckingham Palace to take up the office of Prime Minister. I am at his side, preparing to forge my own path as the 'consort'. To me, this means keeping up our ordinary family life while embracing whatever official duties and charity engagements come my way.

The Permanent Secretary, Sir Nick Macpherson, and key members of the civil service team, like his Principal Private Secretary James Bowler, are on hand to see us out. They handle everything very calmly and efficiently but there is a frisson in the air. The political team are all there to say goodbye as well, and then dash off as they, too, make the move to 10 Downing Street today.

Everything is happening very quickly. I watch Gordon sign some last-minute documents, including outgoing Prime Minister Tony Blair's resignation letter as MP.

This is a moment that I don't know if either of us thought would ever come. I have always understood that because Gordon is Gordon, he has every likelihood of reaching the top in politics. However, the golden rule in politics seems to be to plan and hope for everything – and nothing. So I decided very early on that I would keep up my own interests and maintain a fairly calm reserve for whatever our future together held.

Gordon has been at the very centre of the past decade of government, at the heart of the Labour Party, and part of a small, highly visible team who had seen the Labour Party through its change and modernisation, through its journey to become the party of both fairness and prosperity, of wealth creation and social justice.

His focus has always been on what he could achieve through his work – not always smoothly, not always making it easy for himself – but unquestionably focused on making the world a better place, especially for the poorest and most vulnerable in our society.

For my part, I had known Gordon for more than a decade, and been married to him since 2000 in the full glare of publicity, which came with his high profile. I had met Gordon while doing some work for the Labour Party organising a business dinner for the former party leader, the late John Smith. In the last few years, I had stepped sideways from a successful career of my own, had two young sons, and engaged with numerous campaigns and charitable causes, thereby forging my own new path.

There is a strangeness to the change of leadership today, an odd calm, but also a sense of the massive change to our lives looming on the horizon. I do not feel ready for the change and also cannot predict how different life will be moving from Number 11, Downing Street, as wife of the Chancellor of the Exchequer, to Number 10, as wife of the Prime Minister. But I am well used to hosting receptions, attending government dinners, being a charity patron and going on numerous charity visits. I have also campaigned with the Labour Party for many years so I feel pretty well prepared for whatever lies ahead, without expectations of dramatic personal change.

During Gordon's time at Number 11, I often described Downing Street as a public building with no public access. I felt one of my roles was to open up the buildings to as many different groups of people as possible, so they could enjoy its history and interiors, and celebrate their own achievements and activities. I hope to continue this, and apply the same approach, at Number 10.

Now Gordon is about to walk through the famous black door of Number 10. We leave the Treasury, walking past the open-plan offices and corridors. He had been cheered to the rafters when coming in to the Treasury in 1997 and now, a decade later, is being seen out with tremendous pride and warmth by the staff. Hundreds of staff assemble in the atrium and hundreds more are spilling along the stairwells, hanging off the banisters and railings, clapping and cheering Gordon on his way. The sound echoes off the ceiling – a great big, happy sound from a hard-working team of people who all know they were part of a very special period that oversaw 11 Budgets, the creation of an independent Bank of England, the introduction of a minimum wage, increased investment in public services and strong economic prosperity.

At the entrance to the Treasury building overlooking St James's Park, we jump into the back of Gordon's ministerial car driven by his long-serving driver, and go straight to Buckingham Palace. As we drive up the Mall, we can see throngs of people lining the streets, many clapping and waving us on our way. I suddenly feel quite self-conscious, as though everyone can see us in microscopic detail, even though it is obvious that to the friendly bystanders we will be just a blur whizzing past. This is such an important moment in our lives and it is all happening so fast. I feel quite apprehensive, but still have a little calm part of me that is enjoying it all.

We drive through the palace's gates and across the palace courtyard, where Gordon is whisked upstairs. Someone explains that a BBC documentary about the Queen is being made so our every movement will be captured as part of it. I am taken to a side room and engaged in delightful conversation by the lady-in-waiting. This serves to distract me perfectly from any chance of getting (more) nervous. I am wearing a pretty red floral dress by Katherine Hooker, a cream jacket with matching red trim, and some snazzy

3

red patent sling-backs with quite high heels. It seems suitable given it is a summery June day. I keep wondering whether my skirt will be creased when I stand up again.

Protocol demands that the new PM meets the Queen and that the spouse joins them only at the end, for the final part of that conversation (protocol also demands that the PM's conversations with the Queen stay private).

As we descend the staircase to leave Buckingham Palace, Gordon is now officially the Prime Minister of Great Britain and Northern Ireland and Head of Her Majesty's Government.

The first visible change is the car – a huge armour-plated Jaguar, which is introduced by the new driver as 'Pegasus'. A car with a name; this is new. The security team for Gordon is unchanged, though expanded in number.

The car door is opened for us on each side. I look up and see that a live broadcast film crew is recording every moment, then, as I jump in, I whack my head on the roof of the car. I learn fast that Pegasus has a much lower roof than we're used to, and that its mighty armoured ceiling is very hard indeed! Mindful that this is a good moment for smiling in front of the cameras, I literally fight back tears and grin.

I do not want to miss a moment so I ignore the bump. I don't even tell Gordon, but leave him to go over his thoughts for what he wants to say outside Downing Street. I just sit, looking out of the windows on to the Mall, hearing a great hush. It dawns on me that all the hefty armour-plating means the car is effectively sound-proofed. I can still see people outside waving and cheering but it is as though they are all miming, and in slow motion. We curve around St James's Park and across Parliament Square – passing Winston Churchill's statue – and back into Whitehall.

At the entrance to Downing Street, the familiar black gates open and we stop to get out and walk up the street. The media are stacked three-high on temporary scaffolding opposite the entrance to Number 10. All the cameras and microphones are pointing in one direction – towards that black door.

Gordon stops at the microphone set up in front of the massed cameras. I stand next to him and just listen. I have heard many Gordon speeches in my time, many of them wonderfully stirring, uplifting and wise – calling for political support, offering economic guidance and passionately urging change in the UK and around the world.

Today, his words are simple and heartfelt. He promises, as his own school motto said, 'to do his utmost'. I know that the same will go for me, too.

We turn to the door, greeting the policeman on duty. We do not need to knock. The door opens and we walk inside. It is time to play our part in contributing to what happens next in government and a new life behind the black door.

CHAPTER 2

Crossing the Threshold

Wednesday 27th June

The door opens and Cabinet Secretary Sir Gus O'Donnell welcomes us, giving me a hug. We walk through to be greeted by the tradition of staff clapping their new PM in. Gordon shakes everyone by the hand and warmly greets those he already knows but there are plenty of new faces, too. We both move down the long corridor inside Number 10 beyond the Cabinet Room where, right at the end, our little boys John and Fraser are waiting with other family members and close friends. Here we all take a moment for lots of hugs. But not for long.

Gordon has to turn his attention immediately to the recent floods that are causing such destruction around the country. He heads off to the Cabinet Room and to find his new office while I take the boys up to the flat we live in, a couple of floors up. We actually live above Number 10 while the Blair family have lived until today in the bigger flat at Number 11 in an arrangement agreed back in 1997 to accommodate their larger family numbers. As we calm down after the excitement, my sister-in-law, Clare (an environmental journalist married to Gordon's younger brother Andrew), makes cups of tea, and I reach for the phone to call my mum, Pauline, and stepfather, Patrick, just to check in with them. They came to the Leadership conference a few days earlier when Gordon was elected as Labour leader in Manchester, and we will catch up properly very soon, but it is nice to hear their voices. The boys are happy playing so I turn my attention to what needs to happen next.

One of the first things I have to deal with is the issue of accommodation and security. We have been living in the flat above 10 Downing Street for the past two years, but now we have to decide about moving to the neighbouring flat at Number 11.

The Number 11 flat offers more space for the children and more privacy. A small lift allows visitors to come and go from the back entrance, and the boys can go directly down to the garden without going through the main building. Added to this, the protection team is keen on the move, thanks to a number of added safety features.

I had put off making any decision in the run-up to Gordon being sworn in as PM as, to be honest, it just felt a bit unseemly and frankly unfair on the Blair family while they enjoyed their last bit of time in what had been their main home for a decade. Cherie Blair kindly offered to show me around but I could not believe that she wanted to think about new occupants while she was focusing on her own big move.

So, instead of packing boxes, the first meeting I take is a conversation about personal protection. Since 9/11, the issue of security has been greatly heightened. Visitors to Downing Street have to go through the big black steel gates on Whitehall (installed in 1989 in response to the IRA threat) and a permanent security scanner, after they have been checked on a list and have shown proof of identity.

Gordon has had personal protection since the London bombings in July 2005 when a direct threat was made against him. Prior to that, even as Chancellor of the Exchequer, he managed without, although there had been some uncomfortable moments when just out for a morning run or walking through an airport. Of course, all current and former Prime Ministers have security protection and that won't change.

As a family, we have become very used to operating with Gordon's protection team. I often joke that spontaneous moments have to be thoroughly organised in advance, but the reality is that you have to notify the security team for even a short walk, and intimate dinners in restaurants are a thing of the past. We are delighted to learn that a number of Gordon's team from the Treasury protection team (Gary Richmond, Stuart Lockwood and Craig Rowe) are moving across to Number 10. It is so much easier for the children to deal with familiar adults who lurk about with their dad, rather than strange new men in dark suits with bulky jacket pockets.

I agree with Gordon before my meeting that we will take the advice of the Metropolitan Police and the Home Office. I am mindful that Cherie had had full protection (which continued for some months after she left Number 10), and did not relish the prospect. The Home Office recognise that I am not as high profile as Cherie and are looking for ways to minimise any security issues. Frankly, I think they also see an opportunity to clip a bit of their Budget and please the Treasury, too.

We all agree that I will provide my diary to the police team who will then assign protection if they think it necessary, such as at public-speaking engagements or big government visits. What still concerns them is how I and/or the boys will get away if some incident (of any nature) arises. Left to our own devices we would just walk away and hope to find a taxi or jump on a bus quickly. But this does not exactly qualify as a speedy exit by Met standards. The happy conclusion to this discussion comes in the form of Mr Roy Gibbons MBE. Roy was Gordon's driver at the Treasury for ten years and, before that, Kenneth Clarke's when he was Chancellor. Roy's two decades of government service earned him his much-treasured MBE and we already know him well (his lovely wife, Monica, always remembers our boys' birthdays and makes a delicious Jamaican ginger cake).

As Gordon now has a police driver, it is agreed that Roy will become the driver for me and my family, which means we can have a 'getaway car' instead of full-scale protection. We could not have asked for a better person to get us around the place. I sneakily didn't surrender my Oyster card (though no one actually asked!), because there will doubtless be times when the boys and I will have to go in different directions. I can then send them off in the car with Roy and take the Tube, or hail a cab at the back of Downing Street. As time goes on, this may get harder to do without being recognised, but in all my years as wife of the Chancellor of the Exchequer, I pretty much encountered huge amounts of goodwill wherever I went. I also think that when people are not expecting to see you on the Underground, they tend not to recognise you. However, I was once spotted by a political journalist who said 'hello' in a friendly way, and then duly wrote about it in his Sunday newspaper. After that I was a bit more careful, and kept my public transport travels a bit more discreet, by avoiding the nearest Tube stations and bus stops and walking the last bit back. While not opting for a full 'dark glasses and pulled-down hat' disguise, I do also take care to dress so I don't attract extra attention.

Another important person assigned to look after the family is Clare Cains, our housekeeper. Clare hails from Ireland and lives with her beloved husband John and family in south London, and has worked as part of the Downing Street cleaning staff for many years. The cleaners at Downing Street are all women, all with strong views and a great sense of humour. They have a cleaning rota that lets them work around the building, keeping it spotless without getting in the way of the daily work that goes on there.

About 200 people work in the Downing Street offices, mostly civil servants for the government of the day, and a further team of political staff that the PM appoints. Of course, there are lots of 'pointy heads' – the policy staff and private secretaries who focus on the business of government – but the support teams include clerks and secretaries, IT and digital communications, press officers, events support and the custodians at the famous door. Underpinning all of them are the formidable cleaners.

These women know their way around the whole building, all its staircases and annexes; to this day, I am not sure that I do.

Many of them arrive for work in the early hours so they are rarely seen by visitors, and never caught on camera. Clare got to know all the family's different needs and various habits very well: she would rescue Gordon's suit jackets from the backs of chairs, find Fraser's shoes in the hallway, and know where John had left his homework bag. She takes very great care of us all and understands the pace of everyone's lives, which all too often means that she is literally picking up the trail of various belongings around the flat.

The situation with living in a Downing Street flat is that it becomes your main residence, and the value of living there is charged to you via the tax system. This means that we pay extra tax to allow for the fact that being in a Downing Street flat is an in-kind benefit that comes on top of the PM/Chancellor's salary. This is worked out as the value of having the flat and main bills paid, including some of Clare's time looking after us in the flat. On top of that we, as the 'tenants', pay the council tax to Westminster Council, our family TV subscription, and TV licence. I get asked about this a lot – there seems to be a great deal of public interest in every aspect of our homelife. We are also registered to vote from that address.

Thursday 28th June

As soon as I hear that Alistair Darling is to be the new Chancellor, I get hold of his wife, Maggie, already a great friend, and agree we will make the move to Number 11 but with no great hurry.

Apart from signing up to pay our council tax, my initial time revolves around meeting everyone I can who works in the building and talking about everything; from stationery to access to a computer with a new secure email address. I do break out at one point and take the boys to go and visit my school friend, Ailsa, and her boys, who live just outside London, for a bit of real air and normality. I am already aware of what a bubble it can be in Downing Street, so it is worth the foray out to see the real world.

Meanwhile, Gordon has the exciting job of appointing his new Cabinet and, in the days to come, all the other Ministers. I have to say it is uplifting to see Gordon's own Cabinet all in place, coming in for their first meeting.

CHAPTER 3

First Decisions

Friday 29th June

I am all too aware that my appearance and fashion sense will come under scrutiny. I arrive at Number 10 with a toddler and a baby – John is not yet three, and Fraser is only 11 months old – and am not exactly feeling my fashionable best. Having children definitely changed the way I look. During pregnancy and in the months after birth, I gained weight, found less time for the gym, and even less time for any kind of beauty treatments. I am suffering from the sleep deprivation that many mothers of small children will understand is a tiredness like no other. Some days, brushing my teeth is all I can manage first thing, and brushing my hair comes a bit later, as an added extra.

I know exactly how long it takes to get ready for a red-carpet event, where photographers with long lenses are picking out who appears in the next day's papers. But the idea that I am to find time for perfect hair, nails, spray tan, eyebrow threading and skin-rejuvenating wraps is amusing at best. Some may think I should invest more in my presentation, but it just isn't practical or affordable, given there is no official allowance for the wardrobe of the spouse of the PM (or, in fact, for the PM, either). I decide early on to go for a neutral look that won't do me down, but also won't make me stand out.

I love looking at women in great clothes looking fabulous in magazines as much as anyone, but my definition of what looks great also extends across a diverse spectrum of the way women look. I love clothes and the ever-circulating trends as fashions get reinterpreted for different decades. I worked in Soho for a long time and so was dangerously close to Liberty's and in the same road as Ben de Lisi's studio. I am also interested in how our fashion industry works, how it affects and influences so many people through our designers, our high streets and across multi-media. In Britain, we have some of the most brilliant, innovative designers – both established names and young emerging talent. We also have, I believe, the best fashion education in the world in our colleges and universities.

I decide, where possible, to only purchase British designers and shop in British high-street stores. (Later on, fashion guru and US *Harper's Bazaar* editor, Glenda Bailey, suggests I include the American labels that are packed with British creative talent, which I readily did.)

Having always worn a lot of both designer and high-street fashion, the designer pieces I have fallen in love with over the years have come from Jasper Conran, Ben de Lisi, Nicole Farhi, Margaret Howell, Paul Smith, Paul Costelloe, even Katharine Hamnett (for those who remember the famous T-shirt that she wore to Downing Street back in 1984).

My starting wardrobe now comes from Jaeger, who have bounced back on the high street under Belinda Earl's direction, and I go and meet their buyer, Shailina Parti, to look at what's coming up. I also go to Amanda Wakeley for evening wear. This is a safe but definitely stylish choice as she has a real flair for understanding how to make women look good, whatever their shape and size. I try to work out how many dresses I will need, and quickly realise there is a great call for a different outfit for every occasion. Of course, I can be clever with a bit of mixing and matching of accessories, and for working meetings, frankly, I am all for wearing favourites over and over again. But evening dresses fall into a different category.

I quickly discover that there is no shortage of designers and retailers who will offer you free clothes just so you wear their label.

However, there are many rules that govern what MPs (and spouses) can do with free gifts, not to mention the moral aspect of using your position to grab freebies. So, the Number 10 advisers and I figure out a way that works for everyone. Any clothes, shoes, etc, that I want to keep, I can buy. Any other freely offered clothes, I can effectively 'rent' for about 10 per cent of the retail value, and then return unmarked or damaged, of course. This means I can wear a different Amanda Wakeley dress at every state banquet and Guildhall event without breaking the bank. I also come to the same arrangement with jewellers, Garrard, who prove really helpful at finding good pieces to go with my long dresses, and getting them insured.

There is much discussion about the personal cost of this life borne by spouses, but in all seriousness I have not found the taxpayer falling over themselves to cover the cost of my frocks, and I think I have found a reasonable compromise.

Once I get the hang of how busy my diary is with official and charity engagements, I do opt for one immediate luxury. I ask my regular hairdresser, Australian Mark Pittman, if he will come to the flat to blow-dry my hair – something I just have never managed to work out how to do well myself. He and his wife, Sue, opened their salon, Bibas, in the 1980s in Bloomsbury, and it has thrived ever since, with me as one of their early customers as I had one of my first post-university jobs nearby.

Saturday 30th June

While I have been managing all kinds of domestic and daily office tasks, suddenly something happens that brings a big reality check for the world we live in. News comes through that a bomb attack in London has been foiled, followed by a Cherokee Jeep full of explosives crashing into the main terminal at Glasgow International Airport. The baggage handlers save the day by restraining the men in the car.

Gordon immediately chairs his first meeting of COBRA, the emergency committee that deals with national crises. He has appointed one of the tough, capable women he likes to work with as Britain's first female Home Secretary, Jacqui Smith. She reports that the national terrorism threat level had been raised everywhere – a tough start to a new job.

Monday 2nd July

I'm starting to understand why being the WPM (Wife of the Prime Minister – I think that Sir Denis Thatcher forged his own path as the one male exception so far) feels so tricky. I have no exact status, no official position, masses of conflicting expectations both internally and externally, and a terrible suspicion that at any moment a great mistake will be made by ME!

Over the last few weeks, during Gordon's leadership campaigning time, it was clear that he would arrive with the support of pretty much all the Labour MPs, and so I turned my attention to what I would do once he was made leader. I see my role as supportive, of course; for government events, both professionally and personally, as my husband takes on an even bigger job than the one he had before. I also see – and can look to all my predecessors for this – that there is an opportunity to use the visibility, platform and privilege of being at 10 Downing Street to use my efforts to do something useful and good. I don't want to over-complicate things, but I am very clear that I can have a voice for change if I don't step on any policy-making toes. I have to get the balance right between not being an elected politician myself, while making good use of my own abilities and professional experience. I know that whatever happens, a watchful media will report on my successes, or otherwise. It is not without a degree of personal stress that I recognise that failure on my part will make a good news story, but I am an 'eyes forward' kind of girl and prepared to take the risk.

There is, of course, no formal guidebook for all this, but I have had my 'trial run' at Number 11. Two things strike me at the start:

firstly, that my children are very young, so I need to make time for them and prioritise our family; and secondly, that with whatever time I can carve out after that, I will devote my efforts to supporting causes I am passionate about, and continue to open up Number 10 to as many charity groups and other visitors as possible. I am prepared to work hard, follow whatever rules do exist and totally support our Labour government.

I don't have a formal plan and need to find out what resources are available. A few weeks ago, I did sit in Fiona Millar's kitchen in her North London home sipping delicious Lemon Zinger tea, getting as much advice as I could from her. Fiona ran Cherie's office back in 1997 and became the Head of Events and Visits for all of Number 10, so I rightly figured that she was the closest thing to a guidebook I could find. I am very grateful for the steer she gave me.

To get my own office up and running, I am allowed two members of staff and a place to work with computers – and also a fairly blank slate. After some discussion, an office is provided on the first floor just off a central staircase right between Numbers 10 and 11 (there is another more famous staircase with all the pictures of former Prime Ministers but that is further inside the Number 10 building, just past the ground-floor Cabinet Room running directly up to the state rooms where visitors enter). My new office was previously occupied by Lord Birt, the former BBC director general who came to work for Tony Blair, and is notorious for having the ceiling collapse all over Lord Birt's desk. I am assured it has since been fully repaired and will accommodate me and my team of two. It also has some rather fabulous works of art from the Government Art Collection, but I am warned that these might be collected any time, so to enjoy them while I can.

One odd thing is that the office has no internet connection (only a link to the in-house Cabinet Office intranet system), so I immediately put in a request for an update to the twenty-first century. This is a wonderful but sometimes strange building.

I begin by appointing Konrad Caulkett as my special adviser. Konrad is in his mid thirties, very personable and has the right skills for juggling different events and activities from his former jobs with a think tank and the *New Statesman* magazine. He has a lot of experience in organising events, mailings and visits to political conferences. When he and I meet for coffee to discuss the job further, we realise that we are both on a steep learning curve. He also has a very understanding girlfriend, Victoria, who knows that he will not be doing a 9 to 5 job.

I have a groaning in-tray of welcoming letters, invitations and requests, so we are joined part-time by Pauline Pennington, a civil servant who works in the Honours section, who works her way through them all for me. One of the first small parcels we open contains a card from Fiona Millar wishing me well with the challenge ahead, and a box of her favourite Lemon Zinger tea.

It does look as though Konrad and I will be fairly overwhelmed by the array of events and supportive WPM duties as things stand, but are prepared to figure it out. I also intend to maintain my day-to-day involvement in running the children's charity PiggyBankKids set up in 2002, and to keep up the role of Patron for a number of other charities with whom I already have a role: SHINE education trust, Maggie's Cancer Caring Centres and Women's Aid.

Thankfully, I can also rely on Gil McNeil, who is both a close friend and hard-working colleague – Gil and I have worked together for many years. She is the director of PiggyBankKids, which we set up to raise funds for a range of projects to help vulnerable babies, children and young adults in the UK, including funding scientific research to make pregnancies safer and save newborn lives at the Jennifer Brown Research Laboratory. Gordon and I helped establish the medical research laboratory in Edinburgh in memory of our baby daughter who lived for only ten days after her birth in December 2001.

As Gil lives in Kent, with her teenage son, Joe, she does not come in to London every day to work. In fact, it is often in the evening, after my boys' bedtime, when we catch up on our various activities, compare notes, read over speeches or articles, and look at the workload coming up. I know that I will be able to count on her and call her any time things are extra tricky, or a bit too much for me.

The first charity reception at Number 10 I join as host is for the Down's Syndrome Association. Then, the next day, my first visitors are a group of trade union women, and I also meet a group of war widows for tea, which brought home to me firsthand how brave our service families are. We also see lots of friends and colleagues at a reception for Horse's Mouth, a great energetic online volunteering programme, set up by entrepreneur MT Rainey, that seemed very in keeping with the thinking of Gordon's team. I think there must have been 200 people at the Horse's Mouth event – the building was just buzzing. The level of activity is building up and I am starting to realise how busy I will be.

Wednesday 4th July

Gordon is taking full advantage of the honeymoon period enjoyed by all new PMs, when everyone lets you get on with the job unencumbered. He kicks off with Prime Minister's Questions (PMQs) and announces that the plans for the super casinos are no more, which is greeted with much delight by the general public. A mini-Las Vegas is not on its way to Blackpool, at least not yet.

Thursday 5th July

Another small but welcome change was kicked off when John, an inquisitive and alert toddler, noticed the flagpoles on the roof of Downing Street and complained there were no flags flying. As Gordon pondered the reason for this, he thought that it would be a strong symbolic gesture for all our public buildings to be able to fly their Union Jacks in defiance of the recent terrorist attacks. It turned out that an ancient by-law stated that the Union Jack could only fly a certain number of days a year. So Gordon asked the next question which was to find out how you could change that ruling. It turned out that the answer was that the Prime Minister could change the law. That was handy. He did, and it is a wonderful sight around Westminster, and around the country, to see so many Union Jacks flapping away proudly in the wind.

I get a text message from Piers Morgan, the TV presenter and former newspaper editor, who has been a friend for many years: It reads, 'Love the flags idea ... I feel oddly proud.' Quite right.

Sunday 8th July

I take a short leave of absence to attend a family event. My beloved father, Iain, passed away a few months ago, at the end of March. While my parents divorced when I was a child, my two brothers, Sean and Bruce, and I, have kept in close contact with our dad. We enjoyed many memorable family holidays over the years in Scotland, visiting grandparents and going off on our own camper van adventures. He later remarried very happily and settled just outside Dublin with his wife, Elizabeth, and my two new half-brothers, making Ireland his home for the last 30 years or so.

Although my father had been in poor health for a number of years, it has been a shock for us all to lose him (just around the time when Gordon was giving his last Budget, I remember flying out to Dublin only hours later). With family and friends, we gathered together for the funeral a few weeks later in April. Sadly, my dad missed seeing Gordon become PM, which he would have enjoyed very much – and today I join Elizabeth and my brothers for a memorial mass at St Joseph's Church in Glasthule by Sandycove. While I am not a Catholic, my father had become one and taken great comfort in the Church, and he would have been chuffed to see us all there for him today. I head out at the crack of dawn to get a flight to Dublin and, after the service, spend the day visiting the places my dad loved.

Wednesday 11th July

A large part of the WPM's duties is to greet and spend time with the spouses of visiting leaders and heads of major international organisations. Some visits are in the diary months in advance, while others will pop up at short notice.

My first official spousal engagement meeting is with Ban Soon-taek, wife of the new United Nations Secretary-General, Ban Ki-moon. Gordon has always engaged enthusiastically with international development issues and ways to reduce global poverty. While he talks to Secretary-General Ban about his first UN General Assembly coming up in September, where Gordon is to be one of the opening speakers, I meet Mrs Ban for a half-hour coffee.

I meet her at the door of Number 10, and notice that a red carpet has been rolled out for their arrival. Mrs Ban has been travelling extensively with her husband and must be really tired, but she shows no sign of it. Her own family home is in South Korea, but her new home is now in New York and her English is very good. She is an elegant, quiet and gracious woman and I have a great chat with her about family life, and keeping up with hard-working spouses. I feel I have made a good friend. We agree to keep in touch and find ways to support each other's charitable work.

Monday 16th July

I finally find time to move our belongings over to Number 11, thereby making way for Alistair and Maggie Darling to move into Number 10. We shift over our various boxes and work as hard as we can with the cleaning staff to get it ready for their arrival. That done, I whizz over to our new flat, as tomorrow we have Fraser's first birthday to celebrate.

Amid all the flurry of government business, a house move and more, our children have been terrific. However, Fraser is still small and the wakeful nights and early starts just add to the exhaustion that all mums will understand.

To celebrate Fraser's first birthday I invite some friends with young babies and toddlers over, and we all sit around the hallway on a big blanket playing toddler games. Gordon finds time to sneak away from the office and join us for a while (at least the travel time between home and office is short). Anna Darling (Maggie's teenage daughter) and I spend hours wrapping a baby-friendly 'pass the parcel' and later entirely forget to bring it out. Maggie has made one of her fabulous chocolate cakes while at home in Edinburgh and brings it down on the train. Louise Shackelton comes with her new baby, Isaac, and her husband, David Miliband – the new Foreign Secretary – also calls in via his meetings downstairs. A suitable amount of chocolate cake and chaos ensues, and very importantly, some birthday photos for the album are taken lest anyone think in future years we did not make an effort while we had other distractions on the go.

Thursday 19th July

Gordon and I were reminded about the fragility of life and the courage of those who face illness and difficulty today. We met 12-year-old Liam Fairhurst, who suffers from terminal cancer. He is fundraising for his favourite causes and spreading a great deal of joy and inspiration, and came to visit with his parents and brother, Callum. Liam reminds us of how to turn any adversity into a moment of triumph and achievement, especially by helping others. Somehow I know we will be seeing more of this remarkable family, but I know that Liam has reminded me how important it is to support other families' efforts around the country to do special and remarkable things. Downing Street is the perfect place to recognise people and their achievements, and I hope we can reach out to all kinds of people while we are here.

CHAPTER 4

House in the Country

Saturday 21st July

For us, Chequers is a great treat. It was wrongly reported, when we moved into Number 10, that we had decided not to use the place, but I have never been sure where that story came from, as it certainly wasn't from us.

One of the real privileges of being the British Prime Minister is the use of the country house and grounds of Chequers. It was the gift of Lord and Lady Lee of Fareham, a wealthy couple who decided to set up a Trust to endow the Prime Minister of the day with the exclusive use of this Elizabethan house, fully staffed with local Forces people there to welcome the PM and his family. It is tucked away in the English countryside in Buckinghamshire, only about an hour or so's drive from Westminster. David Lloyd George was the first Prime Minister to use the property and so enjoyed it, that it is said that he was loath to leave it when he came to the end of his time in office.

Before Lloyd George, the Prime Minister was always the type of person who came with a ready-made country estate of HIS own. As the Trust deed set up to fund this gift says: 'It is not possible to foresee or foretell from what classes or conditions of life the future wielders of power in this country will be drawn.' Times were changing by the end of World War I, and Lloyd George, raised in North Wales, had worked his way to the top in political life very much on his own merit.

The Trustees of Chequers – chaired by the leader of the House of Lords and various other grandees like the chair of the National Trust – are very strict about following the Trust deeds fairly. This gift had been made so that it was for the leisure and relaxation of the PM, in recognition of how pressured and relentless the daily job always is. So although we are welcome to invite any personal guests, including other international leaders, and to have our own lunches and dinners there, it is not to be used as an alternative place of work for meetings, photo calls and such like. The Trustees also want to protect the privacy of the place, and so are quite restrictive about what photos are taken and how they are used.

British Museum director Neil MacGregor once vividly described how the building had been lived in when it was first built. The big central hall was once an open courtyard with a fire in the centre where everyone, including animals, would gather for warmth, and to cook food. An upstairs dining room, that was nowhere near the kitchen, would have been where the noblemen and women gathered to eat; this room still has a table and chairs, but meals are eaten on the ground floor, in a room rather more conveniently located near to a modern kitchen. This upstairs room is now used for gatherings like Political Cabinet meetings (where the civil servants get left out) to discuss new ideas and a bit of blue-sky thinking. The Trustees allow this as they feel these have less to do with work, and more to do with ideas exploration, thereby keeping within the terms of the Trust deeds.

It is traditional that after a change of Prime Minister, the outgoing PM goes to Chequers for one final weekend. Very soon after the Blairs went to say their goodbyes, I drove down to Chequers with Sue Nye (the new Director of Government Relations at Number 10 and long-time aide of Gordon's) so that we can say hello and let them know our plans. Sue has vivid memories of staying there in the days when she was a garden girl (secretary) at Downing Street, working for Labour Prime Minister Jim Callaghan. She remembers staying overnight in the little Prison Room where Lady Mary Grey was kept prisoner centuries earlier.

Our family home in Scotland will remain just that – our family home. We won't move our belongings out and will return to North Queensferry during the festive breaks and the half-term school holidays. But, most weekends, where there is not time to travel all that way, Chequers is the perfect option to get away from Number 10 and have a meal prepared for the family with no washing up; enjoy a swim, walk or game of tennis; and appreciate being with family and friends. While Chequers does not feel like an alternative home, it does feel like having the most wonderful country house hotel all to yourself. What gives me added reassurance is that as a charitable Trust set up with an endowment to run the whole estate, this is not a burden on the taxpayer. It would otherwise quickly feel like a great indulgence, no matter how hard earned.

Visiting this weekend with friends, we continue to celebrate Fraser's first birthday. Our American friend, writer and political strategist Bob Shrum – he too is celebrating a birthday – comes to stay with his wife, another writer, Marylouise Oates; as well as author Jo (JK) Rowling and her doctor husband, Neil Murray, with their children. Jo and Bob are thrilled to meet each other: Bob is a great Harry Potter fan ever since I gave him Volume 1 some years ago; and Jo is an American politics fan with a huge interest in the Kennedy family, especially RFK – Bobby Kennedy, and Bob has been a speechwriter, adviser and close friend of the Kennedys since his time as an intern for JFK. I have my camera and capture a wonderful picture of the two of them deep in conversation in the famous Chequers' Hawtrey Room.

Our other friends staying for the weekend include a mixture of friends and colleagues: Sue Nye and her husband, Gavyn Davies, who runs an investment firm with their children, Rosie, Ben and Matthew; and Gil McNeil and her son, Joe – all of whom are to be important people to us for the months ahead. A great pal of

Gordon's, Michael Watt, comes over too, as do Lord Swraj and Lady Aruna Paul. They live close by in Beaconsfield; Swraj Paul is the chair of the Trustees at PiggyBankKids, and a loyal friend. I attend their big family party at London Zoo each year, held in honour of their young daughter, Ambika, who lost her life to leukaemia at the age of four.

While Chequers is there for a welcome break, already we have a dilemma. Gordon needs to broadcast a media statement about the ongoing floods (this June was one of the wettest months on record) without upsetting the agreement over privacy and leisure. I consult the Secretary of the Chequers Trust, Rodney Melville, who explains that Tony Blair had, on occasion, had the same issue. Of course, when the Trust deeds were written it was a different media age. The resolution had been to do a broadcast with cameras from the Hawtrey Room, where another former PM had urgently needed to do a broadcast, without leaving Chequers. This was Winston Churchill, who had made so many world-famous weekly radio broadcasts many from Chequers, and which had provided so much hope during WWII. It had taken place in one spot, just by the main fireplace in that room. As precedent had been set – Tony Blair used this spot, too, with the modern update of TV cameras – Gordon follows suit to make his statement about the floods. If you look at broadcasts from Chequers, you should find that each one has exactly the same background, with a fireplace and the corner of a large sofa – just where the great wartime premier had recorded his words to provide reassurance in a time of crisis.

Our house guests this first weekend are excited enough by Chequers, but further escalation of the general excitement comes as this is the weekend of publication of HP7 – the final volume completing Harry Potter's story. Every comfortable chair and sofa seems to have someone nose down in the book for much of the weekend. I take a great snap of all the teenagers immersed in their new volumes, flopping around on the comfortable Chequers sofas.

Sunday 22nd July

We have lunch today for 22 people, including Ed Miliband (Minister in charge of the Cabinet Office) and Shriti Vadera (a former Treasury adviser highly regarded by Gordon for her brilliant mind and as a friend, now in the House of Lords and promoted as a Minister for International Development). David Miliband is also around at some point, coming in to see Gordon as discussions about the national security issues continue in the wake of the bombing attempts.

In Number 10, the deal is very much that you look after your own domestic and daily family needs within the flat. At Chequers, the staff, which is mostly made up of serving navy personnel from the nearby base, attend to pretty much everything. The key staff members, Pat, David and Harvey, rotate across the shifts over a weekend so that there is always someone we know to call on for anything at all. I suspect the staff will sometimes have to be quite patient and long suffering when we have lots of lively children roaring around inside and out.

The head chef here, Alan Lavender, has served four Prime Ministers: Margaret Thatcher, John Major, Tony Blair and now Gordon. As soon as we arrive at Chequers, Alan is already making a note of favourite meals and seems instinctively to know just when to serve something that you really fancy.

Gordon loves a cooked breakfast and there is none finer than the chef's breakfast. Talking to Alan, I discover that great traditional Sunday carvery roasts and traditional English puddings are a particular strength of his, and quickly decide that our main entertainment can be Sunday lunches for invited guests, rather than late dinners. These can take place in the main dining room, where you can get up to 24 guests around the great table. Sundays will work well for everyone as both we, and our guests, will get the earlier part of the weekend to ourselves, and with the relaxed atmosphere at Chequers, guests can bring their children to eat with our boys and run around afterwards.

Wednesday 25th July

The return to Westminster brings with it another success for Gordon at PMQs. But he is then away all afternoon looking at the water damage from the floods, assessing how best to respond, and seeing our emergency services and flood heroes at work protecting people and their homes. His team is working so hard and doing so brilliantly, and there has been live coverage of the visit on the TV all afternoon.

Gordon makes sure he is back in time to call in briefly at a party for the staff at Number 10. I stay a bit longer as I am still getting to know who everyone is, and help Gus O'Donnell in picking the winning tickets of the raffle (a skill that all political wives – and Cabinet Secretaries, in this case – acquire very early on).

Later on, Gordon and I end up in the sitting room, having a drink. We are usually kitchen-table people but I think we are getting used to living somewhere new and trying out different spaces. He says his abiding image of Change-over Day (exactly four weeks ago) is of John and Fraser waiting at the end of the Number 10 corridor after all the staff clapped him in. No one had told him they would be there so it came as a complete (and welcome) surprise.

Sunday 29th July

Gordon flies to Washington DC today to meet President George W Bush. I don't join him as the focus is on formal working meetings and discussions about the wars in Iraq and Afghanistan. I watch his arrival on television and see footage of President Bush putting his foot down on the accelerator in a golf buggy containing the two of them, just charging around in circles in front of the media cameras. I laugh, looking at Gordon's perplexed expression as he is seated on the moving buggy – I think I can tell exactly what is on his mind! Although Gordon does not know the President and understands that he is following in the footsteps of Tony Blair, who had forged a strong relationship with the US President, the meetings go well and the basis of a friendship is formed to serve them well in the, no doubt, up-coming challenges.

Friday 3rd August

It is our seventh wedding anniversary today. Gordon returns from his US trip and we are ready to head off on holiday. I suggest we stay just one more week in London so that I can get the flat sorted and settle the children in, and allow Gordon to catch up with everyone back at Downing Street (this turns out to be a very bad error of judgement on my part).

We finally set off for a couple of weeks in Dorset, staying with my parents. Everything has been set up there so that Gordon has emergency office back-up, the protection teams are happy that they have the area secure, and all is well.

Gordon heads off early with a very excited John, taking in a visit to Portland to see the preparations for 2012 Olympic sailing, while I follow later with Fraser. By the time we arrive, Gordon has had a walk, read a novel and had a kip, while John has been off to visit a local farm with his grandparents. We all sit down for a family supper and anniversary celebration. At that moment, the phone rings for Gordon. I see his expression grow serious and hear, 'Yes … Yes … Yes … I understand. I will see you as soon as I can.' When he hangs up, he tells us that a case of foot and mouth disease has been found on a farm near Guildford, Surrey. We already know the holiday is over. Total holiday time for Gordon – six hours.

Saturday 4th August

Gordon is driven off to London in the early hours. After a couple of days, we head back ourselves. We decide to base ourselves at Chequers while we establish what the routine for the summer will be, and to support Gordon while he is working with the DEFRA (Department for Environment, Food and Rural Affairs) team, the Chief Scientist and others to tackle the problem.

Thankfully, by taking immediate action, the situation is under control, but the cost to farmers and anyone with associated livelihoods is going to be devastating. With floods, terror attacks and foot and mouth, it has been a tough summer for a new Prime Minister, and for the country. Everyone seems to agree that the government has handled all these crises well, and acted as best it could to address each one.

Friday 10th August

We're ending the summer with a short family break at our own home in Scotland, newly surrounded by police with guns, and with the patient grace of our village neighbours. I always sense myself unwind a bit simply by walking back through the door of our own home, and Gordon feels the same way too. Here we can relax more as a family together, get some fresh Fife air and catch up with nearby family and friends.

Monday 27th August

Back in London, film director Beeban Kidron (director of *Bridget Jones: The Edge of Reason*) calls by in the afternoon. She and her husband Lee Hall (writer of *Billy Elliot*) are good friends. Beeban has her own handheld camera and does a great private interview with Gordon in the flat. She is thrilled to know that there is some footage of Gordon at the start of his premiership just to have on record as she is a great advocate for film diaries.

Lee is also helping Gordon on a follow-up to Gordon's book *Courage* sharing thoughts on profiles of military heroes as Lee has been doing some World War II historical research for a new project of his own.

Tuesday 28th August

There is great excitement that Nelson Mandela and his inspirational wife, Graça Machel, are visiting today. The plan is for a formal photo on the famous doorstep and further photographs in the hallway, before moving to a private meeting in the Number 11 sitting room, excluding all officials. Gordon has asked for a framed picture of the statue of Nelson Mandela that is going up in Parliament Square to be made ready as a gift. Lots of people are not yet back from holiday and it feels quite chaotic at the moment. Nelson Mandela and Graça Machel are the two people whom Gordon and I most admire, and whom we are privileged to count as our friends and, on occasion, colleagues, as we campaign together for common causes. Gordon often cites Nelson Mandela's call to action: not content with climbing one mountain – tearing down apartheid – he set his sights on the next goal, that of providing schooling for the 70 million children who still miss out around the world today.

John and Fraser come in when filming stops, and we have a lovely time chatting with them while the boys are gently bouncing around on the sofa next to the great Madiba.

The Mandelas bring a gift of a beautiful Masai statue. There is a classic moment when I reach for the gift bag, which admittedly I had left to the office to provide, only to discover it contained two small boxes of chocolate and some Number 10 tea. I decide on the spot that I cannot hand these over and hastily explain their gift will come later. It turns out that the idea of the statue photo had been too complicated to produce in the time given (the statue was still under wraps), so someone had opted for the chocolate/tea bag emergency gift. I decide then and there that I will be far more involved in gift choices. I learn, too, that there is a limited budget for gifts, but decide that Gordon and I will just have to provide personal gifts where it falls outside the usual budget.

My mother, Pauline, arrives at the end of the visit, and meets two of her great heroes, which I really enjoy seeing happen. She is here to help me with the next stage of the visit, when we are to host a reception for the Canon Collins Trust in support of the Graça Machel Scholarships, which support the women who may be tomorrow's leaders in Africa.

Gordon has a surprise announcement for Graça – she is to be made an honorary Dame Commander of the Order of the British Empire (DBE), a rare presentation for overseas recipients, but a truly worthy one. At the ceremony, he speaks of Graça's achievements as an Education Minister in Mozambique; as a ground-breaker with her report on the impact on children from conflict, and child soldiers; her commitment to Education for All, a global movement run by UNESCO that aims to get every child in the world a place at school; and her unflagging dedication to seeing women in Africa receive opportunities to thrive and succeed. On behalf of the Queen, he has the honour of making her a Dame, and a presentation is made. (The box is later taken back to send on to her safely. I peek inside it at the very beautiful light blue insignia.)

When Graça speaks, she explains what this honour will mean to people in all parts of Mozambique, and how it will highlight the importance of the scholars she supports, and her wish for them to flourish themselves.

Wednesday 29th August

We walk over to Nelson Mandela's statue unveiling in Parliament Square, which is overlooked by both the Houses of Parliament and Westminster Abbey, and I completely misjudge the weather. I end up palming off my raincoat on to Jo Dipple from Gordon's team, who carries it in the sudden and unexpected heat with no complaint.

I greet Liberal Party leader, Menzies Campbell; Sheila Attenborough (wife of the lovely Dickie); and David Miliband; and seat myself with them. It is odd to see the Tories present too, as their party did so little to combat apartheid. This is really not their day. I say hello to former Deputy Prime Minister John Prescott, who has just announced that he is stepping down as a Member of Parliament at the next election. I had recently sent flowers to Pauline when she was unwell, and was not sure now what to do with this news. I will call Pauline.

It is a very moving ceremony. Gordon describes the statue as a 'beacon of hope', and salutes Mandela as the leader who showed us 'that no injustice can last for ever; that suffering in the cause of freedom will never be in vain, that no matter how long the night of oppression, the morning of liberty will still break through and there is nothing that we, the people of the world, working together cannot achieve'.

Nelson Mandela gives a much stronger than expected endorsement of Gordon, starting his own speech with the words: 'First, personally, please allow me to congratulate our friend Gordon Brown on his new position as Prime Minister of Britain. We are confident that his leadership will not only bring forth Britain's position on the world stage but serve the British people and the world at large with distinction.' Gordon guides Mandela to the podium holding his arm, and the mutual affection of the two men was very evident.

The unveiling of the statue has marked a moving and symbolic moment, best summed up by Madiba's recollection of walking through Parliament Square as a young man with Oliver Tambo (the South African, anti-apartheid politician). They had pondered whether they would ever see a statue of a black man among the greats there in their own lifetime. It seems obvious to us that it should be Nelson Mandela's statue but, as ever, his personal humility prevents him from indulging in his own legend and historic importance. As Gordon says in his speech today, we celebrate 'not just the greatness of Nelson Mandela, but also the goodness of Nelson Mandela'.

At the end, Gordon asks me to make sure that I bring David Miliband over as he had heard that David had yet to meet Nelson Mandela. I know that like so many others, he was deeply honoured to do so.

Michael Jacobs, Gordon's environment adviser, has a great knack of standing in just the right place at the right time and so he was included in the introduction, too – one happy guy.

Friday 31st August

We attend the service at Wellington Barracks led by HRH Prince William and HRH Prince Harry in memory of their mother Diana, Princess of Wales, on the tenth anniversary of her death. Gordon and I sit with the other politicians present, just behind the large Royal party. Alongside Diana's family and friends are more than 100 representatives of the charities she supported. Everyone is deeply moved when Prince Harry describes his loss of 'the best mother in the world'. At the end of the service, there is a long queue to shake hands with the young Princes as we pass out of the chapel door. No matter that everyone must have their busy working day to return to; no one minds the long wait at all, to be able to pass on condolences to these brave young men, a decade after the death of their beloved mother.

Saturday 1st September

Gordon and I have our first visit to Balmoral Castle this weekend. This is the regular annual stay with the Queen and her family on their Highland estate. I am quite nervous about following all the protocol and being the 'new girl' joining a well-established tradition, where everyone else knows the rules. I am perfectly pragmatic about it in theory, but inside feel quite anxious to get it right. Gordon does, of course, have his weekly private meeting with the Queen and over the years has had many more occasions to meet her and other members of the Royal Family. I have joined him at a small number of official events in the past (and vividly remember taking John as a tiny baby to Windsor Castle so I could dart out between a reception and dinner to care for him), but an overnight stay seems in a very different league. As ever, the Royal Household makes sure that we are graciously guided through the myriad protocols that accompany the visit. Our friends, James and Julia Ogilvy, who have a family connection to the Royal Family, are there as guests that same weekend, which is hugely thoughtful and a delight for us. They live not far from us in Fife and we met them when we were both helping at the Maggie's Cancer Caring Centre in Kirkcaldy. Julia has made a real mark chairing the big Project Scotland initiative that has opened up so many volunteering opportunities for young people there. She and I share many similar interests and I always find myself quickly caught up in her amazing energy and determination to help the most vulnerable young adults.

I feel strongly that I should honour the firm views held by Buckingham Palace not to report on private conversations with the Queen and the Duke of Edinburgh. All I will say is that having seen the film *The Queen*, there are elements of the scenes with the former Prime Minister that seem very accurate. There is no picnic but a barbecue to which we are ably driven by the Queen herself, at the wheel of her Range Rover.

Monday 3rd September

Gordon's team returns to the office after a holiday and seem much rested and in energetic mood, which brings a lively buzz to Number 10. Everyone's conversations as I stop to say hello to people in the corridors is about the raft of new appointments being made. Gordon announces that a new group of people are coming in to work with the government; people who are not chosen for their personal politics. This small, new group of ministers hails from other professional worlds and includes a life-saving surgeon and cancer specialist, Ara Darzi, who becomes the new Health Minister; and a former Chief of the British Navy, Alan West, who is the new minister in charge of National Security responsible for preventing future terrorist attacks on Britain. They have been described as GOATs (Government Of All the Talents), and I think the name will stick.

Tuesday 4th September

The Times reports that Labour is only one point ahead in the opinion polls, and that Gordon's leadership honeymoon period is already over. I think honeymoons only ever last about this long.

The media, meanwhile, is distracted by the arrival of a new Downing Street cat, as Maggie Darling has brought her cat, Sybil, with her from Scotland. The YouTube footage of Sybil gets the most views on the Downing Street website.

Friday 14th September

During the summer, Chancellor Alistair Darling has been dealing with a financial crisis at the Northern Rock building society and talking regularly to Gordon. If I have understood the problem correctly, the building society is in serious difficulty as it has borrowed money from other banks and as the system is seizing up that money needs to go back, but it has spread itself very thin with customer loans.

This means that the building society now has no money itself other than depositors' savings, and the problem is understandably starting to panic the public. The Bank of England agreed to guarantee the missing funds today, but there are still queues of savers outside the branches looking to get their money out as they hear news that Northern Rock is on the brink of collapse, thereby taking precious savings down with it. The Treasury is now looking at what it needs to do to both calm the savers and protect their money.

From my perspective inside Downing Street, I can see the politicians and civil servants working flat out to protect people's savings, but it is looking like a big problem.

Wednesday 19th September

We have a visit from Republican Presidential candidate and ex-Mayor of New York, Rudy Giuliani, and his wife, Judith. I have had no briefing for this meeting, so speedily look up some information on his wife to discover she was a nurse who worked very hard – as he did – in the 9/11 aftermath in The Family Center in New York. She did fundraising for the Twin Towers Fund before going into the private sector, but she has not had good coverage in the States and seems inexperienced at US-style campaigning. I discover with five minutes' notice that I am to spend an hour alone with her, while Gordon talks to her husband in the first-floor study.

Gordon steers Rudy Giuliani off for their meeting while I take Judith to the Terracotta Room for our chat. We talk about her work, her trip to the UK and her campaigning role, and I realise that some harsh recent US press coverage has knocked her confidence when it comes to being in the media. Clearly, she will prefer to keep her profile low until the February nomination result.

Gordon's meeting runs on a little so, wanting to be a good hostess, I offer Judith a tour of the main state rooms. We set off to the Pillared Room first. I approach the door and open it with a vigorous tug – ushering Mrs Giuliani straight into a cupboard full of crockery. I simply don't know how to talk myself out of this one, so I just declare, 'This is one of the Downing Street cupboards with our china, and we will now go see the Pillared Room.'

The week ends with a fantastic *Guardian* front page with good numbers for Gordon, but I have a little polishing up to do on my part.

CHAPTER 5

Election Speculation

Thursday 20th September

The Labour Party's Annual Conference is taking place in the Bournemouth International Centre, and Gordon is to make his first speech as Prime Minister on Monday. I go down with the boys on Saturday, who basically get a week at the seaside, plus visits to their grandparents (my mother and stepfather, Pauline and Patrick, who are not far away in Dorset). We also have a great nanny, Melanie Darby, who comes and stays with us every Monday to Friday, and who then escapes back to her own life close to Southampton, in Romsey. As Bournemouth is so close, this makes it all the easier for Mela to take the boys while we are busy with conference activities.

Travelling down, Gordon and I first visit Southampton General Hospital to see first-hand the new cardiac monitoring facility that allows patients to be monitored at home, and the breathtaking new surgical unit that has the technology to even repair blood vessel walls. It feels very close to home for me having lost my dad to a heart attack so recently, and reminds me how fortunate we are to have our National Health Service. I really do feel close to tears at moments throughout the visit.

The last few weeks, even months, have been so busy that I realise I am quite run down. This is doubtless egged on by the broken sleep that comes with young infants and the terrible tendency I have to take on way too much. I have a rotten chest infection, which is affecting my voice, but I just dose myself with antibiotics, and plaster on extra make-up. Rather than face it, I just decide that with my life at the moment, illness is not really an option.

We arrive at the hotel in Bournemouth, which will be our home, office and general base camp for the next few days. Outside is a heaving throng of cameras and a cheering group of welcoming Labour staff and delegates. I have on a new, bright orange Jaeger jacket that looks pretty good as it proves to be a TV-friendly colour when I catch a glimpse of it on the TV moments later, in the hotel room.

Sunday 23rd September

Alistair Darling kicks off the conference today with a solid economic speech that sets it off on a good track. Gordon spends a lot of the day, once we return from church, at work on his speech. He sits at his computer typing at top speed with two fingers, and then has someone come in and decode it. His closest team are around him to talk through speech drafts, phrases and feed in ideas.

Deputy Leader Harriet Harman invites me to speak at the Women's Reception despite my lack of voice. I suspect the only thing anyone might remember is my story about John, who returned to his nursery class in June after our trip to the leadership conference and announced that his dad has just become the 'Leader of the *Lady* Party'.

Gordon and I have taken a decision to keep John and Fraser away from the media spotlight. We have sent a letter to all the editors of newspapers to let them know that it is our choice to not have the boys photographed at any time. I know that politicians can gain quite a boost from lovely family shots and close-up, intimate portraits of family life, but it comes at a price. Our boys are small enough that it will pass by them at the moment, but it won't be too long before it could be an issue at school and with friends. Gordon agrees with me that it is our job to give them a great childhood, and as they already have super-busy parents to contend with, why make it harder for them? I believe that part of my role as WPM is to make an often-extraordinary life as ordinary as possible for myself, my husband and my children. I intend to be good at that.

Monday 24th September

It's the day of Gordon's speech, and everyone is very focused in the speech room. I take the opportunity to switch off a bit and get my hair done with a local hairdresser. I am sure that today will go well, and there is little I can do to contribute anyway.

When we arrive at the Bournemouth International Centre, I join the conference audience, sitting at the front by party workers and next to the airport baggage handler, John Smeaton, who had acted so bravely in stopping the terrorist attack in Glasgow.

When Gordon speaks, he starts by talking about the floods, bomb attacks and other trials that the country has faced in the last few months. There is hardly a dry eye in the house as we recognise the huge impact the government has had on ordinary people's lives in times of crisis and in daily life; an impact for the better. As he finishes his speech, I feel I have heard Gordon give one of his best – and I have sat through a fair few (and count myself amongst his biggest fans).

The rest of the evening passes in a blur as we visit many receptions meeting upbeat, energised people everywhere we go.

Discussions in the media about whether there will, or should, be a general election have been building. It strikes me that Gordon's political advisory team are generally acting as though it is inevitable. I am not going to get involved in the decision but I do wonder why midway through a term you would choose to risk giving up your legitimate parliamentary term.

Nonetheless, election pressure is building. Lots of polls are ordered and the Tories have their conference next week. My mind is mulling it over all the time, so goodness knows what state the advisers are all in.

Friday 28th September

Back in London, and we're hosting a visit from the former Head of the United States Federal Reserve, Alan Greenspan KBE, and his wife, Andrea Mitchell, who is a hugely successful news journalist on NBC, the US TV channel. Both are long-standing friends from Gordon's years at the Treasury and two of the most thoughtful people I know. I love that she pays attention to getting every detail right for him while still pursuing her own career to great acclaim – such a close couple. We used to joke that Alan Greenspan looked on Gordon as a bright young thing whom he was keen to encourage and nurture.

As part of Dr Greenspan's visit, the government is hosting two gatherings for the Prime Minister's new Business Council at Chequers. Tomorrow night will start with a dinner for 24 around the great dining-room table.

Part of the WPM deal is that you are able to advise on hospitality for such events, from menu choices and flowers to place cards and sometimes even seating plans, so I use this opportunity to see how things are done. My own career experience of organising similar scale events means that I have views on pretty much everything and am very keen on the detail. I can see that the events team has a good system and I'm glad that they are open to me adapting it so that it reflects our personal, more informal style. I am always very particular, for example, that name place cards using people's titles and rankings must be 100 per cent accurate, but even Downing Street's system cannot guarantee perfection. So we will move to a new system where only the first and last names are used – the PM's card reads Gordon Brown; no Rt Hon, no Dr, no MP or PM. As our guest, everyone becomes a person, not a job title.

Saturday 29th September

Sorting out the dinner for tonight involves a rather painful process in finalising table plans and taking receipt of the place cards. The hospitality system seems to be run long-distance from London, which means there is no allowance for changes. More than that, the name cards that do arrive are riddled with errors. I need to get this sorted out quickly as we are only hours away from guests arriving, and replacement cards are one hour up the road, back in London. Thankfully, with Gordon's intervention, we arrange for a private secretary to take over and get table cards done in the Chequers garden room that serves as the administrative office.

At dinner, I am seated between Alan Greenspan and Stuart Rose, the Chief Executive of Marks and Spencer plc, whose tenure has overseen a corporate revival to the delight of shareholders and fashion editors alike. Mr Rose is a combination of self-effacement and confidence; I can't quite tell if the self-effacing bit is genuine or done for effect. It does not take long to discover that he is a bit miffed to have received from Downing Street not once, but twice, an invitation addressed to 'Sir' Stuart Rose. While that may well be on the cards for him, at the moment he does not hold the title, and purports to be mortified at the prospect of having a 'Sir Stuart' place card that might lead others to think he was awarding himself his own title. At least we now have a simplified, working system that will avoid future errors.

Stuart asks me about the election speculation, and offers his own advice that we 'leave well alone'. He points out that all businessmen, like politicians, have to ride out bumpier times. I promise to get involved with supporting London Fashion Week for our important British fashion industry, and to come and have a look around the M&S Marble Arch flagship store.

Sunday 30th September

The remaining members of the Business Council are invited to join Alan Greenspan and Gordon for lunch. This totals a further 34 people and I decide to test hosting a Sunday roast carvery with small round tables, so guests can actually chat with each other. It certainly proves popular enough, as the Chequers chef makes a spectacular Sunday lunch.

I sit with John Parker, chairman of National Grid, who tells me his favourite Alan Greenspan story and can't stop chuckling as he tells it:

Question to AG: Do you really need just a man and a dog to understand monetary policy?

AG's reply: Why do you need the dog?

As lunch is ending, a number of Gordon's closest advisers arrive to talk though the election options. Of course, they all keep away from the business guests to avoid piquing their interest.

The team includes Ed Miliband (in charge of the manifesto), Douglas Alexander (who has agreed to be General Election Coordinator), Spencer Livermore, Sue Nye, Gavin Kelly, Damian McBride from Downing Street, plus MPs Ed Balls and Ian Austin (both former advisers to Gordon). They meet for hours to discuss whether or not to call a general election now. Clearly some are veering towards it, but all is not clear cut and certainly no decision is taken today.

Monday 1st October

Gordon has gone to visit Iraq with the Ministry of Defence, and will be away overnight. As the security implications of a Prime Minister's visit to an active war zone are so serious, there has been no advance announcement of his visit. I understand that this is likely to be the first of several military visits by Gordon to countries like Iraq and Afghanistan as Prime Minister, and discover, when talking to Leeanne Johnston, Gordon's loyal diary secretary, that this is the one thing she will not be able to copy me in on in advance. Where possible, Leeanne says that she will tell me and she does promise that he will never be overnight in a dangerous military area without me knowing, even if I don't know the exact location. Recognising the risks, I admire all the more the military spouses, partners, mums and dads who cope so well as their loved ones are out on active service.

The Shadow Chancellor George Osborne makes a speech at the Conservative Party Conference announcing £1 million inheritance tax threshold to be paid by non-domiciles and no stamp duty for first-time buyers. Everyone I speak to seems concerned that it speaks to people's aspirations despite the lack of detail from the Conservatives on how they would pay for it.

Thursday 4th October

Having returned from Basra, pressure is mounting for Gordon to decide about an election, so I leave him to work, and am just relieved that he's back safely. He will make the right decision once he has all the information, but most of his team would like him to go for it, while starting to feel more cautious about which way the voters will go in the marginal seats that have the narrowest parliamentary majorities. Much turns on a dime.

Before the day is out, Gordon has made up his mind on exactly how he will announce that there will be NO election, with a pre-recorded interview on Saturday afternoon. It is one of those decisions a Prime Minister can only make alone even after all the advice.

Saturday 6th October

No matter the political backdrop, I organise an early birthday party for John; we are taking a small group of friends out to Whipsnade Safari Park. The date coincides with four small boys who are John's favourite friends all being around this weekend. Our group spends the day looking at various giraffes, rhinos and elephants through toy binoculars and even getting the chance to feed a few.

We head back to Chequers with some of John's friends in tow to all spend the night. We also have Rupert and Wendi Murdoch coming to visit that evening, their two little girls having joined us on the safari outing. I think that is one of the reasons that Gordon pre-recorded his BBC interview about the (non) election, so that no one could accuse him and Rupert Murdoch of having had an influential discussion on the subject. The BBC exclusive means the press team have to field bitter complaints from Sky and ITV that they did not get an interview with Gordon as well.

Gordon is keeping surprisingly cheerful, and Rupert is not really going near the subject – his papers over the last two weeks have been phenomenally difficult and, I think, rather unfair.

Sunday 7th October

Newspapers are vile today – I can see that there is lots of 'Who is to be blamed?' flying around. I hope they won't fight with each other, as this will only stretch out the story and the discomfort.

Friday 12th October

I have a Friday night girls' supper with my old school friends Ailsa, Fig, Caitlin, Sara, Soph and Zimena. I've known them since we were all 11-year-olds starting secondary school in North London. While we don't see each other every day, it is so easy to pick up where we left off each time we do meet. I cheated and ordered lots of delicious Marks and Spencer food as I knew I would not make time for cooking. Everyone was able to just come up to the flat for supper and, quite late in the evening, I took them round on a tour of the Number 10 state rooms. No visits to the china closet this time, but when I go to retell the story standing by the cupboard, I find out the door is now kept locked!

Saturday 13th October

Gordon did have to spend some of the day reading at Chequers, while I played with the boys, but we manage some time together over the weekend. One of the great privileges at Chequers is the swimming pool, installed in the seventies as a personal gift from the former US Ambassador Walter Annenberg, following a visit by HM The Queen with US President Richard Nixon. We always spend a lot of time outdoors, playing with favourite Lego and Thomas the Tank Engine toys, drawing, reading and just relaxing.

Sunday 14th October

Finally I persuade Gordon to go for a long walk with John in the morning and we have our own swim in the afternoon. Gordon's brother, Andrew, arrives with his boys, Alex and Patrick, for lunch, which delights John who charges around with them. As we get ready to head back to London, Andrew suggests taking John back with them for a sleepover. Much delight all round.

Tuesday 16th October

Libby Purves, the writer and broadcaster, comes in to see me for a coffee this morning. We talk about the death of her son, Nicholas, who took his own life at 23 after suffering years of mental illness. She is about to publish a book of his writings that she found after his death, and it has the most beautiful cover I have seen.

Having lost our own beautiful daughter Jennifer at only ten days old in 2002, I find that I talk often to people who have suffered the loss of a baby or child, and try to be helpful when their loss is recent to them, to help find a way through the pain of it. Today, I am able to learn more from Libby. As a writer, she has a tremendous capacity to organise her thinking and articulate her emotions. I find myself hanging on to her words; her clear expression of things that I know I have felt, too. What resonates with me is Libby talking about the permanent change that a great loss brings – the sense of entering a long, never-ending tunnel. I talk of my experience in turn, and can only hope it was some help. She is an extraordinarily smart, eloquent woman, who understands why her son took his own life but, like any mum, would love not to have lost him.

I remember Jennifer every day and often talk of her with Gordon, but it is also John's fourth birthday tomorrow, so the focus will all be on him.

Wednesday 17th October

John wakes up very excited, but I don't give him a day off school, and take him in as usual. In the afternoon, Gordon does make it back in time to be with the birthday boy. The word from the office is that the general atmosphere is so much lighter with the success of today's PMQs – it has lifted everyone's spirits.

Thursday 18th October

While Gordon is away in Lisbon for the big meeting about the European Treaty, I host a reception at Downing Street in the evening, for the maternal mortality campaigning charity, the White Ribbon Alliance. This is the umbrella organisation that campaigns against maternal deaths in developing countries, levels of which are still so high worldwide, with nearly 600,000 women dying each year due to pregnancy-related complications. I understand more and more that the mother lies at the heart of this issue; that too many are dying in pregnancy and childbirth leaving motherless children, who have such little chance in life in Africa or Southeast Asia.

There has been a huge gathering of politicians and campaigners from around the world at the Women Deliver conference in London today, and many of the delegates come to our evening gathering. I am getting to know all the main characters involved with this issue and am increasingly impressed. I have long focused my charity efforts on children's health, and how newborns and young children can improve their survival chances in the poorest countries of the world.

I have recently joined the international advisory board of the Royal College of Obstetricians and Gynaecologists meeting Jim Dornan, a senior obstetrician from Northern Ireland, who does not pull his punches when he tells me the facts around maternal death. He urges me to use my voice to raise the profile of this neglected issue, and I have already decided that I will.

Tonight, at 10 Downing Street, the White Ribbon Alliance is displaying exquisite and lovingly made quilts from all over the world, each of which tells the true story of a mother's death in Tanzania, in Burkina Faso, in India, in Bangladesh, in Pakistan, in Brazil, in Chile and many more countries. They are stunning, though heartbreakingly sad. The charity already has champions like the great Dame Judi Dench and actress Anna Chancellor, and this evening Douglas Alexander, the International Development Secretary, speaks, having proudly announced this morning the British government's grant of $50 million for maternal health, to include family planning, a critical part of the health equation for women. I join him in welcoming everyone and pledge to play my part in their campaign.

Sunday 21st October

Wandering down to see Gordon in his office, I discover that a parcel has arrived, postmarked 'The Nelson Mandela Foundation', and contains a lovely straw jeep for John and a big wooden gorilla for Fraser, from Graça and Madiba.

A funny story reaches us about a gift John recently wanted to send to Graça in South Africa, which was tucked into the diplomatic bag. The UK High Commissioner, Paul Boateng, had taken receipt of the important package and assumed it was the DBE insignia for Graça that had been presented in London. The High Commissioner duly invited Graça Machel DBE to the Residence for a grand unveiling amongst distinguished guests. As the parcel was opened, out came a great whoosh of glitter followed by John's big shiny card. Graça quickly remembered that she and John share the same birthday, and much laughter ensued.

Wednesday 31st October

Over the past week or so I have started out on my own visits around Britain. I am just back from a trip to the North East of England to visit the staff at the Labour Party HQ in Gosforth, and to visit a health centre in Newcastle with the local MP, our Government Chief Whip, Nick Brown. These new health centres are just amazing with their range of services, easy appointment systems and support during good and ill health. I plan to do more visits to see some of the new government investments in local communities (partly to respond helpfully to invitations to visit, and partly because I enjoy the visits so much).

Now I am back in London, I take some time to catch up in the office. I have agreed to become a new Patron of the women's health research charity Wellbeing of Women and have been getting acquainted with their staff and various projects. I am filling big shoes here, as a previous Patron was Diana, Princess of Wales, in the days when the charity was called Birthright. I will just have to do things my own way, and feel adamant I don't want comparison to anyone else.

It is my forty-fourth birthday today, and having never been a big birthday person, especially where there is no significant 'zero' at the end of the number, I just expect a quiet drink with Gordon at the end of the day. Instead, I discover that Gordon has organised surprise drinks for 20 or so of my girlfriends, including Jo Rowling, Mariella Frostrup, Emma Freud and Kathy Lette. Everyone had gathered quietly (with champagne, so maybe not that quietly) in Number 11, and then crept up to hide in the sitting room in the flat. John and Fraser were there, too, in fancy dress (skeleton and pumpkin respectively) after Trick or Treating around the building. They raised over £120 for charity, choosing PiggyBankKids this year! I get a huge surprise as I walk into the sitting room with Gordon and it does take a moment to realise what is happening. I am even surprised with a 'Spooky Sarah

Brown' cake made by Maggie and decorated imaginatively by my children. Kathy tells me that when they had gathered downstairs, Gordon had walked in and announced, 'Sarah has gone out, but you get me instead,' which they actually believed for a few moments. The whole evening is lovely and I am very spoilt with lots of girly gifts, as well, but I don't make it too late a night as I have an important day tomorrow.

Thursday 1st November

Gordon and I are both up early this morning to pay a visit to the hospital in Selly Oak, Birmingham, where our injured soldiers from Iraq, Afghanistan and elsewhere are treated. This is a very moving visit, mainly because of the evident dedication and professionalism of the health teams and the personal, moving stories of the patients and families we speak to. There is great appreciation towards Gordon in taking time to be there, but the privilege is really ours.

Friday 2nd November

Gordon suggests that he stays in London all day to work on his important speech in the House of Commons chamber that follows the Queen's Speech at the State Opening of Parliament next week. I intervene and insist on getting home to Scotland for a weekend, and lining up whatever help he wants there.

John, Fraser and I set off for City Airport ahead of him and, luckily for us, Alistair and Maggie are on the same flight to Edinburgh. On arrival, Alistair goes off in his car and we take Maggie in ours to do food shopping at the nearby shopping centre, as we will both have bare fridges at home. By the time I get the boys and the food back to our house in Fife, Gordon is already there ahead of us, and admits it is great to be home.

Monday 5th November

I spend much of today rushing around 10 Downing Street from meeting to quick greeting. One treat is to see my Aunt Doreen, my mum's big sister who is over visiting from her home in Pittsburgh, USA. This is the first time she has seen us in Number 10, and I take great pride at showing her round. She is interested, but she also wants to see Fraser who is changing so quickly at the moment, as one year olds do.

Tuesday 6th November

Today is the Queen's Speech and my first time to sit up in the House of Lords gallery to watch the State Opening of Parliament ceremony. I have a great jacket from M&S to wear in a strong on-trend acid yellow, and have found a navy hat at Selfridges that has just the right little bit of yellow in the band to go with it. I have a number of designer outfits earmarked for other events coming up, having just bought a Graeme Black dress from net-a-porter.com, and asked Amanda Wakeley to keep aside a dress covered in Swarovski crystals for the Lord Mayor's Banquet coming up soon.

After any event that is covered by the media, my office invariably gets calls and emails from reporters asking for confirmation of what I was wearing, from coat and dress to shoes and jewellery. As a result – as I choose my own clothes – I always remember to send a quick email to my office about what I have on. Whoever is on duty just keeps a note and will pass it on when asked. My only rule of thumb is to keep wearing British, whether high street or designer.

Maggie and I walk over to the House of Commons together and take our seats in the gallery for the long wait. It's a fantastic vantage point to watch all the various people to-ing and fro-ing in their outfits. The House of Lords chamber is quite spectacular, with the Royal thrones at one end and the link door to the House of

Commons at the other. The peers wear their red robes, the Ladies have their evening dresses and tiaras, and the High Commissioners are there in various national outfits.

The Queen's Speech today covers, in brief, the direction that Gordon wants to take his new Government; to build on the Labour achievements of the last ten years. The speech starts by saying the new policies are 'to respond to the rising aspirations of the people of the United Kingdom; to ensure security for all; and to entrust more power to Parliament and the people'. There are to be new bills and legislation to encourage young people to stay in education or training until the age of 18; for skills training for adults; to reform apprenticeships; to achieve higher levels of employment; to provide services for people in care; and to improve the balance between work and family life. The new government programme is to look at meeting people's aspirations for better education, housing, healthcare and children's services, and for a cleaner environment, and to raising educational standards and giving everyone the chance to reach their full potential. In short, it is a Queen's Speech for people, to enable everyone to improve their own lives, whatever the challenges.

After the speech, I walk back to Number 10 and head to my office to catch up with paperwork. Pauline has returned to the Honours section and I am now overwhelmed by the backlog of correspondence, and don't even have anyone to look after my diary at the moment. Even so, I do nip back at 3 p.m. to watch Gordon give his speech in the House of Commons. Maggie and I have Speaker's passes to sit in the West Gallery, which means that we are sitting over the Labour heads and looking straight at the Opposition benches – a very different perspective. Maggie and I are both quite shocked by the ill-mannered, uncouth behaviour of the Tories. Not because their job is to attack government, and especially Gordon, but because it is done in a very confident, sneery, personal way. I am here to listen to Gordon's speech as he highlights the up-coming changes for the country, but as I sit here just trying to hear his words above the noise, I feel I am sadly coming to understand why people in elected office can become so embittered towards both the media and the confrontational opposition politics in the UK. There is no clear statement of counter-proposals, just attacks of a personal, unpleasant nature. I have heard being in opposition called 'power without responsibility', and now I see why. Still, Gordon's speech goes well, despite the many interruptions, and will, I hope, be fairly reported.

I am not, though, as a spectator, in a rush to come back to the debating chamber.

Sunday 11th November

Today, as it is Remembrance Sunday, we will leave Chequers to return to London. It is Gordon's first time to lay a wreath at the Cenotaph and my first time to attend, although I have always watched the service on television. The staff at Number 10 has provided a DVD of last year's service and written instructions for putting the poppy wreath down, which is surprisingly helpful. The accuracy of following the guidelines feels like an important mark of respect, and all the more so for Gordon, following his visits to conflict areas.

Before we leave Chequers for the service on Whitehall, I take Gordon for a swim very early, without the kids, and afterwards suggest that he practises the stepping up to the Cenotaph on the steps in the rose garden. A bit daft, perhaps, but done for the right reasons.

We walk out of Number 10's front door and straight across the street and through a gate to the Foreign and Commonwealth Office quad. Jack Straw is in the middle of the quad speaking to an assembled group of soldiers, although I don't know why. All the same, we wait in an archway and are joined by a very upbeat John Major, who is very warm to Gordon.

Once Jack Straw has finished, I find my way to the Foreign

Office, and stand, watching events from a window with David Miliband's wife, Louise Shackelton, and the Queen's Deputy Private Secretary, Edward Young. We chat about the Commonwealth Heads of Government meeting coming up and, after a grim, rainy start, the weather brightens and the service passes off very well.

The reception afterwards in the wonderfully ornate Locarno Room in the Foreign Office is very straightforward, reflecting the sombre mood of the occasion. I recognise the Government Hospitality manager who is on duty, and he makes the lovely gesture of offering me my preferred decaf tea – very clever.

Monday 12th November

The Sun has run a photo of Gordon with his eyes shut, saying he slept at the Remembrance Service. This is completely and blatantly untrue. No one expects the positive coverage of the first few months of Gordon's leadership to last indefinitely, but it is shocking how negative some papers are. The attacks are personal and seem designed to occupy a lot of time in being refuted, squeezing down the time needed to do the real job.

It is the night of the big annual Lord Mayor's Banquet hosted for over 1,000 guests at the Guildhall in the City of London. Gordon is back in white tie and tails for the third time since he took over, so perhaps it will be worth the enormous bespoke investment from Gieves & Hawkes. I have black and white diamonds from Garrard to go with my exquisite black Amanda Wakeley dress – both rented, and due back tomorrow.

I am told the five-hour event has been simplified but we still march in to slow handclapping, weaving around the room, a long-standing Guildhall banqueting tradition. The new City of London Lord Mayor and Lady Mayoress, David and Theresa Lewis, are there (this is different to the elected London Mayor).

There are lots of loyal toasts and traditional speeches. Gordon's speech is, as is usual, a major keynote address about Foreign Policy.

It falls to the Archbishop of Canterbury, Rowan Williams, to deliver an entertaining speech full of jokes about the new Lord Mayor. I have only heard him give great sermons, but it turns out that he is also warm, widely read and very witty, too.

Although we get back late, Gordon and I stay up and chat for a bit, which is lovely. He and I both know that he has done really well with his speech. I think that, outfits-wise, we have also both acquitted ourselves well (since Gordon chose to dress formally after the surprising amount of controversy following his personal choice to avoid wearing black tie for the last ten years). And I know that all my efforts to look good will also mean no press coverage – it is only the opposite that will attract comment.

Tuesday 13th November

I join the 'Spouse in the House' reception downstairs in Number 11 for the wives of Labour MPs and Peers. They are a nice crowd and mostly live in the constituencies represented by their spouse, so don't get to meet very often. Maggie Darling was fab, serving all the drinks. Rather wonderfully, the spouses were running the bar themselves. I wish more charities did that when their precious funds are limited.

Wednesday 14th November

Today I have a meeting with Mrs Suzanne Mubarak, the First Lady of Egypt, who is in London for the opening of the Tutankhamun exhibition with the Prince of Wales at the O2 Centre. I have a good briefing on the phone from former government minister and Middle-East expert, Liz Symons, who generously comes and talks me through a basic primer.

Mrs Mubarak is a gracious visitor and I realise I am in the hands of a woman who has, over many years, really worked out how to get so many things done for a number of women's and children's causes in her country. She has been very effective at campaigning for more women to take on their own careers and to take on increasingly senior positions in medicine, law and the public sector.

I thought Gordon was back with us in the flat for the evening, when he is called back downstairs and goes to meet Ed Miliband from the Cabinet Office, and then Alistair Darling. It seems that the Inland Revenue has lost a crucial disk containing a lot of personal tax and bank account information. Everyone is very anxious, especially as the Inland Revenue is not being very clear – they have already provided news that they found the disk, and then said it is not true. It all sounds fairly hideous. Much later, Gordon finally gets a drink and some supper (luckily a favourite – the Chequers steak pie, taken out of the freezer earlier on).

Thursday 15th November

Gordon and I keep a long-standing commitment to visit Lady Wilson at her flat in Westminster to see Harold Wilson's memorabilia. Both her sons, Robin and Giles, are there and say hello, but Giles has to dash off to work. He was a maths teacher but retrained to fulfil a long-held passion to be a train driver. Robin lives in Oxford, teaching maths there and with the Open University (famously established by his father).

We spend a lovely hour looking at all kinds of photos and books. Mary has all his garter seals and things from the Palace. She also has a great collection of biographies. Most interesting are some of the photographs taken with other PMs, Cabinet Ministers and US Presidents (JFK and Lyndon B Johnson). We leave with plans to find a date for Mary Wilson and her family to come and visit Chequers.

Gordon returns to work, and the case of the missing disk. I have a more pleasant engagement attending a lunch hosted by Lynn de Rothschild at her gorgeous home in Chelsea. She has very sweetly put together a group of women for lunch to meet me. Stella McCartney is there, pregnant with her third child, and I warm to her immediately. Trudie Styler, on my other side, is passionate about her work for the Rainforest Foundation. I promise to find her the right people to speak to about a problem faced by an indigenous tribe in Equador.

Monday 19th November

I take John to school and return to the flat with Fraser. He is playing happily while I get ready to join Gordon at an official event. Mela arrives mid morning and takes Fraser so I can head off to the Diamond Wedding Anniversary service for the Queen and HRH The Duke of Edinburgh.

It is a particularly lovely service in Westminster Abbey. Alas, Maggie and Alistair Darling are not there as I had thought, as he is preparing for his Northern Rock statement in the Commons which will be challenging as the situation is not getting any easier. In addition, he has the Inland Revenue data disk problem still rumbling on, as it is so serious that people's personal information may be at risk. As the days go by no one knows if the data disk will ever resurface which if it were to fall into the wrong hands is a good thing, but an end to the matter would be more reassuring.

CHAPTER 6

Off to Africa

Wednesday 21st November

My first overseas visit accompanying Gordon is to the biennial Commonwealth Heads of Government meeting, being held this year in Kampala, the capital of Uganda in East Africa.

The Commonwealth is the group of countries that have at one time counted HM Queen Elizabeth II and her forebears as their monarch. This includes big countries like Canada, Australia and India, and small ones like Malta, who hosted this event last time.

Gordon has always commented that it is such an interesting gathering of countries, and leaders, you can't help but get some useful work done.

I head out today to East Africa, two days ahead of Gordon, as I have an invitation from President Jakaya Kikwete to visit the neighbouring country of Tanzania, where I grew up as a young girl. My dad worked for educational publishers, Longman, while my mum set up and ran a nursery school from the grounds of our home. We travelled out in 1965 (when I was two and my brother, Sean, about six months old) to live first in the village of Arusha, halfway up Mount Kilimanjaro.

During our happy time there, our younger brother, Bruce, arrived to great local acclaim as he weighed in at over 10lbs and had a shock of blond hair. My earliest memory is of the local Tanzanians coming to visit to see this uncommonly large baby and laughing out loud as they set eyes on him.

We then moved to Dar es Salaam, where Sean and I started at the International School there, and Bruce joined my mum's nursery. I vividly remember the look and sense of our home; the local people, including Susannah and Edward, who helped look after us; the sound of Swahili being spoken – I can still recall a few phrases; the long weekends spent on glorious white sand beaches; and memorably seeing wild animals close up in the safari parks from VW camper vans, with family friends including the 'Flying Doctor' (who piloted his own small plane to get somewhere fast in an emergency). Altogether we were there about six years or so, and returned to the UK to live in England in 1971.

This is my first visit back to Tanzania in 36 years and I am really excited. I fly to the capital, Dar es Salaam, to be met by the High Commissioner, Philip Parham, and his wife, Kasia, and then to the airport lounge where I am greeted by the Tanzanian First Lady Mama Salma Kikwete. We start to chat and hope to know each other better. Her first language is Kiswahili, so she struggles a bit with her English and clearly feels very inhibited. I can tell she is otherwise a very feisty and outgoing person, and a good communicator. She talks of her own charitable foundation, Wanawake Na Maendeleo (WAMA), and its work to create scholarships for young women to attend secondary boarding schools, and to communicate with adults to protect children from HIV/AIDS infection.

We are driven to the High Commission Residence, have a quick chat and agree to meet the next day. I am really pleased to have moved from 'Your Excellency' to 'Mama Salma' in that time. Her informality is very refreshing.

It is interesting, too, to meet the High Commissioner and his wife. He is young and has been in Tanzania for two years, and must be ready to move to a new posting. They have six children, who are all back in England at boarding schools. Kasia is a very slim woman, lovely looking, with a warm manner. She is passionate about education and has immersed herself in teaching special needs both at the privileged International School of Tanganyika and the Dogodogo Centre for homeless boys and AIDS orphans.

At supper, we dine on delicious but very un-African quiche on the mosquito-screened veranda with the Parhams, joined by my team including Konrad, plus Clive Gardner and Craig Rowe from the protection team, who were assigned to deliver me safely to Uganda. The Commission staff is delightful and I think we kept them up late – the temptation is to watch the England–Croatia football game, which no one has a good feeling about. I call home and speak to Gordon, John and Fraser. They sound happy, which makes it not too bad for me to be away.

I climb into my bed surrounded by mosquito nets as political secretary Fiona Gordon texts me the football goals from back home (we lost 2–3).

Despite the gap in time since my last stay here, I feel I am in a familiar country. Some of my old memories and senses must still be deeply ingrained in me.

Thursday 22nd November

This morning I was up at 6 a.m., had a quick bath and then break-fasted downstairs in the High Commission. Full English is on offer but I opt for the mango, yoghurt and homemade muesli.

A local hairdresser called Peter is here. I am not sure I need a hairdresser but it would be rude to cancel at short notice. Peter watches the TV avidly as he does not have one at home. My hair gets a quick blow-dry and he wants my autograph.

A little later, I climb into the car and drive to Msese Road to see our old family house of 36 years ago – a white bungalow. I remember so well the garden, the trees and the veranda, and even meet the current residents, a couple from India. The plot of land has been divided into two and a separate house built where my mother used to run the nursery school out of the garage.

Afterwards, I squeeze in a nice trip to some shops to buy trinkets and things for the boys. I think I did well but clearly overpaid as I had no time for haggling. I will have to refund the High Commissioner £90 on our return!

We drive to WAMA after a quick outfit change into my smart, white Jaeger suit that I wore for Gordon's speech at this year's Labour Party Conference, and a draped scarf. I decide to risk low heels although I am warned there is a bit of walking to do.

I meet the First Lady again. She has a nice suite of offices and clearly a good team of women around her, especially Fatima. There are lots of local press and cameras crammed into the room. We exchange gifts (she to me: a large wooden framed carving of Africa, a statue of mother and child and a handmade basket all of which I will be able to keep as they fall within the right limits for official gifts; me to her: a book on London provided by Number 10 and my personal gift, a bright red shiny LK Bennett handbag. I hope she likes it).

There is a strict rule that no gifts worth more than £140 can be kept by the Prime Minister and spouse – not unless the additional value of the gift is paid personally, something we have rarely done (just two pedal cars for the boys if I remember correctly).

We move on to visit the Muhimbili Hospital. Everyone crowds into a meeting room, and there are lots of handshakes and lots of press. The hospital CMO speaks to provide a welcome and we set off. Dr Tony Falconer, both a medical consultant and the new Senior Vice President (and tipped as the next President) of the Royal College of Obstetricians and Gynaecologists (RCOG) International, joins me. He is an impressively focused man who is already proving to be a dream for me to work with. He has travelled out from the UK with Dr Nynke van der Broek from the Liverpool School of Tropical Medicine, who has designed the obstetrics training courses we are here to celebrate. We look first at temporary accommodation for labour wards, high-risks wards, neonatal ward and antenatal clinic, and are told that more permanent wards are under construction.

Childbirth is the most momentous and personal thing, and so it is hard to see so many women faced with difficulties. A highlight is the woman who gave birth naturally to quadruplets (all doing well). She was from Lindi region like Mama Kikwete, who I think plans to help her financially.

In the boardroom, the hospital's Chief Obstetrician Dr Lema introduces me to speak. I focus on the work of the UK government and the role of other organisations like the RCOG. I thank everyone and hand over to Tony Falconer who speaks about the RCOG's work, and the recent successful training course.

Later, our British High Commissioner hosts a lunch for me to meet 14 very interesting Tanzanian women. He invites me to speak at the start. I take the opportunity to explain my association with Tanzania, my visit to my old house and the purposes of my official visits (to hear from the First Lady her priorities, and to follow my own interest in visiting the hospital). I wheel out John's 'Lady Party' joke again. We all get on so well that by the end of lunch the women are still chuckling, and send best wishes to the Leader of the Lady Party. I give everyone a small gift of a Downing Street trinket box.

When it is time to go, I say a warm goodbye to Kasia – it is amazing how you move from strangers to friends in a day.

On the plane to Uganda, Konrad and I are seated next to the Tanzanian President. I have a good conversation with President Kikwete about maternal health and he is both well briefed and talks passionately about tackling the problem in his country. We talk of my childhood in Tanzania, of Gordon and the Education for All initiative, of the President's likelihood to head the African Union next year (he tells me he will accept, if invited in January). He is smart, young and charismatic and will doubtless be a more visible figure on the international stage in the future.

When we land at Entebbe, the President takes the initiative to separate our exits and heads off to great fanfare. I step off the plane a little later, and more quietly, and head off with Konrad to a quiet bit of the airport lounge to wait for our bags. Although we only have hand luggage, the Tanzanian government gifts (the statue and the carving) have travelled in the hold.

I am to have Ugandan police protection all week who now take charge of our transport and take us off to Kampala and on to our hotel. We get to our very new resort hotel around 7 p.m. and are met by hotel manager, Stephen Smith, who turns out to be the brother of my friend, Penny Smith, the television presenter and author – small world indeed.

Once in the room I have time for a nice bath and a bit of TV – oddly watching David Tennant, David Morrissey and Sarah Parish in *Blackpool*. As Gordon and his team don't arrive until after midnight I have supper with Craig Rowe. I have the vegetarian Thai curry, while Craig braves a very undercooked burger, and we go through our itinerary for the time in Uganda. I am to divide my time between the official spouses' programme and other charity visits.

Friday 23rd November

Gordon and I are abruptly woken by a 6.30 a.m. breakfast doorbell. My fault – I booked it thinking Gordon would be up! The press seem to be very grumpy back home. A news story has broken that UK Army generals are personally criticising Gordon rather heavily. It is clearly a purposeful, political and coordinated attack but not to be shrugged off for that. The shame is that Gordon has worked very hard to understand defence and meet its needs, and thought that most relationships were okay. They probably are okay for the most part, but clearly not with the two generals who are speaking directly to the press.

After breakfast, we travel by car for half an hour to a conference centre. Gordon and I go our separate ways after a quick handshake with Uganda's President Museveni, and Secretary-General of the Commonwealth Don McKinnon and his really lovely wife, Clare de Lore, whom we have met on numerous occasions before – notably at the Commonwealth Heads of Government Meeting for Finance Ministers in London when Don was new to the job. I had been seated by Don and Clare at the finance minister's dinner and got on so well that we have kept in touch ever since.

The Commonwealth Heads of Government meetings here seem to have a long agenda, but at the heart of it today is the decision to suspend Pakistan from membership again. A new Secretary-General of the Commonwealth to replace Don, who is retiring, must also be elected. It already seems certain to be the Indian candidate, the current High Commissioner in London, Kamalesh Sharma, which will suit everyone.

In the holding room for spouses, I introduce myself to people and chat to the Maltese Premier's wife who hosted the previous meeting. We are seated again for the opening ceremony in the presence of the Queen who is, of course, the head of all the Commonwealth countries. There is a long wait, lots of speeches, and an unusual dance performance of the history of Uganda.

We move on by minibus to attend a spouses' lunch hosted by the President's wife, Mrs Janet Museveni. The Duchess of Cornwall is the guest of honour as she has travelled with HRH Prince Charles to the meetings this week. I am under strict instructions from the High Commission to attend to the Duchess and to ensure that all goes smoothly. I have no idea why it would be thought that I would not.

As I enter the hotel where the lunch is to be held, *Sun* photographer Arthur Edwards asks me, on behalf of the Royal press corps, whether I will be curtseying. 'Yes,' I say.

'I knew you would, Sarah. The others thought you might not.'

In the foyer, a very nervous spouse of the Deputy High Commissioner waits to greet the Duchess and introduce me. When the Duchess arrives I duly curtsey. The photographers all take their shots and I know the picture editors back home have their story. I am just glad I am wearing a beautiful blue Amanda Wakeley suit.

The rest of my day encompasses a very moving visit to the Ugandan Society for Disabled Children with their patron, Terry

Waite, and a formal evening dinner for the government leaders and spouses. This does not run very late which means a nice early night back at the hotel.

Saturday 24th November

Having discharged my duties on the spouses' programme, I can embark on my own visits, and have a small programme of health visits I have arranged with Tony Falconer and Dr Andrew Weeks from Liverpool, who have flown in to help. We go first to Mulago Hospital, the biggest one in Uganda. Here I am faced with a direct view of the harsh realities of having a baby in Africa. There are simply not enough doctors and midwives, not enough equipment, not enough medical supplies. Two moments stick with me. One is the image of a small delivery room with eight little cots in it. All the babies are alone as their mothers have died in childbirth – all on this one day. I also vividly recall my conversation with Sylvie Numuwange, a young woman with her baby curled up beside her. She is just relieved that they had both survived as she has five other children at home. The Canadian photographer, Thomas Froese, is with us and captures our image together. He asks her permission to publish her photo and urges me to write an article using the picture when I get home.

We fit in another visit, to the Nagura Health Centre. It has more limited facilities and from time to time suffers from electricity failure, which makes surgical work impossible. It is uplifting to see the work of an innovative 'adolescent' clinic that really looks at the needs of young people and educates them in understanding their own health, from HIV/AIDS to pregnancy.

My final visit of the day is to the inspirational Safe Alternatives For Youth project in a slum area. The SAFY volunteers make a huge and touching effort for our visit, and it is quite something to walk through the slum pathways to meet everyone. It is a sunny day so the pathways are dry, but I imagine that when the rains fall these paths are just rivers of mud.

Before we leave, I have an amusing tussle with Sue Nye about a giant box of footballs and kit that has been organised by Number 10 adviser Stewart Wood as a gift from the Football Association. Football is loved so much in Africa and enough kit for two teams will transform many an afternoon for these people. The kit is a mixture of all the Premiership clubs, with a couple of sets from each football team. Sue wants to take out the Newcastle United strips that advertise Northern Rock on the front. Ever mindful of a negative press story, she is sensitive to the fact that by deciding to help out Northern Rock on behalf of the taxpayer (the Bank of England helped them out with their 'liquidity' problem earlier this month), the government could be seen as sponsoring a football team. I try to resist, but Sue wins. I know she is right.

Sunday 25th November

After a final official dinner held at the State House in Entebbe last night, we're heading back to the UK this morning.

The whole UK government delegation travels together on a chartered plane. I settle down, watch a film and then write all my thank-you letters and a whole set of notes on the maternal health issue. Pondering the visit, I feel an enormous sense of pride at the privilege of representing the United Kingdom, our government and, of course, our PM. I also think that with my small team of Konrad, Gil and me, we had put together a great little programme that made good use of the time. I have now seen first-hand the desperate need to address health issues in Africa. We just can't live in a world where mothers suffer and die unnecessarily in child-birth, and no one counts this as important. I know that this is one of the Millennium Development Goals (MDGs are the targets agreed by all the countries of the United Nations to reduce global poverty around the world; and improve human rights, nutrition, access to water and sanitation, education, global health and the environment by 2015) that no one seems to be talking about or acting upon, and I just hope I can do more here myself.

*

We get back to the flat in time for the boys' supper time, and it is just a joy to see them both. Gordon has to head straight off to his office and fine-tune a speech to British industry. I am more fortunate and can succumb to my tiredness and get a good night's sleep.

CHAPTER 7

Festive Greetings

Monday 26th November

I'm really feeling now that Christmas is approaching. Christmas preparations for the Prime Minister are fairly complex, and start months earlier with the design choices for the decoration of the Downing Street Christmas trees – there is one out in the street and at least three more inside to think about.

Also to be decided upon is the design of the official Number 10 card (and time to be made to personally sign hundreds and hundreds of them), and of an additional Downing Street card for staff to buy and send, too. Our Christmas card this year has been designed by renowned children's illustrator, Shirley Hughes (it is the National Year of Reading), and she will come in person to officially turn on the Christmas tree lights at the start of December.

We also need to choose personal gifts from Gordon and me to the team of around 250, including those at Number 10, Chequers and parliamentary staff. We of course have our own Christmas shopping to do for family and friends, so thank goodness for the internet. I always seem to end up ordering presents for Fife when I'm in London, and vice versa – when we first moved to Downing Street I found it wasn't uncommon to place an order and just never receive the goods. When I investigated why, I discovered that because of the Downing Street address, my orders were sometimes thought to be pranks and did not go through. So now my online orders go to a different address, which seems to solve the problem.

*

This is a time of year so many charities and groups ask for receptions, and we try to fit as many as possible in. Over the coming days we have receptions for the Terrence Higgins Trust, for the Stephen Lawrence Trust bursary students, a visit from actor Henry 'The Fonz' Winkler who is a great supporter of dyslexia charities, a temporary exhibition of Sam Taylor Wood's portraits of Maggie's Centres users in Fife, the visit from this year's *Woman's Own* children of courage, and a reception for the flood heroes from our emergency services.

We also set up two photo shoots that get squeezed into the diary on a day when Gordon is definitely in Number 10. The first is with established photographer Tom Miller who is booked to take some official pictures of Gordon, and I have separately booked him personally to take some of me, to use where personal pictures are requested for anything from a charity publication to members of the public. I am really looking forward to seeing Tom as he was at school with me and I have not seen him since, and know he has photographs in the National Portrait Gallery.

The second shoot is with David Bailey, who has agreed to set up his studio at Number 10 to photograph Gordon for *GQ* magazine as part of a political series. As it is the legendary Bailey, I poke my head in to see how the session is going, and all I can hear is Bailey addressing Gordon as 'Fella', amid a sea of busy assistants, which amuses me. I have as a memento a great shot he took of me and Gordon, just for our private use.

The afternoon sees me at a reception to thank all the students and volunteers who helped Gordon in his leadership campaign, when we hear the news that Peter Watt, the General Secretary of the Labour Party, has resigned in order to clear his name during a row about a political donor that is rumbling on. It is very sad to see this happen. I leave the reception to make a call to Peter's wife, Vilma. She will obviously be a tremendous support to Peter during this difficult time for him.

Tuesday 27th November

I attend the British Fashion Awards as Stuart Rose's guest, as he is the current chair of the British Fashion Council. I choose to wear a dress by Britt Lintner, an American based in Britain who created her own label while still working in a hedge fund, and the mum of two small boys. She steers me into a brown velvet dress that even wins the approval of *Telegraph* fashion editor Hilary Alexander. Stella McCartney wins Designer of the Year, and I am delighted that I have picked that night to wear a pair of her shoes. It was, however, one of the worst-run events I have ever been to – terrible food, nothing ran to time, the actual awards were haphazard and a bit erratic, with speeches no one listened to. Then I twigged, of course, that it was exactly as it should be for a fashion event: no one eats anyway, and everyone just wants to talk and network all night, which is exactly what happened.

Thursday 6th December

I have decided to stick my neck out a bit on the maternal health issue, and I have written an article drawing on my trip to Tanzania and Uganda, which the *New Statesman* magazine has agreed to publish alongside Thomas Froese's picture of me with Sylvie and her new baby in Kampala.

Sunday 9th December

Gordon leaves early this morning for a visit to both Iraq and Afghanistan to see our British troops, and take a Christmas message from everyone in Britain that their service is appreciated. This is an important visit for him and I am sure it will be well received on the ground out there. I would love to accompany him to show my support too, but understandably the armed forces limit the visitors to just essential ones, or super VIPs like sports stars, who can really provide a lift to troops in tough times. As usual there is a news blackout for security purposes at the start of Gordon's visit – coverage of his trips to these sorts of areas is only broadcast once he has left them.

Monday 10th December

Gordon came back in the middle of the night. Truthfully, it is always a relief to get him back from any visit to a conflict zone, but the combined disruption to my sleep from anxiety about where he is and the late-night return is less welcome, as I am already coping with some very broken nights and early starts with the baby at the moment. At nearly 18 months old, Fraser is doing terrifically well, but we are not through the night feeds yet, and his days start as early as 5 a.m. I am hoping in the New Year that we will turn a corner and some more sleeping hours will be found. I am very determined to fit in the workload and evening commitments for the charity receptions, but the constant tiredness is beyond articulation. I remember, from similar times with John, that a moment does come when you look back and wonder how you coped, but right now I am in the 'just get on and manage it day by day' phase. Frankly, I have to be optimistic on a daily basis that the change to longer, settled hours is just around the corner – it is the only way to think.

Thursday 13th December

I have the luxury of a few days free. Yesterday, John and I went to see *The Nutcracker* at the Royal Opera House with friends, and he was mesmerised by the dancing (and fighting) mice.

This afternoon a group of us also go out to see the big King Tut exhibition at the O2 Centre. I have strong childhood memories of the Tutankhamun Exhibition in the 1970s, and I see there is something about Egyptology that still fascinates children today.

Friday 14th December

I take the boys down to Chequers for the weekend as Gordon is in Portugal and Brussels for what is an important meeting with other leaders, to sign the Lisbon Treaty (an agreement that amends the two treaties that make up the constitutional basis of the European Union).

When I am on my own with the boys, Downing Street can seem very empty at the weekends, especially if Maggie Darling is away. At Chequers, the members of staff are good company and pitch in with entertaining John and Fraser, and it is easy and lovely to have friends over to visit. We know a few people in the area, too (I was born about 30 miles up the road in Beaconsfield, but left the area when I was two years old so can't exactly claim status as a local).

I have had a pretty good time with the kids today, but I have missed watching the news, something that does give me the opportunity to find out how Gordon's day has gone. By the time he gets back to us, I can spot at once by his tired expression that he has had a long day batting for Britain.

Saturday 15th December

Just a bit of time with the family makes Gordon relax after this pressurised start to the weekend, and he spends a fair bit of time outdoors with John, and then back inside watching CBeebies online and sorting shapes in a box with Fraser. Heaven for me, too, as I put my feet up with a cup of tea.

Tonight, Gordon and I have a small dinner with HRH Prince Andrew, Duke of York, who works with the government as an international business envoy, and the Admiral Lord and Lady West. Alan West, the National Security Minister, is also under scrutiny from the media this weekend but in his case it is an accusation about his private life – of an alleged close friendship with the dark-haired singer from Eurovision supergroup ABBA,

Anni-Frid Lyngstad. The Wests take the story in pretty good humour as Anni-Frid is a friend of theirs (and whom we have met in the past at a dinner hosted on a big naval ship when Alan was still the Navy Chief).

Their good humour helps Gordon further unwind. We have a very jolly night, part business, part fun, and I take everyone up to the library for coffee afterwards. The three guests are all very interested in the history of Chequers and in seeing some of its treasures. I show them the treasured ring that belonged to Queen Elizabeth I and Admiral Lord Nelson's pocket watch. Without thinking, I also open the drawer that holds the wax death mask of Oliver Cromwell to show everyone. There is a bit of a collective gasp, and I suddenly realise that this might not have been the most diplomatically sensitive gesture on my part: showing the face of the Great Protector and signer of King Charles I's death warrant to a member of the Royal Family. Stumbling apologies ensue on my part, although the Duke is, of course, very gracious about it.

I am pretty sure that Alan and Rosie will forever tease me about this.

Sunday 16th December

As it's the week before Christmas, we host a big lunch with lots and lots of children: Cabinet Minister Ruth Kelly, and her husband, Derek, come with their four; Kirsty Young and Nick Jones have their four; and so, too, does Africa Minister Mark Malloch Brown and his American wife, Trish. The kids eat at two separate round tables in the Great Hall and there is a giant platter of home-cooked chicken nuggets, chips and veg for the little ones.

Piers Morgan is also here with his girlfriend, Celia Walden, and finds himself sitting next to PepsiCo chief, Indra Nooyi, one of very few women chief executives of a large international plc firm. Piers is his usual ebullient and talkative self. I sit with International Development minister, Shriti Vadera, just watching his conversation as he puts forward one confident but outrageous view after another to this corporate high-flyer (although he does predict a winning run for Senator Obama at this stage). Suddenly, Indra clearly decides that while she might be very entertained, she has had her fill of the views of Piers, and this sophisticated corporate leader leans forward and tells him that she has identified his type – he is an FOS.

'Oh,' says Piers, 'that sounds important. What does FOS stand for?'

'Full of S**t,' comes the reply.

Shriti and I nearly choke on our desserts we laugh so hard. Luckily, Piers can laugh at himself, too, or lunch might have ended badly.

Monday 17th December

I know the actual Christmas holidays are about to start when I find myself posing for a photo holding up a frozen turkey in the hallway of Downing Street in front of the decorated Christmas tree. I am assured that this is a long-standing tradition, where we receive a great gift of a turkey for our own use, to support Britain's turkey farmers at what is clearly a critical trading point in the year. I meet Paul Kelly from Kelly's Turkeys in Essex, and his wife, Marisa, and we all pose with our frozen bird.

I explain to Mr Kelly that I have kept to our own Brown family tradition for Christmas: I have internet-ordered my turkey to go to Scotland and, as I have done for years, I have ordered from Kelly's Turkeys. It is a small world. We agree that the gift turkey will go up the road to The Connection at St Martin-in-the-Fields – the charity run in the crypt of the church by Trafalgar Square that serves a great Christmas Day meal to those who don't have a home to go to then. Happily, Mr Kelly agrees that he will supply as many turkeys as are needed to serve everyone there that day. Excellent festive spirit.

All kinds of gift hampers also arrive as official gifts, and exceed the threshold for gifts we can receive, so we agree that the contents of these can also go up the road for The Connection's meal, as I can't bear the idea of it going to waste.

Wednesday 19th December

We head home to North Queensferry, with a few days before Christmas in which to sort out food and get the house decorated for our own family time. No matter what else is going on, arriving back in Fife always feels like home, and the place where we can relax as much as is ever possible these days. The Metropolitan Police protection team have settled into their local accommodation and are always on hand when Gordon needs them and are working very well with the local Fife Police.

Saturday 22nd December

I just love waking up at home in Fife where we have our own choice of home décor, belongings, and wonderful fresh air. None of us gets to spend as much time outdoors down south as we do in Scotland. After a hectic few weeks, Gordon is already feeling better after just one good night's sleep, good food and a bit of Fife air. He has to make some final calls before the break, but also takes the time to wander out of the study to watch football, have a mid afternoon kip, and a long relaxing bath.

Now we are home, I am just focused on having a good holiday break with the family, decorating our own tree, wrapping gifts and stocking up the fridge for the festive days ahead. Gordon is able to spend good chunks of time with us switched off, but he is also concerned about the economy; not just Britain's, but worldwide.

While this is a time when people are feeling that things are getting better, Gordon always likes to do his homework. I can see that his holiday-reading pile has a lot of weighty tomes about international economic issues past and present. Having come through the near collapse of one building society, I imagine that he does not want to take anything for granted.

Monday 24th December

We have a fantastic Christmas Eve walk along our favourite local beach with the boys. It's loved by us, as it is where Gordon proposed to me back on Millennium New Year's Day.

Tuesday 25th December

No one is up too early but when John and Fraser finally get to them, the Christmas stockings are a success. Another great beach walk today; this time, John links hands with us and Fraser and says he wants to walk as a family. It is very touching. Good lunch with the boys and my parents – their Grandma and Pops. A gentle, peaceful day.

Wednesday 26th December

We always have a big family lunch on Boxing Day and today is no exception. Patrick and my mum, Pauline, are still here, so too are Gordon's brother John, and his wife Angela, daughter Karen and her husband, Paul. I cook what I always cook: a giant ham from the local Puddledub Pork farm using Delia Smith's classic recipe, served with lots of vegetables including red cabbage. Everyone eats a lot and we chat for hours over the dining-room table. We also take a moment to remember the victims of the terrible Boxing Day Tsunami in 2004, especially our friends Dickie and Sheila Attenborough, who lost so many family members that day.

Thursday 27th December

My mum Pauline and stepfather Patrick get ready to leave us after the holiday festivities. It is Patrick's seventieth birthday and we do try to make a fuss of him, but the two of them are heading off for an evening in a hotel in Yorkshire they have booked. We are planning a celebration early next year when we can get lots of our family together – including those from overseas – to celebrate both their seventieth birthdays, which are just one month apart.

The news of the assassination of Pakistan Premier Benazir Bhutto comes through to Gordon just before it is broadcast by the media. Somehow this is extremely shocking, although there have been recent attempts on her life.

I am not sure I will ever quite get used to knowing details of big world events before they are in the public domain – there is a strange time when the information comes, and you have to be careful who you speak to at that moment until you see it airing on the BBC. It is an odd sensation, and one that is not at all comfortable when it is bad news. Gordon is on the phone immediately, with calls being set up rapidly by the Downing Street switchboard, and speaks to Australia's new Prime Minister Kevin Rudd, and then to President George W Bush, to coordinate their stances against terrorism.

Friday 28th December

Today we have our own time, remembering our daughter Jennifer on her birthday, and are able to visit the churchyard where she is buried alongside Gordon's parents and grandparents in a peaceful setting surrounded by Fife hills.

It is the greatest sadness for Gordon and me that our first-born child only lived for ten short days after her premature birth in December 2001. We had a very precious time with her, and recall every moment, but despite the best efforts of the doctors and midwives she passed away in January 2001. I have learned that the grief becomes a part of you, and I hold on very tightly to the love I have for that little girl. When I understood that I did not have to return to my former self after her loss, I felt a great burden lift – she remains a part of me firmly in my heart. Gordon and I come regularly to visit her grave and to leave flowers, but it is on her birthday that it is the most special time to be here together.

Sunday 30th December

We have arranged to spend New Year at Chequers and many of our family are coming to stay, including both of Gordon's brothers and their families. Gordon's friend, Murray Elder, is also joining us (the two of them have known each other since they attended nursery school together, aged three), and Swraj and Aruna Paul are visitors for afternoon tea.

Gordon has been pretty glued to the phone as he is a firm part of the Kenyan post-election discussion after the violence there on Thursday and has some involvement with the troubling situation in Pakistan in the aftermath of Bhutto's assassination. In both cases he knows a number of the key political leaders, and can contribute to conversations that aim to calm down two different fragile but equally inflammatory political situations.

The chef prepares a wonderful New Year's Day lunch, which we all enjoy, and we do the big walk afterwards. In the afternoon I play with the boys, while Gordon spends more time on the phone. By tomorrow we will be back to work in London, the holiday break well and truly over.

2008

Thursday 3rd January

We have one of those nights where one child is up at 3 a.m. and another at 6 a.m., and everyone greets the day exhausted.

Yesterday, there was an awful fire at the Royal Marsden Hospital. At 9.15 this morning, I hear that Gordon has suggested that we visit the evacuated staff and patients, who are now safely at the Royal Brompton Hospital, and see the fire team at the Chelsea fire station. I am dressed and ready to go by 9.20 a.m., and Mela takes the boys. Just as I am marvelling at my own ability to get ready in five minutes flat I realise I have toddler fingerprints all over my black dress and an unidentified splodge on my red jacket. Such is life. Health Secretary Alan Johnson is travelling in the car with Gordon so they can brief each other en route. This, thankfully, means I can sit in the staff car and dab my dress.

Quietly reading my own briefing notes with Christina Scott, a private secretary from Number 10 and Maeve from the Department of Health, I discover that Royal Marsden Chief Executive Cally Palmer and Chief Nurse Shelley Dolan will be there alongside the Royal Brompton team, and I want to relay this through to Gordon. Both Gordon and Alan have their phones off, so I call Met detective Gary Richmond, who I know will be with them in the front seat of their car, instead. Christina and Maeve comment I'm being a good private secretary.

At the hospital, we meet an amazing team of people who have helped 79 patients be safely evacuated during the fire, including two who were in the middle of surgery, and some who are very sick indeed. The staff is all safe too, and the building has been secured with its most valuable equipment rescued. This includes a brand-new £12 million Da Vinci machine that Gordon and Alan Johnson had visited only a few short weeks ago. We also greet the ambulance crew, and meet the brave but grateful patients. They are all cancer sufferers, with one of them a doctor herself. All were praising the NHS and our emergency services.

Later, we see the Chelsea fire team who are all very self-deprecating in a British way, but it is clear that their training really paid off.

Monday 7th January

Gordon starts the week on R4's *Today* programme, where he announces personal health MOTs. Thinking about the damage the lack of sleep must be doing, I reflect that we all need one.

I start the New Year more mundanely by getting my hair done and then scoot off to my first scheduled meeting of the year. I already see I'll never have quite enough time to catch up with paperwork so I must get better at passing it on to Beth Dupuy, who has joined Konrad in the office to help sort us out. An American, Beth has moved from Washington DC with her husband, Josh, to London recently, and with her experience of working in Senator Edward Kennedy's office has just the right skills to meet the needs of my office.

Tuesday 8th January

David Beckham comes in to see Gordon about football, and young people. He arrives at the flat for a private drink with Simon Fuller from 19 Management and Terry Byrne from his Beckham Academy. Cabinet Secretary Sir Gus O'Donnell, who is a big Manchester United fan, is hovering by the office so Gordon invites him to join James Purnell (Culture and Sport Secretary), Ed Balls (Children, Schools and Families Secretary) and Stewart Wood (whose brief at Number 10 includes sports). Leeanne is delighted that she is able to say the immortal words, 'If you could just follow me upstairs, David,' and have them obeyed!

The BBC is very excited when they realise David Beckham is here, which is obvious from his car number plate, and their reporter, Nick Robinson, catches him on his way out. David says unbelievably kind and generous things about Gordon, just perfect. He says, 'He's a very good man; he's a man that's looking after our country and he is doing a very good job. I'm very proud to be here.' What is also clear is that both men love football, and both love talking about football.

Thursday 10th January

With the holidays well and truly over, I now need to prepare for a visit with Gordon in a week's time to China and India. A big trade delegation is travelling with the Prime Minister's office and there is a packed programme. I am still getting used to how best to handle these kinds of visits, and still feel the need for some sort of handbook. I look at Gordon's schedule for the events where I accompany him, and my office is in touch with the British Embassy in Beijing directly to organise activities for me. I also have to pack, using one of the big sturdy trunks that will travel with us. The trunks for Gordon and me are brought up by Steve and Glyn, the Number 10 messengers who promise to just spirit them away for the journey once they are filled up.

Friday 11th January

John starts nursery for full days from today – my boy is growing up! I still manage to combine taking him to school some days, with Mela doing others. Gordon also takes or collects John about once a fortnight, which both really love.

Quite how Gordon manages to fit in the school runs I don't know, as it is clear that the crisis of Northern Rock is rearing its head again and causing great concern. Despite the efforts of the Bank of England to calm savers' fears, there is clearly an escalating need to resolve the building society's financial difficulty. The Treasury has been looking at what needs to be done, and Alistair has been talking to Gordon. I expect that we will have a few more long evenings ahead where Gordon is working downstairs until late, while I do bedtimes without him.

Monday 14th January

I have an important meeting first thing with Sir Gus O'Donnell who, as Head of the Civil Service, is considering a review of the 'Office of the Prime Minister's Consort', which at the moment means *me*. I manage to be late by going to his office only to discover that Gus is actually waiting for me in the White Room at Number 10.

I have lots of my own ideas of what might be considered appropriate for government funding, to enable the smoother operation of my office. There definitely does need to be some change. I suggest that if he goes ahead with his review I could be involved if we agreed that nothing would be changed until after the next election, so I would not be seen as acting to benefit myself.

My ideas range from how best to achieve the right support both in the office and on trips (currently, for example, no one is earmarked to travel with me on the China/India trip) and there is also huge pressure on having a high-priced designer wardrobe, which has been a great personal cost for many political wives. I explain that I have been able to rent certain clothes like evening dresses, and am very mindful of the ministerial code that is rightly very clear about preventing large unreported gifts. Gus is very good (or perhaps patient) at listening to all the details, including the minutiae of frock rentals, and shopping generally.

I also discuss with Gus how things have gone for me so far. I have a few niggles still about events and various processes in the building, but I agree with Gus I will only bother him with things I can't fix myself. I look forward to hearing what Gus does next, and also to seeing what I can do to represent the government in my privileged, if sometimes hazily defined, position.

CHAPTER 8

Lunch in Beijing, Shanghai and New Delhi

Thursday 17th January

The first big trip of the New Year is an action-packed trade and higher-education visit to both China and India. The entire schedule will be completed within four days, and that includes the travel time. As China and India are arguably the two most significant trading nations for the UK, with giant populations and burgeoning and productive economies of their own, the decision was taken to visit both countries as a matter of priority. A big business and higher-education delegation has been amassed, with no shortage of chief executives and university heads wanting to join the trip.

I have a frantic morning before taking the flight to Beijing. Having run my own business, I have done reasonable amounts of travel in my time, although admittedly with more assistance than now. I don't have anyone from my office coming on this trip, but I have had word from Sir Gus's office that he has come to my rescue for future travel. It has proven very difficult to arrange a trip long distance, and it is already clear that juggling everything, from luggage to itineraries at the other end, can't just be absorbed by the PM's secretarial team. I will get more help next time, but for this one I have to just make it work.

Konrad has put together a comprehensive file of everything he thinks I need to know while I am away. I am combining accompanying Gordon on official visits and dinners, with a number of women's lunches (each with a short speech), and visits to a school, a museum and a health centre all packed into the schedule.

I have also spent time putting together my wardrobe for this visit, ever mindful that there might be some press scrutiny of my outfits. I still carry a fair bit of my new ebullient, post-pregnancy weight, which I am struggling to shift. This means two things: I don't plan on being a fashion icon anytime soon; and I am not my fully confident self, even when dollied up. It is a girl-thing mostly, to worry about weight in a way that affects self-esteem, but there are few women I know who don't care about how they feel when they choose their clothes. I am pretty level-headed most of the time, but a bit anxious about this visit. It is partly wanting to represent Britain well and partly vanity in just wanting to look okay.

I have a nice mixture of things to wear for China. Knowing that everyone will be in very business-like suits – especially in Shanghai – I have some well-cut Jaeger bits, some Burberry, a bit of Marks and Spencer, some Top Shop, plus nice summery Monsoon things as it will be very hot.

At the recommendation of my friend, the Anglo-Indian TV presenter, Lisa Aziz, I have chosen my outfits for India from Abu Jani and Sandeep Khosla, as I know how welcomed it will be to wear Indian-style clothes. I am sticking with salwar kameez rather than a full sari. Beautiful as saris are, it takes a bit of va va voom to wear them, and I am also slightly accident-prone, so don't want to risk any unravelling or tripping-over at an inopportune moment. In another lifetime, I would be a fabulous sari wearer, but this trip I am playing it safe.

I am up bright and early with the kids and spend time with them before John goes off to school. Fraser is there as I leave, so there are lots of big hugs and big mummy kisses.

I travel with Gordon in the back of the Jaguar and we hear over the police radios that there is a breaking news story about a plane from Beijing that safely crash-landed and evacuated at Heathrow. As we board our big chartered aircraft we can actually see the landing site circled with fire engines and airport vehicles.

The TV camera crews on our plane make full use of our vantage point and film out of the windows, while the journalists file their copy directly. Our plane is full of government ministers and officials, company chief executives and university vice chancellors, as well as a big group of media. Everyone is also teasing Sir Richard Branson who is on the trip, and therefore forced to take a British Airways flight.

After we take off, the impending time difference in China means everyone tries to get some sleep. Once in the air, there is not much moving about or socialising, just heads down – or at least, that is what happens at my end of the plane, where I am seated with Gordon and his private office team.

Friday 18th January

On arrival in Beijing, Gordon is immediately off for his first meeting with Premier Wen of China. Mrs Wen does not undertake public appearances with her husband as she works in the private sector, and wisely avoids the conflict of interest that could arise, so I have no official duties while here. Instead, I am taken on a visit organised by our British Embassy and take with me Sue Campbell of UK Sport and Dame Kelly Holmes, who are both here for some Olympic-related activities later on in the trip. Dave Gardner from the protection team is with me and warns that it will be freezing cold when we get to the school for migrant workers' children. It is January and we are in the midst of a Chinese winter.

At the school, I am struck by the sight of these energetic, enthusiastic, welcoming children as they perform their school song in parka jackets, but with no shoes on. They just have cloth tied to their feet. The dorm rooms have trainers and flip-flops lined up under the bed, but they are only worn for PE. Kelly shows the kids her Olympic medals for the 800m and 1500m track events. We are invited to join a PE class so, in my winter boots, I find myself jogging around the playground with a double Olympic Gold athlete and the head of UK Sport.

*

After a visit to the Capital Museum to see a joint exhibition of Olympic posters with our own Victoria & Albert Museum, we move on to lunch. I have asked the Embassy – as I plan to do for all overseas visits when I am 'off-schedule' – to organise a lunch with some interesting local women.

We gather at the Fengshen Restaurant by the site of the old Imperial Palace and are first greeted by an amazing sight of people wheeling around on a frozen lake on giant 'ice' bicycles. I am told they are very popular during this coldest season here in the historic park. The restaurant recreates an Imperial Chinese atmosphere with traditional costumes and dancing. I move around the different tables having a bite to eat at each one and meet a range of feminist and environmental activists and cultural figures, NGO workers and an online bookseller. Much of the talk is overshadowed by a presentation about the food, which is announced as being the old Empress's favourites. That turns out to be chestnut paste with beans, and tasty mini burgers.

Later, I meet Gordon who is joining Premier Wen in the first-ever Town Hall meeting recorded in China, with the audience asking the questions. This is held in the fittingly named Great Hall of the People.

Gordon is one of those people who just keeps going, but tiredness is really kicking in for me in the heat of the room. Despite the rather staged questions, the audience is treated to some very candid answers from Premier Wen. He appears refreshingly open and keen to continue what has evidently been a successful opening dialogue in the private meeting. What is exciting is the moment when Gordon mentions that they have been discussing Burma, and that he has asked for China's help to free Burmese leader, Aung San Suu Kyi, who's been detained under house arrest in Burma for 11 of the past 17 years. I also get a real personal boost when he mentions the importance of addressing maternal health as a matter of urgency –

I know then that he has been listening to me when I have been banging on and on in recent weeks.

The finale is a visit to a massive hall full of thousands of students, to watch a world-class table tennis match between China and Britain's Olympic hopefuls. China wins, but then it is a game at which they excel. I am just grateful that Premier Wen didn't challenge Gordon to a game.

Back to the hotel, but our day is not quite done. I arrive before Gordon as he has a meeting with President Hu, followed by a short banquet hosted by him. When Gordon finally arrives back at the hotel, we pop into a reception to thank the many Embassy staff who have been involved with organising the visit.

Gordon and I are now beyond the point of exhaustion, so I decide not to even order any food before going to bed. As the time difference works out, I phone home to speak to the boys – well, a 'Mama, Mama' from Fraser and a chat with John. I also call Gil to talk through the programme we have coming up over the next few months; with our tiny team, there is no room for slacking off just because I am away on a trip.

It is at moments like this that I have to remind myself that it is me who has insisted on taking on everything. There is no rulebook that says everything has to happen, but it just does seem important to give it all a go.

Saturday 19th January

We start the morning of our final Beijing visits going to the new 'Bird's Nest' Olympic Stadium that still has its seats under plastic wrappers, and a green-energy power station that is also nearing completion. Both are quick visits, and we are soon off again by plane to arrive in a very rainy Shanghai.

In Shanghai, we are bundled into cars on arrival and zoom along the expressway – the roads have clearly been closed just for our journey

– past miles and miles of newly built hotels and office blocks. I chat in the car to Angela Gordon from the High Commission about today's lunch with Shanghai women.

This time we enjoy a Western menu at a big hotel in a nice private room. I meet Chinese women who hail mainly from business, as well as a representative of Save the Children, and a TV presenter. The British Chamber of Commerce's team host a very lively and informative discussion about China's entrepreneurial culture and fast pace of work. As is the case with women everywhere, the discussion comes down to finding the right work–life balance and there are some lively contributions about the empowerment of women in the workplace. The general consensus is that the rate of change in China is very rapid, and that Shanghai is learning lessons from the West faster than they were learned the first time around. Approaches to corporate philanthropy – so unusual to the Chinese – are even beginning to creep in.

My afternoon visits cover a visit to Roots and Shoots, a school volunteering scheme that focuses on recycling in schools and planting organic gardens. It is run by the Jane Goodall Institute, which has been the forerunner for what is coming into our own schools in the UK. I love the handbook on how to run your own school organic garden project so much I take a copy with me.

After that, I join Gordon again for a very swift tour of Ming furniture in the Shanghai Museum and then we go on to an entrepreneurs' summit, where I join in the discussion and hear Gordon's closing remarks.

Back at the hotel, we have a final event with the British business delegation and then head to our room. It turns out, however, that Gordon's day is not quite finished, and he has a number of TV interviews, including a lengthy one for Sky with Adam Boulton, in the hotel suite. Sue Nye and I stay out of sight, tucked in the neighbouring room ordering room service, and thinking of new ideas for the official Downing Street gift list (it seemed an opportune moment and was on both of our 'to do' lists).

Sunday 20th January

Today includes a seven-hour flight to New Delhi. Most people, including Gordon, sensibly caught up on sleep. I stay wide awake tackling some of my speech drafts, and watched a pretty terrible film with an instantly forgettable title starring lots of well-known people. We arrive to great fanfare and rather warmer weather.

I visited India once before as a student, with my university flatmate, Lucy Kneebone, for six weeks of backpacking from Delhi to Orissa to Goa and back up to Kashmir and Nepal. I realise what a privilege it was in the mid 1980s to be able to see so much. I had got a strong sense of the scale of the place when Lucy and I took a train journey to the other side of the country and it took 36 hours. We had wanted to find some sunshine after we were almost flattened, while wearing rucksacks, by the pouring rain of the monsoon.

On this trip, Gordon and I are only in the capital, New Delhi, for a couple of days. We make a quick stop at the Presidential suite at the Taj Mahal Hotel, which is vast and strewn with (New Labour) red roses.

One of the great highlights of this trip for me is the Women's Empowerment event in the Nehru Youth Centre in Chenak. Thousands of women have gathered, after travelling many miles, for a meeting of several days that addresses their needs and interests as women. Many of them are eager to share their stories with Gordon – some in English, most with translation – of the impact on their lives of the economic empowerment that micro-credit brings. The other themes are improving girls' education, raising literacy standards, and action against domestic violence and early marriage. Gordon speaks to the whole audience, using a translator. It proves a very inspiring event.

After the meeting, I am whisked off separately by the High Commissioner's wife, Arabella Stagg, back to the Residence. British Embassies around the world all have their little reminders of things 'back home'. While I get a briefing on the next day's maternal health centre visit, we are served very British tea by the friendly

Nepalese staff. The tea also comes with chocolate brownies, which are of enormous interest to the Residence's bouncy new puppy.

Every moment of this life is accounted for, and I am learning how to adapt to all its different demands, and to accommodate my own requests. One thing I do sort out with Arabella – after several days on the road – is getting in her local hairdresser, who I work out how to pay with my own rupees (there are no budgets for this kind of thing). When travelling in the UK, I have happily used local hairdressers for a quick blow-dry, and trying the same system out long-distance seems to work very well, just as it did in Tanzania. It is the one bit of external reinforcement I do need when travelling, although I am fortunate that, style-wise, I am never after anything complicated. I can think of only a couple of times when an excess of hair mousse and hairspray has resulted in a hairstyle more akin to Margaret Thatcher's bouffant than my own chosen look – and luckily, here in New Delhi, this is not one of those occasions.

Back at the hotel, we are ushered outside by the Indian Trade Minister to see the new £2,500 Tata car. All the press cameras are gathered around as we admire this astonishingly inexpensive car. I realise that we are looking at a show model rather than a 'ready to drive' car when Gordon goes to open the back door, and the handle comes off in his hand. In unison, we both turn to face the cameras, smiling, while he keeps the handle in place as if there is no problem at all. If Tata can get a car on the road for such a low cost, the company deserves the chance to get it right, and neither of us wants to hinder that chance by giving the media a moment to mock it.

We are privileged to have a very private dinner this evening with Indian Prime Minister Manmohan Singh, and his wife, Gursharan Kaur, at their official residence, Racecourse Road, together with some of India's most prominent and influential politicians. I am delighted to see Gursharan Kaur again as we first met in Uganda and find her a compassionate, thoughtful and very smart woman. She is very well informed about the charity projects I work on and shows a tremendous detailed interest in my role, and what I am trying to achieve. With her warmth and support, I feel as if I am talking to a member of my family just willing my success. Her capacity for instant friendship is a lovely quality to have.

I am seated next to Prime Minister Singh. Gordon is opposite us next to Mrs Sonia Gandhi, who is a powerful political force in the country since the assassination of her husband Rajiv Gandhi during his time as Premier (himself the son of the great Indian Prime Minister, Mrs Indira Gandhi). On my other side I am seated next to Sonia Gandhi's son, Rahul, a young up-and-coming politician whom everyone tips to go to the top. The Gandhi family is a great political dynasty in India, but Rahul is also a smart, personable young guy who applies a great deal of thought both to the issues of his country and global cooperation. I am very taken, too, by his sister, Priyanka, who also joins us. Her contributions to the conversation show a real spark and a very progressive approach to politics, though she does claim to have no interest in standing for office herself. I am told that she has been central to organising her brother's and mother's successful elections, so it is clear she has great talent.

There was a fabulous moment when the three Gandhi family members engaged in a heated discussion about the reasons for their party's recent election setbacks in the State of Gujarat. It was like sitting at their family table at home, or at least reminded me of sitting at my own family table!

Knowing that the day may come in the not too distant future when Rahul leads his party, and even his country, I ask him what he thinks would make the difference to India in order to see its real growth as an economic force AND to see the quality of life improve for its citizens. He gives me a simple and, to my ears, welcome answer: 'Women's empowerment.'

While the dinner was fascinating, Gordon and I were very ready to get back to the hotel and put our feet up. Gordon is all the more excited as he has found Premiership football on the television, and can catch up with a Manchester United game from the day before.

Monday 21st January

We start the day with a ceremonial event at the Rashtrapati Bhavan on the forecourt of the Presidential palace, and a wreath-laying at Gandhi's memorial at Rajghat. I have donned one of my Abu Jani outfits and wear a green and cream jacket with green trousers. The ceremony involves listening to both national anthems, and then Gordon inspects the presidential guard. We walk with Prime Minister Singh and Gursharan Kaur to meet the various guests, and I am pleased to see that our business and education delegation have all been included in this event.

There is one potentially tricky moment when Gordon treads momentarily on the back of Mrs Kaur Singh's sari as we are walking along, but amazingly it is not snapped by the media.

A phalanx of formation military helicopters flies overhead which is very impressive, but turns out to be for a rehearsal for the Victory Day parade later in the week.

At Rajghat, we take part in the customary ceremony at Gandhi's memorial. We take a moment for peaceful contemplation and then sign the visitors' book with a message. The area is so tranquil that even a repeat performance of helicopters and stampeding journalists trying to get a photo of Gordon with his shoes off cannot disturb the peace.

Gordon then heads to Delhi University to make a speech that he has been planning for a long time, about global cooperation for the economy and trade, and also for national security. The world has changed and so the thinking, too, needs to keep up with progress. He will also float his ideas about the need to change the big international institutions like the United Nations, the International Monetary Fund and the World Bank. I particularly love his idea that the World Bank needs now to focus not just on rescuing countries in trouble and tackling global poverty, but to include a focus on the environment. Some of the worst damage to our planet may come from industrialisation, but the results often take place in the poorest countries. If we want to keep our entire world green and healthy, and do more to protect both people and the precious disappearing rainforests, for example, we need to do this at a joined-up, global level. I would love to be at the speech but at my own request, the High Commission has organised a trip to visit a maternal and infant health centre.

I am taken to the edges of the city to a suburb called Nangloi, to visit a maternity hospital that will receive the gift of a back-up generator from our own High Commission. I am accompanied by Lord Paul of Marylebone. Swraj talks to everyone we meet here in their own language, so we are able to walk through the slum meeting mothers, and make an impromptu stop at a school, talking to lots of excitable little boys enjoying the novelty of the disruption.

After seeing first-hand in the health centre the good service possible for mothers and babies with even modest resources, we return to the Embassy to talk to someone I am very excited to meet.

I have heard a lot about the head of the White Ribbon Alliance India, and Aparajita Gogoi is as inspirational as I was led to believe, demonstrating just how a grass-roots effort can organise itself to make a real difference to people's lives. She brings with her a group of like-minded people – men and women – to talk to us about a maternal mortality campaign, and I feel much energised by the conversation, which is full of ideas and possibilities for the future.

I return to the formal programme which includes a courtesy visit to meet President Patil of India, and a final event in the form of a banquet at Hyderabad House hosted by Prime Minister Singh, with all the politicians and business leaders from India and Britain. Our delegation is boarding a night flight back to London so the banquet has been timetabled to fit in with our take-off time. This means that we all eat five courses in just under 40 minutes and have no speeches.

At the end of this successful mission, everyone is very chatty and friendly and I get to have a serious conversation of my own with Prime Minister Singh, who has forged a strong friendship with Gordon in the handful of times they have met. I did check with Gordon beforehand if I could raise the maternal mortality campaign I heard about from Aparajita Gogoi, and so discover for myself a very positive response from Manmohan Singh. He is able to talk to me about the recent legislation to enable more women to sit and take part in local government that actually has had a direct impact on the services available to pregnant women. More to the point, these new polices don't cost the Indian government anything, but bring a much-needed opening up of opportunities for able women to join in with their communities' decisions. Good free policies are hard to find and should be cherished by political leaders when they are discovered!

As we left for the airport, we had lots of goodbyes and thank-yous to make as so many people had been involved with the success of this very intensive trip.

Once on the plane, it is straight to sleep for me and Gordon. The time difference going home is in our favour and it is possible to get a fair few hours' kip before we land, and more when we get back to the flat. There is no question that this has been a hugely successful trip for everyone but, arriving home, it is difficult to see what the next few weeks hold for us back in Britain.

Tuesday 22nd January

Having arrived around 2 o'clock in the morning it seemed only a short time before John is padding in to say hello, some time before dawn. Triple sleep-deprivation from the combination of work and travel as well as small children is brutal. It is really a question of mind over matter to get through the days when not enough hours are there to find for sleeping.

Once finally awake, I have a useful day catching up on the endless emails that have built up in my absence (I didn't have any access while I was away), and preparing a speech to give in Davos, Switzerland, for the World Economic Forum at the end of the week. I also have to start looking at the next round of outfits and am talking to designer Britt Lintner about hiring one of her dresses for both Davos and the opening of British Fashion Week the week after. I am so keen to fit in a reviving Pilates exercise session and a resuscitating hair salon visit, and still get some good amount of time with the boys, that I push all thoughts of jet-lag away.

Wednesday 23rd January

I have been invited to a private lunch at Clarence House with HRH The Duchess of Cornwall today, which I am really looking forward to. First I attend the Women's Aid corporate development board meeting somewhere in the City, as it is the first one with Nicola Mendelsohn as the new chairperson. Nicola is a good friend who, apart from being the mum of four great kids, also runs the advertising agency Karmarama. Luckily she has a good snappy chairing style, which moves the agenda on rapidly, so I also have time in the morning to call in and visit one of the primary schools in the Downing Street catchment area, as I am doing the application for John.

I get to Clarence House on time and have a truly delightful lunch with the Duchess. It is just the two of us as she is in London to see her daughter with her new baby. We eat together in a very pretty room and enjoy a healthy organic lunch that I suspect comes mainly from the Duchy Estates. We have no agenda for our lunch other than that, I suspect, this might be a thank-you for the Ugandan curtsey, in which case lunch was not necessary but very enjoyable all the same.

Thursday 24th January

With the start to the New Year I embark on regular visits to see MPs in their own seats, and see at first hand the work of the government. Today I am with Karen Buck MP, who holds the seat of Westminster North and is such a dedicated constituency MP. She treats me to a visit of a wonderful school, Edward Wilson Primary, and I get a sneak preview of the Sure Start Children's Centre that is about to open on the same site. When you see the difference that the investment in children makes, and hear from both teachers and parents how much it benefits their own families and their communities, you know why public service is a great place to be. Oh, I hope Labour keeps this seat at the next election.

Friday 25th January

I join Gordon on the trip to the World Economic Forum up a giant mountain in Davos, Switzerland. This is an annual gathering of the brainy and/or powerful, good and great, and is a regular fixture for many of the world's corporate, academic and political leaders. Gordon has been on several occasions to speak at the formal panel sessions that address world topics like the economy, environment or development.

It is, however, my first time, and I have an invitation to contribute to a 'fringe' event. Not on the formal programme, maybe, but to my mind a great event to be invited to nonetheless, I am to join a group of women at dinner to talk about what difference we can make to help meet the United Nations' global-poverty reduction targets: the Millennium Development Goals (MDGs). The targets I am focused on are MDG 5: the target to reduce maternal mortality by three quarters; and MDG 4: the target to reduce child deaths by two thirds – all by 2015. The rate of child deaths is coming down, but the deaths of mothers have been forgotten, which won't help surviving children at all. My speech for the Davos women's dinner will focus on this forgotten MDG.

To get to Davos, we are up at 5 a.m. to board a flight to Zurich, and we change on to a big army helicopter that takes us up the mountainside (I literally did not open my eyes the whole journey as I am a serious heights wimp). The journey was always going to be quite tight for the start of Gordon's session, and a small delay taking off meant that as we landed in Davos, only two minutes are left until he is due to be introduced on stage to speak in the main conference auditorium. We get out of the helicopter, and someone grabs us and moves us fast into the WEF building. Gordon's feet do not seem to touch the ground but before I know it, he has bounced up on the stage and is being interviewed by Klaus Schwab, the Davos founder. The discussion breezes through the MDGs and how to form partnerships between governments, businesses and others to achieve them, and there is some chat about the reform of global institutions and globalisation. My head is only just starting to clear yet everyone is already going full tilt, including Gordon.

However, I quickly start to get the hang of Davos: everyone is very clear and very fast, all the time, while wearing oddly casual clothes and snow boots and furry hats, even when indoors. I follow Gordon for the rest of the day, listening to his sessions with other government heads, HM Queen Rania of Jordan, Bono, Bill Gates and lots of corporate high-flyers.

I do get a quick moment to leave my bag in my hotel room, which is very Swiss ski lodge with a beautiful view of fabulous snowy fir trees and the surrounding mountains. Gordon is due to fly straight back today, but my dinner is due to run too long for me to make his flight back down the mountain.

The dinner involves some of the most glamorous and powerful women in the world, all crammed into odd wooden trestle tables in the ski lodge. I skid in on the icy path to join everyone at the reception, tucking away my flat-heeled boots to put on some higher heels in the corner. I join a photo line-up with Education for All advocate, HM Queen Rania; Ethiopian model, Liya Kebede; entrepreneur, Wendi Murdoch; PepsiCo chief, Indra Nooyi; World Bank MD, Ngozi Okonjo-Iweala; and, no introduction needed, Annie Lennox. We are lined up as a row of seven women to highlight the one-in-seven lifetime risk of maternal death in Sierra

Leone – the country to have the misfortune to have the highest rate in the world.

I am seated next to HM Queen Rania and we talk, at her instigation, about how challenging public speaking is. Having met at dinner in Downing Street on an official visit, it is fun to talk to her more informally but the subject matter is not too good for my pre-speech nerves. Annie Lennox on my other side is an inspirational delight to meet, and we have an earnest conversation about her commitment to women with HIV/AIDS while I try not to be too star-struck. She gives a short talk to everyone on her work with Oxfam, encouraging women to work together and collaborate on a new women's engagement project called Circle. Queen Rania also addresses the room, speaking from a lectern and introducing a film edited by Comic Relief's Emma Freud to introduce the maternal mortality theme. When it is my turn to speak, after the starter, I find the lectern has gone, the lighting has been turned down low for dinner, and I have to stand clutching a hand-held mike, peering at my typed speech.

I have a good speech with an important message to get across, but I give it so badly. I am not undermining myself by saying this – just reporting the facts. I stumble on my words, turn the pages clumsily and feel fairly mortified even as I speak. I am just thankful that the room is not so brightly lit, as it means I can't see everyone's faces clearly. I have always been a nervous public speaker and I think all my fears were realised this evening. People often say about the challenge of public speaking: 'Well, what's the worst that can happen?' For me, at that moment, I don't think it could have been worse. As I sit down to polite applause at the end, I finally get a lucky break. Konrad sneaks up to me and whispers in my ear that if we move fast, there is a last flight down the mountain and we can get home tonight, travelling with Shriti. Even in my high heels I am off over the ice before you can say, 'Better luck next time!'

We get to the heliport in the nick of time and jump aboard our helicopter. I keep my eyes shut the whole time while Shriti keeps me distracted telling me that she is sure I can improve my public speaking with a bit of practice and by controlling my nervousness, but I am too terrified by the notion that we are whizzing around in the Swiss mountains to even think about my speech any more.

In Zurich we jump into a car that takes us to a plane where I am finally calm enough to chat to our other fellow passengers: none other than HRH Prince Andrew, Duke of York, and Lord Digby Jones. I manage a quick call home to tell them I am coming so there are no surprises when I come creeping in after midnight. By this time I am already thinking of a return to Davos next year to conquer all my fears.

Monday 28th January

I host a lunch today for Mrs Musharaff of Pakistan, set up in Downing Street's Terracotta Room. As she is a former teacher and reportedly passionate about reading, I have invited some women who I think will be interesting to her. My guests include Maggie Darling (who is a former journalist and not long ago completed her own MA back at university); Meg Munn, our Minister from the Foreign Office; Viv Bird from the Book Trust; and Mariella Frostrup, who presents a book programme on both radio and TV. We managed to combine lots of good diplomatic and govern-mental talk with having fun: we do talk about books, but we also talk about shopping in discount malls around the world.

Later that day, I am back behind the black door with Gordon to meet Ernest Koroma, the new President of Sierra Leone, and his wife, Mrs Sia Koroma. Once we have taken the customary pictures on the doorstep, I take Mrs Koroma with me to the White Room for tea. We immediately get on and, as her husband's election was only held in October, she has been in her position an even shorter time than me.

Her husband's predecessor was a widower so she has no one she can follow or compare herself with. We talk together about how the role of the spouse can be put to good use, but how you have to put down the building blocks yourself to mark out what you hope to achieve. Like me, Mrs Koroma has no official, formal role other than as a consort, and no access to her own budget with which to put herself to work. Sierra Leone has suffered so badly during years of war and has much to do to see its people heal, *and* to rebuild so many services in the country, including basic hospitals and schools. The First Lady tells me that she wants to establish a foundation to work with women and children in memory of her mother. Her sister, a lawyer, is advising her and she has a very strong religious faith to guide her.

As we talk, I hear that her strong focus is to create educational programmes and to contribute to public health programmes. She mentions the overwhelming need to reduce infant mortality in Sierra Leone. She tells me the heartbreaking story of her first Christmas as First Lady, when she gave a gift of layettes to all the Christmas babies, only to find that very few survived to actually receive her gifts. We talk about the link between maternal and newborn health, and I urge her to focus also on maternal mortality. As we speak, we realise – prompted in my mind by the speech I have just given in Davos – that the great opportunity for her lies in one terrible fact: her country, as a result of the tragedy of war, has the highest maternal mortality in the whole world: if you are a woman in Sierra Leone, you have a one-in-seven chance of dying in your lifetime as a result of pregnancy and childbirth. Compare that to the UK's statistic of one in 16,025. In a country with 6 million people (more than the population of Scotland), Sierra Leone has only 300 trained midwives and 80 qualified doctors, only three of whom are trained to deal with emergency deliveries of babies.

The very fact of having the worst global figures of maternal mortality means that Mama Koroma can make herself heard from her capital of Freetown, to the United Nations. She can become a powerful force for change. I plan to help her as much as I can.

CHAPTER 9

State Visit

Tuesday 29th January

Britain's place in Europe is surely one of the most hotly contested political issues. We have in the past all got ourselves very exercised about whether we are part of the European Common Market, whether we allow the European Commission to hold certain powers and whether we should or – as Gordon decided in 2004 – should not surrender our beloved pound for an arguably simpler system to have a common currency with other European countries (thank goodness we didn't given that the Euro has proven to be a lot less flexible for the countries that are in it during the global financial crisis).

The most important thing – if you are a Brit – is to get the right balance of being a True Brit: a part of Europe and, of course, a compassionate global citizen AND to keep reassessing what is best for Britain. We have done well to have English be one of the dominant languages of business, and of pretty much anything. At the same time this makes us pretty lousy at foreign languages – myself and Gordon as leading examples – but I hope this is rapidly changing in our schools. My children meet other children whose first language is Arabic, Spanish or Chinese and I hope, as a parent, that they figure out which one or more they think they should learn, rather than relying on speaking slowly and loudly on holiday all their lives.

*

Gordon can't emulate Tony Blair's rather fabulous speech given one time in French, but what he lacks in the second language department, he more than makes up for in the strong relationships he has built up with many European leaders and other senior figures. President Nicolas Sarkozy is a great friend as they both served as finance ministers together (as our Chancellor of the Exchequer is known once you hit Brussels or a G8 meeting). Gordon also gets on famously well with the leaders from Germany, Italy, Spain and across the EU. Having been Chancellor for a long period his experience is valued.

Everyone has become anxious about the possibility of an economic downturn. Gordon is hosting a major meeting at Number 10 for some key European players. A meeting, press conference and dinner has been arranged to kick off the year, with President Nicolas Sarkozy of France, Chancellor Angela Merkel of Germany, Prime Minister Romano Prodi of Italy and the head of the European Commission, José Manuel Barroso. There is much gossip in the air about Nicolas Sarkozy's reported relationship with the supermodel and singer–songwriter Carla Bruni.

I am on call to say hello to everyone as they arrive (and definitely want to know more from Nicolas). There has been much discussion about the order of arrival – bearing in mind that everyone is a VIP – but it must have been resolved as everyone seems happy when they get here. As Gordon meets each person at the door, I chat to them in the Cabinet Room until Gordon is able to come and join everybody. There is a bit of a gap waiting for President Sarkozy, who is famously late for pretty much everything, especially if the cameras are lined up to notice. As he is the last one to arrive, I join Gordon in the hallway to say hello.

He immediately takes us both to one side in the hallway, and whispers the news that he and Carla have just quietly married, but that they are still withholding the news from the media. We whisper our congratulations and agree to keep the secret. What this means is that Carla is definitely joining him on the French State

Visit to London that is coming up in a few weeks, and that I will meet her at some point during that trip. I look forward to meeting her with great interest, and hope we can do something useful together with our time.

Once Gordon and the French President join the others for their meeting and dinner (where it is reported later that Chancellor Merkel chides Gordon and Nicolas for texting at the table, and Gordon for speaking on Nicolas' phone to Carla to wish her our congratulations), I dash back to the flat to say goodnight to the boys, then rush out of the back door to speak at the Ovarian Cancer Action dinner in the City. I had promised former CBI chief/Trade Minister Lord Digby Jones that I would do this, and it lets me recover my sense of being able to speak semi-competently in public after the Davos debacle.

Speech done, I'm actually home to a quiet flat by 8.30 p.m., and opt for a nice bath and a couple of taped episodes of *Ugly Betty*.

Wednesday 13th February

I attend a lunch hosted by *Glamour* magazine editor Jo Elvin with financial whizz Nicola Horlick, San Tropez fake tan entrepreneur Judy Naake and film producer (*Elizabeth* and *Brick Lane*) Alison Owen to discuss careers and how to get on with them. I have not given any newspaper or magazine interviews despite many requests to do so, and doubt I will do many while we are at Number 10. I am unconvinced that this is a good way to let people know who I am, but happy to take tentative steps to speaking up a bit. So, joining a lunch with interesting guests and a serious topic that will afterwards be written up in a big circulation magazine like *Glamour* seems a good place to start.

Thursday 14th February

This evening we have a fabulous reception to mark the launch of the PiggyBankKids books *Mums* and *Dads*. As the charity's director, Gil McNeil's parallel career as a writer and former book publisher has benefited PiggyBankKids enormously, as we have edited a number of anthologies that have contributions from all sorts of well-known people, with all the royalties going to support the charity's work.

We have a great mix of contributors to the books attending, ranging from Joanne (*Chocolat*) Harris to Kathy Lette, and Norman Tebbit and Ronnie Corbett to Alastair Campbell and Seb Coe – a great mixture of people that makes for a lively and very fun evening. The catering team do a first-class job serving drinks and delicious canapés.

Meanwhile, so much seems to be happening with the Northern Rock problem that the working days for Gordon stretch all the way into the evening. The discussions with Alistair Darling have been about the bidders for the company, and the Treasury is looking seriously at the options. So, neither of us takes much notice of Valentine's Day although I do, as always, get lovely flowers. I am astonishingly picky about cut flowers, and in general I don't much like them (I am allergic to lilies, which make my eyes sting, and I think gerberas are truly ghastly with their fake bright colours), but I happily make an exception for a bouquet of roses from my husband.

Sunday 17th February

I have booked a call to speak to Carla Bruni-Sarkozy, who is at her home in France. As we will be under such intense public scrutiny during the State Visit, I want to make the lunch I host for her as great a success as I can.

When she comes on the line and I hear her deep breathy voice, I know that the British will be very charmed when she hits our shores. We agree that we would both like to do something serious at our lunch and I invite her to bring the focus to the White Ribbon Alliance. She agrees readily, as she has an existing interest in HIV/AIDS and the prevention of transmission of the virus from mother to child during pregnancy, which is a vital part of the health story in reducing deaths. I promise her that I will get on with the arrangements and keep her posted on the details.

Monday 18th February

It appears to be a very busy day at both 10 and 11 Downing Street, and I keep a watchful eye on the news all day. At the culmination of many hours' work, the government has now taken over the running of Northern Rock as the only option left to keep it going. I have a cup of tea with Maggie and we agree that both Gordon and Alistair are very calm and level-headed under the pressure.

Tuesday 26th February

I am just coming out of the back of Downing Street to take Fraser on a walk when the police there tell me that suspected gun shots have been heard in St James's Park. Alistair Darling is also walking out the back way at the same time with his daughter, Anna. We are all quickly ushered back inside. One of the police team, Steve Walsh, kindly arranges for someone to drive Fraser and me, leaving from the front of Number 10. That plan is foiled by a flat battery in the car. In the end, Fraser's car seat is moved again and he and I finally depart in an armoured Jaguar. Not the easiest place to escape from sometimes!

Thursday 28th February

Up with Fraser for ages and then spend some time with John, but still I'm out of the door at 8.30 a.m. as I want to keep up my visits around the country to see first-hand what other families are experiencing. Today I go to Hastings to visit Michael Foster's seat. I visit a lovely children's centre in Castle Ward (with a good view of the castle) and see that their work is much needed. Admirably, they have an active outreach programme to find the most vulnerable parents and encourage them to use the centre.

A lunch with party members follows at the local football club. Michael is defending a notional majority of 800 (down from 2,000 with boundary changes), so he will have quite a fight at the next election. It will be interesting to see what happens at the borough council elections on 1st May. We have reclaimed two seats for Labour in recent by-elections, and the local Labour councillors are only two seats behind the Conservatives now. I wish them well.

I travel on to Sittingbourne to a fabulous children's centre attached to a primary school in a very deprived area. A great young guy, as head of the school, works with a fabulous young local woman, who runs the centre. It is so impressive. There is a great atmosphere too, and they are so enthusiastic about what a Labour government is delivering for them. I fear for this seat, however, as the majority is even tighter with only 79 votes in it.

Gil and Konrad are with me all day. It's a long trip but it's actually a lot of fun to be with party members. We meet party stalwarts with Derek Wyatt MP at his agent's house, who are all very positive about the future.

Monday 3rd March

I am writing an article for the *Daily Mail* about inspirational women I have met, to accompany their support for the Inspirational Women of the Year awards. I need to use some real examples of women I have met recently and a number come very quickly to mind. I have just met Jo Baker Watson, winner of the Tesco Mum of the Year awards, who came to visit Downing Street. She is a lovely mum who set up a cerebral palsy care centre for her daughter, Megan, who sadly died before she was able to benefit from it. The Megan Baker Centre helps hundreds of children with a treatment from the Peto Institute in Hungary, which is very effective.

I was also really struck by Gill Hicks, who came to Number 10 with Leonard Cheshire Disability to speak at their reception. Gill is the young Australian woman who lost her legs in one of the 7th July 2005 bomb blasts in London and has not only made a remarkable physical recovery, but is now engaged in peace campaigning, and a true inspiration. So I have lots to write about.

Thursday 6th March

I meet Susie Nemazee, the wife of the UK Ambassador to Paris, Peter Westmacott, to discuss Carla Bruni-Sarkozy's visit, and then fly out of the door for a trip to Oxfordshire. First stop is to my friend Heather McGregor's annual charity lunch and shooting day in Northolt. There are not many natural Labour people here, but there are some nice friendly faces and I find the opportunity to speak to them both about PiggyBankKids, and the White Ribbon Alliance. I leave after lunch before the guns come out.

I also visit Andrew Smith MP's very marginal seat in Oxford East (no by-elections here but a vital seat at the next general election), and go to a school and children's centre to get a fascinating insight into a local project to develop emotional literacy in parents. I take Book Trust book bags as a gift as it is World Book Day. We finish at Andrew and his wife Val's house for a meeting with a wonderful group of party members – they are so supportive of Andrew and known for being one of the best (and possibly even *the* best) organised Labour Party groups in the country. I hope he finds a way to keep his seat as one of the hardest-working MPs around. With this lot out campaigning for him he should stand a very good chance.

I have always enjoyed campaigning, but it is not just at election time that it is important. For MPs, it is not just about providing a good local constituency service, but about keeping up contact with all voters, through a strong network of committed volunteers. I am certainly happy to play my part with phone calls, knocking on doors and even stuffing leaflets in envelopes if needed. This is replicated all over the country, and we will certainly need it for the next general election.

Friday 7th March

I have the boys in the afternoon. I collect Fraser from nursery at the end of his morning session and we then return to school to collect John later in the afternoon. It is Friday and I know Gordon won't get back early, so we go and meet my mum and Patrick, and are joined by my sister-in-law, Clare, too. We all go to a nearby Wagamama noodle bar.

Tuesday 11th March

Jeremy Heywood, who is in charge of Number 10 as the Permanent Secretary here, has arranged for Beth Dupuy to move from my office to join Gordon's private office team. She will report to James Bowler who, having resumed his Treasury role as Principal Private Secretary for Gordon, has had a very positive impact on the organisation of the office. Beth's immense organisational and planning skills will be an added asset to supporting a Prime Minister's complicated schedule and many different activities. But I need to find a good replacement, too. At Jeremy's suggestion I go to meet one of his own former assistants in the White Room. Christianne Cavaliere is bright, keen and comes well recommended. It also turns out she has a PhD, experience working in the United Nations, and is currently tackling a regional UK brief with Minister Phil Hope in the Cabinet Office. I am very happy to have her join my small team and will welcome a really good, full-time person to cope with the growing workload of charity events, campaigns and government visits. All I need to do is persuade Phil to release her from his office as soon as possible, and given his generous nature I know he will do this for me and Christianne.

Emma Freud is in the middle of working as Second Unit Director with her partner, Richard Curtis, on a film about pirate radio DJs hijacking a boat (*The Boat That Rocked*). In between location shoots, she comes to see me to work out how we can come up with lots of new ideas for a global maternal mortality campaign to reach all the international decision-makers. In the last few weeks, I have discovered a lot of like-minded supporters and champions for this issue, and we are progressing our thinking to raise its profile at a rapid pace. I have found an excellent campaigning ally in Emma who, as a Trustee of Comic Relief, is bringing all their power and connections to bear on this issue.

Wednesday 12th March

Budget Day. This is somehow just as nerve-wracking as when Gordon did it. I am reminded that it is not just the banks of media outside, but the sound of helicopters overhead that adds to the air of menace and impending sense of judgement.

Alistair does well with the Budget, cheered on (silently, of course) by his family, who are all watching from the gallery in the House of Commons. I only ever saw Gordon give his final Budget there – I had missed all the previous ones, as I was always then out at work, or at home with small children.

This time, I watch the Budget on TV, and have lined up a take-out salad from the Pret A Manger down the road, a mini Green & Black's honeycomb chocolate bar and a cup of tea. Somehow it is not the relaxed hour watching TV I had imagined, as I'm also juggling files and telephone calls. This is just one of the many times I can't actually tell the difference between my former office-based working life, and my new, fairly office-based working life. And people tell me how lovely it must be to no longer have a job!

In the evening Gordon and I attend the *News of the World* Children's Champions Event. I have joined the judging panel this year, and Gordon has already met all the winners and other judges at Downing Street this afternoon.

I heard that the boys went with him to entertain everyone, and I have it on very good authority that celebrity judge Amanda Holden told one of my boys that he would have glitter in his poo from eating the tiny, glitter-covered fairy cakes we served. While Gordon is chatting to the new England football manager Fabio Capello and top Labour supporter Ross Kemp, I spot Amanda and tell her that I've had my spies on her. She roars her big, throaty, all-too-familiar *Britain's Got Talent* laugh and tries to explain to me that glitter is not actually digestible. She stops halfway through the explanation when she realises I am just teasing and not telling her off.

Later in the evening as we get back, we call in to say hello to Alistair and his team, who are enjoying a well-deserved late drink after a very long day.

Thursday 13th March

Gordon is away for a few days in Brussels, spending time with President Nicolas Sarkozy as they work on an agreement for joint funding of the Education for All initiative, which they'll unveil at the Emirates Conference in London later in the month. What always impresses me is that these two leaders can focus on something that will help the poorest in the world, even while they are also discussing the global economy with all the European leaders.

I have decided I need to catch up with what is in my wardrobe. I have the never-ending, but nevertheless enjoyable job of seeking out the right clothes to wear, and finding a selection of outfits that suit both my budget and what is in the diary.

I meet one of the consultants from the Jaeger team today. I am not a very patient person when it comes to trying on clothes, and having spent so many years being a thoughtless size 10/12, but now bigger post-babies, I am unimpressed by how I look in most things. I have that classic avoidance of anything requiring a glimpse in a full-length mirror and always explain to myself that I am just TOO busy. I decide to take the store adviser's suggestion for a black and white outfit from the Jaeger London collection to put to one side for the forthcoming French State Visit. I am not entirely decided but – perhaps with the pressures of being a mum of a very young son – I seem to have lost my sense of my own taste just for the moment. I also take a lovely hot-pink dress with a long black jacket that has the same electric pink lining to wear to a Labour Party fundraising dinner tonight.

I go home to spend time with the boys and leave it to the last minute to get changed. When I do, I realise I have cut it very fine with only ten minutes before departure, including putting on some make-up. Far too late I discover that the magnetic security tag is still on my hot-pink dress. This causes huge frustration and the fastest turn around for a new outfit ever. Ta da! And yes, boring black.

Gordon has had little time to prepare a speech for this evening and asks me what he should focus on. I just urge him to speak from the heart. He has the popular and super-talented actor, David Tennant, to introduce him, which he does very warmly. They both share that 'Son of the Manse' upbringing, as well as a passionate sense of social justice that comes with the territory. David is at the height of his success with the *Doctor Who* series and the two of them are absolutely mobbed by the gala dinner guests. John O'Farrell is hosting the dinner with his effortless non-stop joke-telling – he is as funny in person as he is in his books. Gordon stands at the front of the stage and talks personally and magnificently. I don't think anyone is unmoved. Arabella Weir stands up and does a very good ask for pledges of support. All in all, it is a very good night.

Tuesday 18th March

I'm sitting in the flat having my regular catch-up meeting with Gil and PiggyBankKids manager Joe Hewitt on the charity when Beth and Konrad walk in with the very sad news that Anthony Minghella has died following his recent cancer operation. This is terrible for everyone but I am concerned for Gordon, who has found a close friendship with him. I immediately try to call Gordon directly and via others' phones, and finally get through to

Number 10 chief adviser Stephen Carter, who is able to tell me that Gordon has already received the sad news.

In his subsequent statement to the press, Gordon describes Anthony as 'one of Britain's greatest creative talents, one of our finest screen writers and directors, a great champion of the British film industry and expert on literature and opera'. He was all that, and a generous, warm-hearted and loyal friend to Gordon – and to the Labour Party, having directed the 2005 Election Broadcast.

I go to find Gordon when he is back at Number 10 and even join him in his meeting around the Cabinet Room table with the Speaker of the United States Congress, Nancy Pelosi, who is visiting with her husband, Paul, and a large delegation. Towards the close of the meeting, Gordon invites me to contribute to the closing discussion about the MDGs to explain the lack of sufficient focus on the maternal mortality issue. Speaker Pelosi is hosting a Capitol Hill event in April and invites me to speak at it, which is a huge honour. I very much hope I can find a way to be there.

Wednesday 19th March

After a busy day for Gordon, we find time to visit the Black Britannia exhibition – portraits of black Britons by *Mirror* photographer John Ferguson. It turns out to be really enjoyable, and I run into Mike Fuller, the only black Chief Constable in the UK, now running the County of Kent's police force. I met Mike some years ago when he was with the Met, and called on him to contribute to my PiggyBankKids anthologies. I have a great piece by him written about his dad.

Monday 24th March

Gordon says that after ten years of Labour government, he's realising that every problem that arrives will be called his fault. I suspect he might be right. There have been some highly contentious debates in Parliament about stem cell research that always polarises opinion. MPs' expenses are also a growing issue that he is giving a lot of thought to, mindful that this is a system that badly needs improvement and, of course, the economic climate is worsening as a result of the global financial situation. All fall under the watch of whoever is the PM of the day!

Tuesday 25th March

An endless office day for me, broken by popping into Gordon's reception to present awards to the 'Bevin Boys', who served in the mines in WWII. This is a lovely thing to do, to honour a group of people who gave tremendous service but who have long not received the true recognition that they deserve. I think everyone there seems happy to be part of the celebration.

Wednesday 26th March

Today is the start of the French State Visit to London. I feel quite nervous about the various parts of the programme, the formality, and the huge media and public interest in the visit, never mind getting hair, outfits and posture right standing next to a super-model (which actually bothers me less, whether wisely or not). I imagine that Carla will be feeling equally nervous, and she has so much at stake as this is her first official visit with her new husband.

President Sarkozy is speaking at the Palace of Westminster in the afternoon, which is our first commitment. As it is a full State Visit, the Sarkozys are the guests of the Queen and have been staying at Windsor Castle.

It is not until the early afternoon that I am ready, in a pink Louise Kennedy coat, and go with Gordon to the House of Lords, where President Sarkozy will address the members of both the Houses. We wait outside the main chamber to greet the President and the new Mrs Sarkozy when they arrive.

Gordon and I get a warm greeting from his old friend and I give Carla a hug as she looks so anxious. She looks so terrific in her chic dove grey and navy Dior; she has pitched it just right for her serious trip to London. I sit in the front row next to Gordon – we risk terrible pictures by wearing the translation headphones in order to hear the speech – and Sarkozy speaks in French throughout, giving a wonderful speech that will go down well as he has put in a lot of references praising Britain, which is very smart. Harriet Harman sits on the other side of me. We scoot out at the end quickly to wish the Sarkozys goodbye for the time being.

A short while later we are ready for the evening engagement; this time I am wearing a long blue Amanda Wakeley dress with a Garrard white gold, diamonds and aqua necklace and earrings set – Gordon is in white tie – and we set off for the ride to Windsor Castle.

The State Banquet passes off well with all the usual fanfare. The long length of the banqueting table is exquisitely and lavishly set up with gleaming silver, sparkling glassware and perfect flowers. The only mishap is when Gordon is misdirected by someone, down the wrong side of the banqueting table, and so he arrives late at his table place. We are kindly allowed to leave early and get back by 11.15 p.m.

Thursday 27th March

Mark Pittman comes in early to redo my hair and I don the black and white Jaeger London suit and my usual heeled patent shoes. Gordon and I are down in the entrance hall on time to greet the Sarkozys. The whole day begins with the photographers' flashing light bulbs for their arrival at the door of Number 10.

We escort them both up to the main function rooms. Nicolas tells me that he is excited that it is Carla's first visit to Downing Street. He and Gordon retire to their meeting and Carla and I go to the Terracotta Room and talk on the sofa – with cameras flying in for a short period to capture some footage. So far, I think for two people who have only spoken briefly on the phone, Carla and I get on very well.

Carla's mother is with her on this visit and so I have asked my mum, Pauline, to join us too. The British Ambassador's wife, Susie, is there, as is Lady Susan Hussey, the lady-in-waiting who will be looking after Carla during her day with me.

After tea and a chat, Carla explains she is worried about the speech she will give at the White Ribbon Alliance charity lunch. The two of us leave our group and go alone to the nearby study to look over our respective words. Beth has already mentioned to me that Carla has discussed with her aides the possibility of pulling out of speaking. I hope I have provided her with sufficient reassurance but don't think I should mention that I am as nervous as she, and have no great track record in great speech making myself. I have already agreed with the media and events teams at Number 10 that my speech can be filmed for television, which now seems quite a bold decision.

We are driven to nearby Lancaster House, the spectacular mansion managed by the Foreign Office, just close by in St James's. Here we meet the French delegation including the French Prime Minister's wife, Penelope Fillon (in the UK, we often forget that the French have a Prime Minister as well as a President). Then it is time to run through the presentation lines with Kirsty Young, who will be introducing us to speak. Emma Freud is there and gives Carla a fabulous 'You'll be great' confidence-building pep talk as the nerves are showing again. I feel boosted even hearing it one removed.

The guests at lunch today are 120 powerful, interesting and active women. It is being sponsored by the Vodafone Foundation rather than by a government budget; they have been generous with the lunch and table arrangements, and an already spectacular dining room looks exquisite.

Kirsty introduces a two-minute DVD that sets the scene for the theme of the White Ribbon Alliance's work then, rather formally, Carla and I walk into the dining room once everyone is seated. We are greeted with warm applause from a friendly crowd. I speak first, introduced by Kirsty, and after walking up to a lectern set up in front of an intimidating bank of cameras. I really am quite far out of my comfort zone, but this time I am very determined to get the message across about a sorely neglected health issue that I think will move the audience, all of whom can help raise its profile. I also have a strong and rather patriotic desire to 'not let the side down' in representing Britain with my small part of this State Visit programme. I think I speak well enough, and certainly acquit myself much better than my Davos moment, which remains forever the low benchmark in my mind. What I realise as I speak is that everyone is listening very intently, and I believe that for many of the women invited today, this will be the first time they have been made aware of the avoidable deaths of mothers who we can help.

Following me, Kirsty introduces Carla, who gives a shorter speech, but does so with her mesmerising, melodic voice and her wonderful accent: she has us all joining up to 'ze coze' (the cause).

Finally our guests are able to enjoy their delicious lunch from top caterer Alison Price. Each table of ten women has one seat taken by a representative of the maternal mortality campaign whether US director Theresa Shaver, UK director Brigid McConville or a Patron, like Diana Quick. Each of them led a conversation about the campaign over lunch, looking for ways our guests can follow up on the issue and play their part. Of course, there is much chat and gossip to get through, but there is plenty of time for that, too.

I let Carla eat most of her main course – and send and receive a couple of texts to her husband – before I start to take her round the room to meet as many women as possible. Everyone wants to say hello and she makes every effort to reach everyone. I have invited some fashion editors like Lisa Armstrong (*The Times*) and Hilary Alexander (the *Telegraph*) who, of course, all know Carla from her modelling days at the international fashion shows. Hilary is there in a flash to speak to her, her notebook out, to discuss the Christian Dior wardrobe for the visit.

I also have included lots of government and other high-profile women including Leader of the House of Lords Cathy Ashton, Annie Lennox and Lynn de Rothschild, as well as the Cabinet spouses who are my friends like Louise Shackelton and Alice

Perkins (Jack Straw's wife). They have all been a huge support in giving me encouragement for the day, knowing from their own experience just how much detailed preparation is needed, and how much pressure there is to avoid mistakes.

Carla and I do manage to look ahead to when we might meet next as the French delegation heads home today. The forthcoming G8 summit ('Group of Eight', a forum for governments of eight countries in the world: France, Germany, Italy, Japan, the United Kingdom, the United States, Canada and Russia) in Japan is one opportunity, and while I will definitely be going and taking my campaign there, Carla is caught up in recording a new album that will be ready for release around the same time. She tells me that she had not thought of going, but is not uninterested if her schedule can allow for the time to visit Japan.

One remark stays with me after she leaves. When I ask her how she manages to make time for writing music and her own work, now that she has married Nicolas, and is part of his life at the Élysée Palace, she says, 'The only thing I miss is my loneliness.'

Friday 4th April

As important as the European discussions are, there are also obligations to build relationships with leaders from other continents, too. One such big gathering for international leaders is the Progressive Governance Conference. The Australian Prime Minister Kevin Rudd has flown in, and is staying with David Miliband at the big country house Chevening (available to the Foreign Secretary of the day). This gives me the opportunity to meet his wife, Thérèse Rein, a remarkable woman with a powerful reputation for founding and running a successful international business that secures employment for people with disabilities.

My first impression is that she looks like I remember myself six months ago: quite blinky as you hit another entirely new, slightly pinch-yourself experience. Luckily, I am all set to give her an unscary, easy experience coming to Downing Street for the first time. With her permission, I have invited a number of maternal health experts to brief her who will be joined by some fellow Australians who have settled in London.

I take Thérèse to the Terracotta Room in Number 10 to meet the small expert group comprising Gill Greer of the International Planned Parenthood Federation, Roxy Philson of Bono's ONE campaign, Emma Parry of Comic Relief and Brigid McConville of the White Ribbon Alliance. The Australian contingent has been assembled by my entertaining and reliable pal, Kathy Lette, who has brought the unique Barry Humphries and *Rabbit-Proof Fence* film director Phillip Noyce, with his beautiful Nigerian wife.

Together we watch an extract from a film on Burkina Faso, talk about maternal mortality and the challenge it poses, and then lighten up a little as we eat cake and chat. My boys run in to say hello (and find the cake).

By the evening, I make it down to Chequers where Gordon has about 14 or 15 heads of government from the conference coming to supper – a feat of coordination with cars pulling up in the driveway, each to be met separately and photographed on arrival. There is an endless stream of inspirational figures walking through the door: John Kafour of Ghana, Kevin Rudd of Australia, Jens Stoltenberg of Norway, Michele Bachelet of Chile, Ellen Johnson Sirleaf of Liberia and Helen Clark of New Zealand.

There is some concern when Peter Mandelson, who is the EU Trade Commissioner, does not turn up. When someone calls him he is reported to have replied that he had not been invited properly. Gordon's adviser, Justin Forsyth, steps up to the plate to take his seat but just as he is going forward, one of the other guests turns up with an unexpected UN guest. So Justin gallantly nips out again and joins the sherpas and advisers who all eat together in the Great Hall of Chequers, just outside the dining room. What I love about Justin is that, despite his senior status, he just does not make a fuss about this kind of thing – a rarer quality than you would think.

Saturday 5th April

Gordon and I attend Anthony Minghella's memorial service, which takes place at St Thomas More church in Hampstead. It is a heart-breakingly sad occasion – the family are suffering so deeply, as are his film world colleagues. Gordon and I are thoughtfully seated at the front – next to artist and film director Sam Taylor Wood, who I know from our work with the Maggie's Centres – and near a door, as the family understand that we need to be the first to leave, with so many international leaders visiting London.

The service comprises readings and addresses from writer Michael Ondaatje, producer Harvey Weinstein, and Gordon, as well as actors from Anthony's most famous films: Matt Damon and Jude Law (*The Talented Mr Ripley*), Juliette Binoche (*The English Patient*), Renée Zellweger (*Cold Mountain*) and Alan Rickman with Juliet Stevenson (reading part of *Truly Madly Deeply*), plus a personal address from Anthony's scriptwriter brother, Dominic Minghella.

Everyone is very emotional – most noticeably the actors, which I suppose is their due. Richard Curtis stands to introduce the speakers and hold everyone together. Harvey Weinstein gives one of the most informative and inspirational addresses I have ever heard – he makes vivid Anthony's daily working life and the whole process of starting a film and bringing it to the screen.

Renée Zellweger's address is extraordinarily flamboyant: she takes her coat off, adjusts papers, and talks at a high emotional pitch about Anthony's influence on her. Gordon is next up, and nudges me to whisper that he wonders how his short Biblical text will work to follow that. Actually, its simplicity is what makes it so moving. Gordon says of Anthony that he was a great man, but also a good man and that the text he had been asked to read reflects his values. His reading is one of the Beatitudes recorded as the words of Jesus in his Sermon on the Mount, from the Book of Matthew, which starts, 'Blessed are the meek, for they shall inherit the earth.'

At the end of the service we sneak out of the side door into waiting cars. Gordon was loath to leave ahead of the church Mass, but when we get into our separate cars, I call him to say that though I know he would have wanted to stay it is just a fact that while he does his current job there are many things that he is going to have to leave early, or not go to at all. A case in point is tonight's dinner with George Clooney, which Mariella Frostrup and her lawyer husband, Jason McCue, have invited us to attend. It is not possible to go for a whole evening as the workload is too great, and at times when it isn't, an early night would be top of the list.

As it turns out, Justin Forsyth is able to attend the dinner and returns, suggesting that Gordon actually find 20 minutes to meet Clooney and McCue to talk about their campaign work for the people of Darfur, Sudan.

Gordon's diary secretary Leeanne once joked that she would consider her posting with him complete once she had diarised appointments for both David Beckham and George Clooney. So far we are one down, and one to go. I promise to see if we can arrange for Clooney to come and see Gordon to talk about Darfur, but do request it be in the office so we can keep our promise to Leeanne.

Tuesday 8th April

I have decided to tackle head-on the problems I am having with public speaking. I think that I am getting better, but I still suffer from panic attacks and need to equip myself with ways of getting over this. Gil suggested I sign up for a couple of sessions with speaking coach Polly James whom I had met during my time working at communications consultancy Brunswick Arts. Polly works within the Brunswick Group of companies advising CEOs on their presentation techniques, but she is best known for her other career as an actress, and was hugely famous in the early seventies for her part as Beryl in *The Liverbirds*. Needless to say, she is properly trained and has also worked with the likes of John Schlesinger and Peter Brook, so I know that I am not going to emerge with a Liverpudlian accent.

Polly comes to the flat to do a session and takes one look at me – or rather a quick listen – and comes up with some easy breathing exercises that are immediately helpful. My top tip from her is to concentrate on my full breath all the way through my body – she even has me lying on the floor of the sitting room, huffing away. Whatever it takes!

While I'm taking deep breaths in the flat with Polly, the rest of the building is taking deep breaths and full-on swoons at the visit of George Clooney and a human-rights legal team. In the last five years, fighting in Darfur between rebel forces and a government-backed militia has led to the deaths of at least 200,000 people and left 2.3 million people homeless and without their livelihoods, living in camps in poverty and often in great continuing peril. Even the biggest aid and humanitarian relief agencies have found it difficult to gain access to them, and both the rebels and the government have ignored the United Nations Security Council's requests to protect civilians caught up in this terrible war. Clooney has long shown a personal interest in the plight of the people of Darfur, and of refugees in general. At the start of this year he took up a role as a UN 'messenger of peace', using his tremendous high profile to shine a light on this tragedy.

Clooney and his colleagues arrive before 9 a.m. to meet Gordon and get right down to a discussion about what action can be taken using Gordon's international contacts, and Clooney's megawatt media power. I am not trying to be cool or rude, but I am not part of the meeting and so continue in the flat with Polly and the boys. Then I get a call from Leeanne asking if I will take the boys over to say hello to George and Jason McCue (whose kids know my two). I happily grab Mela and off we go. Of course, Mr Clooney is very charming, and a properly professional famous person. By this, I mean that he has that way of paying attention to everyone who walks into a room, looking to control what happens so that the experience works well, that conversation is good, that he is liked. It is not a bad thing, it is just noticeable among very famous people, and Mr Clooney seems to be among the best at this.

Luckily for me – as I am wearing a very 'comfy' lime green M&S cardie – the photographer present is only taking private snaps. I get one of the boys with Clooney for their scrapbook. Needless to say Leeanne and Mela are included in one of the pictures for their personal albums, too.

Word of Clooney's presence goes round the building and when I leave the room, people are hanging around in the corridor and leaning over the banisters. Clooney is so much the professional superstar, he makes time as he leaves to walk around and say hello to everyone, and is a good sport about visiting the press office and having his picture taken with pretty much everyone there.

Gordon is pretty unfazed by super celebrities and, despite the cynicism that can surround celebrity support, always welcomes their involvement with charitable or social issues as the attention they bring can help shine a much-needed light. From Angelina Jolie to Matt Damon, he has worked with a number of Hollywood folk who are inclined to support anti-poverty initiatives in Africa. Clooney's interest in the wellbeing of the people of Darfur is well documented. The ongoing difficulty is how to engage the rebels in talks that will move things forward to a solution. Clooney reports later from the Dorchester Hotel that the two of them had discussed whether a fund could be created to provide helicopters to provide better security.

Gordon has also offered to host talks with the Sudanese rebel leaders in London if they are needed, which Clooney tells the media after he leaves Number 10. He is very positive about this outcome, but both Douglas Alexander and David Miliband are pretty furious that Gordon made the offer without consulting the International Development team or Foreign Office respectively. But as Gordon so often says, when you have a chance to help you need to grab it. Sticking to protocol is less important than making progress.

CHAPTER 10

Visit to the White House

Wednesday 16th April

My first trip to the White House to visit President George W Bush and First Lady Laura Bush with Gordon has been set to coincide with a series of meetings with the Presidential candidates for the forthcoming, ground-breaking electoral contest. It is also our nanny Mela's birthday, but all we can do is wish her a happy birthday and then leave her to celebrate with our two children. This was possibly not what Mela had planned as her family are all arriving in London to see her today, and with two small boys is opting for more of the cake- and less of the wine-type celebrations, but she has been beyond understanding about our schedules.

I started out feeling jet-lagged before the day began due to small people waking in the night and needing an extra bottle. Added to this, I am travelling to Washington DC without Gordon or security protection, so head out to the airport with only Konrad and our luggage for three days (and 14 different events). I always say that when you travel with the PM, you get to tarmac-it all the way. This means just leaping off aircraft on to the tarmac and straight into cars. Travelling without the PM is a different business altogether.

At the airport, I am slightly embarrassed that I have a too-large bottle of nail polish remover that must be ritually confiscated. The security officer searching my bag sweetly apologises for the inconvenience and asks me how long I have been working for

Konrad. I tell you, we girls have some way to go in the world to find equality.

As soon as we step on to US soil, we are surrounded by three US security service personnel to watch our every move, as well as our own Gary Richmond from the Met for protection. We also have the full flashing blue police lights as we drive into Washington DC – all I could think of at that moment was how much my boys would have loved those police lights. There is definitely something about being the mother of small boys – I just notice every emergency service vehicle and every earth digger with appreciation.

My first official appointment is on Capitol Hill for the White Ribbon Alliance. I join Speaker Nancy Pelosi for her reception to celebrate Representative Lois Capps's bill to take a resolution through the House (1022) to call for better maternal health in ending maternal mortality for the US and abroad, through greater financial investment and the recognition of good maternal health as a basic human right. It is a big deal to see that the US administration wants to join the call for change to save women's lives. I am delighted, too, that my work has been acknowledged, and my time with Nancy Pelosi back in London when she visited was well spent for us both. Her fabulous husband Paul is also there and I congratulate him on being so supportive. He explains that he is actually in town for the Congressional Spouses Lunch, and for the visit of Pope Benedict XVI who is to be the star of a White House dinner.

I know that this bill in Congress does not change anything on the ground yet, but this is a start and encouraging to learn that some of the important, progressive people are listening. Next stop for me will be to find out if the White House wants to listen, too.

I move straight on to the Four Seasons Hotel bar to meet my long-standing American friends Marylouise Oates and Tammy Haddad for tea who I catch up with whenever I am in the States. Tammy, a former live TV chat-show producer, has started a new business, Haddad Media, of which she is President, doing interviews with a handheld steady cam – the Tam Cam as it is called. She lives in Washington DC with her husband Ted Greenberg, a brilliant lawyer who chases laundered and counterfeit money, and their two children, David and Rachel. Marylouise and her husband Bob have already visited us in Downing Street and Chequers, and are based in New York, both teaching at New York University, but she has been lured to Washington for our get-together. Marylouise had a few months ago had the terrible news that her beloved sister Jane faced cancer treatment, but there is good news now and the treatment signs are very optimistic. It is reminder, as always, of the fragility of life and the passion with which we must live it.

When our 'doing a little Georgetown shopping and having afternoon tea in the hotel' time is up, I am driven to the British Embassy Residence and, in the early evening, catch up with Gordon at a reception hosted by the British Ambassador, Sir Nigel Sheinwald, in Gordon's honour. Gordon reports a series of good meetings today in New York at the UN Security Council, where he had lined up in agreement with President Kikwete (of Tanzania) and Secretary-General Ban Ki-moon to take a tough stance against Robert Mugabe and the dreadful election stand-off in Zimbabwe, which is damaging that country so much.

Once the reception is over, I have committed myself to joining a White Ribbon Alliance dinner at the magnificent home of journalist Elsa Walsh in Georgetown. Elsa is well known for her marriage to the legendary Watergate reporter Bob Woodward (played by Robert Redford in *All the President's Men*), but is herself an accomplished journalist and author. She has gathered together some women who might engage with the issue of maternal mortality, from celebrated columnist Sally Quinn to Patty Stonesifer from the Gates Foundation, and a former Homeland Security adviser. She tells me President Bush had been quite struck by Gordon's case for investment in education in Africa as a necessity for national security, not least because he has seen evidence of al-Qaeda filling the gap by providing their own schools in Africa and elsewhere, with their own teachings.

I am invited to address the room by Elsa who introduces me in a gentle, personal way, sharing how the love she has for her own teenage daughter must be reflected by every mother as their child is born. I have given a number of speeches now about the need to focus on maternal health internationally, but this time I realise I am speaking privately to a group of highly professional senior women who between them can make a world of difference to literally thousands, if not millions, of lives around the world. I follow Elsa's introduction about her daughter by explaining the depth of loss I feel in not having my daughter, Jennifer, with me, in our family, enjoying her own life. It is an unfathomable sadness to lose a child, one that always stays with you. I explain how the love that Gordon and I felt during the short time we had with Jennifer had the deepest impact on us, and just those ten days opened our eyes to why the fight for life, for the best chances in life, are so important, and why our actions to provide that for all people should be at the core of the humanity of us all.

After speaking, I move around the different tables speaking to everyone. On the last table, I talk to Judith Helzner from the MacArthur Foundation, who is working with her boss Jonathan Fanton to donate a further $50 million for maternal mortality projects – now that is a good sum to start the week with. And for my final chat I find Sarah S Brown.

Before I married I don't think I ever met another Sarah Macaulay (my maiden name), although my younger brother Bruce married a Sarah so I do know one now, but I collect Sarah Browns everywhere I go. (It just fascinates me, the range of things different people do with the connecting thread of the same name. Remember Dave Gorman, the comedian who spent a year tracking down everyone with the same name as him? I am a bit like that, just not so full-time!) Sarah S Brown is a legend for her groundbreaking educational work tackling the high statistics of teenage pregnancy as the CEO of the National Campaign to Prevent Teen and Unplanned Pregnancy.

Congress Representative Lois Capps stands at the end to say

that she is more convinced than ever that the US needs to address its own gaps in maternal and infant mortality, and lead by example for the rest of the world.

I get back just after 11 p.m., which is really about 4 a.m. UK time. Unsurprisingly, Gordon is fast asleep.

Thursday 17th April

We kick off today with a thought-provoking power breakfast with Alan Greenspan and Andrea Mitchell at the Embassy, overlooking a view of its cherry blossom-strewn lawn. Gordon is asking Alan for his take on both the US economy and the global economy. They speak a lot about the role of the Middle East, whether increasing Saudi oil supply would help (even in the short term) and much alarm is sounded over food prices and the growing global food crisis.

Our ambassador, Sir Nigel Sheinwald, comes to get Gordon and me for his next series of meetings. Gordon is to meet each of the Presidential candidates, so one way or the other we will be talking to the next President of the United States. It is clear that Senator Obama is the emerging Democratic favourite, but Senator Clinton is putting up a great fight and has just triumphed in the previous night's televised debate in Pennsylvania. Senator McCain has already secured the Republican nomination but is entering the election as the underdog.

The arrival of the three Presidential candidates at the British Embassy all goes like clockwork: Obama at 9, Clinton at 10, McCain at 11. I join Gordon in greeting each one as they enter the study in the Residence, and on each occasion Gordon and the candidate leave the room to walk down a long corridor in front of cameras, and into a private 45-minute meeting.

Obama is tall, striking and has obvious charisma, but waits for someone else to get the conversation going. He does, however, turn to me and ask me about juggling family life, and was the only one of the three who gave me the opening to talk about my push on maternal mortality. He warmly assures me that he and his wife, Michelle, would take this issue up if successful.

Senator Clinton is open and friendly, and immediately fell into an easy conversation about Northern Ireland asking Gordon about a conference he has coming up. They do, of course, know each other from previous meetings when her husband was President.

John McCain is jovial but seems very tired. When he was asked to join Gordon for the walk past the media cameras, he joked as though muttering to himself, 'Okay, mustn't drool.' I realise that age is his barrier, in the same way as being black, and being a woman, serves as an issue for the Democratic contenders.

After joining Gordon at his morning meetings, I am now ready to go out for my first meeting with the US First Lady, Laura Bush. I am greatly looking forward to this, but a little worried that I am not quite myself. I noticed at last night's reception that I was getting slight balance problems and feelings of panic. I had passed this off as jet-lag combined with the nervousness I experience before speaking publicly. Once I had spoken I was fine, but today I notice it creeping back again as I set out to meet Mrs Bush.

My meeting has been arranged as something called a 'courtesy visit'. I am interested to meet this dignified and gracious woman who has so diligently championed the enjoyment of reading and beating illiteracy with great passion, and been tenacious in pursuing better life chances for the women in Afghanistan. I understand that she will be keeping up her causes after she leaves the White House next year.

Our offices have agreed on a visit to the Smithsonian exhibition at the Washington DC Patent Office Building, about the second inaugural ball of President Lincoln. I arrive in good time and join the large number of executives of the museum, who are all eager to see her. I really am now feeling very over-tired and actually strangely unsure of my balance. If I stand for any length of time unsupported I start to feel pretty wobbly on my feet, and a bit 'whooh' in my head.

When Mrs Bush arrives I say hello and join her as we are taken round the exhibition. I just creep along, leaning against walls where I can – hanging on in there. The curator talks to everyone throughout the exhibition tour, keeping their attention throughout. We then have a short walk to the main courtyard with its new undulating ceiling designed by British architect Sir Norman Foster. Alas, I can hardly look up, but it is interesting to see and hear the excitement of the visitors as they notice the First Lady standing nearby. She very sweetly waves to a young guy in a wheelchair who catches her eye, but she and I have hardly spoken a word throughout the visit.

After that, I get out into the fresh air to clear my head and decide that I can keep going. As I recover from my nervousness, I feel much steadier on my feet – this is very strange, and quite restricting. I carry on and attend a pre-arranged meeting with US Ambassador Mark Dybul who runs the major AIDS organisation PEPFAR, and whom I have long admired and wanted to meet. We both attend a meeting at the British Embassy chaired by David Lane, head of the ONE Campaign, which Gordon has convened to look at how the global poverty reduction targets can be reached with the different partners from NGOs, the US administration and the private sector working together. I even manage to make my contribution at the appropriate moment in the schedule.

Once the event is over, we have less than half an hour to get ready for a White House dinner. I have with me a lovely grey dress and pink jacket from Amanda Wakeley, which looked great in London, but for a 'semi-casual' dinner now makes me feel a bit dressy and self-conscious. I remind myself that it is, after all, the White House, so a bit dressy seems okay, but I live by the motto that my greatest mistake is still ahead of me – and our media can be very mean when they want to be. I also have high heels and am very conscious that I am still quite wobbly on my feet.

We leave the Residence in the big, black limousine Gordon has been using and speed along cleared roads with outriders. The

Bushes are waiting in front of the White House entrance and we all pose briefly for photographs. President Bush asks me if I have visited the White House before and I say only once, on a tour many years before. He kindly takes us on a personal guided tour to see the main function rooms, showing us the room where the Pope's State Dinner was held the night before (without the Pope, as it turned out who it is reported was quite tired after a long day).

Our tour continues through the various anterooms, including the ground-floor Oval Office, and we see all the recent refurbishments overseen by Mrs Bush. We also look at the various portraits, including the haunting one of JFK with eyes cast down, which was painted after his death. President Bush explains his portrait will hang opposite his father's in the downstairs entrance where President Clinton's portrait currently hangs.

From there, we are taken up to the sitting room in the private residence of the White House – past a large, modern portrait of the President on an easel that he says has just arrived, and that he is trying to decide what to do with. It looks pretty good to me.

In the sitting room, we are all seated on a sofa – the President at one end next to Gordon, and Mrs Bush in an armchair next to me. Our conversation is very easy going and uncomplicated. The President talks more of his retirement plans, which include writing a book about his 15 big decisions in office, undertaking speaking engagements, and creating a new Library/Foundation on Freedom in Texas by raising $250 million after leaving office.

He knows about his unpopularity, but is unmoved by it. Mrs Bush asks me about JK Rowling as she talks enthusiastically about children's books, and about the boys and my charity.

We dine in front of the most spectacular view (stopping off to visit a balcony where we can see an unpainted bit that shows marks made by the British in the days when we attacked the White House, and certainly did not have a special relationship!) The discussion returns to the President and his leadership style (he believes in lots of delegation). His mood is reflective and includes his thoughts on people who have lasted the course (not many), his admiration for Condoleezza Rice, and his long-standing friendship with Bill Gemmell, a businessman from Scotland who is the head of a sizeable oil company, and whom Gordon also knows.

Gordon and President Bush seem easy in each other's company but then both men are good at this kind of thing. They talk a fair bit about books they are each reading and I notice that President Bush is a great lover of works by British historians. We also talk about their daughter Jenna's upcoming wedding, which is clearly a much-looked-forward-to event. We are due to leave at 8 p.m. but dinner goes on to 8.45 p.m. as we dine on an excellent meal that includes Texan beef and a very delicious chocolate dessert. While the President does not drink, the rest of us enjoy a glass of wine. I think we all had a good time.

Friday 18th April

Gordon starts the final day in DC with another power breakfast, meeting Ben Bernanke, the current head of the Federal Reserve. I say a quick hello but both men look like they have a lot of business to discuss so I make myself scarce and join the Number 10 team in the main dining room eating with Jon Cunliffe. Jon is the person who leads all the international negotiations at the G8 and other significant meetings and is highly regarded by Gordon. There is no one who can do the job quite like he does and he is admired and feared in equal measure – all for good reasons.

I avoid the newspapers generally, but even I can see the striking pictures of Gordon with the three candidates yesterday, laid out by the breakfast table.

The tradition of thanking all the Embassy staff for their support always astonishes me, as it reveals quite how many people are involved behind the scenes in a PM's trip. Once we have shaken hands, we head out by car to Andrews Air Base and board the chartered plane. We are on a rather interestingly furnished Titan Airways plane to go to Boston as the Visits team are ever mindful to keep the travel budget down (generally speaking, we do seem to use a mixture of scheduled and chartered flights from British Airways, Virgin and some private airlines with smaller planes, while as a family we just board a regular scheduled flight when we are going to the constituency in Scotland). Today's craft is a vision of orange and brown, and styled as a 1970s throwback. You half-expect *Jaws*, *The A Team* and *Charlie's Angels* – the original versions – to be on the film menu.

I often encounter people (always Brits), who tell me very passionately that they believe the British government should have its own version of the US President's Air Force One in order to enhance our country's status when we travel overseas. However, as impressive as the mighty Air Force One is, it does cost an absolute fortune and there are other things higher up the spending list that take priority, and I suspect always will be.

Style considerations aside, though, and more importantly, the Titan Airways plane is safe, comfortable and the in-flight staff are terrific. Everyone on board – the Number 10 team, various accompanying visitors and the press pack – settles down quickly and easily for the journey.

We soon land in Boston. This great city is notorious for its terrible traffic jams that bring everything to a standstill at rush hour. We all disembark and get into cars that take us on a very strange journey across the whole city to the far side, with absolutely no traffic in our way at all. An entire tunnel is cleared to let us through – a once-in-a-lifetime experience I suspect – and there must be some serious behind-the-wheel cursing going on in some of those vehicles affected.

We arrive at the John F Kennedy Presidential Library and Museum on Columbia Point on the edge of Boston in record time. The building is dedicated to the life and times of the USA's thirty-fifth president, with exhibitions about his life and legacy, and has students and scholars from all over the world visiting to see the collection of historical materials held there.

The view from the museum of the water is spectacular, and it is the most stunning day. Gordon and I reminisce about Cape Cod holidays we have had in years gone by. We have never been as a family with our little boys, but hope to some day. The last time we came was the summer after we lost Jennifer and, looking back, I am not quite sure how we got through those months. Perhaps that is partly why we have needed some distance before returning.

We get a warm welcome from Senator Edward Kennedy and his wife Vicki, who are long-standing close personal friends and great political supporters, and from JFK's daughter, Caroline Kennedy, whom Gordon knows. We immediately begin a quick tour of the exhibition, which shows film footage, photographs and memorabilia of JFK until his assassination in 1963, his brother Robert F Kennedy, also assassinated as he ran for President in 1968, and other members of the family. When we stop to look at footage of JFK with his young children, Vicki and Ted gently tease Caroline – but I feel tremendous sadness for her, losing her dad as a young girl, and most recently her mother, Jacqueline Kennedy, and brother, John. A great deal of loss in that family.

The head of the Kennedy Library, Paul Kirk, stands up to introduce Senator Kennedy just as the Senator reaches for the microphone himself. The Senator steps down from the stage and seats himself again allowing Paul to continue with his fulsome introduction. When Senator Kennedy finally gets to speak, he does so with the splendid opening line: 'To think I tried to stop that introduction ...' He gives a very moving and highly complimentary introduction, describing Gordon as 'a leader of great principle, integrity and courage' and prefacing Gordon's speech by saying, 'he knows how to confront the difficult challenges before us in today's demanding and ever-changing world'.

Gordon's speech covers some really big themes as he starts to map out his thinking from his speech in India – his vision for 'a new World Bank; a new International Monetary Fund; a reformed and renewed United Nations'. As he stands in the Kennedy Library he pays tribute to President Kennedy's recognition of our interdependent world back in 1962, but highlights the 'sheer scale of the new

Arriving with Gordon through the black door, 27th June 2007

Our wedding day, in front of the media in our back garden, 3rd August 2000

Giving my bouquet to bridesmaid Rosie Davies, with my stepfather Patrick behind me, and my mum by his side

With my brothers.
From left to right: *Kit, Patrick, Bruce, Nico, Sean, Iain Alasdhair*

LESLEY DONALD

We made the conscious decision to give our children privacy despite the very public world of Downing Street. This photograph became the only official family photograph when Fraser was born in 2003

TOM MILLER

An official photograph by Tom Miller, 26th November 2007

At Chequers with Uncle John, my mum and Auntie Doreen, 7th June 2008

Almost our first visitors at Number 10 – President Nelson Mandela and Graça Machel, 28th August 2007

Attending the tenth anniversary memorial for Princess Diana at Wellington Barracks, 31st August 2007

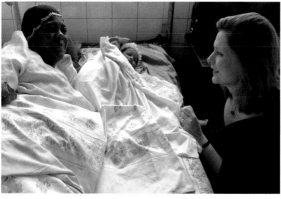

In Kampala, Uganda with Sylvie Numuwange and her new baby taken by photographer Thomas Froese, 24th November 2007

Revisiting my childhood home in Dar es Salaam, Tanzania, 22nd November 2007

Hosting the first reception for the maternal mortality campaign. Talking to Rose Mlai and Betsey McCallon of the WRA. Konrad Caulkett is in the background on the right, 18th October 2007

The girls at my surprise birthday party organised by Gordon, 31st October 2007. Left to right: Nicola Mendelsohn, Amy Gadney, Kathy Lette, Helen Scott Lidgett, Lisa Aziz, Maggie Darling, me, Sue Nye, Susan Boster, Mariella Frostrup

My Halloween birthday cake

Left to right: Maggie, Helen, Melanie Darby, me, Amy, Mariella, Gordon (hidden), Jo Rowling

Christmas is coming with the traditional frozen turkey photo. This first year was with Paul Kelly of the famous Kelly's Bronze turkeys, 17th December 2007

Here with Carla Bruni-Sarkozy at the lunch I hosted for the White Ribbon Alliance at Lancaster House, on the occasion of the French State Visit to London, 27th March 2008

An unexpected photo taken in my green M&S cardie with George Clooney, 8th April 2008

On the Number 10 doorstep with US President George W Bush and First Lady Laura Bush as they came to join us for a dinner with British historians, 15th June 2008

It was wonderful to be able to take part in many overseas visits. Here at the Aida Refugee Camp in Bethlehem, Palestine and at the Hall of Names at Yad Vashem in Jerusalem, Israel, 20th July 2008

And we fit in a visit to the Beijing Olympics the following month. Back row, from left to right: *Helen Etheridge, Clive Gardner, Stewart Wood, Tom Fletcher, Ambassador William Ehrman.* Front row: *me, Gordon, Lord Coe, Mayor Boris Johnson, David Beckham, 22nd August 2008* global challenges that our growing interdependence brings'. Gordon talks of the 'urgent necessity for global cooperation' and makes clear that he believes that we all have a shared moral sense that we are all responsible for each other. The point of calling for the reform and renewal of our big international institutions is to use the opportunity to create a 'global covenant' and build a new global society 'grounded in the great values we share in common'. This means all the world leaders finding a way to work together for us all, which will be the real challenge in the months and years ahead.

At lunch, I sit next to Governor Deval Patrick who has been campaigning hard for Barack Obama, so I hear first-hand why he believes that Senator Obama would transform politics. He has known Senator Obama a long time and both studied at Harvard Law School, and he is very certain that as President, Barack Obama will mobilise the country to help itself across all communities, while providing good leadership from the top.

Gordon and I present the Senator and Vicki Kennedy with a reproduction of Winston Churchill's speech on receipt of his honorary US citizenship from President Kennedy in 1963: 'In this century of storm and tragedy, I contemplate with high satisfaction the constant factor of the interwoven and upward progress of our peoples.'

In return we receive a lovely box with US and UK flags on it, which contains a tea service with a pattern Jacqueline Kennedy used. I know that we will really treasure this gift.

After leaving the Kennedy Library, I think we are all set to go straight home, but instead Gordon pops into the Kennedy School of Government for a quick discussion about the speech he has just given, to a packed room of academics, whom even I have heard of (they all write best-sellers these days).

I have no idea how Gordon has the stamina for the session but it goes well and we walk out into the glorious sunshine to the Harvard Coop bookshop. Gordon has the unusual freedom of browsing in a shop, and promptly puts his purchases on my credit card. As we walk away I realise I am feeling far better than I have in days just for a bit of fresh air and exercise.

Monday 21st April

Still not quite recovered from the US trip, I attend a reception for Tottenham-based community football club Broadwater Farm United, where the children are about to participate in a tournament in Tokyo. Nice reception with Secretary of State for Culture Andy Burnham MP, David Lammy (the local MP in Tottenham), and the cultural attaché from the Japanese Embassy. The kids, in smartish British Airways-sponsored tracksuits, are very focused on the food, piling through platefuls of it.

I still feel rather jet-lagged, so give myself an easier afternoon. I go and visit M&S with their head of communications, Flic Howard-Allen, and PR chief, Tania Littlehales, who expertly steer me around the floors scooping up clothes. We use the press area as a changing room for me and I show them any clothes I want a second opinion on. I get a nice cup of tea while my credit card disappears off to settle my account – of course, I have bought far more than I planned to. Flic and Tania both tease me about the lime green M&S cardigan I was wearing in the George Clooney photographs which, of course, appeared in the press and were not left as private at all!

Back at the flat, I put John and Fraser to bed and start on some emails and letters while it is quiet. Gordon heads off to an evening meeting with the Parliamentary Labour Party where our own Labour MPs are very concerned about the effect of a withdrawal by Gordon of a 10p tax rate on some of the lower paid (done by him as Chancellor before leaving office last year). This could be a difficult meeting, but I get a couple of positive texts from his advisers so it sounds as though it has gone well after all. Clearly, the MPs feel that he does understand their concerns – 'I get it' is the quote from him.

At the end of the day, I finally catch up with him myself. He seems together, composed, quite sure of himself despite the upset.

What I know, perhaps more than anyone, is that he is the person who has given most time, thought and energy to reducing poverty as Chancellor, and that what he and his colleagues have achieved with tax credits provides a pathway to poverty reduction much more than any tax rate large or small ever could.

Tuesday 22nd April

As we settle back after the US trip, I spend an hour with Leeanne and Beth going over the diary, while Gordon is in the weekly Cabinet meeting. I am able to find dates where I can accompany Gordon on his visits, and secure some down time for quieter evenings (events notwithstanding), and suppers with friends or colleagues.

I have an appointment with Fraser for a check-up at the wonderful Great Ormond Street Hospital so miss the important service for the fifteenth anniversary of Stephen Lawrence's death at St Martin-in-the-Fields church in Trafalgar Square (just two minutes from Downing Street). I am very sad to miss this, but hope that as a mum, Doreen Lawrence will understand the choice I make. Gordon goes with Oona King instead as, despite the busy day, this is an important service to attend.

Later on, Gordon also prepares for a tricky PMQs tomorrow, and is still negotiating over 10p tax issues with Labour MPs. I creep out late and go to Shriti Vadera's house for supper. She has a group of her friends from the development world there, including Richard Curtis, Emma Freud, Bob Geldof, Justin Forsyth from Number 10 and Phil Bloomer from Oxfam. I am really pleased to be included. I have a long chat with Richard who is missing his Comic Relief work while shooting his new film, and hoping to do more for Botswana. 'Sir Bob' asks me to write a short piece on the maternal mortality campaign for the issue of Japanese daily newspaper *Asahi Shimbun* he is editing, to come out just before the G8 Summit in Japan.

Konrad is already on the advance visit to Japan to scope out how we can achieve another packed schedule there.

Wednesday 23rd April

Today is a big day for Gordon with PMQs and final negotiations with Labour rebels over the 10p tax issue. I meet Panamanian First Lady, Vivian Fernandez de Torrijos – her party arrives very late after her car shoots past the gate to Downing Street. Then both her and the Panamanian Ambassador's jackets unzip and lose a button respectively. Christianne Cavaliere, who is just about to start work full-time in my office, witnesses all this with some horror. We assure her the comedy levels are not typical. The meeting is very fun and we get on very well. Vivian is searching for charitable activities to reinforce healthcare among indigenous populations in her country, and is already a strong and well-known international advocate on disability issues. We agree to help each other at the UN meetings in September.

Thursday 24th April

Icelandic Prime Minister Geir Haarde visits to meet Gordon, and I spend time with his wife, Inga, who tells me all about Iceland. The country has a total population of 300,000 (about the same as Wigan) and there are fewer people now earning a living from fishing than from energy. She tells me everyone in Iceland loves the arts. She does not mention banking.

Gordon and I then jump in the car to go on a visit to Wolverhampton, where I witness the new political team at work. A crew from Saatchi's are filming for the Labour Party alongside a documentary team from Channel 4, with a new Number 10 broadcast officer, Nicola Burdett, who I thought was very impressive, if first impressions count.

An unknown someone has told Nicola that I will insist on avoiding all personal shots of myself, so she will have to work around me. I never find out who it was, and Nicola is far too discreet to say, but I promptly knock that rumour on the head and elbow my way into a bit of footage; I am not much bothered if I am in a shot or not, but am more than happy to join in and do my bit.

Gordon will be spending at least one, usually two days a week, travelling across Britain (unless overseas) to hear about local issues, visiting homes, workplaces, schools, hospitals and community centres throughout his premiership. (Much of the daily ministerial work will be done on trains, so that there is no backlog back at Downing Street.) On this trip, we fit in a visit to a printing business, a Sure Start Children's Centre and a party members/trade union meeting.

There is a little nervousness among the political team about the terrible press coverage we are getting, and a fear of what happens next. I so wish them well in turning the political feeling around, and our own confidence.

I trust Gordon's political antennae absolutely and, as we leave the members' meeting, he worries that they weren't quite with him. A YouGov poll this weekend puts us 18 points behind, which is even lower than the polling just before Gordon became Prime Minister. I feel great frustration as, to my mind, we have the finest leader imaginable.

Once we get back to London we call into the Archbishop of Canterbury's annual reception held in Lambeth Palace, just the other side of the River Thames from the Palace of Westminster. I get stuck with a female journalist who reminds me just how poisonous and disingenuous someone can be when they have made up their mind to oppose you. More amusingly, veteran rebel MP Frank Field bounds up in very cheerful mode to say how much he enjoyed talking to Gordon about the 10p tax issue, and share his delight that everyone reached an agreement in the end.

Thursday 1st May

It's Polling Day for many local councils, as well as the election of the Mayor of London. Ken Livingstone is standing for re-election as the Labour candidate and has had a tough campaign with the *Evening Standard* vociferous in its support for Tory candidate Boris

Johnson. Gordon and I walk over early to the Methodist Central Hall in Westminster to cast our votes.

The political team has been quite downbeat all week, but Gordon's mood suddenly changed yesterday. He had such a successful day: a good meeting with former World Bank chief Jim Wolfensohn; a good Radio 4 news interview; a strong PMQs session; and a lively question and answer session at the Institute of Directors. He seems very certain of himself, his message and his ideas. It is funny how the outside world's depiction of Downing Street is very different sometimes to the rather smoother job going on inside. No one expects a good election result for Labour but I think we all recognise that we will deal with the consequences and start afresh tomorrow.

In the afternoon, Gordon asks me to join him to meet with Mr and Mrs Hicks, with their two sons and a family friend. Their son, David, was killed in Afghanistan and they have just collected his Military Cross from Buckingham Palace. Gordon has been in correspondence with the Hicks family and invited them to visit. They are an ordinary, noble and dignified family who have made a huge sacrifice. It is an honour to meet them. I know that Gordon feels their loss very deeply, but I can see that as a government we don't have Mr Hicks entirely on our side. It troubles me that we don't have the support of a man like him.

After Gordon departs for a meeting with US Secretary of State Condoleezza Rice, I show the Hicks family around Numbers 10 and 11 and introduce them to John and Fraser. I tell Mr Hicks that we will start again with a clear slate on 2nd May after the voters have judged us, and take it from there. I think he understands that it is a reasonable place to start.

Friday 2nd May

The results are either as bad as expected, or arguably even worse than anyone had thought. Labour has lost 250 council seats. Gordon is amazingly stoic. I half-expect a silent phone, but there are many calls and texts of support.

CHAPTER 11

Campaigns and Celebs

Tuesday 6th May

I'm pleased to see the campaigns I am backing are gaining momentum. I have agreed to take on a number of speeches for the maternal mortality campaign and a number of other speaking engagements for various charities, as well as the Downing Street receptions.

My office is really up and running with Konrad and Christianne on top of the letters coming in, the charity receptions, visits to Number 10, and more. I am very reliant on Gil being available at the end of the phone, not just for the political office but to talk through my diary and often my day. We are a very small unit but now have a good connection with Beth Dupuy following her move to Gordon's private office, and an invaluable relationship with Gordon's diary secretary, Leeanne Johnston, so we can coordinate our movements, as well as Barbara Burke, who organises all the overseas trips for the PM and his office. I still have to conquer some of my fears of public speaking, and in a perfect world would get a bit more sleep every night. It is sometimes just sheer stubbornness on my part to get everything done, and the things that slip are gym visits, when I have seen too much dawn light with a small boy.

My greatest ally for my work is Gordon, who lends me all his support; I am often amazed he has the time or even brain space to take on my issues, too. Certainly, any of the UK campaigns focused on helping people most in need or the international development work targeting global poverty or education will always get his attention. So I am delighted when he includes me on the guest list for the gathering of business leaders at the Millennium Development Goals' Call to Action meeting at Canary Wharf. A scarily impressive group of CEOs have come together to look at what the corporate world can do to help meet the targets. What Gordon has been saying, as have others, is that if as a world we are serious about keeping the promise we made to reduce global poverty then it will not be enough for governments on their own to act. This is what I have found interesting – finding ways to bring together all kinds of diverse groups in a common endeavour. The assembled CEOs hear from the President of Rwanda, Paul Kagame, and the President of Ghana, John Kafour, both giants who have achieved so much in their countries and are now looking to bring Africa into the twenty-first century. They both know that they have a good friend in Gordon.

I am seated between Mark Malloch Brown, our Africa Minister, and fashion designer Ozwald Boateng, and am able to tell him that we included one of his ties in our recent gift to President Bush.

With so many VIPs in town, there are numerous invitations later in the day to cocktail receptions to support the different aspects of championing the MDGs. The smartest event is the Malaria No More event at the Dorchester Hotel hosted by News Corporation President Peter Chernin, and the UN Special Envoy for Malaria, Ray Chambers, who has flown in especially for the occasion from New York. I realise that Ray is someone I can work with as there is such an overlap with my cause – many pregnant mothers and their infants are vulnerable to malaria. Teaching mothers good malaria prevention could be so key to helping eradicate this terrible killer. We all understand that we need some pretty vocal high-profile champions for these causes. I will be as noisy as I can be, but I know my limitations so I will be recruiting others.

Wednesday 7th May

A few weeks ago I had been invited to join Carla Bruni-Sarkozy for a private lunch at the Élysée Palace, and jumped at the chance to meet her again (and see this extraordinary building in Paris). Today is the day agreed for the meeting, and I'm looking forward to seeing her again.

Carla is charming and welcoming. She looks as spectacular as ever in pinstripe trousers and a strappy little white top. We chat first in her office, comparing notes on political life. She is trying to record her music album and get used to her new married life. We eat lunch out in the Palace gardens, which are rather idyllic. President Sarkozy appears at one point, literally from behind a bush – I think he had spotted us from his meeting in another part of the garden. I have brought him a box of (unofficial) biscuits made for the forthcoming G8 meetings in Japan, which Konrad had brought back from his recce. The box depicts cartoons of the eight world leaders sitting naked in hot springs (presumably famous to the region where the G8 takes place). Actually, the seven male leaders' cartoons are drawn naked but Chancellor Angela Merkel has a discreet towel wrapped around her illustrated form. I think the French President looks a little aghast at the box and wonders just how many of these will be distributed, but certainly saw the funny side.

Over coffee, Carla and I agree to contribute to each other's campaigns – she is hugely supportive of the maternal mortality campaign since her visit to London and will keep up the initiative with her dedicated focus on preventing mother-to-child transmission of HIV/AIDS. Since the untimely death of her brother from AIDS, she has been very moved to make her charitable contribution through tackling this epidemic, and her interest in the maternal health campaign allows her to combine the two. On my way out, I meet *Vanity Fair* writer Maureen Orth who is here to interview Carla for the magazine, and get swept into the interview to add my comment on her.

*

While I am in Paris, I also call in to see Penelope Fillon, the wife of François Fillon, France's Prime Minister. Penelope is herself British, but has lived in France for many years. Her sister is also married to a senior French politician, who happens to be PM Fillon's brother.

We take tea and eat macaroons in the garden of the Hotel Matignon, and agree that the French are really very stylish.

Wednesday 14th May

While Gordon is away attending to a US/Northern Ireland investment conference, I use the time to meet a number of the big charities to recruit their support for the maternal mortality campaign. From Comic Relief, Oxfam and Save the Children to FIGO and the ICM (two organisations representing obstetricians, gynaecologists and midwives around the world) everyone is joining in. The next step is to sort out the campaign messages we all agree to, and recruit some well-known faces to convey the messages.

In the meantime I am also working with a number of UK charities. One of them, Wellbeing of Women, exists to support medical research to improve the health of women. It is the charity that has funded ground-breaking research over 80 years, including support for the first ultrasound pregnancy tests, and all kind of cancer breakthroughs. I want to use my position to promote health and wellbeing for women and their families, and being their Patron is a perfect fit for me. I have already signed up to speak at their regular annual women's lunch. The charity is also the beneficiary of the fundraising dinner for the WoW/*Daily Mail*/M&S Inspirational Women Awards. I present the award to Dr Carrie Herbert of the anti-bullying charity Red Balloon that provides intensive support for badly bullied children. The successful auction raises lots of funds including seeing Heather McGregor (the 'Mrs Moneypenny' from the *FT* magazine) bid £10,000 for breakfast in a fancy restaurant with Sir Stuart Rose. I enjoy seeing the astonishing women who are honoured that evening. I also see Paul Dacre (editor of the *Daily Mail)* showing great enthusiasm for the event, which he rewards by carrying it on his front page the next day. Everyone hopes to repeat it next year.

Thursday 15th May

I have my first meeting with Naomi Campbell who comes to Downing Street for the first time with her PR manager, Alan Edwards, to discuss her Fashion for Relief events and to explore whether the next one could support the maternal mortality campaign. I feel a certain sense of trepidation at meeting the notorious Miss Campbell and remember all too well the long saga of how Naomi successfully sued Piers Morgan for revealing details of her private life when he was editor of the *Daily Mirror*. But then I have only heard Piers' side of the story (who hasn't?) Then Naomi was back in the press again for an 'air rage' episode aboard a BA flight, which was taken to court. But I have seen the success of Fashion for Relief in the United States and can only believe that someone with a very good heart would put that much personal time and effort into a fundraising event to meet the needs of crises like the Hurricane Katrina disaster.

Naomi Campbell in person was rather more friendly than the myths and legends. She is, of course, extraordinarily beautiful. She is very direct about her interest in the campaign and exactly why she thinks she can help. I am used to meeting well-known people but this woman is offering to roll up her sleeves and get down to business. We meet in Gordon's study. This is the room that was formerly Margaret Thatcher's office but is used for private meetings now, as Gordon works from an open-plan area in another part of Downing Street. The study is now lined with books, formal portraits and, unlike the more decorative and ornate reception rooms, smells very masculine due to the leather chairs in it. Gordon calls in to say hello and Naomi presents us with a copy of her book about her visit in 1990 to see Nelson Mandela, who is clearly enormously fond of her.

Saturday 17th May

Gordon is working long hours at the moment so it is tricky finding decent amounts of good family time, or just for me to see him. He flies up to Edinburgh to address the General Assembly of the Church of Scotland – his father was a Church of Scotland Minister so this invitation is very meaningful to him. I take the boys off to London Zoo, which is one of our favourite run-around spaces apart from the obvious animal attractions. We hear Gordon giving his speech on the radio – he is talking about Burma, and the power of the internet and mobile phones in protecting people's freedoms there, and the importance of a leader like Aung San Suu Kyi. His voice is so soft, but powerful; you could hear his personal commitment to this issue in his every word. The boys, though small, ceased their usual chitchat and just listened and listened as we drove along. It was an unexpected but rather amazing moment that stayed with me.

In the evening, Gordon and I receive the devastating news that Senator Edward Kennedy has suffered a stroke and been taken into emergency care in a hospital in Boston. Bob Shrum calls, sounding very anxious, and it is clear that this is very serious. We send our best to Marylouise and he promises to keep us posted with further news.

Tuesday 20th May

When Bob calls again this morning I realise that he – and all the family and friends close by – must have been up all night. I can't imagine what Teddy's wife, Vicki, is going through right now.

I finally meet David Muir who has joined Gordon as one of his most senior advisers and whose work will be critical to the general election, whenever it happens. He is a brilliant guy who joins from a big advertising agency with a great reputation for political strategy and reading the polling information, which is such an important indicator in campaigns. From now on, if I want to know how we are doing, I will just ask for David's latest numbers.

I am not involved with the strategic planning of the election campaign, but I do want to be out there campaigning as I have done in past general elections, and in the recent by-elections, helping get our Labour vote out. I make calls to our supporters in Crewe and Nantwich where we have a by-election following the sad death of Gwyneth Dunwoody MP. All my conversations are very good, but I hear from David that we do have reason to worry that we might not hold this Labour seat when the vote is counted later this week.

Wednesday 21st May

May is a big month in the preparations for the London 2012 Olympic Games. The International Olympic Committee (IOC) is visiting London to check on the progress of the building at the new site, and all the other plans. Olympics Minister Tessa Jowell, who has been part of this from the start, has a lot on her plate. Gordon and I join her for a reception at Lancaster House to welcome everybody with the London Mayor, and tomorrow will go to visit the site itself.

Thursday 22nd May

Exercise-wise in our house, Gordon has a new trainer coming in, and so all our mornings seem to start very early. There is a small gym at the top of the flat that must have been installed some years before we arrived here. We have put in our own treadmill, Pilates reformer machine, and various other weights and balls. I tend to go out to a place called Pilates off the Square as I like the sociability there, as well as the exercise, but Gordon opts for a trainer who puts him through his paces at 6 a.m. When we are in Scotland, we go out to a nearby gym and swimming pool, but in London it is more restrictive for him so this new routine does work well.

As soon as Gordon's trainer leaves, we head down to the Olympic site in Docklands. The overwhelming first impression is how much rapid progress has been made in just a matter of months.

One of the most enjoyable aspects of this visit for Gordon and me is the opportunity to speak to some of the young athletes as they purposefully pursue their dreams. Perhaps unfairly I find the speeches rather less fun. There are far too many of them for a start, including one by London Mayor Boris Johnson, in which he inexplicably quotes Latin text, and then lectures me afterwards about the importance of Latin. I went to a great school in North London that did not teach Latin so was unable to comment.

On the way back to Westminster we take a detour and join the Patient Safety Conference with Health Minister Ann Keen. The *Today* programme presenter John Humphrys is chairing the conference. We know him, of course, for his abrupt and often cynical questioning of politicians on the early-morning radio show. Gordon leaps on to the platform and gets a great laugh when he says, 'I am delighted to be able to speak next to John Humphrys here today … without fear of interruption.'

Friday 23rd May

The Crewe and Nantwich by-election result is disastrous for Labour with a 17 per cent swing against us. It coincides with a break in Scotland for us over the parliamentary recess, which couldn't come at a better time.

Gordon spends the time over his break sleeping, thinking, reading, resting and spending time with me and the boys. I visit Gordon's old school, Kirkcaldy High, at the invitation of the very dynamic head teacher, Lindsay Roy, who is turning the fortunes of the school around at a very rapid rate. We take the boys to find the local pancake house to have lunch with our friends, Pete and Marilyn Livingstone. Pete was at school with Gordon and works for Business Gateway Fife. Marilyn is the local Member of the Scottish Parliament for Kirkcaldy. Both have lived and worked here all their lives and are always here for us when we come home. I enjoy the brief interlude to just be with people who know us well, and love us no matter what is happening in the outside world.

Monday 26th May

Back in London we are up and running straight away, with a jam-packed diary and the unfolding events of the day. Right now there are important issues for Northern Ireland to address, to ensure the peace process continues within the Assembly there. Our Secretary of State Shaun Woodward is a very able pair of hands for Gordon, and always supportive. I am starting to understand that there is always something going on in the background on Northern Ireland and from time to time it gains Gordon's greater attention. This was such a problematic political situation for so many years that no one wants to take anything for granted, and there is still work to do.

I am very buoyed up in my work by the confirmation that I have a fantastic new adviser for the maternal mortality campaign in Emma Parry, who comes to me from Richard Curtis's office (she and I first met there and I had invited her to the tea I hosted for Australia's WPM, Thérèse Rein). Emma has cut her teeth on Make Poverty History and is very bright and hard working. The White Ribbon Alliance is able to support her on the maternal mortality campaign, which gives me such a valuable new resource.

Later, we go off to a black-tie do at Windsor Castle for the Olympics committee but on the way down there, it turns out I am not actually invited to it. As we are already travelling in that direction, I agree to sit and wait in the car. While this is not very elegant, it suits me fine as I can talk to Emma on the phone from the car park in relative warmth, and the evening passes quite quickly. Emma's background as a high-flying McKinsey consultant is quite daunting, but she is very down to earth, very stylish and has such a genuine core of 'super niceness' you almost think she can't be real. She is very well liked across the development world, and this will be a great help at banging on doors to get everyone signed up in support.

Monday 2nd June

After a courtesy pre–G8 meeting with Japan's Prime Minister Yasuo Fukuda and his wife (they are the G8 hosts this year and are visiting London), I leave Downing Street to travel up to Glasgow for the Royal College of Midwives annual convention where I have accepted an invitation to speak. There is a fabulous moment when I arrive and I am escorted by someone who does not quite know the big convention centre; I am marched straight into a cupboard. I do helpfully explain I'm a big cupboard-tour guide person myself.

The convention hall is full to the rafters with 3,000 midwives from across the world. It is quite daunting to even enter the room, never mind walk up on to the stage. What I know is that this is an audience that will be totally behind my message of achieving safer pregnancy to protect families around the world, and fully back the call to take this message to the G8 to find out what the world leaders plan to do to achieve the forgotten MDG 5. I am generously rewarded by the, for me, very moving moment of a standing ovation, complete with whistles and 'Go Sarah'. I love these women and will have their strength in me when I make my way to Japan for the G8.

In the evening I get back from Glasgow and do a quick turnaround to attend the *Glamour* Women of the Year Awards in the pouring rain, in a great marquee set in the middle of Berkeley Square. I am seated between *Glamour* editor Jo Elvin and the ubiquitous Piers Morgan. We are set to present various awards during the course of the evening.

Lily Allen calls by our table on her way up to the stage at one point, to tell me she is supporting Labour and Gordon all the way. She is in one of her trademark vintage dresses that, on closer inspection, reveals a pattern of headless Bambi-like baby deer.

Rather to my alarm, there is a set of pristine, but deathly-looking white stairs with no handrail leading up to the stage, which gets progressively wetter from the muddy shoes as the evening wears on, and I watch in true alarm as writer/actor James Corden looks like he is about to jump off the stage rather than risk the stairs. Piers seems to manage the journey up them fine, but comes back down to report that the going is absolutely lethal. Needless to say, my presentation to Annie Lennox as Campaigner of the Year is second to last. I seriously consider taking my high heels off to get up there, but after taking advice from the table, know I have to take the risk. Piers puts the case succinctly – if I go up barefoot I guarantee a picture and bad coverage; if I go up in high heels I only get a bad photo if I fall over. However, all ends well – as I put one foot on the treacherously slick stairs, presenter Paul O'Grady gallantly reaches down, grabs my hand and airlifts me up. Who knew that Lily Savage had such super strength? Obviously Annie Lennox pretty much floats up and gives a divine speech about the fight against HIV/AIDS in Africa. The good news is that we depart the stage from the back.

Once home, Gordon is still up, frustrated by a sticking point in the Ireland talks – this seems to be the pattern of these talks through the decades. In addition, having come through the critical votes on the 10p tax, and an embryology (stem-cell research) bill, there is now controversy over the House of Commons votes on the proposal to detain terrorist suspects without charge for up to 42 days. Gordon is determined that he is following the right path for the security of Britain, but it will be difficult to secure a majority. Of course, the Opposition parties will find reasons to oppose it, so we will need to secure every Labour vote we can to get this one through. More than for the other votes, this one will really count for Gordon's position as Prime Minister. I am not sure what will happen if he loses this one.

Thursday 5th June

I manage to extract Gordon from his calls to MPs to take him to the National Theatre to see Lee Hall's play *The Pitmen Painters*, directed by Max Roberts. Gordon is tired and not really in the mood, but I insist. We go with friends, Paul and Alison Myners – he is Chair of the Tate Trustees and she the Chair of the Contemporary Arts Society, so they should enjoy it. The play tells the true story of a group of miners in the North East of England who became an acclaimed painting group. Lee, who made his name with *Billy Elliot*, is a great writer, and the performance is as diverting and entertaining as I had hoped.

Saturday 7th June

This weekend I have invited Lady Wilson, the widow of former Labour Prime Minister Harold Wilson, with her family to revisit Chequers. Mary Wilson is now in her nineties, but as bright and vivid as ever with her memories of her time as the PM's spouse in his two terms: first from 1964 to 1970, and again from 1974 to 1976. When Harold Wilson was PM in the mid seventies, their twin granddaughters were christened in the Long Gallery at Chequers and she brings with her some of the photographs from that day. It is amazing how unchanged the room is, right down to the sofa covers that are, admittedly, a little more sun-faded today. Mary came with her son, Robin, and his wife, Joy, and her twin granddaughters with their husbands and children. Head chef Alan Lavender makes a special lunch for them and we walk in the rose garden. It seemed to be a very enjoyable trip down memory lane for her.

Sunday 8th June

Today is a day I've been looking forward to for ages, as it's all about family. Gordon and I have my brother, Bruce, to stay on a visit from Australia as a surprise treat for my mum, Pauline. We have a big family lunch to celebrate the seventieth birthdays of both my mum and my stepfather, Patrick, with one of the chef's celebrated Sunday roasts. Alan also makes their favourite dessert, a spectacular tiramisu complete with decorated birthday greeting and a couple of candles. My Aunt Doreen has flown in from her home in Pittsburgh, and my mum's brother, my Uncle John, has travelled from his home in West London. Also with us are Patrick's brothers, Mark and Jasper, plus Patrick's two sons (my step-brothers) Nico and Kit are all here with their families.

I am sure that our big family gathering will be as fondly recalled as many of Mary Wilson's best Chequers memories, although I am a great believer that it has more to do with the people than the place, lovely as Chequers is.

Monday 9th June

Back to London, and tensions are mounting over the 42-days vote. Gordon is engaged with lots of calls to talk to MPs so they hear all his arguments before they finally decide whether to oppose the government. This is exactly the time when the most loyal and helpful MPs get the least attention – but I suppose that happens in so many other workplaces, too.

During the working day, of course, other government business continues. The Commonwealth leaders are in London for a meeting with Gordon, and government heads such as President Kikwete of Tanzania and President Museveni of Uganda are all in Number 10 for a reception.

Foreign Secretary David Miliband is hosting a dinner afterwards as we have other plans for Gordon this evening: everyone is in on the secret, even the African leaders. It is the twenty-fifth anniversary of Gordon's election as an MP, and we have brought in people spanning all those years for a surprise party, and I smuggle the boys down in their pyjamas to join in, too. Sue Nye, together with Number 10's political events managers, Rachel Kinnock and Lisa Perrin, have organised everything, tracking down all kinds of people. As they all arrive, they come in at the big front door and creep quietly down the hall and out to the back garden. Gordon's attention is fully taken up with his meeting and reception with the Commonwealth leaders. Once all the garden guests are in the back, someone prompts Gordon to see all his other visitors off to their dinner. Gordon immediately gets on the phone to the Chief Whip, Nick Brown, to get an update on how things are looking for the 42-days vote in two days' time. Nick keeps him chatting without saying that he is one of the people standing in the back garden waiting for the big 'surprise' moment – Nick entered parliament himself on the same day as Gordon and has been a friend ever since. Finally, we get John to go up to his dad, get him off the phone and say, 'Dad, as you have been an MP for twenty-five years, I have come to take you to your surprise party.' I don't think he guessed at all, and is even more delighted when we promise that there will be no speeches.

The weather is perfect, the political office is serving all the food and drinks, and Glenys Kinnock and Rachel have made cupcakes iced with 'GB' on top, and other initials for the MPs also there celebrating the same anniversary, from Nick Brown to Dick Caborn, Margaret Beckett and Tony Lloyd. Everyone who has ever worked for Gordon is there, from researchers to former ministers. It is a lovely boost at the end of a long and tricky time, and a reminder of all that has been achieved even as we face tough times ahead.

Wednesday 11th June

The day of the big vote regarding the 42-days bill. The result is due around 6.30 p.m. but the way the House of Commons works it could be any time up to 10 p.m. before we know the result. I see Gordon off in the morning and keep myself busy with a committee meeting for Women's Aid, and a briefing from Liz Symons on the key women in the Middle East who might want to join my international campaigning. I pop by the Make a Wish Foundation reception to meet some great kids celebrating the charity's twenty-first anniversary.

Sue Nye gives me a call at lunchtime to say that PMQs has gone spectacularly well, which helps get me through the first half of the day. After some time with the boys, I get ready to go and speak at the CBI First Women Awards which honours high achievers in business, finance and the public sector. All I know is that Gordon is working furiously on meetings with MPs in the House and that this is going to the wire.

My phone rings and I can see I have a message I have not picked up. I call back to listen, assuming it is something old I have missed before but it is Swraj Paul, and the first words I hear are 'Congratulations!' Then I spot a text from Baroness Mary Goudie (a Labour Peer and also one of my Trustees at PiggyBankKids) saying the same, and then my phone starts pinging away. Phew!

I look up the BBC news website and see that it was pretty tight. But a win is a win in politics, and we are back in business.

CHAPTER 12

Dinner with the Historians

Thursday 12th June

With the forthcoming visit of President George W Bush on his valedictory world tour, my office is called on to support the Number 10 events team. The Americans field so many people on their advance visits, it is all hands on deck just to hold conversations with everyone. I play my part by dealing directly with the US Ambassador's wife in London, Maria Tuttle, who is very straightforward to deal with and a woman after my own heart; keen to cover every single detail so that the visit works well for everyone.

Along with these big visits, the charity receptions continue as does all the other daily work. My office is overwhelmed by requests and invitations from around the UK – to visit constituencies, to see Sure Start Centres, new school buildings and polyclinics, to look at environment and green projects, all springing up around Britain.

My small team of two in Downing Street work their socks off every day, and are well complemented by support from the private office, events team and others around the building, depending what expertise is needed at any given moment – whether IT backup if the computers get stuck or to find out some essential fact from a policy person to respond to a letter. We are fortunate that our team all get along very well.

Both Konrad and Christianne have very long-suffering partners, Victoria and Cele, as many are the days when they don't manage to make it back in time for 'their turn to make dinner'. I am fortunate that Victoria and Cele are both as supportive as they are, and take it all in good humour.

Both Gil and Emma are often in the (originally) one-man office also, so when I am there, too, it is a real squeeze. Mostly I work at a computer set up in the flat as I am sure we would be breaking a fair number of European working laws otherwise.

As we don't have any big travel commitments until the G8 Summit in July, we are all using the breathing space to plan the next round of charity receptions and UK visits by responding to all the invitations we can.

Friday 13th June

Wendi Murdoch is back in town and helping me with some of the activities for the maternal mortality campaign being held in New York in the autumn, to coincide with the UN Summit.

Wendi has an idea to build on the Davos women's dinner with Indra Nooyi and HM Queen Rania. She comes to Chequers with a group of mutual girlfriends. It is a girls-only night and we have the excuse of celebrating Wendi's up-coming fortieth birthday. The guest list includes Emma Freud, Shriti Vadera, Claudia Winkleman and Kirsty Young, as well as Elisabeth Murdoch and Rebekah Wade who both have fortieths to celebrate, too. Word gets out and the event is duly reported in the newspaper diaries.

Wendi, Emma and Shriti arrive early. Shriti has the most extraordinary intellect that enables her to understand the development agenda and all the possibilities for the many countries of the UN, and her experience is invaluable to me (as it is to many others). Wendi has a wonderfully cool way of getting things done with no fuss. The girls all arrive looking very glamorous and we enjoy a wonderful light dinner of asparagus, sole with spinach, and the chef's own special recipe: Turkish Delight ice cream served with berries and a pretty butterfly-shaped biscuit.

*

The Chequers housekeeper Pat Evans had greeted me earlier with the memorable words, 'The cheese seller and the magician have arrived.' It turns out that Rebekah has sent a platter of gourmet cheese and booked the guy who sold her the cheese as he happened to be an out-of-work magician.

After dessert, the cheeseseller/magician, who's French, comes out and performs some clever card tricks. Someone else brings flavoured vodka so those that want can warm up with a shot or two, and then we all play a game called Celebrity that was hilarious but the rules all too immediately forgettable. Much laughter, much fun, and even better that no one has to travel home that night (Chequers has ten bedrooms).

Saturday 14th June

Everyone heads off this morning, after breakfast. I get back to London and join Gordon to welcome all the High Commissioners stationed in the UK, and then watch Trooping the Colour, the annual pageantry and spectacle of the Queen's Birthday Parade, held on Horse Guards Parade just to the back of Downing Street. We can all step out of the back gate of the garden and straight into stands, with a wonderful ringside view for all our guests. There are always a few spaces left and we offer them to members of the Cabinet and their families.

Sunday 15th June

Tonight we are hosting a dinner in the State Dining Room at 10 Downing Street for President and Mrs Bush, who have just arrived in London. In order to make it interesting for the President, I follow up on his obvious interest at our White House dinner in British historians, and invite some of our most eminent historians. Our stellar line-up includes – in no special order: Alistair Horne, Andrew

Roberts, the Holts who chart out the maps of battlefields, Piers Brendon, Linda Colley and David Cannadine, Max Arthur, Sir Martin and Lady Gilbert, and Simon Schama. The Cabinet Ministers in attendance are Chancellor Alistair Darling with Maggie, Foreign Secretary David Miliband with Louise, and Defence Secretary John Hutton with Heather. Lord and Lady Williams also join us, as I thought that Jane Williams would be of great interest as she was Winston Churchill's PA during his time as Prime Minister and has wonderful stories to tell. The President's long-standing friend from his stay in Scotland many years ago, Bill Gemmell, is also invited.

The great chef, Anton Mosimann, creates a wonderful British meal serving Scottish salmon, a summer pea soup, beef, and a summer fruit trifle. The US security detail checks everything, and the chef literally has the Secret Service standing over him while he cooks the President's meal.

Gordon and I greet the President and Mrs Bush on the doorstep. Although I have now stood on that famous step numerous times in front of the cameras, I do have a moment of thinking 'Wow!' at being there, especially with the US President and First Lady. There is a scale to a Presidential Visit like this that reminds you just how far, globally, these images will travel.

We escort the Bushes down the corridor, up the famous staircase and into the reception room to join the other guests. I have opted for an unusual format in our dinner seating. Rather than bunch all the historians together, competing for the attention of the politicians or vice versa, I have laid out the room in four separate tables of ten. The President and Gordon will move around the room – joining a different table for each of the four courses – in order to talk to each of the historians. I am sure that any single table would make a whole evening fascinating, but we are trying to cram in a lot in one night. I know that the President is delighted to meet or renew acquaintance with some writers he admires, and will meet many that Gordon rates too.

The President and Gordon start with Simon Schama and Alistair Horne, who seem to balance each other well (Schama has been openly critical about the war in Iraq). Then, a move with the soup course to Max Arthur and the Holts, and with the main course they see Cannadine, Colley, Sir Martin Gilbert and Piers Brendon. Each time they move, one of the Cabinet Minister couples switches places with them and sit at a new table. The Ministers have had all their briefs to tell them exactly who they are sitting with at each point. The waiting staff keeps track of wine and water glasses as the switches take place, and it all moves along very smoothly.

Finally, at the dessert table, I move things back to a more conventional format so that President Bush is seated by me while Gordon sits next to the First Lady on the other side. President Bush also has the chance to speak to Andrew Roberts on the final table.

I have a fast and very intense conversation with the President, which manages to cover his own reputation, life after the Presidency and praise for the productive working relationship he has established in a short time with Gordon. He takes the time to ask me about Scotland and our children, whom he has not yet met. Then we move on to the G8 Summit. The President asks me to explain to him very directly the case for the maternal mortality campaign and promises his support for health workers. He asks me what else he needs to do. I reply that I think his job is to deliver G8 funding for sufficient quantities of health workers, the 4 million people that the global health campaigners are calling for. He says he believes that health workers would make a difference. He suggests I also speak to Mrs Bush about the campaign when we have time together, and also makes mention of his particular support for the eradication of malaria and for eradicating some of the Neglected Tropical Diseases (NTDs) from the world. I remind him that while both are huge medical concerns, it is only by connecting up good health, education, sufficient food and clean water too that any of the health goals can be reached, and quality of life improved. Health workers can do a lot more than just administer vaccinations.

At the close of our discussion, the President says that he admires people who are loyal and hold strong marriages. I then receive a final Presidential Fist Bump as he says he has enjoyed our conversation, and is looking forward to the G8.

All the guests rise to go through to the Pillared Room where a photograph is taken of all the historians together with Gordon and the President, who jokes that he might make this the next White House Christmas card. I take the Bushes to meet Anton Mosimann and then they take their leave back to the US Residence in Regent's Park.

Monday 16th June

The school run is complicated this morning by the road closure for the President so we had planned for Mela to take the boys out extra early for juice and muffins. This is their preferred treat on special days like the State Opening of Parliament. As it turns out, the boys go down instead to meet President Bush who comes in extra early to start his meetings with Gordon before their press conference. It is being reported that on arrival, President Bush turned on the doorstep to the mass of media shouting out questions and replied, 'You can kiss my ass.'

I meet Laura Bush at the British Museum. She had taken herself earlier to the little-known Dickens Museum, and now together we look at some of the precious artefacts from Afghanistan and Burma with the curators there. Mrs Bush has already taken an interest in the people of these countries, and I feel very proud showing her the wonderful collections at one of our finest museums. The curators take great care explaining the history of what we are looking at, and we wear gloves to handle the artefacts themselves. Even after so many years of being First Lady, Mrs Bush still shows the interest of someone discovering something new; she has a grace and politeness of manner that never falters for a moment. I imagine this goes some way to explaining her enduring popularity, even as her husband has faced his harshest critics.

I return to join Gordon to rush out to Northolt Airfield and take a private plane out to Belfast's army airport. It is our job to be on the ground ready to meet the President and Mrs Bush for their visit to Northern Ireland. We make it just in time to see Air Force One landing right in front of us. Air Force Two has already landed, bringing out their own vehicles for travelling – it is quite a sight to behold.

I receive a most elegant thank-you letter. Andrew Roberts and his wife Susan Gilchrist clearly had a great time at the historians' dinner and got a rapturous welcome from the President, leaving everyone speculating whether Andrew might write about the Bush Years in time. Alistair Horne is rather less gracious, writing an article in the *Independent* asserting that the initiative for the dinner 'manifestly came from the White House, with the President suggesting that he might like to meet a group of us Brit historians'.

Rather mean to steal the credit away, especially when I had invited him to suit the President's interest, as Horne's politics are certainly not mine. That said, I don't think the evening was about changing hearts and minds, as I rather think everyone there was already set on their chosen path.

Tuesday 17th June

Gordon attends various meetings in Brussels and visits Paris to have lunch with President Sarkozy. As Ireland has just voted no to the Lisbon Treaty, doubtless as a reaction to the economic downturn, the implications for everyone else are being discussed. I think that Brussels meetings can go on a bit and certainly the dinners continue until about 11.30 p.m. I always get a weary Gordon on the phone at the end.

Once he is back we retreat to Chequers for a weekend to recover our energies. Roy drives the boys and me off a bit later than usual, and we get stuck in some Friday night traffic. We then hear the familiar sound of motorbikes coming up behind us, and move off with the rest of the traffic to allow 'Dad's Car' and its police escort to go by as it comes straight past us in the traffic queue. There is definitely a bit of teasing of Dad later.

Gordon's school and university friend, Murray Elder, is staying with us this weekend, and is the easiest, most low-maintenance house guest you could ever want. Gordon is mulling over what is coming up, and thinking of a reshuffle in September.

We have a fish and chip supper and an early night.

Wednesday 18th June

After Gordon's evening off last night, he is whisked away today to go to Jeddah for the oil summit. I notice that Gordon is robustly defending our EU Trade Commissioner, Peter Mandelson, on the trade talks, after Peter was attacked by President Sarkozy.

While Gordon is away, I take the boys to Lord and Lady Paul's much-loved annual party at London Zoo. It is held for hundreds of families each year in memory of their little daughter, Ambika, who had loved the zoo very much in her short life.

We stay right until closing time at the zoo. By the time I have got the boys back home and in bed, Gordon is back from Jeddah. I dread to think how much he has packed in while he has been away.

Tuesday 24th June

President Mandela and Graça Machel arrive in London for several days to honour his forthcoming ninetieth birthday (which falls the day after Fraser turns two). We are involved in many aspects of this visit and want to be with them as much as possible.

We go first as a family to visit them in their hotel suite at The Dorchester. Gordon is able to present a cheque for £25 million from the UK Government for the fight against HIV/AIDS to honour the special birthday.

It is often the way that the most important things all end up being booked for the same day. We squeeze in some time at John's last party at the very wonderful Tachbrook Nursery School before he leaves in a few weeks. Then leaving the boys with Mela, I drive up with Roy to North London to a small event at the Edgware Reform Synagogue. I am there to hand out the graduation certificates and awards for their Schule Leadership Course. I had wanted to do this as it has been organised by the Alan Senitt Trust. Alan Senitt was a young man who was destined for a very bright future with close family and good friends, but he was murdered in Washington DC on 9th July 2006 as he walked out in the street one evening with his girlfriend. His family and friends have reacted to this senseless murder by investing in other young people to help support their futures. When Alan's mother, Karen, asked me to come, I thought that on the day that Nelson Mandela arrives in town with his message of peace and cooperation, I could not say no.

Only the previous week we hosted a reception for the Tom ap Rhys Pryce Trust set up in memory of another bright young man, a lawyer engaged to the woman he loved, murdered in the streets of North London for his mobile phone. Adele Eastman, his fiancée, and his parents have raised funds that support projects for exactly the kind of youths who killed Tom.

After leaving the synagogue I have time to call into a very different event. My long-standing (she would be most unhappy if I said old) friend Penny Smith has her book launch at a nightclub in Soho. She has written a sequel to her romp around the world of TV studios. I catch the tail-end of the party but Kathy Lette, Fiona Phillips, Ian Hislop and Penny's boyfriend, actor Vince Leigh, are still there so it is on lively form. We do many snaps for the gossip photographers and I hope she sells lots of copies of the new book. Penny and I met at the well-known PR chief Roland Rudd's wedding (in the days when he was just a rookie financial journalist, back in July 1991) and have stayed in touch ever since. My brother Sean, his friend Toby Young and I had been asked to give her a lift from the B&B, but somehow failed to make contact. My first sight of Penny was her marching up to us at the wedding reception saying 'Thanks a lot!' in a loud, sarcastic voice. We have got on much better than that ever since.

Wednesday 25th June

Piers Morgan invites himself over to visit and I take him into the flat to give him a cup of tea. He returns the hospitality with some advice: 'Right now you would lose an election,' he says. 'Bold daily announcements are what you need. Take England cricket away from Zimbabwe.' It turns out – though not because of Piers! – that we do pull out of the cricket that day AND strip Robert Mugabe of his knighthood. Both acts are well received but certainly not front-page news, and not much credited to Gordon who initiated both. Still, Piers is broadly right – a bit more momentum is needed, and a bit of luck.

I receive a courtesy visit from Cindy McCain, wife of John, the US Senator. She is in London to host a fundraiser with Henry Kissinger for her husband's presidential campaign. She is tall, slim and attractive and has just undertaken a big trip to the Far East with no apparent jetlag. She is fascinating – she has made a huge commitment all her life to international charitable work in conflict-torn countries; not the easiest option she could have picked. Emma Freud joins me for the meeting, and we work hard to recruit her to our causes.

This evening Gordon and I are to attend the first of a number of special events to mark Nelson Mandela's ninetieth birthday – a glittering gala dinner in a giant marquee in Hyde Park.

Gordon and I, together with ex-President Bill Clinton, are invited to join Graça and Madiba early and help them greet their guests. As overawed as I always am by the charisma and presence of Nelson Mandela and of Graça, I am hugely confident and more than up to the social challenge of greeting the good and the great alongside them. I am always pleasantly surprised by what a favourable difference it makes to my personal confidence to have people around who communicate an infectious positivity. I am still watching myself for any further dizzy spells arising from stress and overtiredness, but today I feel great.

It also helps that I have on a fabulous Graeme Black dress. I have well-groomed high heels and polished hair (okay, other way around, but the point is, I have not done my usual ten-minute dash for dress, hair and make-up). Unfortunately, the first thing I do as I leap excitedly out of the car is snag my tights on a bit of Hyde Park greenery. The tear is gaping. Thankfully, I am carrying a spare pair – very pleased with myself for that – and Gordon's event maestro, Helen Etheridge, whisks me around to the Ladies. After that nifty change, I make it back to the advance guests' VIP tent where alongside Madiba and Graça, Bill and Chelsea Clinton, and Gordon, we are to all collectively greet guests and do photos.

There is a stellar line-up of amazing Hollywood folk who have flown in specially: Forest Whitaker, Will Smith and Jada Pinkett Smith, Denzel Washington, Robert De Niro, Oprah Winfrey and more, many more.

Gordon and I are seated at the 20-strong top table. At his end, President Clinton, President Mandela, Graça Machel and Gordon. At my end, Oprah Winfrey, Forest Whitaker, me, and Will Smith. I spend all evening talking and talking to people – and it feels as though they are my regular chums. Everyone is chatting about families, holidays coming up and work–life balance as we all do as married folks and parents. There seems to me to be an unspoken rule when celebrities meet each other that as they already know each other by reputation, they can already be good friends as soon as they shake hands.

Forest Whitaker has taken a high profile as a Malaria Champion joining the global campaign to eradicate this terrible killer, inspired to do so by his time in Africa filming *The Last King of Scotland,* and I get a brief chance to talk to him about this work.

Gordon gives one of the main speeches of the night ('No injustice can endure for ever' is the line that sticks with me), so does Bill Clinton, who has that unique way of taking one individual's story and using it wonderfully to make his point. No one eats the food as they are all too busy frantically networking, despite it being Gordon Ramsay's finest. I have to report though that the dessert is – I kid you not – chocolate mud huts.

Once all the guests are seated, Nelson Mandela enters the tent in a wheelchair and there is first a hushed awe and then a never-ending ovation. When a microphone is brought over for him, he addresses everyone from our table, and speaks movingly and powerfully, not missing the opportunity to attack Mugabe in his speech, nor, by inference, those leaders who might act on the world stage to oppose what is happening now in Zimbabwe. He described it as 'a tragic failure of leadership'.

I am seated at the far end of the table and realise that my prime position (between Forest Whitaker and Will Smith – did I mention that already?) is blocking the photographers from getting their perfect shot. I move, tucking in snugly next to Will Smith, and Mr Dave Bennett, photographer of the stars, must surely thank me for evermore because it is his beautiful photograph of President Mandela, Graça Machel, Bill Clinton and my husband that graces every paper the next day.

Auction house Christie's then leads an auction of unique Mandela items for his foundation, and Oprah pays £1 million for a picture she says she will hang on the wall of her school in South Africa. The threshold has been set and no one, but no one, wants to go below £1 million. Will Smith has a go at auctioneering the next autographed item, but ends up bringing the hammer down on a final figure of (a mere) £400,000 divided between himself, Uma Thurman and Emma Thompson. He sits back down next to me saying, 'That did not go according to plan.' Emma T pleads her case delightfully as an 'unwealthy English actress' and ends up agreeing to do a voiceover instead for the Nelson Mandela Foundation.

Gordon is surrounded by people all evening who wish him well for his unswerving support for international development and the poorest people in the world. Gordon has a great chat with Sir Elton John and David Furnish – they are very knowledgable on the state of UK parliamentary legislation and know how much a Labour government has done on gay and lesbian issues, and are also keen on our government's track record on tackling HIV/AIDS in developing countries.

When Gordon and I get back to the flat we are wide awake after such an amazing experience and end up using the energy to talk about his office, and how to get things right. We are caught between Gordon's capacity to do a GREAT job, and an external reported perception that no longer allows for any success stories. Gordon always shows what he is feeling and there is no doubt he is adversely affected by things – he would not be human otherwise. But he still gets up every day and does his best as he promised on the first day. He knows – as I know – his full potential, and I hope we all find a way to allow him to reach it.

Thursday 26th June

I visit Millbank Primary School, where John will start next term, for my parents' induction. We are fortunate to have a wonderful local community primary school close to Downing Street with an exceptional head teacher, Alyson Russen. Even if assuming that I was just being polite by going to an induction (so no one thinks I am seeking special treatment), I discover it is actually very useful.

We are all ignoring the fact that it is the Henley by-election today, where a successor to out-going Conservative MP and new London

Mayor, Boris Johnson, will be chosen. The result is pretty much a foregone conclusion for another Conservative. What comes as worse news later in the day is that the serving Labour MP in Glasgow East is choosing to stand down. This brings us a by-election that really needs our attention as it is a seat we would not want to lose.

Friday 27th June

It is a year since Gordon became Prime Minister, but we are all too busy to think about it. There are many more challenges to face before we could consider celebrating being at Downing Street.

I join Graça Machel one last time to meet some of the scholars supported by the Graça Machel Scholarship programme, the fund that supports young women who could be future leaders in Africa. She says she set it up 'as a birthday present to herself'! Gordon and Graça share a rather uncommon perspective that it will be women who will build, run and essentially save a better Africa as the continent of the future.

I have to take my leave and give my apologies for missing Madiba's pop concert in Hyde Park this evening. I can hardly believe I am turning down my front-row seat with such a fabulous line-up of performers. However, I have one opportunity a year to host a charity event at Chequers and this evening is my first one. The dinner is for the Maggie's Cancer Caring Centres and our line-up includes actress Kim Cattrall as compère, powerful speakers talking about the charity, and great auction prizes including walk-on parts in *Sex and the City II*. Kim is a great sport, entertaining everyone and encouraging the auction bidding upwards by adding in a dress of her own from the film. The evening eventually raises £750,000 towards building new Maggie's Centres around the country.

Gordon arrives towards the end and is able to regale everyone with stories of his evening at the pop concert. It is quite something to think of him sitting by Nelson Mandela, explaining who each of the acts were. The great statesman showed considerable interest in Amy Winehouse, who despite everything has a magnificent voice. At one point, she announced that her husband Blake (Fielder-Civil) and Nelson Mandela had a lot in common as 'they have both spent a lot of time in jail'. At the finale, when all the artists joined together to sing the classic song 'Free Nelson Mandela', Amy was seen singing her own version – 'Free Blakey My Fella'.

Saturday 28th June

Despite his night out rocking with the Mandelas, Gordon is up bright and early for John Sexton, the visionary head of New York University who is joining him for breakfast. NYU is a university with campuses all over the world, from Manhattan to Abu Dhabi. Gordon is passionate about the role of education, and sees its importance to Britain as something we can export successfully and also offer educational opportunity to all our young people. There are a number of great university heads with this scale of vision, and John Sexton is certainly one of them.

Afterwards Gordon is really energised and upbeat, and we are joined for lunch by ministers Shaun Woodward and Tessa Jowell, as well as leading figures from the arts world including actor Alan Rickman, director Richard Eyre and poet Andrew Motion. It makes for a most relaxed and enjoyable occasion – we almost feel off duty!

Sunday 29th June

Back in London, Gordon meets Peter Mandelson to find out what role he might have in a general election. Shriti was with them most of the time and told me later Peter appeared very cool about it. We have supper that evening with Alastair Campbell and Fiona Millar in our flat. I thought that any political discussion would have to wait until after the Euro 2008 final on TV that evening, but Alastair and Gordon have such a good conversation about the political difficulties of the moment, and the potential to move ahead, that they don't abandon the table for the football until the last half-hour of the game: Spain 1, Germany 0 as it turns out.

It seems clear that both Peter and Alastair will bring all their experience to bear for the next election campaign. For my part I am always happy to see Fiona who is keen to hear how I am getting on in my office and whether any of her advice was helpful. It certainly gave me a good place to start.

Monday 30th June

I have completely fallen for the clothes of Scottish designer Graeme Black. I visit him at his Chelsea studio and hope that I can get away with some of his designs. Bearing in mind that Victoria Beckham is another fan, we are talking a different body shape, with all due respect to me. His clothes are beautiful though, and I hope to find something to suit me for the busy autumn schedule I am already looking ahead to. I pick out a few great dresses and leave a very happy girl.

Tuesday 1st July

The month begins with a massive historic moment to celebrate. Our National Health Service was created on 5th July 1948 by Health Secretary Aneurin Bevan under the leadership of Labour Prime Minister, Clement Attlee. The NHS is one of the things that I am most asked about when overseas. In countries where the cost of healthcare is an ever-crippling burden to individuals, people invariably offer their admiration of our system. I imagine that everyone in Britain has their reason to be grateful for the safety net of the NHS at some point in their lives, or life of a loved one. Gordon and I are certainly no exception: an operation in his early twenties saved Gordon's sight and I needed the NHS very much during my pregnancies and childbirth.

Gordon starts the week by speaking at a huge dinner hosted by the *Health Service Journal* at the Science Museum with the Health

Secretary, Alan Johnson, and I am looking forward to the service of celebration tomorrow.

Wednesday 2nd July

I join Gordon for the service at Westminster Abbey, which revolves around the stories of some of our NHS heroes, who have already been in to visit Downing Street. I was very touched by the words of 23-year-old Ed Mayne, who speaks about his speedy diagnosis and successful treatment of tongue cancer, and it is moving to hear the archive recording of Aneurin Bevan himself.

We arrive at the service next to empty seats, which are only just filled up in the nick of time. I wonder if Opposition MPs would be keener on arriving on time if it was not a celebration of a great Labour achievement.

In the evening, Gordon and I host a reception at Number 10 for the NHS workers who have been there today, along with Health Secretary of State Alan Johnson and his ministerial team: a former Treasury colleague of Gordon's, Dawn Primarolo MP; cancer surgeon and GOAT (Government of All the Talents) Lord Ara Darzi, and former nurse Ann Keen MP. There is something rather brilliant about having health professionals on the Ministerial Health team. The popular opera soprano Lesley Garrett is a guest this evening (she comes with her GP husband, Dr Peter Christian) and has arranged with Gordon and Ann to surprise everyone by singing. I have to say that when she sings 'Impossible Dream' in the Pillared Room, everyone is moved to tears. As her voice, and the collective emotions of everyone there, soars, I am reminded that our Labour governments have so much to be proud of across the years, and have achieved so many things for ordinary people all over the country.

CHAPTER 13

Tea in Tokyo

Saturday 5th July

After a hurried drive to the airport, I land at Tokyo Narita airport at midday – about 4 a.m. my time. I have travelled ahead of Gordon to join the UK Embassy's event for the maternal mortality campaign just ahead of the G8 summit in Japan's Hokkaido.

We are met by our UK Ambassador, Graham Fry, and his wife, Toyoko. He immediately qualifies as the most down-to-earth ambassador I have met. This may be because we are his last job before retirement back to the UK, but he is very welcoming, nonetheless. He takes enormous trouble on our journey in from the airport to point out all the landmarks of Tokyo and their context to the city. As we approach the Embassy, we see the red Tokyo Tower rising up, which will be the only thing I can consistently recognise – everything else is a blur of flashing glass and twinkling neon.

At the Residence, we greet the staff and hand over our bags, and then we attend the British afternoon tea hosted by Graham Fry, for the White Ribbon Alliance. The Japanese First Lady, Mrs Fukuda, is the guest speaker. She explains how Japan prides itself on turning around maternal and infant health care. At the end of World War II, Japan was a defeated nation recovering from two atomic bombs dropped on major cities. Its maternal and infant death rates were no different than those of the survival rates in the poorest countries in Asia or Africa today. Yet in ten years, Japan reversed its health decline by focusing on child nutrition, and investing in health education. These days, every mother in Japan is given a booklet when she becomes pregnant to chart both her own healthcare and then the baby's through feeding and growth, vaccination and pre-school. Mrs Fukuda had brought along her own booklet from the time when her children (now grown up) were born. I am very touched that she is taking this so seriously, just before her husband chairs the summit.

There are lots of presentations and photos from the White Ribbon Alliance; from its Japanese membership group JOICFP (Japanese Organization for International Cooperation in Family Planning); from Women Deliver, who hosted the conference in London that first got me going on this issue; and from Oxfam, who have brought their ambassador, actor Bill Nighy. I keep expecting him to be funny as he is always so entertaining both in person and on screen, but this is a serious event and he is appropriately sincere and gentle. He tells me he is travelling up to Sapporo (where the famous beer comes from) to join Oxfam at the gathering of all the activists and campaigners who want their messages to be heard by the G8 leaders. Sapporo is the closest town they can reach just outside the security ring surrounding the G8 location in Hokkaido. It makes me realise just how fortunate I am to have an invitation to get inside, and a government behind me backing our campaign.

To thank the Ambassador for hosting the event, I happily agree to visit an exhibition the Embassy has been supporting at the Science Museum in Tokyo. The exhibition was created by British artist David Buckland, who invited painters, sculptors and installation artists to travel with him on a fishing boat called *Cape Farewell* to see the effects of climate change first-hand, going even as far as the Arctic. The gallery is full of works from artists around the world, including Brits like Antony Gormley and Turner Prize winner Rachel Whiteread. I give a speech as invited to do so, but do not quite get the hang of the translator on hand who, if I follow my instructions properly, will speak after every sentence. I completely forget to take the right pauses, and pretty much give a speech to a room full of uncomprehending faces all wondering when I will stop talking. Only at the end are they enlightened, when the translator gets his chance to speak.

Sunday 6th July

After a breakfast with JOICFP, I fulfil a promise to my friend Tim Shriver to visit a group of young Japanese Special Olympics athletes and their families, who have made a wonderful film of their visit to the Special Olympics World Games in Beijing. Speaking to the mothers I gain a better understanding of the philosophy of Tim's mother, the Special Olympics founder, Eunice Kennedy Shriver: 'Namely, the belief that people with intellectual disabilities can, with proper training and support, enhance their individual abilities, enjoy equally with others the joy of sports and prove to society that: IT NEEDS THEM.' Good to know that this is as true on this side of the world as it is on mine.

Konrad and I have time for a little shopping in the Oriental Bazaar (to buy sumo wrestler and ninja T-shirts to take home) and to buy little Japanese toys for the going-home bags for Fraser's birthday party next week. The multi-storey Kiddyland has an entire floor dedicated to Hello Kitty, and another given over to more Snoopys than you can possibly imagine. While I know that there is much to absorb of historic Japanese culture here in this city, I have to admit that I am equally enjoying the veritable feast of Japanese popular culture. The fashion district is also a real eye-opener, with every major brand represented in street after street. A real shopper's paradise if you don't mind what your bank statement says afterwards.

The ambassador treats us to a traditional Japanese lunch at his club, with a spectacular view of the city and the grounds of the Imperial Palace. Our pal, Murray Elder, had already forewarned me, from his earlier visit to Japan, that the ambassador was bold in his food-ordering choices so being a food weed, I opt for a vegetarian menu. That turns out to mean a bowl of delicious miso soup and a main course that was actually chicken! Konrad, on the other hand, has the eel, the jellyfish and the seaweed slices. I can see that I will be on a miso soup and green tea diet for the next few days.

We head for the airport to fly to Hokkaido for the summit, and I manage to catch the boys who have gone to stay with Mela and her family in Romsey for the weekend. I also speak to Gordon, who has just met the organisers of the (Gay) Pride March in London, including the award-winning actor Sir Ian McKellen, who is one of my favourite actors ever.

Gordon has become very serious about the UK economic projections and is even saying that recession looks unavoidable. He now says that he thinks the global economy is worsening. Japan's Prime Minister Fukuda had hoped to make the theme of his summit climate change and global health, but world events are dictating that instead, the priority discussions will be about food prices, oil prices and the economic downturn. Gordon suggests I don't get my hopes up too high about maternal health getting much time on the agenda. I am not giving up yet.

On the flight I pick up a copy of *Nikken*, a business newspaper that carries an advert designed by Freud Communications for the White Ribbon Alliance, with the signature and picture of 30 famous women including Annie Lennox, German model Claudia Schiffer and a famous Russian astronaut. It also runs in *The Times*, the *Wall Street Journal* and a German newspaper. The French publications were unyielding with their high prices so I am not sure we have got this under President Sarkozy's nose yet.

I am writing an article for Monday's *Times* newspaper, too. It has been started off for me by Christianne and Emma, so I have an outline of the key facts about MDG 5 and our campaign, and I add my personal touch. I send it back to Damian McBride in Gordon's press office to cast his eye over it – he returns it with a whole host of comments and changes. Very, very annoyingly, I can see that his comments are all good and worth including, although I don't know how he even has time to look at my piece, never mind understand the intricacies of the campaign. Damian has a reputation for being a tough operator with journalists and politicians, but I never see that side – perhaps because I am neither.

Catching up with the news, I can see that Senator Obama has declared he is a patriot (he is the darling of the American public and much of the media) and that Oxfam protestors in Sapporo are dressing up as G8 leaders with giant masks on. As part of my absorption of Japanese culture and news, I also read that an American man called Joey Chestnut has beaten the Japanese title-holder to become the new Hot Dog Eating Champ by guzzling 59 hot dogs *in their rolls* and then a further five hot dogs in a nail-biting overtime heat, which he wins by a single bite. This last story makes the front page of the *Japan Times*.

Once we land in the northernmost part of Japan, on the island of Hokkaido, we drive 90 minutes to the Windsor Hotel, a hilltop retreat worthy of a Bond villain, with huge sweeping vistas in all directions. I am welcomed with flowers and elegantly whisked in moments before Prime Minister Berlusconi of Italy's arrival.

Monday 7th July

Gordon flies in separately and we meet at the start of the day but soon go our separate ways again as he heads off to meetings with the various other G8 leaders. I start with the spouse programme at a lunch in the hotel restaurant, meeting Svetlana Medvedeva of Russia, Margarida Barroso whose husband heads the European Commission, and Laureen Harper of Canada, for the first time.

I am touched that there is a moment's silence at the start of the lunch in remembrance of the 7/7 London bombing victims of 2005.

Mrs Fukuda explains that she has created a very personal programme for the spouses, introducing us to the traditional Japanese crafts and activities for which she holds a great passion. Together we watch a 12-layer kimono demonstration, and join Mrs Fukuda's tea-ceremony teacher of the last 30 years to have our first attempt at the tea ceremony ourselves. The hospitality is superb and runs faultlessly. For me, though, it is a bit like going on a school trip without your friends. You have the opportunity to do new things but no one to turn to in order to share the moment or have a bit of a laugh. And, of course, there are also cameras on us the whole time, and no one wants to make a mistake or inadvertently do something daft.

During the evening, the leaders and their spouses are entertained with an outdoor energetic dance performance and stunning firework display (but in the pouring rain under umbrellas). I stand watching with President Bush. Defying my personal expectations, I find him very easy to talk to. Perhaps he is more relaxed as he approaches the end of his term in office, but the President has a knack of getting right to the heart of an issue with direct questions.

We move inside for a traditional Japanese meal seated on the floor. Conventionally, we should tuck our feet underneath ourselves and sit that way at the table for the evening, but thankfully there is a hidden hollow beneath the table so we can sit with our feet dangling down in it, which is clearly designed to be more comfortable for us inflexible Westerners.

I can see that Gordon is sitting opposite Angela Merkel of Germany and both are engaged in earnest conversation. I am between Nicolas Sarkozy of France and Stephen Harper of Canada, and opposite Silvio Berlusconi. Everyone speaks French, which I can just about keep up with. Berlusconi tells the oft-told tale of the young person visiting Parliament, who points at the benches opposite and asks, 'Is that your Enemy?'

'No, that's the Opposition,' comes the reply. 'The Enemy are on the same benches.'

I have a long conversation with Canadian Prime Minister Harper about how best to balance a high-profile political life with raising kids. He explains he had been working in the private sector when he was invited to be the Leader of the Opposition, with no expectation of being in government. He only came to power when the government led by Gordon's close friend, Paul Martin, fell. He tells me he will shortly be meeting the Conservative Party in London as 'they are our sister party'. I say that I do not believe that there are, or should be, 'sister parties' between countries and that the old divides do not exist in the same way. 'Of course,' he says, 'government leaders all work together as only they can understand the burdens of office.'

Sarkozy seems quieter than usual, perhaps because Carla is not here (she has stayed in France to prepare for the release of her album). He talks about his hopes and ambitions for his time in office and his wish to be fearless about future re-election, in order to pursue what he wants to do. We also talk about our boys – my kids, his kids, Carla's son. I think that this is what leaders talk to spouses about. It is certainly enjoyable for me to have a normal family-oriented conversation, and I hope he calls Carla later to say the same thing. The dinner ends early as everyone has had a long day, and there is a longer one to come tomorrow.

Tuesday 8th July

Even before I head out this morning, all the advisers are gathering in Gordon's room as the key British negotiator, Jon Cunliffe, has been up most of the night redrafting the communiqué text (this is the written version of what can be discussed and agreed when the leaders meet together and takes many hours to produce behind the scenes).

All the other leaders appear to see international development as an added extra to the summit, and not as central to what happens to our whole world. Gordon is also looking ahead to the United Nations annual meeting in September, which assesses the progress made on each of the Millennium Development Goals, and sees what is needed from the G8 to make this productive. The commitments made in 2005 at the G8 summit in Gleneagles in Scotland to invest money in development for the poorest countries are still holding, but the struggle to get all countries to actually write the cheque is just that, a struggle.

Berlusconi is hosting the next G8 and he has already upset everyone by saying he thinks development investment is a waste. Canadian Prime Minister Harper, whose country hosts the 2010 summit, holds the hardest attitude. He has expressed a not unreasonable concern about governance, and how much development funding reaches the people it is meant for. With that approach, though, my wish to see maternal health make it on to the G8 agenda for the first time might not come to pass.

The day ends dramatically when advisers looking through the window of the meeting room see everyone in a turmoil, jumping up and down, and gesticulating. It turns out that Gordon had torn up the rulebook and is setting out new proposals for sanctions on Zimbabwe. Everyone agrees to these so the meeting does, in the end, finish on a high.

Bob Geldof has somehow made it in, past all the security rings, into the heart of the summit (I'd be very surprised if Justin didn't have something to do with this). I join Bob with Ambassador Fry in the café. I have already seen the copy of *Asahi Shimbun* he edited that included articles by both Gordon and me, which looked terrific translated into Japanese – I was very proud to be included and very happy to be able to report on the maternal mortality campaign in another country. Bob has just set up meetings for himself with Bush and Merkel, although both have offered him the same time slot. Rather than choose between them, Bob has managed to get them to meet him together. He will certainly be making the case for helping the world's poorest in his own unique and persuasive way.

Later, I go to hover near the official Heads of Government meetings taking place, to see if I can get any word on what happened about getting maternal mortality into the official documentation. This is vital, not least as it has never been discussed by G8 leaders at a summit before, never mind achieved any official commitment, but without their leadership I don't know how the rest of the world can be expected to take the issue seriously. It has truly been the forgotten goal amongst the MDG targets.

While I know Gordon will, of course, support any discussion on maternal health, it must be one of the other leaders who must raise and pursue the issue. Prime Minister Harper had been mentioned as one possibility but I hear no word via Gordon's advisers that this has happened. I ponder on the fact that the number of mothers dying in pregnancy and childbirth has not changed in over 20 years, precisely because it is not even recognised at the highest political levels. With no political will, no change can take place for these women dying on the floor of huts, in fields, and in their own homes in the saddest of circumstances. I feel that if nothing happens today then my campaigning journey will have reached a sad end, as I don't know what else I can do to make a difference.

Tom Fletcher, Gordon's Foreign Policy aide, comes to tell me the good news. President George W Bush has emerged as the surprising champion for these women and their families. He has not only raised the issue, but insisted that a section on health workers for better maternal health be included in the communiqué. I talk to Jon Cunliffe who confirms more details for me, and who is off to check the final wording.

I know that many women's organisations around the world have not seen eye to eye with President Bush, but today he has done a good deed that we can all build on, so that never again will the lives of mothers be so at risk. Now many activists, concerned professionals and policy makers can count on planning for change. I think of all those people who have travelled to the nearby town of Sapporo to bring their message, and wonder how they will join in celebration when they hear the news of a small, but good step achieved tonight. They can all pat themselves on the back as the many years of advocacy have finally paid off today.

I tear myself away from all this activity to rejoin the spouses' programme. We visit a snow energy facility and an eco house, featuring traditional demonstrations of textile gift wrapping, including my favourite top tip on 'How to wrap a watermelon' and 'How to carry two bottles of wine'. Ever mindful that I am one camera-click away from some terrible mistake that will haunt me for ever, I steer clear of the invitation to drive small electric cars around (as, luckily, this coincides with my scheduled call home to talk to the boys before John goes to school).

Back at the hotel, I arrange to deliver my gifts for all the spouses. The gifts include a beautiful compact mirror from Jaeger; as well as an original Antony Gormley piece for each spouse, signed by Antony Gormley, Bob Geldof and Richard Curtis, that Richard had arranged for me to bring out. The budget is still fairly modest for official gifts and I still just arrange gifts myself personally, but this time the Jaeger gifts were approved, and I think that between Richard, Bob and Antony, they have absorbed the cost of theirs. I find Sue Nye, who is here on this trip, and we take a walk for a general gossip and to get some fresh air. We head to the ski lift with a lot of security detail in tow to see the full view and then are offered golf buggies, so we take a speedy tour of the grounds.

Dinner for me tonight is with the spouses – a full, nine-course Japanese meal with the noodles being prepared in front of us. Margarida Barroso, the wife of the President of the European Commission, has said that she would like to say a few words to us about Laura Bush, who is here on her last G8 summit. Just as she rises to speak, the doors open and a whole group of press with cameras pour in. No one looks more shocked than poor Margarida. The press corps is duly ushered away, to return at a better time when we watch an *ikebana* (flower arranging) demonstration.

It is a strange relationship for all the spouses to just meet inter-mittently and as a constantly changing group. We are all very different but do share similar experiences as political spouses, and everyone is open to getting to know everyone else. I can see that it is a sad moment for Margarida to goodbye to Laura Bush after eight years of international meetings together. I think that at the start we must all feel a bit shy – I certainly do – but we are all in this together and are treated to some wonderful experiences. Certainly our introduction to traditional and contemporary Japanese culture has been led by a gracious and thoughtful host.

I feel I have got on well with all these interesting and accomplished women, and have formed lots of good – while obviously diplomatic – friendships. What I really have to get the hang of is interpreters. It is necessary to speak to Svetlana Medvedeva with an interpreter, and it does take some getting used to as the conversation is necessarily slower paced. And I have to consciously remember to watch Svetlana talk in her own Russian, rather than be tempted to watch the translator who speaks over her in English. Svetlana is a great ambassador for her country as she happily describes with great passion lots of aspects of Russian culture and society.

Even as I form friendships, I do always push my campaigning cause – oh, they can see me coming a mile away but as a group have been very supportive!

Wednesday 9th July

The final day of the summit, and we visit a volcano centre, meeting the young delegates who attend the 'J8' from all the G8 countries, and watching a tree-planting ceremony. There is much quiet chuckling as Ken Gambrill, my UK protection officer, spots that one of his burly Russian counterparts, who has been big and tough all week, is now carrying Mrs Medvedeva's bright blue handbag while she plants her tree.

At the end of the G8, the UK is delighted to have helped secure a good agreement on health workers. We now have a firm figure to work with to fulfil the maternal mortality reduction targets (and other interrelated aspects of global health too), which means the money can be raised globally and the job started. A figure of 2.3 per 1,000 is agreed – for every 1,000 people in a country, an average of 2.3 people will be trained and employed as doctors, nurses, midwives and supporting health staff. There is not actual cash yet, but it is still a major step forward for international leaders to acknowledge that maternal mortality lies right at the heart of the MDGs.

All has gone well at the G8, but the UK news coverage is mostly about domestic issues, including a number of knife-crime incidents. I join the team on the 767 plane home, which Visits Coordinator Barbara Burke has hired from the Dallas Mavericks basketball team. No one can say that we aren't looking at saving costs where we can.

Thursday 10th July

The vast majority of passengers are apparently wide awake when the plane stops off in Novosibirsk in Siberia, where much vodka is drunk and caviar eaten. I sleep through it all, oblivious.

As soon as we are back, Gordon is straight off to make a statement about the G8, attend the Police Bravery Awards and then we both go to Wembley Stadium for the Labour Party's annual sports gala.

Thursday 17th July

All my Hello Kitty and other Japanese toys came in handy for Fraser's second birthday party, which he is celebrating with his cousin Isabel, who was four yesterday.

Mela has got much of the food ready with Maggie Darling, who has set everything up in the Number 11 state room, which is far enough away from the offices and means we can use the Number 11 front door for our guest arrivals. I have, as ever, just kept inviting people and now we have 65 kids coming. That is a lot of jelly and cake, I know.

My brother, Sean, is visiting us from Los Angeles with his wife, Caroline, the birthday girl Isabel, and their other daughter, Honor, who is just one. My boys are ready to pounce as soon as their cousins arrive. Within moments they are all playing in the big, soft carpeted hallway of the Number 11 flat with Peppa Pig and the Ben 10 aliens, joining in a big game together.

Maggie has made a phenomenal cake for Isabel that has a full-size Barbie standing up on it, wearing a pink sparkly skirt. Fraser has a more traditional chocolate cake sporting the whole of Pooh Corner.

I feel confident we can cope with an invasion of 65 kids as we have booked our favourite children's entertainer, Mr Marvel. I cannot explain the magic of Mr Marvel. He does all the usual stuff – puppets, tricks with a rabbit, balloons – but somehow keeps the children sitting in rapt attention or bent double with laughter for as long as you want. He then sends them off to eat, and afterwards neutralises the sugar high by running a kids' disco with a bubble machine, so they can bop about like mad.

The first time he came to Downing Street, we had terrible difficulty working out how to get the live rabbit into the building without putting her through the security scanner. In the end, Mr Marvel arrived at the back rather than the front of Downing Street, and the rabbit effectively arrived the same way catering supplies arrive, but with no danger of heading to the kitchens.

We book Mr Marvel over and over again for charity and family events, and no one ever seems to get tired of his routines. I would put 'First-class children's entertainer' on the top-ten list of essentials for any WPM.

Once the party is over and the kids are settled down, I leave Mela to babysit and sneak out to Celia Walden's book launch in a new bit of the private members' club, Soho House. I take my friend, Vivienne Dyce, visiting from our local village in Scotland with her teenage daughter, Megan, and tell them that I will show them a bit of cool London, as this is pretty much their first trip to the city. My brother, Sean, comes with me as he knows Celia's boyfriend, Piers

Morgan, from years gone by, when they both worked on *The Sun* together.

My moment to show how cool I am is rather dissipated when I ring the bell of Soho House and no one answers. Finally, a girl appears to say that she can't see my name on the list. It takes a fair bit of persuading to prove I am not there to gatecrash and we are let inside. We tell Piers about the entry mishap and he can barely hide his delight. I realise that without question, I will have the opportunity to read about it again. What makes me laugh the most is when I consider the range of things that are happening in my life at the moment. One minute I am the honoured accompanying guest at a G8 summit, and the next I am nearly kept out of a book launch.

CHAPTER 14

Both Sides of the Wall

Saturday 19th July

My day starts with a glorious lie-in (to 7.30 a.m.) with both my little boys cuddled up in the bed. Then we all get going again and off in our separate directions.

Today, I am heading off to accompany Gordon on a short but very packed programme in Israel and Palestine. As is becoming the pattern, I make my own journey outwards – Gordon has travelled ahead to visit Iraq en route.

I am trying out the new BMI flight to Tel Aviv and discover that the BMI chairman, Sir Michael Bishop, is travelling on the same plane – this guarantees that the service will be good. (It is not such a coincidence as he is joining the PM's business delegation for a number of meetings in Israel and Palestine.) I have no complaints about the flight bar a surprisingly lousy movie selection (long plane journeys are one of the few times I get to watch a film all the way through). Instead, I read my huge briefing file on the trip and immerse myself in what lies ahead. The big picture of all diplomatic efforts in this region is, of course, the peace process, but this trip is focusing on economic development. We have seen the lessons from Northern Ireland ourselves, where progress towards peace speeded up when it became clear that everyone was more likely to thrive and prosper by ending the hostilities.

Apart from individual meetings with the two Prime Ministers (both former Finance Ministers, whom Gordon knows well from his days as Chancellor), the highlights of the visit include a meeting of the Israel–British Business Council, and the launch of a new Palestine–British Business Council, which will have both Palestinian and Israeli business executives attending. There might be something to this economic path to prosperity, as the arrangements go very well. Up to speed with my own schedule I put the file away. I also discover that I can watch recorded TV shows and am quite happy for the last hour or so watching episodes of *Gavin and Stacey*.

We meet the British Ambassador, Sir Tom Phillips, on arrival, and I manage to ruffle feathers immediately by requesting that we also organise a car ride for Sir Michael Bishop, as he is part of our UK business delegation (I just think it is terrifically rude not to offer one of our leading company chairmen a ride when he is here to support the UK). Konrad beetles off to sort out our passports and fix the situation. In the end, the ambassador waits to meet Gordon on his separate arrival, and Sir Michael comes in the car with me all the way to the King David Hotel in Jerusalem.

Sunday 20th July

We set off very early with an endless diary sheet full of extraordinary first-time experiences for me. We start with a visit to Yad Vashem, the Holocaust museum in Jerusalem. Gordon has a long-standing family relationship with Israel (due to his father, who visited many times), and organised the grant to the Holocaust Education Trust that has enabled two school children from each UK secondary school to visit here every year, or to go to Auschwitz. As soon as we arrive, we speak to a number of guests invited by Gordon, who he thought would enhance the visit, including Sir Martin Gilbert, the esteemed historian who has written numerous books on the Holocaust, and his wife, Esther. The Director of Yad Vashem takes us around the whole of this heartbreakingly necessary place that brings its visitors a meaningful connection to the people whom it honours and remembers.

I feel very honoured that our friends Ronnie and Sharon Cohen are with us, especially as we stand in front of the exhibition about the *Exodus*, the ship that carried Holocaust survivors to Palestine the year before the state of Israel was created. Sharon's father was Yossi Harel, the brave commander of that ship, and it is fascinating to hear her memories of him standing there in front of all the images of the ship and its traumatised passengers.

Yad Vashem also has a school, a synagogue, a cultural centre and a memorial to the 1.5 million children who were murdered or perished in the Holocaust. Gordon is invited to light the eternal flame at a ceremony within the memorial and lays a wreath of remembrance. A choir sings a beautiful, haunting song by the Hungarian Jewish composer (and parachutist) Hannah Szenes, who joined the British army parachuting into Yugoslavia to help save other Jews there during World War II. She was captured and executed in 1944, when she would not reveal other names under torture, and is celebrated as a great heroine in Israel today.

Gordon has always been fascinated by such bravery and has written in his book on courage about that seeming fearlessness in the face of great danger in order to protect what is good and right about our world. I am pretty sure that he has exactly that kind of courage to face down the greatest injustices while risking his own life. For myself, I have no idea whether I could be that brave; I would love to think I could be, but really, I just don't know.

The power of Yad Vashem is that it enables you to think deeply about human beings and what they are capable of. It reminds you starkly of the consequences of such cruelty in humankind, and finds a way to uplift and offer promise, even as it devastates with its story of the Holocaust. The magnitude of what happened is so hard to comprehend and stays with us for a long time afterwards.

From Yad Vashem we drive directly to the Presidential Palace to meet President Shimon Peres of Israel. After a personal meeting, Gordon and President Peres hold a joint press conference. The President is generous in his praise of Gordon and urges him to continue his work on the 'economic road-map to peace'. In short, this means finding a path for countries to be more prosperous and people to enjoy a higher quality of life through living together in peace, rather than by fighting each other.

I am delighted that all the UK business and higher education delegation is present to hear President Peres speak so highly of Gordon.

From Israel, we travel to Palestine to meet Prime Minister Salam Fayyad of Palestine. This means we drive to a checkpoint at the entrance to the city of Bethlehem just bordering Jerusalem, and then all change to armoured vehicles. Gordon goes in one car with Prime Minister Fayyad, while I jump into another vehicle and the safe hands of Dr Khouloud Daibes, Palestine's Minister of Tourism and Women's Affairs.

Khouloud is my age and the mother of three children. She left Palestine for 14 years to live in Hanover, Germany, but explains that she returned home in 1993 with a great surge of optimism for a better life for Palestinian people.

She has since raised her family under severe visa restrictions, set by the Israeli government, and struggles daily with the notion that her children are unable to even travel to the seaside 40 minutes away under the current rules.

She has been doing her current ministerial job for 16 months when I meet her. She looks tired, but still enthusiastic and determined. She has found out that I like to use my own time to meet local women and hear what is going on from their perspective, so she has gathered together a group of four Palestinian women who each run different voluntary sector groups for women and children.

One woman involved with a domestic violence charity is clearly feeling the strain as the link with an economic downturn (and lack of work) goes hand-in-hand with an increase in domestic abuse in the home. As always, I recognise the power of women's achievements in all kinds of circumstances to protect and nurture their families and communities.

Khouloud then takes me to visit one of several refugee camps in the area.

We visit Aida, a camp that runs alongside the rather oppressive wall (or 'security barrier' as the Israeli government calls it) that divides Israel and Palestine. I am taken up to a rooftop so that I can see the scale of the camp, but I notice that Gary Richmond, the protection officer with me, is unhappy. There are a number of press cameras there, looking for something to publish back home, so I pose for about ten seconds and then Gary whisks me back inside. I have no idea if the press got their snap.

It is sobering to have only to walk a few metres from this kind of potential danger from rooftop snipers to visit the camp's children's centre. It is the school holiday, so the children are attending a summer camp, but within the grounds of the overall refugee camp – they can't travel anywhere, of course, but activities are being organised to keep everyone busy and entertained.

I am now in the hands of the UNRWA (United Nations Relief and Works Agency for Palestine Refugees in the Near East) head, Karen AbuZayd, who has worked here and in Gaza for the last eight years. Karen is one of those immediately impressive UN types who give so much of themselves to their work. She has a large group of UN people with her and together we watch the children dance, and play a game called Fruit Salad, which involves me joining in. Fruit Salad is a bit like Musical Chairs, but with no music and no chairs – and my popularity as a visitor rises when I lose! My visit here does not last very long but I think my hosts have given me a sense of how people live in a place like this, and how onerous the restrictions can be for daily family life. It is unimaginable compared to the relative freedoms that my family and other British families enjoy.

My next stop is to join Gordon at his meeting with Prime Minister Fayyad. They are now at a large hotel built when Bethlehem (as the birthplace of Jesus Christ) was celebrating the year 2000 AD. We are offered the most British-looking cheese salad sandwich, and one of the best nectarines I have ever eaten. The business delegation is in full swing with their conference, and now the two Prime Ministers join them to make their speeches. Gordon is again talking about economic cooperation to get people working together. He has made an announcement of £30 million to the Palestinian Budget and launches the Palestinian–UK Business Council. Everyone is very chuffed that so many Palestinian business leaders have turned out for this event. What impresses me, too, is the turnout of eminent Jewish business leaders who have travelled from the UK and Israel – Lloyds TSB head, Sir Victor Blank, Sir Ronnie Cohen and Sir Trevor Chinn to name just a few. When everyone is under one roof talking to each other and working together, it brings the greatest hope.

We depart in our armoured vehicles for a final treat on this side of the wall. We draw up in Bethlehem Square to visit the Church of the Nativity. The sun is shining down and I think the large array of flag-waving kids must have been there for a while. The children all wave and cheer, looking very pink-cheeked in the heat. As soon as Gordon walks towards them he is completly mobbed with hugs and handshakes. There is something about Gordon that just makes kids smile, and something about kids that makes Gordon beam. I have read all the comments about how Gordon smiles, whether it looks real, whether it is his best look, many comments barbed and cruel – what I know is that put him with a bunch of kids, and you just get a giant grin from him, and them. I often wonder if children who still hold their natural optimism have that extra sense, not yet lost, to instinctively recognise a good person. Whatever it is, I just feel rather honoured at that moment to move out of the way and avoid the crush.

At the entrance to the Church of the Nativity, we meet the three leaders from the Catholic, Armenian and Greek Orthodox churches that are all present here. We bend down very low to go inside and enter a darkened, cool, peaceful place with vast high ceilings, a long nave and what looks like architectural digs in the floor. On closer inspection these turn out to be original Byzantine floor mosaics that have only recently been uncovered. We approach the altar and Gordon is presented by His Beatitude with a replica of an ancient religious picture. His Beatitude then presents me with a cross, blesses it and puts it around my neck.

We then descend to the cave beneath the church, believed to be the exact place of Jesus' birth, and we can see the Holy Crib. The Catholic Father also briefs us on the Christian service held every year and we light a candle and take a moment to pray.

Finally we go through the Catholic Church and meet all the Franciscan monks who continue to work, though in decreasing numbers, in Syria and Jordan, and in Palestine. The church is very light and bright, and so familiar from televised Christmas Eve services, when you see the bambino placed under the altar then.

After all the security arrangements, there is a bit of a moment when we discover that neither Khouloud nor I can return to my car as the driver has locked it with the keys inside. It happens to all of us, but I suspect this is not a good moment for our driver. I can see both my handbags and the Tourism Minister's bags sitting on the back seat. Rather reluctantly, I leave in a separate car to go back to the checkpoint. One of the aides from the Consulate very nobly stands by the locked car for two hours until the door is finally opened and personally brings my bags back to the hotel.

While Gordon meets the Israeli–UK Business Council, I meet a group of British Jewish students who have just spent three weeks in Israel thanks to the UK-based youth and education charity UJIA (United Jewish Israel Appeal). I want to ask them lots of questions about their experiences, only to find myself the subject of their inquisition. What are my first impressions? What are my thoughts on culture and identity? These 18-year-olds are a friendly but tough crowd – they want answers from politicians and anyone who spends time with them. I am impressed.

*

After an hour catching my breath back in the hotel room, I follow Gordon to meet the Israeli Prime Minister, Ehud Olmert. What I have noticed is how much Gordon's experience and time as Chancellor is helping him. With Olmert and Fayyad as former Finance Ministers themselves, their backgrounds also mean that they are pushing in the same direction to each get the best benefit for their own countries, including Britain, who is a good friend to both.

I join Gordon at the Israeli Prime Minister's residence, and meet Ehud Olmert for the first time. Martin and Esther Gilbert are also there, and it is a rare treat for everyone to have someone with his historic expertise on hand. I meet Aliza Olmert too, and immediately warm to her. She is attractive, beautifully dressed, and has fabulous paintings of cypress trees on the wall that, it turns out, she painted herself.

She has returned to her own social-worker roots to establish an Early Years programme in Israel. Oh, I just love her. One of the things that I am most proud of in our Labour government – as is Gordon, who was so personally behind this at the Treasury and about which I receive the most positive feedback abroad – is our early years Sure Start programme. I am a passionate believer that the investment in our youngest citizens is vital to realising the promise and potential of everyone. How we raise our babies, how we engage and play with our toddlers, how they start off at school can, I believe, bring about the greatest opportunities for young people. Life throws a lot of curve balls and how we cope with what happens, and how we make our choices, is what matters.

Sure Start was first suggested at the start of the Labour government in the late 1990s, and we now have over 3,000 children's centres in the UK, starting in the poorest areas, but now spreading around the country. There has been a fair bit of criticism and opposition from all sides of the House, not least because they are relatively costly to run, but investing in children pays huge dividends later on. We are now at the stage where we can measure properly whether they are working, and every indication tells us that they are. Aliza and I immediately talk about her work on Early Years while we wait for the PMs to finish their business ahead of our dinner.

Word comes from the Israeli team that the planned press conference will be cancelled because they are concerned they will have too many difficult questions about their domestic issues from the Israeli press. I find Stewart Wood (who has many areas of expertise at Number 10, including the Israel/Palestine issue) and Foreign Policy aide, Tom Fletcher, to get their view on what is happening. Like me, they are just astonished and laugh out loud at the imagined notion that we might ever suggest to our British Press that we are cancelling a press conference to avoid tough questions. As it is, Prime Minister Olmert heads a very fragile coalition in his Parliament (the Knesset) and he is under a lot of pressure to defend some funding accusations made against him for a previous campaign. Despite these concerns, the press conference does go ahead, outdoors, and eventually everything calms down.

Gordon and I dine on our own with the Prime Minister and Aliza, on a meal made from local food with a south-east Asian fusion thing going on: Thai soup with raw vegetable bean shoot salad, an aubergine and sweet potato plate, and steak. The dessert is a fruit granita that arrives in swirling mist of dry ice – I have never seen anything quite like it. At the end we meet the chef to congratulate him on his culinary success. He immediately responds by listing every single Gordon Ramsay restaurant – clearly quite a fan. Olmert then tells a fabulous story about Roman Abramovich being sent by Putin as Governor of Kochoko in Siberia to purchase the Russian enclave in Jerusalem, and being prepared to write a cheque for $100 million on the spot.

Whatever the future for Prime Minister Olmert in politics, he is fulsome in his praise for his working relationship with Gordon, recalling the time, years before, when Gordon arrived for a meeting in Israel and had just stepped on to the tarmac when he got a call to say he was needed in London for a crucial vote. What impressed Olmert was not only that Gordon diligently returned for the crucial vote, but that he got right back on another plane and returned to Israel to attend the meeting.

Monday 21st July

I accompany Sharon Cohen to a rather special place she has told me about. I have been kindly issued with an invitation to speak at the awe-inspiring Rachel Nash Comprehensive Breast Cancer Clinic, Hala, run by Rabbi Michoel Sorotzkin. This is a small place where women on low incomes can come, whether Jew or Arab, and receive first-class treatment to check for signs of breast cancer.

My grandmother died of breast cancer at the age of 70. I have lost friends and acquaintances to breast cancer, and also know those who have survived treatment and continue to keep good health as both diagnosis and treatments are improving all the time. Not long after I turned 30 I had day surgery at St Thomas' Hospital, London, to remove a breast lump. I was fortunate as my lump was benign. And I will always remember the doctor explaining to me what the biopsy might show before the three-week wait for the results began. My mind explored all the possible outcomes before my all-clear came, and that memory stays with me vividly now. That was the early 1990s and since then, the most amazing progress in treatments has been made in our NHS and elsewhere, including Israel; it is devastating for people to suffer because of a late or difficult diagnosis.

Rabbi Sorotzkin is one of those exceptional individuals who, for personal reasons, was moved to create something like the Hala centre. It is hard to explain why one place stays in your heart. I visit so many wonderful charities, hospitals and community centres. I think a little piece of each one lodges in me, and certainly reaffirms my optimism for the universal kindness of people. But one or two strike a chord and make a lasting connection. In the UK there are the Maggie's Centres, and now in Jerusalem I find the Hala Clinic.

Gordon has been offered the great honour of being the first serving British Prime Minister to address the Knesset. I arrive with Gordon in the blazing sunshine in front of the Israeli Parliament building, and accompany him as he walks up the red carpet to a great fanfare. We hear our respective national anthems, and perform a guard inspection. We enter the building past the greatest and certainly the largest Marc Chagall painting I have ever seen.

Gordon's speech follows Prime Minister Olmert and Benjamin Netanyahu (who used the opportunity as Opposition Leader to be quite political and criticise the government). Gordon speaks authoritatively about the UK's position as a firm friend of Israel. He talks about his own father's strong and binding relationship with Israel as a church minister. He would take back slides for Gordon and his two brothers and show them all the places he'd visited. I remember Gordon coming with his brother Andrew a few years ago and revisiting all those places that they had previously only known from the pictures projected on the dining-room wall.

Inevitably, Gordon chooses to raise the controversial subject of the settlements and there is an audible sigh of relief when only one politician in the room gets up and walks out. At the end, Gordon receives a very warm standing ovation.

Back in London, we head straight to Downing Street to attend a political reception of MPs and their spouses in the garden. What a great atmosphere, with lots of positive feeling about Gordon. The MPs that are here are backing Gordon all the way and wanting to try very hard to win a difficult, perhaps even impossible, fourth term, whenever the election is called.

CHAPTER 15

Summer Ups and Downs

Tuesday 22nd July

As we approach the summer break, there is always a flurry of events to complete before the Houses of Parliament rise for the recess and the diary quietens down. Of course, this is also the start of the 'silly season', when anything can turn into a major news story.

One memorable moment comes at a charity reception for the Sheila McKechnie Awards for social justice campaigners. The late Sheila McKechnie was a friend of Gordon's since university, and a brilliant campaigner for social change as the director of Shelter and the Consumers' Association Which?

Gordon is presenting the awards when a commotion breaks out. I see a man dart away from Gordon, who steps back laughing and brushes down his suit. It is clear by the look on his aide's face that something strange has happened but it is difficult to tell as Gordon just continues handing out awards. The man is quietly escorted away only to start another kerfuffle outside.

The police later explain that as part of a protest against the new airport terminal at Heathrow, our plucky campaigner had decided to superglue himself to the Prime Minister. When that didn't work, he tried to superglue himself to the big black gates outside only to discover he hadn't enough glue left. The protestor said he failed in his plan because he couldn't get the PM to stand still long enough for the glue to set. I think we should have expected something like this when I see that our runway rebel has called his campaign 'Plane Stupid'.

Wednesday 23rd July

Prime Minister Odinga of Kenya and his wife Ida call in to see us at Downing Street. This is an important visit for the Kenyan PM, who wants to pass on his gratitude for Gordon's role in the negotiations when Kenya was experiencing violence in the wake of their elections last year. I take Maggie Darling and Emma Parry from the maternal mortality campaign team to host Mrs Odinga and her staff at breakfast. She has a great interest in how Africa handles the growing problem of cancer diagnosis and cancer care and, of course, expresses an interest in what she can do to support the White Ribbon Alliance Kenya.

Mrs Odinga also expresses a great interest in what we are doing in the garden with the Royal Parks Agency gardeners. With all the recent rain the colours on the flowers are looking quite vibrant. We talk about the enjoyment and therapeutic value of gardening and I share with her my idea to get the kids growing things if I can negotiate a small space with the gardeners.

We meet the winners of *Five News'* Britain's Kindest Kids and it is no surprise to me that I discover that our friend Liam Fairhurst, whom we met this time last year, is among the nominees. It is great to see him and his family again, and I am delighted to discover that he is the overall winner, too.

Thursday 24th July

Looking at the diary for today, I can see that it will unfold as one of those days that shows the best and worst of what we do and are. In the morning, we watch the splendid sight of hundreds of purple-clad bishops on their Walk to Witness march from Westminster to Lambeth Palace. It is gloriously sunny, which is just as well, as many bishops are spending the day in large marquees set up at the back of Lambeth Palace. I join Gordon and we meet the multifaith group that includes Richard Chartres, the Bishop of

London for the Anglican Church; the Chief Rabbi Jonathan Sacks; Cardinal Cormac Murphy-O'Connor, head of the UK Catholic Church; and the heads of the many other faith groups of Britain including Muslims, Sikhs, Hindus, Baha'is and the Jains. We also meet His Beatitude, the Greek Patriarch whom we last saw in Bethlehem.

The conference is being hosted by Archbishop Rowan Williams and his wife, Jane, and the theme is to 'Halve Poverty by 2015'. Faith groups have been some of the greatest champions of the anti-poverty drives that have influenced world leaders in recent years. The Make Poverty History campaign was spread far and wide by church groups in the UK, to name but one example. I even remember Gordon's mum and her friends in the local village in Aberdeenshire posting their Christian Aid cards to Gordon at the Treasury, urging him to take action to Drop the Debt in African countries (much to the mailroom's amusement as they spotted them among the thousands received).

Gordon follows the Archbishop of Canterbury on to an outdoor platform to address the audience of bishops. He speaks at his finest – just a very powerful piece of oratory, with no notes, perhaps not much different from a minister's style, giving a call for all faiths to continue the work to reduce poverty. He calls on the past successes over wrongs that were said to have been impossible to right: slavery, the Cold War, apartheid, world debt and, of course, poverty. He cites the vision of Isaiah in the Bible – 'to undo the burden of debt and let the oppressed go free' – and the words of Amos, that 'justice will flow like water, and righteousness like a mighty stream' to declare that there is nothing that we cannot do for justice if we do it together.

When I look at the audience – who don't normally set much store by politicians – they are visibly moved and a number have tears rolling down their cheeks. I see Justin Forsyth and Tom Fletcher turn to each other and say in unison, 'And that's why we work for him.'

*

After a few hours with PiggyBankKids at the flat, I travel to Stratford-upon-Avon for a long-ago booked production of *Hamlet*. It is the first night and we are due to see the performances of two very fine actors, and coincidentally long-standing Labour supporters, David Tennant and Sir Patrick Stewart.

Gordon is preparing for the National Policy Forum which takes place tomorrow; an important meeting for the Labour Party and one of the few places where the party leader really has to demonstrate what they are doing. As a result, Gordon is inevitably delayed more than he wants setting off for the theatre.

Daily Mail editor Paul Dacre and his wife, Kathy, both great Shakespeare enthusiasts, are there, as is Number 10 adviser Stephen Carter, with his wife, Anna. Stephen and I talk about how we expect the election result in the Glasgow East by-election to go, as the result is due about the time the play ends. This has been the toughest by-election we have fought, defending a Labour majority of 10,000, and we have seen a massive swing of support going to the Nationalists. We expect a desperately close outcome and both chuckle at my untimely decision to have booked a Shakespearian tragedy as an end-of-term treat.

The play is very well done, nicely edgy with a classic, on-the-edge-of-manic performance from David Tennant, and an excellent lose-yourself-in-that-magnificent-voice performance from Sir Patrick Stewart as Claudius. The rest of the cast excel and for a first night, I can't spot any bits that don't run smoothly. Gordon arrives just before the interval so he gets a chance to see everyone before he sits down for the second half.

Afterwards, we go backstage to congratulate David, Patrick and the rest of the cast. Just at that moment, Stephen's pager beeps, bringing the terrible news that the by-election has probably been lost by about 300 votes. Gordon calls the political team and gets this view confirmed. We quickly say our goodbyes and drive off in our car.

We creep into our hotel room in Stratford and realise we are quite stunned by the news of the defeat. To lose a seat like Glasgow East is terrible news for Labour. We both have a long and restless night with pretty much no sleep. It is not enough to look at the organisation or make excuses for local politics, we need to look deeply at what we are doing overall, and we need to find better ways to have our messages reach people. Most of all, we need to pick up our confidence and work together successfully, and fast.

This does feel like the lowest point ever.

Friday 25th July

I stay with Gordon as he gets ready for a visit to the Jaguar factory en route to the National Policy Forum meeting. His speech will need to be on a par with the one for the bishops just yesterday morning.

When Gordon returns to Downing Street it is clear from what the team are saying that he has performed as well as could have been expected all day. This is a tough, tough moment and would have felt very different if we had got away with holding the seat.

Much as I wanted the win, I do wonder if this loss might also be a sharp awakening before the summer, and the chance to think things over and return afresh.

I am much cheered up by the arrival of my brother, Sean, and Caroline, and the girls, Izzy and Honor, who are back from visiting my parents in Dorset, to join us on holiday. As soon as they put their bags in the spare room, we all gather round the kitchen table tucked in its nook and catch up on each other's recent news. The cousins are all very excited to see each other and we talk about the house we have rented for our holiday, and all the freedom we will have on the beach, riding ponies. No one talks politics.

Senator Obama is due to visit us tomorrow, and our holiday is set to start the moment he leaves. But that does not mean we are not greatly looking forward to his visit – not least my American house guests.

Saturday 26th July

Even from inside our flat, you can hear the hubbub that happens every time the media congregates for an exciting arrival or departure at the Black Door.

From our back windows, the children peek out into the garden to see Gordon with Barack Obama, the man with the 'audacity' to hope to become the first black President of the United States. The two men are sitting on cane basket chairs on the back terrace having tea. We can see Gordon speaking earnestly with lots of hand movements to emphasis his points. Obama is leaning forward just as earnestly, taking in whatever is being said, and occasionally adding his own comments. From what I can see, these two men are getting on just fine, while their advisers from both sides are also meeting inside the building. Everyone is very taken with key Obama strategist, David Axelrod, who arrives dressed casually carrying a backpack, and heads straight for Gordon's key election adviser, David Muir.

Mid morning I take the boys, together with Sean and his family, over to the White Room to say hello to the Senator. We talk about impending holidays and the Senator says he is looking forward to his summer break in Hawaii. Gordon and Obama stand by the fireplace to pose for an official photo, only for Izzy to poke her head through Obama's legs. Having two daughters himself, Obama takes it all in his stride with a big smile.

Yet again, Obama raises with me the issue of maternal health, and tells me he looks forward to my meeting his wife, Michelle.

Meanwhile, outside the room, one of Gordon's aides is very cross that Gordon and Obama were able to go outside the garden walls and wander around Horse Guards Parade when this had been expressly forbidden earlier. I am, however, very sympathetic to the custodian who unlocked the gate. It would be very difficult to say 'no can do' when it's the PM standing there with the favourite Presidential candidate. Certainly, the unsuspecting tourists and passers-by got a bit of a shock.

After a final, unscheduled extra meeting in the study between Gordon and Obama, the visit ends and goodbyes are made. Obama holds a short press conference for the assembled media outside. When asked about Gordon's popularity he says it is just a natural reflection of being in office: 'There have been months when I'm a genius and months when I'm an idiot if you read the newspapers. It seems [to me] I'm pretty much the same guy during this process.' Just in saying those words, today I think he is a genius, and understands political life all too well.

Half an hour later, we are in our car and off to Suffolk for a fortnight. We have rented a big house near Southwold. Amusingly, our landlord is a successful paparazzi photographer called Dave Hogan, famed for his celebrity portraits and famous pictures from Live Aid. A separate house on the grounds is able to house the protection team and back-up from the PM's office.

Sunday 27th July

The phones don't stop ringing for the first days of the holiday. The newspaper fallout from the by-election defeat is very negative for Gordon. Separately, the World Trade Talks are continuing and Peter Mandelson calls in to keep Gordon apprised of the slow but occasionally positive progress being made with some countries, such as Brazil and France. The holiday is also interrupted for a few moments by excitable calls from London about an article David Miliband has written in the *Guardian*. It seems like speculation follows us wherever we go now but, as usual, Gordon responds to it by focusing on the big stuff: I try to keep up when he talks to me about Ben Bernanke's thesis on the US depression of the 1930s. Gordon has brought his usual huge pile of holiday reading material with him – this year the novels are noticeably fewer in number, and the history books on past recessions far more noticeable.

Gordon has booked himself a local personal trainer, Millie Dobie, to keep up his running and take up Pilates, too. Poor Millie feels the sharp end of our tabloid press when they start to pry into her private life. I imagine they just went for her because she is an attractive, fit-looking woman. Whatever they print, she is clearly a good trainer as Gordon is looking fitter than ever.

We have several friends nearby, and join up with Emma Freud and Richard Curtis and various other families to combine children's activities and meals together at the end of days on the beach, or pony riding, or visiting the giant maize maze. We have a memorable outing to the Dingley Dell pig farm with a full tractor-trailer tour.

Tuesday 29th July

We join Richard and Emma at their house for dinner in the evening with nearby holidaying friends, including director Paul Greengrass and Jo Kaye, food critic Tracey MacLeod and writer Harry Ritchie, for a meal. As we arrive, Richard takes great delight in introducing us to his Suffolk neighbours, Emma's cousin the novelist Esther Freud and her actor husband David Morrissey, who played Gordon in the TV drama, *The Deal*. This gave Sean the opportunity to say, 'Gordon, I would like to introduce you to ... Gordon.'

Although both of us have enjoyed many of David's performances, *The Deal* is one that we actually missed – though we have been told often that David was unnervingly good in the part. Thankfully, he seems to have warmed to Gordon from his close study of his early years in Parliament and they hit it off straight away. I can't imagine what it must be like to meet someone you have 'acted', and meeting someone who has pretended to be you is pretty weird, too.

We have a wonderful meal seated around a big table in the centre of Emma's barn, and finish the evening with one of Richard's legendary, heart-warming toasts. Richard singled out the work done by many people around the table for international development and particularly for Africa – he was especially generous about Gordon and me, but we do all go back many years with this work, and there is still much to do.

*

Our boys have the happiest of times, playing with friends, and lots of time with their dad, too, down on the beach. The highlight is possibly the trip with Dad and fellow Raith Rovers fan Harry and his sons to the Hollywood cinema in Lowestoft to see the latest kids' summer release.

Sunday 3rd August

Our eighth wedding anniversary falls in the middle of the holiday. As ever, Gordon asks me if I want to go out somewhere lovely for dinner and I think of a romantic table for two, and a cosy neighbouring table of detectives, and I decline. So, as usual: he asks, I decline, we stay in and have a meal. Mela has timed her arrival from her own holiday break perfectly and immediately instructs us to go out to the garden and have a drink while she takes charge of the boys. This is bliss – feet up in a garden chair, glass of cold white wine and the company of my husband with no talk of work or anything dull and domestic. A little precious moment to treasure.

Wednesday 20th August

We return to London and one of the first people Gordon asks to see is Shriti, who has been keeping a close watch on the global financial situation. There is clearly a growing problem and a large number of the world's heads of government are enquiring about Gordon's thoughts for the solution to the economic downturn. I think that this is all Gordon and Alistair Darling must think about at the moment.

We get ready to travel to Beijing to attend the closing of the Olympics and the official handover to London 2012. As we are still in the middle of the school holidays I have also booked seats for John, Fraser and Mela to travel with us which makes it a great treat for everyone.

Our flight goes first to Oman where we wait for a day and a night while Gordon goes off to visit our brave troops in Helmand, and meet President Karzai of Afghanistan.

Gordon returns full of admiration as ever for our troops, who are working in tough conditions. They are clearly all enjoying the British success in the Olympics and the Afghan people have been really uplifted by their first ever Olympic medal – a bronze in Taekwando. Gordon also met President Karzai's little son, who is Fraser's age, and was quite taken by the little chap, who leads a difficult life in the high-protection presidential compound.

Friday 22nd August

We receive a wonderful warm red carpet welcome in Beijing and Gordon starts his visit with a long private meeting with President Hu of China. Then we head off to find out the latest on our British athletes, with Tessa Jowell and Lord Coe. Our tally so far is 15 golds, and 35 medals overall.

We meet in the Fencing Hall to watch Heather Fell in her Pentathlon efforts. Simon Clegg, head of our UK mission for the British Olympic Association, brings us up to speed on all the behind-the-scenes organisation. I discover that in Simon's former life he was the minder for ski-jumper Eddie 'the Eagle' Edwards, at the Calgary Winter Olympics. My brother Sean is working on a film script about Eddie the Eagle's life, so we have much to talk about there.

Our next treat is to watch the 500 metres canoeing final, and to see Tim Brabants win Britain's sixteenth Gold. His coach Albert Woods is seated next to us and can't quite get an angle on the finishing line when it is crossed. I can see clearly that Brabants has won but Albert needs the reassurance of the scoreboard before he breathes again.

Gordon alternates his meetings between the British athletes and the Chinese Government. He meets Chris Hoy, complete with his three cycling gold medals that have captured the attention of everyone back home. He is modest, full of praise for the rest of the cycling team and chats happily to Gordon as they pose for photos.

Before the day is over we visit the National Stadium, our first time back in the Bird's Nest now that it is finished and full of cheering people. We watch our British relay team, and see Usain Bolt of Jamaica win a new world record. The afternoon count for Team GB is now 18 golds and 42 medals overall.

Saturday 23rd August

Today, we see Tom Daley diving in the architecturally breathtaking Water Cube. We have a full tour of the Olympic Village where our athletes stay in their B&Q sponsored mini-apartments, and we watch football seated with David Beckham back in the Bird's Nest. He and Gordon just talk football and no one else in the stands – not me, not Boris Johnson, not even Lord Coe – can get a word in edgeways. Gordon is exploring how we can create a British football team for the Olympics, meeting with either great support or great opposition whoever he talks to, but never indifference.

Our final commitment is to attend the spectacular closing ceremony in the National Stadium. This is a big show featuring many, many performers, but the sight of the athletes marching out their flags is the most moving thing. Our London set is quirky but grows on you as it unfolds from a red double-decker bus.

We then join Tessa Jowell, Lord Coe and others at London House for the official moment of handover to Britain. As we walk inside Gordon is faced with the unexpected but nonetheless welcome experience of Jackie Chan popping up to offer himself as the first unpaid volunteer for 2012.

The moment for the handover duly comes with all the TV cameras focused on the Mayor of London, Boris Johnson, who waves the Union Jack four times in line with IOC rules. He then gives a jocular speech claiming that though the Chinese may excel at table tennis it was, in fact, invented in Britain, to be specific, in the stately homes of England. Gordon congratulates the Mayor on his flag-waving and teases him about his efforts to further Anglo–Chinese relations.

He goes on to congratulate China on their success as 2008 hosts, and to open up our own Olympic welcome: 'London is proud to be Olympic London. Britain is proud to be Olympic Britain.' With the cheers at the end someone is heard shouting, 'I love you, Gordon,' and glitter cannons shoot off prematurely just as Gordon finishes speaking to a huge cheer from the crowd.

We all face great wrath from the Mayor's team who are convinced that someone from Gordon's team has set them off deliberately. It would seem the cannons were actually set to go off when the Mayor concluded the handover with another flag wave amidst a glitter explosion. Truthfully, I don't think anyone did it deliberately but there is no way to assuage the Mayor's team's belief in our magic powers.

Wednesday 27th August

Once we are home in Scotland, I set the TV to record some of the speeches from the Democratic Convention. I am interested to hear Michelle Obama's speech, which is strikingly proficient. A recent article reported that Mrs Obama goes to the gym four times a week. If true, it has certainly paid off – she looks terrific.

Hillary Clinton has already conceded her defeat in the Presidential Race and gives her speech to support Barack Obama at the Democratic Convention today and I think it is one of the best, most moving addresses I have ever heard. It certainly speaks to me. I love her reference to Harriet Tubman, who led the call for the fight against slavery. '[She] had one piece of advice: "If you hear the dogs, keep going. If you see the torches in the woods, keep going. If they're shouting after you, keep going. Don't ever stop. Keep going. If you want a taste of freedom, keep going."

'And even in the darkest of moments that is what Americans have done. We have found the faith to keep going ... And remember, before we can keep going, we've got to get going by electing Barack Obama the next President of the United States.' Huge applause.

Cut to me on my sofa at home, tears pouring down face.

Later I talk to Gordon and say I wonder if, maybe, just a thought, no need to decide, if I could, should, maybe, speak at the conference, perhaps to introduce him. He is immediately interested in the idea, asking what I think I want to say. I haven't decided yet, and the idea of speaking at such a huge event is very scary, but it is a thought that I can't shake since listening to Senator Clinton.

CHAPTER 16

Global Financial Meltdown

Saturday 13th September

Baroness Thatcher is a guest for lunch at Chequers today along with her trusted private secretary, Mark Worthington. All politics aside, it is a privilege to invite her back to Chequers, where she has not been for many years. She seems to enjoy the lunch, which has been chosen as one of her favourites (chef Alan Lavender, who started at Chequers during her premiership, keeps a record of everyone's preferences). We are joined by historian Sir Martin Gilbert and Esther, his wife, who both join Gordon in talking to her about her favourite moments in office. There is a classic moment when discussing Ronald Reagan and Lady T says, 'It all worked because he was more afraid of me than I was of him.' Another favourite Lady T quote comes when discussing her role in ending the Cold War with Presidents Reagan and Gorbachev: 'Oh, I could be very determined at times.' Quite so.

In the evening, reinforcements arrive to give Gordon a bit of support: Kirsty McNeill, Gordon's new head of external relations and a talented speechwriter whom he first spotted when she combined a leading role in Make Poverty History with securing a big swing for Labour as a candidate at the last election; and David Muir, his chief political strategist who seems to understand instinctively that Gordon's biggest strength is his authenticity – that he's not a celebrity. Rather he is a clever, tough guy who is focused on the big things that matter to families.

A small number of MPs are ordering nomination papers, which is the only way a serving Labour leader can be removed if enough do it. While no one thinks these MPs will get anywhere near enough nominations, it is a very damaging thing to do to the party as a whole. The newspapers can only report an awful story for us, and Gordon and the government still need to focus on what needs to be done to run the country in these challenging global economic times. It is disturbing that this is our own party – and former friends – who are doing this to us.

Sunday 14th September

Jo Rowling calls me to say that she wants to do something to support the Labour Party, and specifically Gordon's leadership. What a woman. I love it that she does what she believes – and hats off to her and Neil for supporting us. I tell Gordon, who is visibly moved by the news, and agrees that she should speak to the election fundraiser, Jon Mendelsohn, to follow up on whatever she is thinking. I alert Jon to expect his phone to ring with a call from Jo so he does not think that it is a prank call.

Gordon is hard at work on the telephone, speaking a lot with Alistair Darling, Jeremy Heywood at Number 10, and Shriti. They all know that the investment bank Lehman Brothers is going into meltdown tomorrow, and that the mighty Merrill Lynch has already had to be rescued by Bank of America.

When Gordon and I talk later, I suggest that his command of the global financial situation might well overshadow the rebellious behaviour of some short-sighted MPs. Gordon is particularly worried about HBOS (Halifax Bank of Scotland) and the need to amend legislation to allow relevant takeovers if a big problem does arise.

How can one person be smart enough to do all these things and think ahead *and* worry about division in the ranks, too? I want him to be better supported internally but on talking to Kirsty and David, they are much more positive and reassure me that Gordon has a team of real talent – it's just a question of pointing them in the same direction and focusing on the big questions. Right now, these are about how we can save people's jobs and homes and businesses.

Monday 15th September

As Lehman Brothers files for bankruptcy, this is obviously top of the economic agenda. Surprisingly, the Labour rebels are still getting a fair degree of coverage in the UK media.

Gordon goes with Jeremy Heywood to an event at Citibank in the evening while I keep to the Downing Street programme. It is London Fashion Week and we are holding an event at Number 10 for the fashion industry. I am most excited about this. It is not just my interest in fashion and the prospect of meeting so many of our brilliant designers, but the feeling that this is a moment for the industry to engage seriously with the trade organisations and government departments (not to mention a good time to sound out some potential 'faces' or contacts for the maternal mortality campaign). Hilary Riva, the dynamic CEO of the British Fashion Council, speaks to a select group of their representatives about the fashion industry's agenda. Then the front door is opened up to a full house of designers, models, stylists and media. The room is very buzzy, and I am followed around by reporters who are literally taking down notes on every 'Hello' and 'How are you?'

Tuesday 16th September

Gordon starts the day with first a full Cabinet meeting and then a political Cabinet meeting (where the civil servants are banished for their own good). Gordon's main priority is HBOS, which looks certain to go under – though he does seem to have a plan, and there is a strong sense of momentum building for plans to tackle the banking meltdown.

The political Cabinet meeting is important, as a junior minister has just resigned from the Scotland office in protest at Gordon's leadership (although I fear he may have thrown his whole career away for nothing). It seems pretty certain that the financial crisis is going to become everyone's top priority.

Wednesday 17th September

Today Lloyds Bank looks like it will rescue HBOS as part of a merger, so the big focus today is on whether this will work.

Rather incongruously, given everything that is going on back at Downing Street, I am due to join Naomi Campbell at her Fashion for Relief event at the Natural History Museum, as part of London Fashion Week. Given the fashion industry's role as a leading contributor to our powerful, creative economy, I am more than happy to support the evening. Naomi is also dedicating the funds raised at the event to the White Ribbon Alliance, which makes her a girl after my own heart.

Once again, I get equipped to cope with being in supermodel proximity with high heels and a little red dress. Two weeks ago, I turned up for the promotional photo to find myself squeezed between Naomi, Erin O'Connor and Jade Parfitt. I am about 5ft 9in, and I still felt like the short person in that line-up.

On arrival, I do various TV clips explaining where the Fashion for Relief fund will go, and then position myself backstage. Trudie Styler is hosting the proceedings and after an introduction from the British Fashion Council's Harold Tillman, I address the crowd to explain the cause they are supporting tonight. I then get a front-row seat to watch the cavalcade of supermodels, famous faces and socialites parading down the catwalk. The 'walkers' range from Lizzie Jagger and Tyson to Ronan Keating and Victoria Pendleton wearing her Olympic medals. Vivienne Westwood and Tracey Emin bring the crowd to their feet as they walk out together, and the finale arrives with Cilla Black and her amazing legs. Then the bidding starts for the clothes, raising extraordinary sums despite the economic uncertainty.

Thursday 18th September

Approval comes from Barclays to buy the remnants of Lehman Brothers. But the stock market prices are tumbling again and the world is feeling very weird. The Governor of the Bank of England is across in Number 11, so plenty of Treasury people are buzzing about.

I head off to host a reception for 100 or so volunteers from the charity Wellbeing of Women. The coming year will be very challenging for their fundraising but these women have an indomitable attitude that might benefit many of the City stockbrokers. The Chair of Wellbeing of Women is actually Sir Victor Blank, who is also the chairman of Lloyds TSB bank, so he is excused from attending the charity gathering tonight as that would have really caused confusion for the Treasury officials inside, and the media outside the black door.

In the evening I speak at the annual Women's Aid gala dinner in a big marquee in Berkeley Square. It is possibly the worst night in years to be holding a fundraiser. Gordon is coming with me for the reception, but it takes a while to extricate him from the stream of international phone calls. We travel in the car with full flashing lights and woowoos, which adds to the sense of impending disaster, but as soon as I arrive I realise that at the very least, this event will be just fine.

Gordon and I pose for photographs with Gordon and Tana Ramsay, who are the hosts. The marquee is beautifully set up with low lighting and sparkling glassware on the tables. It has the feeling of being out in the middle of nowhere, or perhaps on an ocean liner; the feeling that these are the only people left in the world. Gordon chats for about 20 minutes with the guests, who all crowd around him with high expectations that he will fix the financial crisis somehow. I recognise Paul and Alison Myners, Trevor and Daniela Pears (from the Pears Foundation), MT Rainey (from Horse's Mouth), Mariella Frostrup and Stuart Rose. After that, Gordon has to disappear quickly to take a call from President Sarkozy. News breaks quickly that he has taken decisive action to ban sales of short shares.

The dinner goes smoothly enough and everyone is gripped by Gordon Ramsay's sister, Diane, as she speaks movingly about growing up in a household terrorised by domestic violence at the hands of their alcoholic father. Even so, the auction is hard work, and the money raised amounts to about half the previous year's dinner. Surely a sign of what is to come.

Friday 19th September

I travel up to Manchester for the annual Labour Party Conference to meet Gordon, and see the reports that share prices have recovered about 70 per cent of their loss. All is more cheerful in the financial world but by no means back to normal. Gordon is more or less permanently on the phone.

We stop to visit a wonderful sports academy and secondary school in the North West, another example of a great Labour achievement, before we arrive at the Radisson Hotel. The latest polls show that Labour is trailing 20 points, which means that there is a lot of work to do.

After sorting out where Gordon and the kids will stay, I slip out and return to London. I had promised some time ago that I would be part of the Maggie's Centres' annual Night Hike, so Konrad and I take the train south, and join the walkers late in the evening.

Saturday 20th September

Having jumped back on a train up to Manchester first thing this morning, I arrive back to find out that everyone is greatly boosted by the news of JK Rowling's £1 million donation to the Labour Party. Much-needed funds and a real show of confidence from her in what Gordon is doing.

Gil McNeil arrives and we talk about whether I might introduce Gordon ahead of his speech on Tuesday afternoon. I have asked the view of a few people: Sue Nye, Charlie Whelan, Emma Freud and even Jo Rowling. They all respond positively, but they also know that, in the end, the decision should be mine and Gordon's, and his closest political team. No one actually says, 'Sarah, that's a terrible idea,' which is what I had half-expected. I pick a moment in between international calls and ask Gordon again. He thinks it is a great idea but only if I am really comfortable in myself. We decide to ponder it some more.

As I think about what I would say if I was up on the platform, one phrase bubbles up in my head: 'I would like to introduce my husband, our party leader, your Prime Minister – Gordon Brown.' I think this says it all.

If I think too much about the reality of getting up on to the big conference stage in front of all those cameras, and the people and the weight of expectation when they spot me there, I feel anxiety rising and I just want to push it away from my mind. I wonder if I am avoiding a final decision about my speech so I can reduce the amount of time in advance I have to feel gut-wrenchingly nervous.

Sunday 21st September

The Labour rebels have failed to recruit any more support but there is still a sulky, aggressive tone to the presence of this small group at the conference which, you can tell from the general chatter, is bugging the other attendees.

I go off to speak at my first fringe event for Labour Women's Network with some of our key Labour women parliamentarians:

Barbara Follett, Gilly Merron and Glenys Kinnock. The session is on the maternal mortality campaign and invites lots of questions from the floor. What impresses me is how much my fellow speakers and the audience are all already doing to engage with the campaign. It seems to connect with women everywhere.

Gordon and I both attend the conference church service and visit six receptions before returning to our room.

Monday 22nd September

Gordon is very focused on the final run-through of his speech before turning his attention back to the financial markets. Much seems to rest on the success or otherwise of a Lloyds TSB deal with HBOS.

Back at the hotel, Gordon raises the subject of whether I might introduce him at the conference tomorrow and after a quick heads-together with his team, he says YES. I find a computer and settle down to write. I am very clear about my purpose in introducing Gordon: I want people to see him through my eyes – as the great gorgeous man I know, who cares and works hard and does a good job for the country. As I write I don't feel nervous; I just have a very heightened sense of anticipation, but I expect the nerves to start to show tomorrow. Without question this is the most crucial public speaking event I have ever done to date.

David Muir and Stephen Carter make small suggestions to my draft but leave it pretty much unchanged. As it is a personal address, it need only be the words I want to say. Stephen never stops encouraging me. He has rightly identified that it is my confidence that needs building up. He also gives me a great piece of advice: that I should already know in my head how I will handle the reception when I step out on to the stage; how I will stand and smile while the audience applauds.

*

Alistair Darling does very well with his speech to the conference. I know that Maggie will able to relax a bit now, but not me quite yet. Gordon and I have an evening of 14 different receptions and then some sleep.

Tuesday 23rd September

Finally, the day of Gordon's speech dawns. I am determined to keep myself busy so I go for a swim, and book the hairdresser from the lobby salon to come and do my hair. Someone books a make-up artist for me, too, as the HDTV close-ups are pretty remorseless.

At 1.30 p.m., Gordon and I walk across to the conference hall, where the sound and lighting people have made some last-minute timing adjustments to accommodate me. I feel my heart pounding in my chest, and silently remind myself over and over again that I am not the one making the big speech today. I want to do this so much, but also feel pretty terrified. As the backstage waiting room is rather tiny, I leave Gordon on his own and have a final pep talk with Stephen Carter.

I am then ushered to the side of the stage and told I have a minute to go. I can feel the adrenaline surging through my body and feel ready to run a mile or more. Then the minutes stretch to two, and then two more. As the adrenaline subsides and crashes, I feel a bit sick and start to hyperventilate. I feel Gil grab my arm and walk me round in circles. I am very pale, then very flushed, and then pale again.

I just keep walking until suddenly it is time to go on. I walk out on to the giant stage and look out at the huge audience beyond the teeming mass of cameras. People slowly start to recognise that I am not walking towards my seat, but directly to the podium instead. I reach the lectern and the cameras all swivel their lenses on to me in one big movement as the audience rises to their feet and start clapping.

As I smile and hold the lectern, I have time in my mind to thank Stephen for his advice. I can spot Neil and Glenys Kinnock,

John Prescott, Swraj Paul and Mary Goudie in the front row. Neil gives me a thumbs up and silently urges me on, even though I don't think he has a clue what I am about to do.

Looking the other way, I see the Cabinet Ministers seated together and fix on Yvette Cooper, seated by her husband Ed Balls. They and the Kinnocks suddenly remind me of parents at a child's first school play: however well I do today, they will think I have done the best thing ever. When the clapping stops I start to speak, knowing that I am saying exactly what I want to say:

> *Good afternoon, everyone. I asked if I could have a chance today to talk briefly to you, because one of the privileges of my life over recent years has been the opportunity to meet so many different people and extraordinary people. These have all been great moments, often private ones, but always meaningful, and I thank you all. I remember the warm welcome you gave me and Gordon at Conference after our wedding. And I'm so proud that every day I see him motivated to work for the best interests of people all around the country.*

I then introduce the film showing Labour's achievements and move back a bit to watch the big screen. I can feel my legs shaking, however, and move back to the lectern for a safe hold.

At the end of the film, I introduce 'my husband, the leader of the Labour Party, your Prime Minister – Gordon Brown'. The music goes up – '(Your Love Keeps Lifting Me) Higher and Higher' – and Gordon comes on stage, beaming, and gives me a big kiss.

I sit in the front row and watch Gordon give the speech of his life – everything is brilliant: the content, the presentation, the man. There are standing ovations all the way through it. A huge roar goes up at the end and I join him on stage.

The rest of the day passes in a blur with many more receptions and meeting people everywhere. I know that today we have both done well and I hope Gordon's confidence is buoyed by the reaction – we will need it to see us through whatever lies ahead.

Wednesday 24th September

The 747 to New York is full of Britain's team for the United Nations General Assembly (which Gordon is to open this year with Ban Ki-moon) and Gordon's team for his many meetings with bankers, economists and world leaders in both New York and then Washington DC. I have my own packed programme for my campaign to get maternal mortality properly recognised as part of the poverty reduction goals.

Some of my fellow campaigners are on board with us (we found a clever system where they could buy up the spare seats on the official plane so that no cost was incurred by Number 10, other than for my government duties). Both Health Minister Ann Keen and Women's Minister Barbara Follett are here, but so too are Sarah Ferguson, Elle MacPherson and Heather McGregor. The press are very intrigued by our extra on-board guests, but I notice when Elle goes to brief them on the campaign not many serious questions get asked.

I start the New York visit with the Important Dinner for Women that follows the one held in Davos. This time we are in the Tao Restaurant and I am hosting the event with HM Queen Rania and Wendi Murdoch. I am definitely flying the British flag fashionwise with a black sparkly Graeme Black dress, diamond hoops from Garrard and the highest Brian Atwood heels.

The new US Vice-Presidential candidate Governor Sarah Palin is the surprise guest at the pre-dinner reception so our photographs all include her. I don't get much opportunity in the scrum to talk to her so am not entirely clear if she knows she is at an event for a campaign whose support for maternal health includes available family planning.

At dinner, I am seated between Dr Margaret Chan, the head of the World Health Organization, and Susie Buffett, a wealthy philanthropist and daughter of the legendary financial investor, Warren Buffett. My table includes Sarah Ferguson and Elle, but also

Gursharan Kaur, the gracious wife of the Prime Minister of India, and the heavenly Tammy Haddad who films everything as she goes for her Tam Cam and literally files the story to *Newsweek* from her table.

I spent time talking to Aerin Lauder (from Estée Lauder cosmetics), Vera Wang, Whoopi Goldberg and Martha Stewart, who all pledge to help the campaign. Wendi welcomes everyone and reduces us to silence as she speaks of her own Chinese grand-mother dying in childbirth, leaving her mother alone as an infant. Queen Rania gives a confident, polished address, quoting poetry, and we watch a film made by Richard Curtis and Emma Freud with the song 'Every Time We Say Goodbye' running hauntingly on the soundtrack.

I give my speech and ask everyone to play their part in the campaign, showing images of all that we have achieved so far with our gatherings and demonstrations around the world.

When I sit down I realise how far I have come with my public speaking. It is not that I don't feel nervous any more – I certainly do – but it is more that I can channel that nervousness and adrenalin into a good performance, looking straight at my audience, rather than a toe-curling, anxious-making, mumbling monologue directed at the floor. Today I feel good that I have got my message across and it is really heartwarming how many women come and tell me how moved to act they are by the message they have heard tonight.

Diana Taylor (the girlfriend of the Mayor of New York) does a final call to action and starts collecting the pledges for help. The $2 billion from USAID announced this week rather tops the lot, but many articles in newspapers, donations, and other ways to support are offered.

At the end of the event, as I say goodbye to all the wonderful women who came this evening, I sit with a glass of cold white wine and see my old school friends, Jane Brien and Suzi Price, who have come along, and my old university pal, Lucy Kneebone. They tease me a little bit about the evening, just to remind me not to think too highly of myself for consorting with the powerful and the famous!

*

When I get back to the hotel room Gordon is already asleep, having held endless financial meetings ahead of the impending collapse of capitalism (I'm only half-joking) *and* he has to open the United Nations General Assembly in the morning with Secretary-General Ban Ki-moon! I realise I have not eaten at all this evening and raid the fruit bowl, and find an emergency Kit Kat before turning in, too.

Thursday 25th September

The New York trip is jam-packed. My itinerary for today goes something like this:

8 a.m.   Maternal health breakfast with First Ladies
10 a.m.   Meeting with heads of the UN
12 noon   Lunch meeting on gender issues
2 p.m.   Education for All event with PM Kevin Rudd of
                Australia
4 p.m.   Session on malaria hosted by Ray Chambers, the UN
                Special Envoy
6 p.m.   Meeting with the national heads of the White Ribbon
                Alliance and Christy Turlington Burns (with filming
                for her *No Woman, No Cry* film)
8 p.m.   Dinner with Mayor Bloomberg and Bono and business
                leaders
9 p.m.   Small dinner for our campaign champions at Soho
                House, New York. Joined by Bob Geldof, Richard
                Curtis, Emma Freud and Christy Turlington Burns.

A long day.

Friday 26th September

I attend a breakfast on autism, and then head out to Columbia University to the Mailman School of Public Health to meet medical heads and academics to look at how they can play their part, too. I am greeted by Professor Lynn Freedman, who has been one of my heroines in this fight and I am thrilled to meet her. I have loved the fact that as an academic she is still unafraid to bring feminism into her work in looking for intellectual solutions to the problem of mothers and babies dying unnecessarily.

Lynn and the acting Dean, Linda Fried, have also set up a very important call for me before the meeting starts, so I have the privilege of speaking to Professor Allan Rosenfield, the Dean Emeritus and the man who wrote the original article back in 1985 entitled: 'Where is the M in MCH?' (maternal and child health). He was the first to correctly identify that maternal health was being ignored with all the focus going to child health, and that losing mothers was of no help to the surviving child.

Professor Rosenfield is suffering cruelly from last stage ALS, a disease of the nervous system that is robbing him of his ability to move and speak, but not to think. I talk to him on the speakerphone with the help of his wife, Clare, at the other end. He thanks me for the work that I am doing to raise the profile of the issue and to make it visible to government leaders. I explain that I think this is the moment when people can listen, and I am ready and willing to be the noisy person. He is very well informed about our work, and about the achievements of the UK's Department for International Development. As I talk to him, I am sitting in his office, looking at a photograph of this handsome man taken at the height of his professional life. I reflect on how we just never know what will happen in our lives, and why it is so important that we all look out for each other as human beings.

I finish my day with a private meeting with the UN Special Envoy for Malaria, Ray Chambers, who counsels me to keep the focus on community-health workers so we can all support each other. Ray has done so well and I listen to him very hard.

*

I also get a flying visit from my godmother, Irene Skolnick, my mother's great pal from her university days who hails from Manhattan. We meet in the lobby of the hotel where Gordon is speaking on stage to the Clinton Global Initiative. As he gives the closing speech, Irene and I chat, and then I am dragged away, back to our giant 747. I suddenly feel very tired.

The flight takes off and lands an hour or so later in Washington DC, where Gordon is to stop off and meet President Bush at the White House. Despite the pace at which everyone has been working, no else is ready to stop and seem all charged up, ready for a big White House meeting. I, on the other hand, have reached my physical limit for today and make my excuses to Gordon who completely understands that enough is enough for me. I don't even think about the fact I am actually declining a visit to the White House! I don't think I will offend anyone protocolwise, as I am pretty sure my economic views are not required for this meeting. So after Gordon and his team disembark, I have a quick meal with Christianne on our little tables and then put on flight pyjamas, brush my teeth and tuck myself up in an airline seat until they return.

I experience a tiredness like nothing I have ever quite felt before: despite the heating on the plane, I am almost shaking with cold and my fingers and toes are literally going numb at the tips. I have definitely passed the point of no return. I vaguely remember everyone returning, and certainly remember nothing of the actual flight until being woken up for landing.

Monday 29th September

Home again, and Gordon brings his familiar big bag of papers and handwritten notes with him to the flat and continues working.

We turn on the TV and watch as the international action in the global financial crisis continues. When we go back downstairs, we can see that everyone is mesmerised by the TV coverage of the US Congress voting down TARP, the US financial rescue bill. US Speaker Nancy Pelosi and Senator Chris Dodd are speaking on TV.

Having had such decisive action in the UK, it seems an extraordinary system that the US has, which has taken ten days to achieve a plan, and then only to see it fail to get the votes.

Tuesday 30th September

Ireland announces its financial plan today to protect savings.

Thursday 2nd October

Another long day in the history of the global financial crisis. Everyone has been working flat out for so many days and weeks now that I just don't know how they all keep going. I hope that people across Britain understand what a solid job they get with Gordon and the current government team in charge.

Ireland passes legislation to guarantee bank deposits, and the US Senate now comfortably passes its $700 million Wall Street Rescue Plan so it can go back to Congress, where everyone thinks it will now get through.

As a separate news story, but striking me as a stark reminder of how badly politics can work, I also hear on the car radio that the Metropolitan Police Chief Sir Ian Blair has resigned in what appears to be a row with London Mayor Boris Johnson. As soon as I get back to my office I put through a call to Felicity Blair at her home to tell her how sorry I am this has happened. She is furious, feisty and rather magnificent.

Friday 3rd October

Today Gordon is announcing a Cabinet reshuffle, but I am busy with a special assembly at my son's school.

I get a surprise when I discover that Gordon has appointed Peter Mandelson as his new Business Secretary. Strange as it may seem to others, I don't really know Peter, other than to say hello. This is because he and Gordon have not been close for many years, and certainly not in the length of time I have known Gordon, so there have been no occasions when we have spent time with each other. As the European Commissioner, Peter has also been based in Brussels, which has taken him away from Westminster for some years, though he and Gordon have spoken, mostly by phone, a fair bit in recent months about Trade issues.

We have a small yellow bear in our house that plays John Lennon's 'Imagine' when you pull the string in its tummy – it was a gift from Peter sent when John was born in 2003. It is a great favourite, and reminds me that some friendships do run very deep – even across a separation. So, too, does Gordon's first act on hearing of the death of Peter's mum some years ago, in the midst of a time when they had lost contact. He had picked up the phone straight away and called to offer condolences. I remember asking Gordon why he had called – instead of just writing – and he had replied: 'Because I know just how much Peter loved his mum.'

I discover through the day that everyone has a view about Peter's return to the UK government, divided equally between those passionately in favour, and those firmly against. I am entirely open-minded, and look forward to what happens next.

In the evening, Gordon and I dash off to a reception at Lancaster House hosted for the Olympic athletes. It is a wet Friday night and no one has been asked to bring a guest, which seems a shame. Still, everyone is there, and we take great delight in congratulating the athletes we saw win medals in Beijing. We give Rebecca Adlington a lift to the station; the least we can do given the weather.

Wednesday 8th October

Lots of people at Number 10 and the Treasury had to work through the night last night. I certainly did not hear Gordon get back to the flat, as I was long asleep by then. I hear that Shriti went home at one point, showered, changed and returned. Alistair Darling was woken at 2 a.m. and was immediately hard at work.

Gordon comes up to the flat to get a bit more sleep in preparation for tackling the financial rescue strategy. It is clear that the crisis is getting quite hair-raising and the numbers very big. Gordon is up again at 5 a.m.

Rather unusually, he wakes me, too.

Gordon tells me that I should be prepared to leave Downing Street. I don't feel even a bit startled by this news, despite not knowing the details of what he and the government are preparing to do. The backdrop to the global financial crisis has been so immense that it has felt throughout as if I should expect any outcome at any stage, and probably whatever I least expect. What Gordon knows at this point is that the announcements that he and Alistair Darling will make today are so huge that resignation will be the only option if things do not work out as the day unfolds.

What transpires, however, is that Gordon has the best day of his premiership so far, with the faultless announcement of the UK's huge rescue package that has taken so many days to prepare. Gordon holds a joint press conference with Alistair and does PMQs to follow Alistair's statement as Chancellor of the Exchequer in the House of Commons.

Even this week's Parliamentary Labour Party meeting had gone well, so the rebellious unrest of last month is quietening down as the seriousness of the financial situation hits home.

Thursday 9th October

Having had the rescue package well received, Gordon and his team are already talking about what will happen next, and predicting which banks will need large sums of money. It is already clear that some of the heads of the banks will need to resign and new people take over the helm.

Alistair Darling is off to Washington DC to the International Monetary Fund to build support for this bank recapitalisation plan.

The general consensus seems to be that Gordon and the team around him are the only people with the relevant experience to tackle the crisis. It is certainly stretching him, Shriti and the others to the limit. Shriti has been one of the big driving forces behind the rescue package, but it is no secret that Treasury officials find her challenging to deal with, so I doubt she will get much credit from them for her input at the moment.

Friday 10th October

This evening, our boys are off for a sleepover with their Auntie Clare and their cousins, which is exciting for them, and gives me an evening with Gordon. I insist that he come out to the theatre and demonstrate a bit of Blitz spirit, by showing that a cultural life can go on in the midst of a banking meltdown. There is a play at the Royal Court set on the eve of a US general election called *Now or Later*. It turns out to be both a terrific play and packed with excellent performances (and not overly long). We have the added bonus of running into Kevin Spacey, who is the creative director at the Old Vic, and Russell Brand, who we don't know, but it is amusing, nonetheless, for me to introduce Gordon to him. Actually, Russell does none of his bad-boy routine and is very charming to Gordon.

Monday 13th October

In any biography of a prime minister's spouse, there is always the story of officials walking into the bedroom with urgent news. In over ten years at Number 11, this never happened to me, but early this morning, poor Shriti comes upstairs with the duty clerk at 5 a.m. and tentatively knocks on the door. I think it is John, who does not always want to stay in his own bed, and say rather grumpily, 'Seriously, not now, you need to go back to bed and let

Dad sleep,' only to look up and see Shriti standing nervously in the doorway. She has some urgent new figures that Alistair wants conveyed to Gordon directly. Gordon wants the information straight away so she talks from the open door, and then leaves him to get ready to head straight back downstairs to the office.

What happens to the banks today is something as close to nationalisation as I have ever seen. Billions of dollars and pounds are spent on shares. Many of the banks' senior executives are losing their jobs, and massive restructuring of the banks is taking place. It is also Margaret Thatcher's birthday today and while I don't think she would like the renationalisation one little bit, I think, dare I say it, she would be among the first to recognise Gordon's achievements these last weeks and months.

Fortunately, the banks recover massively and overall the strategy has been considered a success. The new Nobel Prize economist Paul Krugman announces that 'the Brown government has shown itself willing to think clearly about the financial crisis, and act quickly on its conclusions' in the *New York Times* and concludes, 'luckily for the world economy, Gordon Brown and his officials are making sense. And they may have shown us the way through this crisis'. Hank Paulson, the US Treasury Secretary, announces his plan to adopt a similar plan in the US, as do many European countries.

CHAPTER 17

On the Stump

Tuesday 14th October

Throughout the turmoil of the recent weeks, I have kept going with all the various charity events and WPM diary commitments that are needed more than ever in the financial downturn. These range from presenting an award to the girls' education in Africa charity, CAMFED (Campaign for Female Education), with Joan Armatrading, to hosting a Wellbeing of Women patrons meeting and joining Maggie Darling at her Dress for Success reception supporting women getting back into work after unemployment.

I have been working long hours, too, on Labour Party visits and keeping on top of all my paperwork and correspondence. I have school half-term soon and also plan to get involved with a by-election coming up near our home in Fife, both of which mean a chunk of days away from the London office. My long-serving project manager at PiggyBankKids, Joe Hewitt, is leaving to head to a new digital communications job, and his successor, Victoria Keene, has just had her first day. So we have a tearful goodbye for Joe, and a big welcome for Tor, at the PiggyBankKids Trustees meeting.

Friday 17th October

It is John's fifth birthday and we have a special weekend in Paris with Fraser, and John's best friend with his family. Gordon is able to travel with us, together with his Foreign Policy aide, Tom

Fletcher, as they have a lot of work to do together. As it is the weekend I suggest that Tom's wife, Louise, and little son, Charlie, join us too, which delights Fraser.

Saturday 18th October

We leave Gordon and Tom to work and the rest of us all head to Disneyland Paris for the day, which is a very welcome distraction and a great birthday treat. I do run into a few fellow Brits who stop and say hello, but most of the day is spent in a lovely, normal, entertain-the-kids way.

When we return to the Embassy we join Gordon and Tom again, and our hospitable and charming ambassador, Peter Westmacott and his wife, Susie, lay on a scrumptious traditional birthday tea, complete with little sandwich triangles and heavenly and (very French) chocolate gateau.

Tuesday 21st October

I am hosting a lunch in the State Dining Room at Number 10 for David Mixner, the renowned American gay rights activist. As I personally have no official budget for hospitality, I host this event myself. David is in town to take part in an Oxford Union American Debate, and I invite some of our own prominent gay and lesbian government ministers and advisers to meet him. I have a terrific response and a guest list that includes the Chief Whip Nick Brown; ministers Ben Bradshaw, Angela Eagle and Chris Bryant; Labour Party General Secretary Ray Collins; MEP Michael Cashman; and government aides Spencer Livermore, Seb Dance and Kirsty McNeill; plus basketball player John Amaechi, alongside Terrence Higgins Trust head Nick Partridge and Stonewall UK director Ben Summerskill. My corporate friends John Roberts and Stephen Whitehead also attend, plus Steven Guy, the LA writer who is en route to work with the brilliant charity Mothers2Mothers in South Africa. Not a bad line-up.

David shares with us the American experience of gay rights, and we all feel rightly proud that Britain has achieved so much more – with civil partnership, the repeal of Section 28, an equal age of consent, and much more. David speaks to the group, and we are all struck by his personal tale of being thrilled to be invited with his partner to a swanky Hollywood producer's house for dinner, only to find on arrival that they were the only two served their meal on paper plates. But there is a laugh when David Mixner asks me why I have not been more visible at lesbian, gay, bisexual and transgender (LGBT) events and I reply truthfully that I've never been invited. Everyone promises that this will be corrected.

During lunch, we determine that there has never been a lunch, dinner or even a snack in the history of Downing Street to recognise the LGBT community. Number 10 has held events for women, ethnic minorities, faith groups and differently abled people, but nothing for the LGBT community. Earlier in the year, Gordon did meet the Pride march organisers, and there was a charity reception for the Terrence Higgins Trust, but nothing that properly acknowledged a very large part of our community. When Kirsty and I tell Gordon, he immediately asks for this to be corrected and Kirsty is already looking at plans for how best Downing Street can recognise LGBT History Month next year.

Within 15 minutes of our guest's departure from Downing Street, there is a full and fairly accurate report in *Pink News* with a nice quote from Ben Bradshaw, and an invitation for me to next year's London Pride march.

I have a pretty good track record at not getting myself in too much trouble with the media and I do try and avoid controversy, but my brother Sean has invited me along to the UK premiere of *Anvil! The Story of Anvil*, a film he was involved in making. It is a sort of 'real-life Spinal Tap' biography of a failed heavy metal band from Toronto with the added bonus, after the screening, of a live performance.

I invite along my girlfriend Kathryn, and as an afterthought call my mum and stepdad for added family support. On my way out, I mention to Gordon's press guy that I am off to see *Anvil! The Story of Anvil* with the band. He looks slightly aghast and says, 'Sarah, whatever you do, just don't get photographed with the band.'

I head off with Kathryn, meet my parents and we all approach the crowd-control barriers at the cinema in Leicester Square, rather puzzled that this band would get so much attention. It turns out that Keanu Reeves is introducing the film, which explains the screaming girls. I try and creep around the edge to the entrance but am spotted by the film's PR woman. Before I know it, I am meeting the band on the red carpet with all the cameras clicking away. Too late, I spot that the band members are doing 'devil horn' fingers above my head. How bad can it be?

I go ahead and watch the film which turns out to be very funny, surprisingly moving and, of course, loud. I don't last the course as the band hits the stage with 'Metal on Metal', but my mum stays for a quick peek.

Wednesday 22nd October

Sure enough, my Anvil pics are in today's papers, but luckily for me the paper editors take it in good heart and make a bit of a joke about it.

It is time to head to Scotland for a couple of weeks over the half-term school holiday. I want to help out in the up-coming by-election in Glenrothes, called due to the untimely death of much-loved MP John MacDougall. I set off a couple of days ahead of the boys and Gordon so I can get out on the streets, knocking on doors.

I promise the security guys no brightly coloured handbags as we remember the Russian protection officer in Hokkaido.

Once there, I'm off with the Labour candidate Lindsay Roy (the headmaster of Kirkcaldy High School), and we get a good reception on doorsteps everywhere, with people just wanting us to say hello to Gordon. But, on turning the corner into a new street, we find a huge media pack waiting to take pictures. I wonder if my arrival had been slightly over-played as there is a limit as to how thrilling door-knocking will be on TV. It soon gets very frenetic with the press pushing each other, shouting questions and leaning over garden walls to record our conversations with the residents. In the end, the police decide it is best to pull me out early.

I get back to our home in Fife and am thrilled to discover in the post that Fraser has won £50 in the premium bonds. But the house feels too empty without my family in it, so I have an early night.

Thursday 23rd October

I speak to Gordon and the boys first thing on the phone. Gordon has just done an interview with Jo Elvin at *Glamour* magazine, and is off to speak to WACL (Women in Advertising and Communication, London), which sounds fun. My friend Nicola Mendelsohn texts me later to say that he was fabulous and very funny. A different kind of day for Mr Brown.

I start off in the Glenrothes campaign office joined by my friend Vivienne Dyce from the village. We do some calls to voters – they either tell you straight away they are solid Labour, or just won't say at all. I still don't yet have a handle on how this campaign is going, and usually like to think I can tune into campaigns quite well.

Later on, we get out with Lindsay to do a blitz around more doors, but it is very wet and windy. The press is more restrained today and we get a great picture of a dog for the *Daily Record* ('Walkies with Mrs Brown' reads the headline). My favourite moment comes as I am out knocking on doors with a camera following, and I am chatting to a woman who asks me to send Gordon her best wishes. Just then my mobile phone goes and I see it is Gordon, so I answer and pass the phone over to suggest she tells him herself. She just beams at me as she talks.

Friday 24th October

Alistair Darling has been on the radio and TV this morning confirming that the UK will enter a recession, but hopes that with the measures taken we will all weather it okay.

I still keep up the campaigning every day once the boys are up for their holiday. I am either on the phones, out on the doorsteps or joining Lindsay on a visit.

Saturday 25th October

Gordon visits Glenrothes. He, Lindsay and Scottish Secretary Jim Murphy meet to talk to local people in a café. It so happens we have picked the café that serves the best Malteser cake in Fife, possibly in all of Scotland.

Friday 31st October

It is my birthday. Gordon and I pop into the campaign office where I am surprised with a cake. All the Labour Party staff and local volunteers come together for a round of 'Happy Birthday to You' and we all enjoy a piece of cake with a cup of tea in a Vote Labour mug, before returning to canvassing and leaflet stuffing.

Later in the day, once we are back home, we get to enjoy a bit of family time by playing with the kids, going for a walk and having a kitchen-table supper, as Gordon is off again first thing tomorrow.

Saturday 1st November

I watch Gordon intermittently pop up on TV as he visits Saudi Arabia. The polls are now showing that Labour and the Scottish Nationalists are neck and neck in the by-election, which for us is a definite improvement, but I want a win here. Right now, Glenrothes seems more important than the US Presidential election.

Monday 3rd November

My last campaigning day in Glenrothes. I finish with a walk through the Kingdom Shopping Centre, then go round the Redcraigs area, stop at the school gates in Kinglassie, and have a final round of door knocking. I spend the evening on the phone, while wrapping gifts for prisoners' families that the local church have requested, and some gifts for the local Women's Aid refuge that Gordon's constituency office has asked for.

Tuesday 4th November

I have an early start to fly back to London and actually feel quite exhausted as I sink into my aeroplane seat.

Once back I have a lot of catching up to do and a terrifying in-tray.

I meet Lottie Davies, the photographer we have picked to shoot the famous front door for this year's Christmas card, complete with the most beautiful wreath from McQueens florist. The building is undergoing its first 'facelift' for 40 years and the front door looks as perfect as it is ever going to look, before the London air grimes it up again.

Wednesday 5th November

The forty-fourth American President has been elected – Barack Obama. What a moment in history for that country. I do so look forward to meeting him again and I hope to work with Michelle Obama as the new US First Lady. Senator McCain handles his defeat, as Gordon says, with characteristic dignity.

Many people in Downing Street look decidedly tired. They clearly stayed up too late watching the returns and speeches on the television.

I am still pretty exhausted after my by-election campaigning and finally realise I have put my back out. I book an appointment with Juliet, my favourite genius osteopath, who clicks me back together. I feel straight and steady, if a little fragile. Even I can tell that I am pushing my luck at the moment and I've promised myself to relook at my diary.

This evening, though, is a very special occasion for the charity, Wellbeing of Women, of which I am Patron. Under its previous name, Birthright, Wellbeing of Women was one of Diana, Princess of Wales's favourite charities and this year HRH Prince William is the Royal Patron of its Lord Mayor's Appeal. The Prince is the chief guest at this evening's event and it marks the culmination of the appeal.

I arrive feeling pretty awful, however, and realise quickly that I am in serious trouble. I talk to Konrad and tell him I think I can manage a quick set of hellos, but then we have to leave.

However, as I am talking to charity Chair of Trustees, Sir Victor Blank, in the reception, I realise that I am about to commit the worst kind of breach of protocol by fainting. I lurch up to Konrad who escorts me out of the room, and an usher finds me a small waiting room. It is not long before there is a tap on the door – one of the Prince's aides has been dispatched to enquire after my wellbeing. My head is in my hands; I feel so grim, but I still find it in me to be fairly embarrassed. I just can't move. Very kindly, I am offered a mask and told to breathe in from an oxygen tank with nice steady breaths.

Slowly, I come back to life, and finally reach the point where I take note of my surroundings and the kind aides standing protectively by the oxygen tank. It slowly dawns on me that I am using a bit of kit that forms part of the Royal medical back-up that must accompany HRH wherever he goes. I am not so unwell that I don't manage to feel totally mortified. As soon as I can stand up, I mutter a round of apologies and walk myself out of there, fast. I get into the car to go back to the flat, head still in my hands.

Thursday 6th November

The next day I am diagnosed with a bit of exhaustion and told to rest. I have to cancel my engagements for the day and start with a call to my friend Stephen Shields, the director of SHINE education trust, to let him know I will miss his big gala dinner this evening. He is so good about it, but I feel terribly guilty letting him and SHINE Chair Jim O'Neill down at short notice. I stay in and write notes to all the various people at the charity, and the Lord Mayor's office and Clarence House to apologise. I especially make my apologies to the Royal Household with a personal note to HRH Prince William – not one I ever imagined penning. All I say is that I plan not to do that again.

Today is also Polling Day in Glenrothes so it is a big day of judgement for the government and especially for Gordon. After the polls close at 10 p.m., Joe Irvin, recently promoted as the new Political Secretary, calls to say that he has been advised that the by-election will be lost by about 200 to 1,000 votes, in a repeat of the Glasgow East result. I am stunned. I had hoped for better, based on the warmth on the doorsteps and in phone calls.

I lie awake pretty much the whole night wondering what on earth else Gordon and I and the rest of the team can do to win the next general election.

Friday 7th November

At 6.30 a.m. Gordon gets up and goes to get his messages. He comes back into the bedroom ten minutes later and says, 'Sarah, we won the by-election by 6,000 votes.'

'Goodness me, that's more like it!' I jump out of bed with a quick prayer of thanks. All day long I get calls, texts and emails to say congratulations. What a brilliant and conclusive result. I am sure we are now back!

Saturday 8th November

I attend the Remembrance Service at the Royal Albert Hall. I always suffer a bit from vertigo in the boxes here, but this year I am particularly anxious that I don't repeat my falling-over trick from midweek. I am separated from Gordon who gives me reassuring glances all night, and just sit tight next to Air Marshal Ian Macfadyen.

Sunday 9th November

The annual Remembrance Sunday service at the Cenotaph. I am watching this year with Louise Shackelton (Miliband), Maggie Darling, Alice Perkins (Straw) and Reggie Davidson, the wife of our Solicitor General. We arrive at the Foreign Office with our respective spouses who are then peeled off to join the group outside in Whitehall, right in front of the Cenotaph.

The rain, thankfully, holds off as I always worry about all the veterans who come so far and stand for so long. It is always a moving service, but it is the faces of these proud servicemen and women as they remember fallen colleagues that never fail to bring a lump to my throat, even more so than the music.

Monday 10th November

Bright and early before school starts, we all meet Sarah and Chris Charlton, and their little daughter Kairen. The Charltons have been chosen by breakfast show *GMTV* as a typical family meeting the worries of the recession. They have agreed to meet all the political leaders and hear the different choices available to them. Our job is to impress them, but we are actually bowled over by these lovely, thoughtful and generous people. It is really helpful to hear how the Charltons are coping with financial pressures and tackling them as a normal working family. It is a regular part of our daily lives to meet people from across Britain, but it is not often that they are here to question us.

Wednesday 12th November

Lindsay and Irene Roy arrive for the first time at Downing Street as he goes to take up his new seat in the House of Commons today. This is such a boost for our MPs. The tragic story of the death of Baby P is at the top of the news today, and dominates everyone's thoughts in the building too from the Prime Minister's private office to the messengers' room when I call by for a chat – we are all talking about it.

Thursday 13th November

Gordon is all set to travel to Washington DC today for the G20 meetings that are being held there (London will host the summit in April next year). Before he goes he calls to ask if I will pop in with Fraser to say hello to President Karzai of Afghanistan. Having met his little son in Kabul, Gordon wants to introduce Fraser.

Fraser is immersed in a dinosaur Lego Duplo game involving small Lego cavemen battling a green T-rex and brings his little figures with him as we walk across to the state rooms to say hello.

I bring with me an educational gift I had bought for the President to take back with him. The President comments that Fraser's small swarthy Lego men look like Afghan people, and asks Fraser what they are doing. Without a second's pause, Fraser bashes his two little people against each other and says 'Kill, kill, kill … dead!' There is silence from me and Gordon as we take in the President's reaction. Of course he knows that Fraser is talking about dinosaur world, but there is a lesson in there somewhere for us all.

It reminds me of the time that Fraser asked US General Petraeus to show him his marching, which he did not, but he did give Fraser a special souvenir medal coin to treasure – smart General.

Wednesday 19th November

We had dinner in the flat with Alan and Ann Sugar this evening. I don't know them at all well but she is wonderfully cool and elegant, and the perfect counterfoil to his bluff direct manner. I loved being with them, and even if I didn't, I would still think well of them – they have been terrifically loyal supporters of Gordon's over many years.

When I think of the well-known people that say they are our supporters, I do think we have the best of the lot, from Jo Rowling to David Tennant and Eddie Izzard. Even Cheryl Cole and Lily Allen are on the record as Labour supporters.

Tuesday 25th November

I still host weekly small charity receptions and was delighted that the Caron Keating Foundation has found a date to suit them. Some time ago I met Gloria Hunniford, who had enquired about doing an event here. I was more than delighted to offer her an evening for the charity set up in memory of her daughter, Caron, who died of breast cancer in 2004, leaving two young boys and a distraught family. I remember Caron from Bristol University where we both went in the 1980s. She was a little older than me, but I remember seeing her around, a very beautiful and vibrant young woman, and soon to be all over the TV as her career took off. My connection to Gloria lies in our shared understanding of loss so it was my privilege to have her there, with her family and friends, to thank them for their support now and in the future for the foundation.

Thursday 27th November

I start the day with a call to my mum to wish her a happy birthday, but our diary holds a more solemn event today. Gordon and I attend the Damilola Taylor Memorial Service to remember victims of knife crime, at Southwark Cathedral.

Richard Taylor, Damilola's father, has consistently championed the campaign to combat knife crime ever since his loss. Today's service brings together many groups and we hear from young people through their singing and speeches. Gordon speaks and is able to share some of the poignancy of being a parent, 'to know that there's somebody whose happiness will always matter more to you than your own. That there's someone you'd do anything to protect. That there's someone who will always be the first person you think about when you wake and the person you say a prayer for just before you sleep'.

At the end, I see Doreen Lawrence, mother of murdered teenager Stephen Lawrence, and give her a hug. I don't have any words for the loss she bears or the dignity with which she carries it. I think of Gordon's words for the bereaved parents: 'while nothing can ever replace that which they have loved and lost, we will do all that we can to honour the dreams that they had for their children'.

Tuesday 2nd December

The annual Muslims for Labour dinner is being held at the Natural History Museum for 400 guests. There is a charged atmosphere and a galaxy of great speakers. I am seated by *Dragons' Den* star James Caan and the food magnate Sir Gulam Noon. Gulam has just returned from Mumbai where he was actually caught in the hotel bombings there and is understandably very shaken by the experience. He tells me that the threat to people's lives was so grave that he actually wrote a long letter to his family believing he had met his final hour. Poor man.

Wednesday 3rd December

This morning is taken up with the State Opening of Parliament so the boys are out early with Mela to beat the road closures. I have a nice expensive Jaeger grey wool suit and some patent Russell and Bromley heels with a fashionable small platform.

I had put off finding the time to go out and buy a hat until yesterday, when I took Fraser into town for an appointment and was faced with the choice of dragging him round shops, or calling in to see my mum for a cup of tea. Walking across the Brunswick Shopping Centre to my mum's flat in Bloomsbury, a purple beret in the window of New Look caught my eye. The only thing that made me hesitate was the price tag – not because it was too high, but at £7, I wondered if it was too low. Then I thought how ridiculous it was to want to pay more for the sake of it when I was looking at the perfect hat for my outfit. I bought the beret with a matching clutch bag for a grand total of £15.

I sit in the gallery with Maggie Darling and enjoy both the spectacle and the never-ceasing joy of hearing the Queen give a speech full of Labour commitments to fairness and prosperity.

The press coverage of my purple 'austerity' beret provides some light relief in the early evening papers – not least as the intrepid reporters have already identified its origin and modest price. I am holding my head up high – it is a great colour and why pay more!

Thursday 4th December

I find myself posing for the annual photo with the frozen turkey from the British Poultry Council and know that Christmas is coming fast.

The Downing Street Christmas tree is lit by Girl Guides and Boy Scouts, gifts are distributed around the building accompanied by mince pies, and I sign hundreds and hundreds of Lottie's beautiful cards.

Tuesday 9th December

I go to New York on my own for a few days to attend the memorial service of Professor Allan Rosenfield, the guru to everyone for maternal and child health. He passed away after his long illness and I want to be there at Columbia University to join the appreciation of his life.

The memorial in the university sports hall is full, and the speeches – from Columbia University head, Lee Bollinger, to designer, Kenneth Cole – are testament to a life well lived and a great legacy left.

Wednesday 10th December

Among my schedule of charity meetings in New York, I attend Wendi Murdoch's fortieth birthday dinner at the Gramercy Park Hotel, and am seated next to Rupert Murdoch. He is a very solicitous host and very touching in the affection he shows for Wendi on her special night. Film mogul Harvey Weinstein is on my other side, which means I am guaranteed good company for the whole evening. His wife, Georgina Chapman, has been a great supporter of the White Ribbon Alliance through her successful fashion business (Wendi is looking amazing in one of her dresses this evening).

My previous encounters with Harvey have been with him as Mr Chapman accompanying Georgina to the British Fashion Awards. He does a great job at dinner pointing out the guests I don't recognise, and explaining who everyone is. I am very grateful to have his gruff, fun company throughout dinner.

Gordon will also just be home from his trip to Afghanistan to visit our troops before Christmas. There is, as ever, a news blackout for much of his trip. He has also been in Pakistan for a big conference and confirms that Pakistan links do exist with the terrorist attack on the Mumbai hotels. This follows on from the sadness of the three Royal Marines killed in Afghanistan by a 13-year-old suicide bomber.

Saturday 20th December

We finally get home to Fife for the Christmas break. We take the boys to church to take part in the nativity play, and to the Kirkcaldy farmers' market to sort out fruit and vegetables for Christmas lunch. As usual, we've ordered a black-feathered Kelly's Farm turkey via the internet, and got a Boxing Day ham from our fabulous local pig farm.

Wednesday 24th December

This Christmas Eve, Santa has been left a mince pie, a glass of wine and a Jaffa Cake. We are now at the stage where both boys get very excited about the prospect of Santa coming and it takes them a very long time to settle (not so Gordon, who's fast asleep by 10 p.m.) I call Gil McNeil to chat while I wait until it is safe to sort out the stockings. Like me, she has a quiet hour on her hands and we end up having a ludicrously useful conversation about the office and all we need to do. I see the time has gone past midnight and decide it must be safe for 'Santa' to deliver the stockings.

Friday 26th December

Over Christmas and Boxing Day we enjoy a lovely family time with all the excitement of opening presents, enjoying good food, lots of walks on the beach and classic telly. Times like this are so precious for everyone, but I appreciate them all the more now while the rest of life is so hectic.

Sunday 28th December

This is our day for remembering Jennifer. Today would have been her seventh birthday. We visit the cemetery to lay flowers and later take a walk in a favourite spot along the beach. Both of us can recall every single precious moment of her all-too-brief time with us, and while I think of Jennifer every day, it is on her birthday that I go through all the details in my mind again. There is much happiness and love mixed up with the sadness – something those who have suffered a similar loss always readily understand. Today is simply a very important day for Gordon and me, and all our family.

CHAPTER 18

Upping My Game

2009

Saturday 3rd January

Downing Street gets back to normal very quickly in the New Year with its 200 staff all back and busy. We are honoured to receive a visit from 50 sergeants and warrant officers from 2 Parachute Regiment, just back from Helmand Province in Afghanistan. The staff is surprised to see Gordon take everyone off after the group photo to see the Cabinet Room.

I am in a spring-clean mood and use my burst of post-holiday energy to get on top of all kinds of things. PiggyBankKids has a continuing appeal for the Jennifer Brown Research Laboratory so we set in train a host of events for the year. I am now Patron of six other charities and like to be involved in some of the ideas and planning, and not just attending receptions for a bit of PM's wife ribbon cutting and photo ops.

Another New Year task I undertake is to go through all the official gifts. Beth and I go through everything to work out where they will go. We follow the system already in place where high-value gifts are taken off to … goodness knows where (storage, I suppose) while other items, valued at under the threshold, can be donated to charities as long as they are not personalised or readily identifiable. Some, of course, can be given as gifts to members of staff who would like a memento of a particular trip, and who in turn make a donation to charity themselves. Gordon and I have kept those gifts that have been personally chosen, and they will always hold a big sentimental value for us.

We have also amassed a wealth of unusual gifts from various visits including lots of pictures and 'sculptures' from children or from maternal alliances around the world, so have made a lively display of these on the tops of filing cabinets.

We also look at our own gifts that we will give to people visiting Number 10 or take with us on our visits around the world. Number 10 keeps a number of gifts in stock, like ties by UK designers and the Jaeger compacts that I bought for the G8 First Ladies. It also has items personalised with the Downing Street crest, such as china trinket boxes, silver picture frames and even a Downing Street teddy bear. Beth and I add a few new things like a rose-scented Downing Street candle (as the gardens have such pretty roses), and a tub of Downing Street chocolate-chip cookies. Compared to other governments, I imagine our supplies and range are pretty modest.

I have agreed to guest-edit an issue of the *News of the World*'s colour supplement, *Fabulous*. Deputy editor Jane Johnson comes in to see me and we map out our ideas. I want to theme the magazine around women's health and encourage better awareness of health signs, and better self-esteem in response to body image issues. Wellbeing of Women has agreed to partner with me, and Jane has set herself a target to raise £500,000. Former newspaper editor Eve Pollard is the vice-chair of Wellbeing of Women so we get her in with charity director Liz Campbell to share our ideas, and work out who might grace the front cover. Chef Jamie Oliver already does the magazine's cookery page so we hope to approach his wife, Jools, for the cover shot and an interview about health, pregnancy and keeping gorgeous as a busy mum. I think I could get the hang of this, and look forward to a rummage in the *Fabulous* fashion cupboard for some 'purple' clothes to match the charity's logo and colours.

Wednesday 14th January

This afternoon, I jumped on an RAF flight with Gordon to join President Sarkozy and Carla for a private dinner at Carla's house in Paris, meeting all their neighbours on our way in. My real treat is that I get to meet her son, Aurélien, about whom I've heard so much. We sit in their dining room eating the most delicious cheese fondue and drinking wine. Much of the conversation leans to the economic situation and the Middle East, but we do get time to just chat.

Carla is now the Global Fund's ambassador for HIV Mother–Child Transmission, and I urge her to chide her husband for cutting his international aid budget. I know it is important to steer clear of interfering in politics when not elected, but I do think global poverty is different – anyone should be allowed to speak out against it; in fact, it is their duty to do so. Gordon doesn't disagree, and I have yet to meet anyone, even a hardened newspaper reporter, who thinks this is unreasonable.

Monday 19th January

The scale of the banking crisis is really affecting everyone's confidence. Gordon is still thinking his way through the problems, as are so many others, but the solutions are not obvious. A quick response is needed, but only if the right judgement is made. So far Gordon has called it right each time, and other world leaders are still turning to him to find out what he will do. That is a lot of pressure.

Gordon and Alistair host a press conference, unveiling the rescue package to get the banks lending again. 'I will not sit idly by and let people go to the wall because of the irresponsible mistakes of a few bankers,' says Gordon. It is well received, but there is no resting on laurels and everyone goes back to work straight afterwards.

Gordon is on a visit to Glasgow with Scottish Secretary Jim Murphy when he takes a call from America's new President (rather excitingly, we discover that Gordon is the first call to an international statesman that Obama makes in his new position). Jim is thrilled to have been there to catch the moment and tells me there is a kind of perfection in seeing Gordon, in the middle of a group of Glaswegian apprentices, chatting on the phone to the US President about working together globally.

Thursday 29th January

I travel with Gordon to the World Economic Forum meetings in Davos, mindful to pack my warmest boots and a big coat.

Out here, we are back in 'I'm accompanying a rock star, mind the crush' mode, where everyone wants to talk to Gordon about his handling of the financial crisis. It is all very incongruous, as we have fallen 14 points behind in the polls back home.

I use my time to meet with all the maternal mortality campaign champions – from Tammy Haddad and Heather McGregor to Ban Soon-taek (of the UN), and Wendi Murdoch. In our different ways we have all been keeping up the pressure so that the maternal health issue can climb higher up the political agenda. Even in the financial crisis it is important – arguably even more so.

I talk a lot to Melinda Gates when Gordon and I join her and Bill for a meeting to compare notes on our thinking, and hear what the Gates Foundation is planning. She is right there on the issue of maternal and newborn health, which is terrific. Gordon heads off to another meeting and I tell him I will meet him at the reception for the malaria campaign and to not worry about what time he and his aides get there if they are busy.

When I arrive, I fast-realise that this is a sit-down meeting and a serious one too, with Bill Gates; Peter Chernin, head of Malaria No More; and, of course, Ray Chambers. But I can't think how to get hold of Gordon's team as mobile phones get no signal on this mountaintop. I can only wait as the time ticks towards the moment when Gordon is needed to speak. Gordon walks in literally at the point of introduction, with an entourage and a great grin on his face, ready for a mingle and a canapé. But he catches my eye, sees my face, and continues on up to the stage where he seamlessly launches into a speech about the fight to eradicate malaria and how we will achieve it. Oh, my goodness, big respect from me for that one, and it's also why I am not in charge of his diary.

The centrepiece of Davos for me (and many of the women there) is the Important Dinner for Women again – number three this time. It is still not yet on the official Davos programme, but there is a big push to get more women's events recognised here. The dinner entails a walk along an icy street (with one of my heroines, the CEO of online news site Huffington Post, Arianna Huffington, who is uncomplaining in a long dress, high heels and no coat) and up the mountain in a cable car to a restaurant on the side of the mountain. I join PepsiCo CEO, Indra Nooyi, and Melinda Gates in addressing the guests.

My job, as always, is to bring everyone up to speed with the maternal mortality campaign's progress and to call for the next stage of support. I am very mindful of my 'overpowered by nerves' performance of last year and hope I have put in enough practice in between to pull it off this year. Cherie Blair is one of the guests and I use the opportunity to pay tribute to her achievements while at Downing Street (which is met with great affection in the room by her international friends): 'Cherie was a breath of fresh air. She campaigned for issues for women and children as a lawyer and as the wife of a prime minister. She took a bit of flak for this sometimes, but it has never stopped her from championing issues around the health, safety and rights of women and children … I really appreciate her support in attending the Davos women's dinner to recognise the importance of the success of the MDG goals to women, and particularly maternal mortality.'

Many more pledges come in from these powerful and connected women for the campaign, and I don't see how we can fail to get attention at the highest government levels around the world.

Monday 2nd February

There is a welcome, positive article published this morning by economic commentator Anatole Kaletsky about the Davos visit. It starts 'Gordon Brown has saved the world yet again' and goes on to outline how Gordon had offered a way out of the financial crisis that was very persuasive about the 'business leaders unanimously recommending cutbacks in public spending and predicting doom for every business but their own'. Kaletsky's article offered an analysis of the facts that will govern the cost of the recovery process. I am no economist, but I do agree that we have had a successful visit to Davos.

Back in London, and we resume our usual routine. The boys have their school friends Mohammed, Sam, and Sam's brother, Max, over to play. We have kept up all our friendships regardless of where we live, and it has been easy to have friends slip in and out of the back door unnoticed and straight up to the flat without interrupting anyone at work. The children can also use the garden any time, and the trampoline and the Wendy house out there. I imagine that the sight of bouncing or gardening children can provide a welcome, fleeting distraction sometimes from the pressures of government business. Certainly the kids seem very popular around the building, and I wonder sometimes if they know more people's names than I do.

Friday 6th February

Television presenter Jeremy Clarkson has attacked Gordon while in Australia as a 'one-eyed Scottish idiot', and is not much kinder about Australian PM Kevin Rudd. I assume the BBC will suggest he apologises, but whatever happens, his comments are unpleasant and inappropriate. The Scottish press have reacted badly, interpreting his comments as racist, and this cannot be good for the BBC, whatever his ratings. People like that just make me shudder.

*

Britain is in the middle of a huge snow-storm and on our weekend trip to Chequers, our car comes to a stop outside the main driveway. We have to be rescued by staff from Chequers who carry in our bags and Fraser, while John and I wade through thigh-high drifts. After that, I call Gordon's team and suggest a four-wheel drive vehicle to get down here.

Gordon is in one of those periods where there are just so many different issues to deal with. One person he is missing is his diary secretary, Leeanne, as she is off on a three-week jury service duty. I think we are all missing her efficiency and cheeriness in the office.

The Governor of the Bank of England, Mervyn King, joins us for lunch with his wife, Barbara, but we try and keep it informal; even governors need a day off sometimes.

Monday 9th February

Elle editor, Lorraine Candy, has offered the White Ribbon Alliance a platform at this year's *Elle* Style Awards. The catch is that I have to follow all the fashionistas onstage and address them on a serious subject, just as the party is about to start.

I am wearing a Ben de Lisi dress that Ben bowled me over with by giving to me after he attended a Centrepoint charity reception at Number 10. I used to go to his Soho warehouse sales years ago to get evening dresses when I worked nearby in Poland Street. I went through the horrors of whether I could receive it as a gift – in the end, I didn't, but I could still borrow it. I have also borrowed some mighty Brian Atwood heels from Britt Lintner and some giant earrings.

I know that many of the guests will have spent all day getting ready for a red-carpet, flash-bulb entrance, but I have to be realistic and condense my prep time to under an hour (not bad by my standards).

I meet British Fashion Council Chairman, Harold Tillman, who is my escort at the dinner, and do all the necessary photos. Balshen Izzet, the 'up-on-fashion' press officer with me this evening, also asks me to have my picture taken with newly discovered *Slumdog Millionaire* actress Freida Pinto.

I find the audience more than receptive when I speak and thank the fashion world for getting behind our cause before it is fashionable, and still in need of attention. I also ponder aloud why my job always seems to entail getting photographed next to the likes of Naomi, Christy, Claudia, Jade, Erin, Liya, Elle and Carla. I say it is a reflection of how much I believe in the cause that I would do this time after time! Bless the beautiful people in the room as they gave me a huge round of encouraging applause.

Meanwhile, back in the outside world, everyone is agog watching the RBS and HBOS bankers present their parliamentary evidence, all the while busily protecting their own bonuses and pensions.

Wednesday 11th February

Inspired by my meeting with Freida Pinto, I get Gordon to take me out to see *Slumdog Millionaire* when we are home in Scotland for a mid-term break. We don't get to go to the cinema very often (who does with young children?), but have never let Gordon's job stop us using our local cinema in Fife, where everyone is always friendly and treats us very normally (a great compliment, I always feel). That said, cinema outings don't work for us as a romantic-date option, as we still need to sit with a clutch of protection officers. So we all really enjoy the film; Danny Boyle and his cast rightly deserve the accolades that have poured in for them.

Wednesday 18th February

We leave for a short visit to Rome where we are to visit the Vatican and meet His Holiness the Pope. We have Mela and the boys with us as we have been invited as a family. Gordon's entourage also includes many of the Catholic members of his team, as this trip will be very meaningful for them.

We are driven directly to the Vatican and as I leave the car, I place a black lace mantilla on my head. Gordon is greeted by a great line of cardinals alongside the Papal Swiss Guard in their distinctive yellow and blue uniforms. We walk along the hallway with our heads angled back to look up at the ceiling as it is lined with exquisite Raphael cartoons and a large El Greco painting. Having studied art history at school and visited Florence and Rome in my gap year, I could spend hours walking around here.

We wait while Gordon has a 20-minute private audience with His Holiness. Everyone is looking extremely smart, especially my two lads in their 'Dad-style' navy suits and large 'David Beckham-style' ties.

When we are taken through to meet His Holiness, I am very struck by his tremendous presence and his immediate kindness and gentleness to our boys. He takes Fraser's hand, who immediately bows his head and says, 'Hello, Holy Father' very sincerely. The Pope is also very inclusive of the rest of the entourage and is insistent on meeting everyone.

Afterwards, Gordon is taken to his meeting with the Cardinal Secretary of State, who is effectively the Prime Minister of the Vatican. While the rest of us do not have time for a visit to see the famous Sistine Chapel, we are instead treated to a short tour of the Vatican Museum and a walk down a private corridor illustrated with frescoes of maps of the world by Michelangelo. On closer inspection, you can see the whole of Australasia is missing, simply because no one knew the continent existed back then when Michelangelo was painting.

Once we leave the Vatican, I go with Christianne (who is accompanying me on the trip) on a visit to the Sant'Egidio Community to hear their presentation on their work with HIV/AIDS treatment centres in Mozambique, and elsewhere in Africa. The community is a network of people volunteering their time, money and goodwill to help others as part of their Catholic faith, and while they continue with their own daily lives. I am very struck by the leadership of the community, and want to explore who to engage with to get the

Catholic world into the maternal mortality campaign, without compromising their reservations about some of the family-planning strategies involved. On the way out of the modest church attached to the centre, I am shown the small cupboard with a revolving door that connects the inside and outside of the building where, in the past, unwanted babies were left to be discovered by the priests. A small but striking reminder of the challenges that unmarried mothers have faced in the past, and still do in some parts of the world.

Monday 23rd February

As the end of London Fashion Week approaches, I go with writer Kathy Lette to the hat designer Stephen Jones's exhibition at the V&A. As trivial as a hat exhibition sounds, this is an extraordinary collection of hats selected by Stephen, and a glittering guest list turns out for the opening. Hats seem to be compulsory and I have a great little hat from Japanese–British young designer Misa Harada. Stuart Rose from M&S is there, and comes up to say nice things about Gordon: 'He is a classic case of "Cometh the hour, cometh the man."'

Tuesday 24th February

My friend novelist Sian Busby comes in to see me for a cup of tea and I give her a tour of Number 10's various pictures and treasures. Sian has had a busy life writing, raising two boys, with a husband working at the BBC; pretty much the perfect life until she was diagnosed with lung cancer and then a brain tumour. She has a wonderful spirit and having suffered through her operations and treatment has recalibrated her life to focus on what matters to her most. We talk about loss and suffering, but also about precious times with family and friends, and how we find personal fulfilment. I hope she enjoyed her visit to Downing Street but I think that I had the more enjoyable time and was certainly left thinking about what matters most in life.

*

Later, I join Gordon for a short trip to the Mall to join the Queen for the unveiling of the national memorial to Queen Elizabeth the Queen Mother. It is a cold day but I have on a warm Jasper Conran coat with a matching beret made by super milliner Stephen Jones from spare fabric. There are rather splendid images of war time, when the Queen Mother was such an iconic figure to the nation, and images of a great love of hers, horses.

Meeting Prince William again, I mutter my apologies about keeling over at the Lord Mayor's event and nicking his oxygen, and he just chuckles.

Gordon offers his sympathy to Prince Harry who has just been through an awful run with the media. Prince Harry replies humorously that it is either the Palace or the government who gets it, so with all due respect he is quite happy when it is the other way around. Gordon replies that we should not forget we also have the Mayor of London, who could take a turn. Prince Harry roars with laughter.

Wednesday 25th February

The tragic news of the death of David and Samantha Cameron's son, Ivan, reaches us early and I immediately cancel my appointments. This will be a heartbreaking time for them. Gordon acts quickly to cancel Prime Minister's Question Time today. It is at times like this that you can tell that all politicians just want to be kind.

Saturday 28th February

Over the weekend I leave Gordon with the boys and I head out of London to visit my friend Ailsa's house for a surprise birthday party for her forty-fifth. I get there to discover the added joy that my old school friends, Zim, now a TV producer and human rights advocate with Amnesty, and Caitlin, a novelist, have made it there, too.

I have known Ailsa and Zim (and my friend, Jane, who lives in the US and who I just saw at the women's dinner in New York) since I was 11 years old and we all tipped up for the first day at Acland Burghley secondary school in North London. Caitlin went to a nearby school and I met her a year later. I had just moved to London with my mum and brothers to our new home with our new stepfather and his sons. We had a lovely home, but also a lot of newness to get used to in a big city and a move to secondary school where I knew no one.

We formed firm friendships that lasted through teenage years and adulthood, and as we all fanned out in different directions with careers, families and various dreams to fulfil, we have always kept in touch. What I love is being able to connect up again after long periods, as though there has been no real absence. Thinking back to classroom days, I can remember working out what age I would be in the year 2000, and pondering on what a great and unimaginable age that would be. The year 2000 was the year I got married, and now I am a mum and living a life I never would have dreamt of at school.

Sometimes I think I want to return to my earlier state of much less self-awareness about the ages and stages of life. But seeing my old school friends for an evening almost achieves that!

Tuesday 3rd March

Gordon heads off to give the prestigious address to the Joint Session of Congress and the Senate on Capitol Hill following his meeting with President Obama at the White House. I take my own flight the next day (so I can fit in John's school play too), which will get me to Washington just in time for my courtesy visit to meet Michelle Obama at the White House.

I get ready for my White House visit while still in the air, which means a tight squeeze in the in-flight loo to change unglamorously. I have a wonderful air hostess looking after me who is almost more excited than I am about my destination. I have chosen my favourite grey Britt Lintner belted dress and gorgeous Astley Clarke opals by British designer Pippa Small. I have some favourite burgundy patent heels that I know how to balance in, though I am not planning on any more wobbly moments on my return to the White House.

Having watched the new First Lady give her Convention speech on television last summer, and seen all the coverage to date with her arrival in Washington DC, I am thrilled to at last be meeting her. I have fast learned that there is no predicting how any first meetings go, but I have no doubt that we will have an interesting chat. As it is a private meeting, I don't have to worry about being nervous and can just look forward to our time together.

Upon arrival, I meet the new Social Secretary, Desiree Rogers. She is a beautiful, immaculate and powerful woman in charge of all the guest lists and has already garnered a very high profile from her appointment. I wish her well in the spotlight but imagine it won't be easy.

She takes me up in the lift to the private floor and I step out into the First Family's private apartment. The new First Lady's opening words to me as I walk out are, 'At last, a normal size person.' She has a tremendous statuesque beauty borne of many hours in the gym, and a wonderful natural bone structure. More than that, she has a face that speaks of friendship and personal connection, which draws me to her. She has already connected with the people of America, and many more around the world. She has a huge burden to carry but brings with it a great opportunity to do some real good. I am willing this woman to succeed in her time in this historic position.

She guides me to a sofa area and, as we sit, indicates that a photographer will just take some pictures at the start. We are positioned behind a giant bowl of flowers, which look likely to take up the foreground of any photograph. As tea and tiny sandwiches are served, it is clear that we are surrounded by a formality that neither of us necessarily requires. Fortunately we have an hour together and so are able to chat about our respective experiences as a political spouse. Michelle is taking notes on living a governmental life, and of a mind with me about keeping our children's lives as ordinary as possible, while letting them share in the special moments.

As we talk about the global health campaigns I have supported, we also cover her thoughts on both healthcare and citizenship in the USA. I do know that this conversation is privileged and represents her early thoughts, which may yet change and evolve as she settles into her role. We make time, too, for a more practical discussion about what to expect at this April's London-based G20, and what she and I might do together when she visits London. She also confides that she would like to bring her daughters, Malia and Sasha, to London in the summer and we agree to meet again then too. I enjoy meeting her two girls and seeing their favourite places in their new home.

When I leave I get the big Michelle hug before I jump back in the car, and I hope I have made a new friend.

Back at the Residence, the first thing I do is call home to get news from my mum on her big day. She has been at her graduation ceremony at the University of London, Institute of Education, to collect her hard-earned PhD in Social Anthropology. What an achievement at any age, but she is collecting her degree at age 72. When we left Tanzania all those years ago and settled in England, my mum had retrained as a teacher. She went on to be a great headteacher of an infants' school in North London, tackling all kinds of social injustice and engaging the whole community in early learning for their little ones. She always said that she wanted to study more for herself, but it was not possible during those years of working hard and raising a family first on her own, after my parents divorced, and later living as a bigger family with my stepfather Patrick and stepbrothers Nico and Kit. Now at last she has achieved her dream. No matter how far away I am now, I want to speak to her and send lots of love.

*

Gordon's meeting with President Obama has gone well, as expected. The President has very kindly described himself and Gordon as sharing 'spectacular wives and wonderful children'.

The UK press corps is generally unhappy as the original press conference had been cancelled then rearranged by the White House to take place within the Oval Office, to correct any impression that this was meant as a slight to the UK. The press corps will have none of it and has already decided – as a collective pack – that this will be reported negatively.

Wednesday 4th March

We are greeted in the Congressional building by Speaker Nancy Pelosi, and run through the details for entering the Congressional chamber. It is a highly prestigious and rare honour for Gordon to be able to address the members of both the Congress and the Senate. I am seated in the gallery to watch alongside my American relatives, who have travelled from Pennsylvania and Virginia to join me: my Aunt Doreen, and my American-born cousins, Caroline and Trevor. I am thrilled that they can be with me to hear Gordon speak at an event which really shows the ties that bind our two countries together, and attest to a very real special relationship.

Gordon is escorted into the Chamber, as is traditional, by those Congressional representatives and Senators who choose to enter with him; Gordon has a group of 42 with him which seems to impress those who know about such things. The audience already holds a copy of the speech in their hands, and 18 standing ovations later I know that we have all heard a great, uplifting speech that may yet form the basis of how we all move forward as a world in peace and prosperity: 'Friendships can be shaken, but our friendship is unshakeable. Treaties can be broken, but our partnership is unbreakable. And I know there is no power on earth than can drive us apart.'

We have just a short time with my aunt and cousins afterwards, and then join the Speaker for lunch. We eat what I think might count as my most delicious lunch ever – a goat's cheese salad; a vegetarian strudel with vegetables that was indescribably tasty; and a chocolate, pistachio and pear dessert. The only blow was the sweet peach iced tea: I can never understand how Americans can drink it with a meal.

Our timing is so tight we don't get to stay for coffee, and have to rush off immediately to catch our flight home.

Thursday 5th March

We do not get home until 2 a.m. UK time, but there is still a full day ahead when we get up. Somehow we both get through the day without flagging, and then get a second wind by the time our evening commitments come round. Tonight, Gordon hosts the promised reception for the LGBT community, and makes a sincere speech of tribute to the fight these people have had to make to get proper recognition. His greatest cheer comes when he says, 'You can't legislate love.' There is still some way to go, but there was a good partying atmosphere tonight, not least because it turns out we were celebrating comedienne Amy Lamé's hen night as she has her civil partnership ceremony with her partner, Jenny, tomorrow morning.

Friday 6th March

Reports come in that a woman has just thrown green custard all over Peter Mandelson, the First Secretary of State. I feel very outraged on his behalf – there must be that awful moment when it first lands when you just don't know whether what has been thrown is designed to embarrass or to actually harm – like acid. He is phenomenally cool about it and follows the first rule of 'being egged', which is to look down so that the television cameras don't get a clear shot of your horrified face to run for the rest of the day. Peter disappears then reappears all cleaned up, with a great one-liner at his disposal: 'I don't mind having the Green Revolution on my shoulders, but I don't want it all over my face.'

Friday 13th March

Chancellor Angela Merkel of Germany and her professor husband, Joachim Sauer, visit us at Chequers this weekend. Gordon has spent a lot of time with Chancellor Merkel, but not knowing either of the couple I have been looking forward to this meeting. What strikes me immediately as we are doing photographs in the Hawtrey Room is what a palpable steady charisma and ease of manner the Chancellor has. She comes across on TV as very stern, but in person she is most congenial, as is her husband, too.

Over a Friday night fish supper, our conversation divides evenly between the global economic situation, and talk about favourite holidays, favourite walks and favourite music (of course, they love Wagner). We sit over coffee in the Library chatting until late. Chancellor Merkel has her own general election coming up in September and very much wants to win again. She operates in a fragile coalition and her country's tradition dictates that she cannot start campaigning until the Opposition makes the first move. She talks a lot about her upbringing in the shadow of the Berlin Wall, and invites us to Germany for the twentieth anniversary of its destruction.

CHAPTER 19

First Tweets

Tuesday 17th March

Having been at Number 10 for a year and a half, I've started looking for other ways to communicate the work I am doing. There is no budget for me or my already stretched little team to do anything extra, but we have a good relationship with the digital communications team and I suggest I might write a blog whilst at the G8.

I also have a hunch that 20 minutes with internet entrepreneur Martha Lane Fox will give me a better sense of my options. Martha has always been a heroine of mine. She boldly went into the dotcom business with a university friend and made a great success of lastminute.com. Since then, she has used her success to campaign against all kinds of human-rights abuses, and has a personal drive to widen internet access to everyone, while still finding time to run her own karaoke business, Lucky Voice.

She comes to see me at Number 10 and we sit down at my PC in the flat. For security reasons, the Downing Street system does not fully access the internet, so I have my own computer set up separately for personal emails, internet shopping and so on. Martha shows me all kinds of good sites, and for social media she suggests Facebook and most of all Twitter. Looking at the Twitter site I realise that as long as I write it myself, Twitter will be perfect. Each message has a limit of 140 characters and I immediately joke that this should be within my concentration span.

What I think Twitter can do is give people a glimpse into my daily life and the world of Downing Street without having to do a newspaper interview, which frankly scares me, as the media can take the smallest thing and twist it beyond all recognition. At least with Twitter if I get into trouble, it will be for something I have actually said. I decide to mull it over for a few days.

I head off to a reception in the Pillared Room in Number 10, hosted for the London Jewish Museum that is due to open soon in Camden Town. I speak at the reception and talk to all the guests and benefactors accompanied by Wendy Levene, who has steered the fundraising to make it all happen.

She kindly gives me one of the gifts that each guest will receive as they depart: a book about the museum and a tiny box of cakes. Konrad takes them off me to quickly log them in to the gift register before he goes home, and I head back to the flat. Moments later he sends me a text that reads: 'Did you read the box?'

It turns out that the side of the tiny cake box reads 'Lunch with Boris Johnson for the Museum on 25.06.09'. The heart of the Labour government is advertising an event for the Conservative Mayor of London. It's too late to do anything, so we decide it's best to laugh about it instead.

Wednesday 18th March

The work has started in earnest for next month's G20 preparations. My office takes on the arrangements for the spouses' programme, including various charity and cultural visits and a spouse dinner in Number 11 while the leaders eat in Number 10. Having worked in the private sector on all kinds of gala dinners and conferences, I realise I know exactly how to do this with a small but really competent team. We add Jill Sharp, an events organiser from the Foreign Office, to our team and enlist Maggie to co-host the spouse dinner using her big state room at Number 11.

Our core team expands to a grand total of five, while the USA team for the Obamas' visit, we are told, will comprise a total of 500 people. This is not a direct comparison but it serves to make the point about how fabulous my tiny team is.

One of the first people to write to me when the G20 was announced for London was Alexandra Shulman, the editor of British *Vogue*, to offer involvement. We meet and agree that *Vogue* will photograph the spouses together in the splendour of the Royal Opera House. I choose this beautiful, central, and security-conscious venue after a quick call to its Chief Executive Tony Hall, who did not hesitate for a second before promising to help arrange a memorable cultural event for the spouses.

Saturday 21st March

With event planning for the G20 taken as far as it can go for now, I decide to brave my new Twitter account. I realise it is a bit of a leap of faith as social media is developing so quickly (Twitter was invented in 2006 and already has two billion tweets a quarter).

I am sitting quietly at home in North Queensferry when I register. I discover there are quite a few Sarah Browns already, so I opt for @SarahBrown10 just to get going. I see there is a language of #hashtags, #Follow Fridays, #CharityTuesdays, smilies ☺, and asterisks that *need to be learned* to really engage with all its possibilities!

I duly type my first tweet: SarahBrown10: Want to help sign up one million mums? http://www.millionmums.org

As I explore, I learn that Twitter has a sense of humour. It can be mean, but it is essentially friendly, so meanness does not work for long. You are not under pressure to reply, but there is an etiquette ('Twittiquette') which encourages Twitter to be about what you put out, not what you demand back.

I set up a Facebook page, too, but I can already tell that it is Twitter that I understand immediately. By the end of the first day I have seven friends on Twitter, and four on Facebook. Two of them work in the same building as me, but you have to start somewhere.

Monday 23rd March

I have breakfast with Shelagh Bright, this year's *GMTV* mum of the year winner, who comes with her daughter Leanne George, herself a mother of two. Shelagh has suffered the loss of twin sons and not long ago lost her husband. Now Leanne has been diagnosed with a terminal brain tumour. The pair of them are here to enjoy their day and we have a chatty breakfast and tour.

We all face the possibility of unimagined fears around the corner, and for Shelagh and her family, those fears have been realised all too often. I know that feeling but I also know it is important to never let fear take hold of you for long. We can honour and remember those we have lost, but must embrace life and those around us too. Shelagh clearly has not lost sight of this and I am very struck by these two women and the courage and humour they both have.

The Reverend Jesse Jackson Jnr also visited Downing Street with his wife, Jacqueline, today. He has been reading the British newspapers while travelling in from the airport and is very struck by the tragic death of *Big Brother* star Jade Goody. I hope that Jade will be smiling at the thought that the Prime Minister and the Rev Jesse Jackson are talking about her and her sons so kindly.

And for me, it has been quite a day for pondering the joy of living.

Tuesday 24th March

Gordon sets off on a globe-trotting tour to meet numerous world leaders as part of the consultations for the G20 meeting. I travel with him first to Strasbourg where he is addressing the European Parliament. The President of the European Parliament, a right-wing politician, greets him and says, 'I never thought I would see a time when I support Labour more than the Conservatives, but that time has come.'

Gordon's speech seems to hit all the right notes and gets a standing ovation from everyone from all European nations, apart from the small British contingent of UKIP representatives. They actually boo from behind their desktop Union Flags when the Lisbon Treaty is mentioned. It just doesn't seem to me a grown-up way to behave in a democratically elected Parliament.

We then fly to New York where Gordon is meeting numerous bankers and economists, and speaking at events with the *Wall Street Journal* and at New York University.

Wednesday 25th March

I use my day in New York for a charity lunch, and also a meeting with the great Glenda Bailey, editor-in-chief of *Harpers Bazaar* US. Glenda, a Brit, has been very influential in getting the fashion industry behind my campaigns and I take the opportunity to congratulate her on her recent MBE. We talk about the British Fashion Council and the wealth of young British talent that resides in American labels like Banana Republic, Kate Spade and Gap. She promises that she will come for London Fashion Week for the first time in years, which is a massive boost as it looks like US *Vogue's* editor, Anna Wintour (another powerful Brit in New York), will also be attending. Glenda and I are firm friends by the time I leave my camomile tea in her giant atrium coffee area, and I expect we will work together soon.

Thursday 26th March

Next stop is Brasilia, the capital of Brazil, where Gordon has a long meeting with his great friend President Lula for an important G20 discussion – Brazil is one of the world's emerging new economic powerhouses. I use my time here to visit Dr Adson, the man charged with reducing maternal mortality in Brazil, for a detailed briefing and have a short meeting with the country's Health Minister, too. A fascinating insight into the country, its achievements and remaining sizeable public health challenges. Memorably, I am given a popular Brazilian fizzy drink and discover it tastes exactly like Irn Bru!

We are soon off again to the huge city of Sao Paulo in the south of Brazil, where a conference is taking place in a rather exquisite private house. Peter Mandelson is speaking on the stage as we arrive, and as he steps down I chuckle as 'The Girl from Ipanema' is played over the loudspeakers. Gordon is up next and the music changes to something rather less flamboyant. We have an overnight stay here, and are off again first thing.

Saturday 28th March

On arrival in Chile's capital of Santiago we are greeted with a diplomatic mishap. Peter Mandelson and Douglas Alexander are first off the plane and the chief of protocol (or some such title) greets them loudly and clearly with the words, 'Welcome to Chile on behalf of President Pinochet.'

There is a silence and then a loud cough. 'Errr ... on behalf of President Bachelet.' There could not be a more different leader in charge of this country. Michelle Bachelet is their first woman President, a doctor of paediatrics and a major force for social reform.

I have a schedule for Chile that allows me to see first-hand the positive difference being made to women's and children's health care that has totally reversed the mortality figures in just a few years. A country like Chile shows us what can be done for those who are sceptical about health-care development.

Throughout the trip I have logged on to any computer I can find to follow my Twitter account and put out messages about the various visits and people I encounter. I discover that I am a bit cautious about starting off. All the obvious social anxieties that arise are not dissimilar to the thought of going to a party on your own when you might not know anyone. What if no one signs up to follow my tweets? What if all I get is negative messages, or worse still, ignored? And for me, what if everyone just uses it as a sounding board for government issues which I won't be in a position to respond to? And what do I want to tweet about?

I discover that the best way forward is to have a go. The process develops its own dynamic quite quickly, and my follower numbers start to creep up slowly every day. I find that if I just look at my day – whether the excitement of an official visit in a fascinating country like Chile, or just an ordinary office day or day at home with the family – there is always something to say.

There are also other interesting things being posted on Twitter and I am very keen on the RT (retweet) button to share information with my followers.

My first important moment of Twitter recognition is a tweet from Tech Crunch Editor, @mikebutcher saying, 'Welcome to Twitter Mrs Brown, or should that be SarahBrown10?' Recognising my inner geek – I am very excited by that!

The best top tips I receive to get me going are: to put up a photo (either my own pic or something quirky); to have a chirpy, witty or thoughtful bio – mine says 'Signing up a million mums' for the new campaign I am fronting with the White Ribbon Alliance; and to just get going as the tweets will come and people will find you. It is clear that following people brings followers back.

Finding my own Twitter voice that lets me be myself in just 140 characters is the key, though. Looking at any of the big tweeters with the giant follower numbers, I notice they all have a distinctive tone and you can see quickly why it works for them, whether they are the current number one tweeters: @aplusk (actor Ashton Kutcher); @stephenfry; @eddieizzard; or @downingstreet (Number 10's Twitter feed reporting Gordon's daily moves is approaching a million followers after less than a year).

Sunday 29th March

Back in London, and we catch up with family (and sleep). This means rushing in to see the boys, playing with them, going out to the garden or sneaking off to the park, and sitting down together at meal times.

In the flat on our own, I cook for everyone and we often have Andrew and Clare, and the teenage cousins, Alex and Patrick, join us for a meal, too.

Sunday is the last calm day before the arrival of all the world leaders for the G20. We approve menus, sign off on table plans, and decide final numbers for the many interpreters and aides. I do what I always do which is take advantage of the fact that homelife and worklife are next door to each other, and jump back and forwards between the two. Luckily I find that despite the proximity, wherever I am, I am immersed in what goes on there – if I am with the family that is all that matters, and once I walk just a few steps through a door and down a staircase to my office, my mind completely moves to work mode.

Monday 30th March

This evening, I accompany Gordon to Buckingham Palace for the State Visit of the President of Mexico, Felipe de Calderón, and his wife, Margarita Zavala de Calderón. Gordon gets on his white tie with minutes to spare – the arrival times are very precise for these occasions. I wear another Amanda Wakeley dress – dark green silk embellished with little brass rings that clank ever so slightly. I am seated between Ian Luder, the delightful Lord Mayor of London this year, and the Mexican general in charge of State and Presidential Security, who turns out to be a great Beatles fan.

Tuesday 31st March

I join Gordon at St Paul's Cathedral for an event organised by the St Paul's Institute on Trust, Faith and Morals. We meet fellow speaker Kevin Rudd and his wife, Thérèse Rein. PM Rudd starts off by calling Gordon 'Prime Minister Brown', from the platform, then moves on to calling him 'Gordon', and at the end of the session is referring to him as 'mate'. I think in Australia that is a compliment.

Back at the flat, we prepare for a very busy few days, starting with President and Mrs Obama's arrival through the black door first thing tomorrow morning.

CHAPTER 20

London Calling

Wednesday 1st April

The London G20 summit is about to kick off and our team at Downing Street has worked night and day to get everything ready. Every single person in the building and across many government departments has contributed to getting ready for this meeting that will address the challenges of the global economy and the financial crisis we all face.

Everyone understands how important this is to Britain. The leaders from the G20 countries represent 85 per cent of the world's economic activity, and their job is to take action collectively to 'stabilise the world economy and secure recovery and jobs'.

All the scaffolding from Downing Street's big restoration is gone, so the building is spotless inside and out. Even the custodians' buttons shine a little bit brighter. The boys watch as the first camera crews move into position on the media platforms opposite, where they will hardly move for several days.

Inside, the day starts with a normal breakfast although the traffic through our kitchen is a bit busier than usual. My mum and stepfather are here to join the initial meeting with Michelle Obama, which is to be very informal. I butter some toast for the boys and pass it to my mum, asking her to check it is all eaten up. When I turn back a few moments later I see my stepfather is munching it! Not quite what I had in mind! I hurry to feed the boys but everyone is a bit distracted by the commotion outside.

Fortunately both Gil and Mela appear, so I rush upstairs and finish getting dressed and put on some make-up. I have a pretty, navy ruffle-fronted Britt Lintner dress and a great pair of high, but comfortable, purple patent heels. We are meeting tall people today, so heels are good.

I am downstairs at 8 a.m. sharp. The Downing Street staff line the hall corridor down to the Cabinet Room as they did on the day we first arrived. This is the 'special relationship' tradition for the first visit of a US President, and many remember the same welcome for Presidents Bush and Clinton. Sue Nye even remembers clapping for President Jimmy Carter when he came to meet PM James Callaghan.

The Presidential armoured limousine pulls up and we all greet each other warmly. President Obama enters Number 10 and shakes hands with as many people as possible. I am thrilled when he reaches my driver Roy and grasps his hand, as Roy so wanted to have this moment.

The President and Gordon are then led off to the Pillared Room for their meeting, while I take Michelle to the White Room for us to have a chat. I have also invited Elisabeth Murdoch, the TV company boss. Elisabeth (an American married to a Brit) hosted the biggest UK-based fundraiser for the Obamas' election campaign. This provides a welcome opportunity for Michelle to thank Elisabeth for her support. We talk about that campaign, the changing nature of politics as people's needs change, and how we can understand better what people want.

It is not long before the First Lady and I have to depart, heading out past the multitude of cameras. On our car journey, we can catch up a little more privately about family news and the activities coming up during the summit.

I am delighted to take Michelle to visit the Maggie's Cancer Caring Centre in Fulham, and meet some of the centre users. Maggie's is an extraordinary charity of which I am very proud to be the Patron. Their cancer care centres across Scotland, with more on the way in England and Wales, are very special, each one a unique design by a world-class architect. The Maggie's London centre, with its uplifting bright orange exterior, was designed by Richard Rogers and Ivan Harbour, who are here today, together with the talented landscape designer, Dan Pearson, who created a tranquil garden for the centre; an oasis of calm in the city.

The charity's chief executive, Laura Lee, is there to meet us and take us inside to meet everyone. Charles Jencks is there: he was married to Maggie Keswick Jencks who started the first centre when she set out, during her own cancer treatment, to find the 'joy of living' in the 'fear of dying'. So, too, is Maggie's son, John, alongside our Health Secretary, Alan Johnson, and our government Cancer Tsar, Mike Richardson. Everyone is here to welcome our special visitor today.

Michelle Obama meets a mum suffering from cancer and her young children and envelopes the whole family in a giant hug. We talk to three men who all speak about some of the special difficulties surrounding male cancers, and then watch a Look Good, Feel Better beauty and make-up session.

We also have time to go to the emotional heart of the building, its kitchen, where River Café chefs Ruthie Rogers (the architect Richard Rogers's wife) and Rose Gray have made a special cake to celebrate the building's first anniversary. I put on the kettle and make a pot of tea so we can all sit at the table and hear more about what makes a Maggie's Centre so special.

When it is time to leave, there are more hugs from the First Lady. As Michelle explains, 'Hugs; they're what I do. When you are big and tall, you don't want to be scary, so hugs are what I do.' Hugs work for me, and for everyone else, too.

Back at Downing Street, I go over the final arrangements for the evening with the Number 10 team. The tables are laid, the flowers have arrived, the staff is hard at work. I look over everything I can and know it will all run smoothly.

*

My hairdresser, Mark, comes in to sort out my hair for the evening, and as an extra treat to myself, one of the beauticians from his Biba salon comes to do my nails. I will be wearing a plain chocolate brown belted Britt dress, an extraordinary beaded brown jacket from Graeme Black and nice Jimmy Choo stiletto heels, the exact match of my dress (Gordon has a smart new outfit, too: a Gieves & Hawkes suit and a British designer tie). I have a crystal necklace I have owned for years that sets it all off perfectly. I always say my job is to look tidy and not fall over. This evening, I am as tidy as I can manage.

I meet up with Gordon at the end of his bilateral meetings with individual leaders and, once he has changed, we are driven the short distance to Buckingham Palace where the Queen is hosting a pre-dinner reception. As we arrive, we are ushered into a room to greet the Queen and the Duke of Edinburgh as they come out of their private audience with the Obamas. We can see as they walk through the doorway that Michelle has her arm stretched out behind the Queen rather protectively, and it is clear the meeting has gone well.

We accompany everyone back to the main reception in the Picture Gallery where I go on stand-by mode as the main photograph is taken of the Queen with all the G20 delegates.

With that done, Gordon is whisked out of the room and we are back to Downing Street double-quick to be in place to greet the first of our dinner guests.

This is a moment of nervousness. We have a protocol-ordered set of arrivals and we are to greet each couple jointly on the doorstep. Where the spouse is not arriving, only Gordon will step outside to make the official welcome and photograph, and I will greet the guest inside the door. Each photograph taken will be heavily used back in each guest's country of origin, so we need to make sure that every meeting goes smoothly.

Our guests start to arrive, walking down the red carpet past the huge array of cameras and lights. Gordon greets each one by name, and I welcome them and explain the instructions for the photo.

Fortunately, we had our dress rehearsal with the Obamas this morning so it all goes smoothly and there is such a pace to it that I have no time to be nervous. When the Obamas arrive there is, if possible, an even greater flurry of shouting and camera clicking.

Once through the front door, the Leaders head off to the State Dining Room, while the First Ladies turn left and go off to Number 11 through the connected doorway. We have four tables of eight for the spouses' dinner, one hosted by me, one by Maggie, one by our House of Commons Leader, Harriet Harman, and one by our House of Lords Leader, Jan Royall.

I have invited a number of eminent British women, who are all suitably excited to be part of the occasion – just like me, really. My guest list is: author, JK Rowling; Olympic gold medallist, Dame Kelly Holmes; Paralympian gold medallist, Dame Tanni Grey-Thompson; philanthropist, Dame Gail Ronson; charity director, Emma Freud; supermodel, Naomi Campbell; film director, Gurinder Chadha; publisher, Gail Rebuck; child-development expert, Dr Tanya Byron; internet guru and entrepreneur, Martha Lane Fox; human-rights activist, Jasvinder Sanghera; *Gavin and Stacey* writer and actress, Ruth Jones; and educationalist (and also my mother), Pauline Macaulay. I am delighted also that we are able to persuade Dr Ngozi Okonjo-Iweala, the managing director of the World Bank, to join our women's dinner. The list stands or falls with me, but I chose the women to ensure an interesting mix, led by my personal choice combined with a knowledge of some of the other spouses' personal interests.

The room is very buzzy with chatter as drinks are served and lots of introductions made. Once the spouses have all arrived, we do a quick check to see that everyone is there. Naomi Campbell admits to me that she arrived at the back entrance, and I ask if she wouldn't mind nipping out and re-arriving through the front door to catch all the photographs properly. We poke our noses out of the Number 11 door and see all eyes are looking the other way. Naomi nips over to the red carpet as if arriving for the first time, and all the camera flashes go wild. (We laughed later that she must have seemed supermodel-late, even though she'd been inside with us for ages.)

I stand for a moment in the doorway and look at all the wonderful women in the room. Many are here because of who they are married to, but everyone is someone doing something very special with whatever circumstances they've found themselves in. I can see that Michelle is radiating her charisma and special girl-power status at a great cluster of women around her. With everyone in their finery and looking very sparkly, we do try to gather together as one big group for a photograph. That is fairly chaotic as everyone would prefer to be chatting, not posing, so goodness knows what will come out. With the arrivals and photos done, we can now relax.

We move upstairs to the Number 11 State Dining Room, a simple but still rather grand room overlooking the gardens. I am very used to this room, having hosted numerous events there while Gordon was Chancellor, and it is a really good space to entertain in. From the Government Art Collection, Maggie has hung paintings by young artists such as Darren Almond and Anya Gallaccio on the cream walls, alongside contemporary giants like Howard Hodgkin and Scottish artist Joan Eardley. The tables look exquisite, decorated with late spring British flowers that fill the room with their scent. Everyone is seated and chatting away, so I simply welcome them all, with some special thanks for my other table hosts.

I am seated between the First Ladies of Russia and Korea. Our chefs for both dinners are being organised by Jamie Oliver, who is here to make sure that his apprentices create a memorable meal. We have Scottish salmon, a slow-cooked Welsh lamb stew and a rustic Bakewell tart made with English raspberries (afterwards, Emma Freud admits that they had a Comic Relief thank-you dinner a couple of weeks ago, where Jamie used them as guinea pigs for his G20 menu). Truthfully, I talk too much to eat a lot, but it all looks and smells divine.

As soon as dessert is finished, I invite everyone to follow me back down the stairs, along the corridors and up the Number 10 staircase to join the G20 leaders for coffee as they emerge from their working dinner. The men – and Chancellor Merkel – look momentarily distracted, and then suddenly click into a more sociable mood for a cup of coffee and petit fours. I introduce as many of my guests as I can to Presidents Obama, Sarkozy and Medvedev. Many already know Gordon so he is able to pop around and say hello himself. Gordon also calls Jamie Oliver and his apprentices out from the kitchen to thank them for their delicious meal. I know that Jamie is absolutely busting to meet the new US President and I take him across to introduce him. Jamie does not miss the opportunity to share his own US plans and is rewarded with the President's good wishes. He also has to head home quickly as his wife, Jools, is expecting her third baby imminently, so everyone gives him their congratulations before he goes on his way.

Before she leaves, Ruth Jones admits to Gordon that she actually binned my first invitation thinking that it was a hoax from one of her comedian friends.

With a busy day ahead, we wrap things up quite quickly and send everyone home. Gordon is straight off to get his head down, clutching the draft communiqué. I am rather less disciplined and take Jo Rowling and Emma Freud up to the kitchen to unwind with a cup of tea and a debrief on an incredible night. We all have a chuckle as we'd spotted Prime Minister Berlusconi asking Naomi for her phone number.

Thursday 2nd April

While Gordon is today chairing the first day of the G20 London Summit at the Excel Centre in Docklands to get everyone in agreement on the communiqué for the Global Plan for Recovery and Reform, I am hosting the start of the spouses' programme.

The main event of the day is at the Royal Opera House, where Tony Hall and creative director Deborah Bull have created a wonderful selection of 'tasters' for us, from school students in the Chance to Dance programme to the innovative Ballet Black. Mariella Frostrup anchors the event and JK Rowling reads the story 'The Fountain of Fair Fortune' from her new little book *The Tales of Beedle the Bard*.

After one contemporary dance piece I am, however, told off by a Foreign Office official who says that there was too much 'flashing buttock' for some of our more conservative guests. Eek!

Our 'official G20 spouse' photograph is taken by the great Mario Testino, who has all the First Ladies lined up on the great stage of the ROH with the lights behind. In addition, *Vogue* editor Alexandra Shulman has arranged for the women to be given the full 'Mario treatment' in a group photo, styled by fashion director Lucinda Chambers and destined for the pages of the next issue of British *Vogue*. This is to be my treat to send on to everyone afterwards when it is published.

I get a special thrill in introducing the talented young Korean singer Ji-Min Park to our two guests from South Korea. We end our cultural feast with a quick peek at the last rehearsals of the ballet *Giselle*.

Back at Downing Street, I wait for news from the summit itself. Finally, word comes that full agreement has been reached. There are cheers and whoops from the staff and the mood visibly lightens. It has been a great slog to get everything ready and also a big risk, with quite a few external commentators questioning whether it could be done.

Gordon and his private office team arrive back at 6 p.m. to full cheers and a great welcome, with the drinks coming out. The head of events, Helen Etheridge, who has steered all the arrangements and logistics at the Excel Centre, enters an hour later to equally large cheers and rightly so. Drinks in hand, everyone turns to the news reports to see what is coming out. Gordon is quoted as saying: 'This is the day that the world came together to fight recession – not with words, but with a plan for economic recovery and reform.'

That plan is to strengthen the financial system with an unprecedented $1.1 trillion to support credit, growth and jobs across the world. The headlines show that a historic global agreement has been reached, and Gordon's chairmanship is widely praised around the world, not least for the preparation required in pulling all the different elements together.

President Obama's press conference goes very well, apart from *The Sun*'s newspaper reporter who surprises everyone, after the BBC, Sky and ITV ask big economic questions, with a person-ality-based question seemingly designed only to undermine Gordon. The reporter uses his moment, at the height of Gordon's successful day, to question the new US President by asking if he has any advice to help Gordon win the election, despite trailing poll numbers.

It is a sign of what is to come. *The Sun*'s front page shows a picture of Gordon digitally remastered as the Austin Powers character, Dr Evil, with the headline, 'And to save the world, I demand … one tril-lion dollars.' It is an insulting, immature response to a remarkable day and leaves everyone in the office rather stunned as to why such a professedly patriotic paper would choose to undermine Britain, never mind the government or Gordon, on such a historic day.

Fortunately, the other headlines are more level-headed and Anatole Kaletsky in *The Times* writes that 'the main thrust of the G20 response to the crisis has been absolutely right'.

Saturday 11th April

It is just the four of us quietly at home in Scotland for the Easter break, and it is lovely. But I should know from experience not to trust these kinds of days. As we are settling down with washed, pyjama-ed boys in the sitting-room, there is a call from Damian McBride, one of Gordon's press officers. All I hear after a long silence is Gordon saying, 'Well, you know you will have to resign, don't you?' Damian has called to tell Gordon that some private emails he sent will be appearing in the newspapers tomorrow, and these will put Damian in a very bad light for suggesting ways to maliciously attack, and even slander, individual MPs on a website.

While the idea does not seem to have been taken any further, it sounds pretty awful, and not something that an employee at 10 Downing Street should be doing.

Monday 13th April

We get back to work even though we are still in Scotland. At breakfast, Fraser says to me, 'Look, today you are the prime minister.' When I ask him why, he says, 'Because today you are wearing the suit.'

If only it were that easy.

What I am enjoying about being at back my desk, though, is catching up with Twitter; my 30 followers, at the last count, have now risen to a mighty 600.

Amid the awfulness of the press coverage following the publication of Damian's emails, there is one cheerful moment. We watch Susan Boyle's magnificent performance in *Britain's Got Talent* on YouTube and can see that already over one million people have watched this, too. Bless her, and we do wish her well.

Also on the upside, I hear that Jo Rowling is writing a profile of Gordon for his entry in this year's *Time* magazine list of the 100 most influential people. I will let that be a surprise for him as he is currently writing, at *Time*'s request, the profile for President Obama's entry in the same list.

Wednesday 15th April

I stay in Scotland a little longer and have a good clean-up of our garden toys from sandpit to pedal tractors. I tweet about this on my computer and get a tremendous response. I have also been planting lots of tomatoes, peppers and sweetcorn in our Downing Street planters with the boys. I report on that, too, and get a great set of replies back. My Twitter followers rise to my all-time high of 1,900!

CHAPTER 21

Flying the Flag in LA

Sunday 19th April

After a couple of weeks' breathing space, I am ready to take off again, this time to attend the African First Ladies Summit in Los Angeles, to make the keynote speech. It is a fair distance to go for just a few days, but I am thrilled as my brother Sean lives in LA. I will get to see him in his own home at last.

I fly out with Christianne and we work on my speech much of the way, as well as reading up on Africa's First Ladies. The flight is so long, though, that I also manage to fit in watching both *The Reader* and *Vicky Cristina Barcelona*. On arrival, we are met by our LA Consulate General and are to stay at the UK Residence there. The rest of the day is a blur due to jet-lag.

Monday 20th April

As I am really hit by the time difference, I start gently with a visit to Sean and Caroline at their lovely home in Sherman Oaks, with a spectacular view over the San Fernando Valley. I see my gorgeous little nieces Isabel and Honor and come bearing gifts – from Boden, of course – of swimsuits and summer dresses decorated with appliqué strawberries and bunnies. The perfect Brit look in fashionable LA and something that makes me a very popular Auntie Sarah.

From there, I dash off to meet California's First Lady, Maria Shriver. Maria is married to Governor Arnold Schwarzenegger and has made a huge success of the Women's Conference, growing it into an annual event that attracts tens of thousands of women. She is the sister of my friend, Tim Shriver, the chairman of the Special Olympics. I first met Maria in Cape Cod when she was partnering Gordon for some doubles tennis against Tim and Senator Edward Kennedy. Both of us remember the match they played, where Maria and Gordon were all set to succeed as Tim's partner, the Senator, just stood in the middle of his side of the court and reached with his racket if the ball came close. Tim played his heart out around the Senator and ultimately triumphed, much to his opponents' chagrin.

We meet in a hotel, and Maria introduces me to her university student daughter, Katherine. Maria and I are there to talk about our different women's campaigns and she wants to hear more about the maternal mortality campaign. As we talk, Katherine starts to contribute some terrific ideas to engage women her own age with the campaign. By the end of our meeting, I am urging her to play a bigger part, and she agrees to take on a youth ambassador role.

That evening, Sean and Caroline come with me to have dinner with Wendi and Rupert Murdoch at their Bel Air home. There is a gathering of friends from the film business, including Robert Iger, the head of Disney, and his lovely wife, Willow Bay. There is also Arianna Huffington, last seen on the Davos slopes in a ball gown, who is always so vivacious and positive. She regales us with memories of her romance with the writer, Bernard Levin, saying, 'He was twice my age and half my size. I would have followed him anywhere.'

After drinks at sunset on the terrace, we go in for dinner and I am seated next to Rupert. At some point the conversation turns to the general election in Britain, due in 2010. He tells me very seriously how much he likes and admires Gordon, but he does not know if Gordon can win the election as it is just a time for change.

I don't know what conversations he has had with people from other political parties, but I don't think anyone is counting on his papers supporting Labour again at the next election. It was a very pleasant evening nonetheless.

Tuesday 21st April

Christianne, Emma Parry and I are driven to the Skirball Center for the African First Ladies summit, where we get a terrific reception on arrival.

The conference kicks off with a video message from former First Lady, Laura Bush. I then give my speech setting out the challenge to save the lives of mothers and children, and a call to action to the African First Ladies to adopt the cause in their own countries. Public speaking is still daunting to me, but I have had a good amount of time to rehearse. I feel I deliver the speech as well as I possibly can and I am rewarded with an overwhelming standing ovation and great hugs from the First Ladies when I return to my seat.

I spend the rest of the day meeting various experts, academics and campaigners at the conference. I also take a group to meet with Melanne Verveer who is Secretary of State Hillary Clinton's trusted adviser on women's issues.

At the end of the afternoon, we hold a very touching event with Naomi Campbell as she is announced as the new ambassador for the White Ribbon Alliance. Since our first meeting, when expectations were low, Naomi has continued to surprise me with her commitment to the charity with real work, and not just tipping up to show support. She has also done something that is far more rare than you would think from celebrity supporters; she has actually raised a good amount of money for the charity herself. It's not too much to say that she is revered by the African First Ladies.

A round-table conversation allows the First Ladies to express their thoughts in turn about maternal health and women's issues, to draw on their own experiences, and to identify what best they can achieve in their own countries.

In the evening there is a gala night at the Beverly Hilton where everyone arrives in their best finery and national costumes. The guests include inspiring speakers like my friend Zainab Salbi from Women for Women International. Zainab tells the audience about her meeting with a woman in the Congo, who had been brutally beaten and raped. 'I asked if I could tell her story and she said, "Yes. Go ahead and tell the world – just don't tell my neighbours."' A reminder about how these sorts of issues and happenings can be spoken about and used to make useful points globally, but that one must always remember that they are a personal, individual issue, too.

Despite the sober messages, the evening is designed to be diverting for all the First Ladies, after two days of intense conference sessions and working groups.

My brother, Sean, is with me at the dinner, as is Emma Parry. Naomi sits down next to Sean and her opening introduction is, 'I've met your mum!'

She then turns to Emma and admires her dress, asking which designer she had chosen. Emma admits it was a high-street sale purchase, but is chuffed at the compliment. As we are all seated, Naomi plonks a spoon in her champagne and said, 'That stops the bubbles. It's the bubbles that get me into trouble.' As the champagne was much in evidence this evening I stood prepared to change my mind about Naomi, but she was as good as gold.

After we've eaten, and when I come off the stage after presenting various awards, I am told by an organiser that Paris Hilton would like to meet me. I have no idea why, but am perfectly happy to say hello. She comes and joins our table for a while and I have no real preconceptions. She is actually very chatty about her life and her business, which is basically Brand: Paris. We don't really have enormous overlap in our interests, but she does ask good questions about the charity and about the summit. I get the impression I am talking to a smart woman who is running a successful enterprise and mostly enjoying herself. She tweets about our meeting from the table, showing all the non-tweeters how to do it.

Wednesday 22nd April

Ahead of my flight home, I have a lunch invitation from Piers Morgan to join him at the famous Ivy restaurant in Beverly Hills with a few fellow Brits. Sean, Caroline and I turn up to find our ebullient friend perfectly positioned at an outdoor table out front. He looks every inch the super-famous person he has become since offering to take the newest superstar Susan Boyle out on a date. He has invited his chums Sharon Osbourne, Katherine Jenkins and June Sarpong to join us for a house chicken salad, a corner of a chocolate brownie (it is LA, you can't be seen doing more than nibble) and a rather more British large glass of white wine in the middle of the day.

Everyone is on spectacularly good form and soon sharing their favourite stories of celeb mishaps. My brother Sean wins hands down with his tale of first meeting JK Rowling in my kitchen and not recognising her. When he asked 'Jo' what she did, and she modestly replied she was a writer, he magnanimously offered his creative advice: 'The important thing, love, is to finish your first draft—'

'Shut up!' exclaims Mrs Osbourne, in her familiar TV judge tones. Sharon is much warmer and more approachable to meet in person than her TV persona would suggest, and rather beautiful.

Katherine and June are both working hard in LA and content just to watch the lunchtime show that is Piers and Sharon today.

Just before 3 p.m. I have to shoot off to catch my plane. As we leave, Piers makes a point of telling the waiting photographers not to make a fuss – which pretty much guarantees they do exactly that. He is one of those people who truly loves being famous. So big hugs and lots of air kisses to my LA friends and I am off again.

I phone home to Gordon and warn him to expect that I may pop up in the British press as the trivial person off having celebrity lunches while the Budget is being presented. Gordon is fairly robust about this as he knows that we are doing good things at the summit too, and it is not as though Ivy lunches are an everyday thing for me.

As if to prove this point, when Emma and I get on the plane together with 6ft Tammy Haddad, we are all assigned a different middle seat somewhere at the back. I have been very insistent about flying economy during the recession so this is just the deal, but it is a knee-locking four hours in the air to Washington DC, more meetings, and then home.

Friday 24th April

I join Gordon in attending Sir Clement Freud's funeral at St Bride's Church on Fleet Street, today. He was truly a man who could be described as a national institution. The order of service reads: 'Sir Clement Freud. Born 24.04.24. Best Before 15.04.09.'

We go straight on to the Labour Party Conference in Swansea to hear a brave, bold and uplifting speech from Gordon that has everyone up on their feet at the end. Gordon is facing a lot of leaks about Labour's private election strategy talks, which is disturbing as it means someone on the inside is doing it. It's the worst of the worst when this happens.

Monday 27th April

Gordon has just returned from a visit to Afghanistan over the weekend, but we are ready to travel again almost immediately. We have long looked for a date when we could visit the Holocaust death camps of Auschwitz and Birkenau to pay personal tributes. We travel first to Warsaw where we will stay tonight.

Tuesday 28th April

While Gordon has official meetings with the Polish President, I travel with the Ambassador's wife, Alison Todd, to the Presidential palace and find her a wonderful guide for pointing out important landmarks. We meet the First Lady, Mrs Kaczyński, who takes us out on a visit to a local primary school that prides itself on its special green ecology status. It makes me realise how brilliantly our UK head teachers are doing, too, with their own green measures, helping to engage the children in gardening and outdoor projects.

From the Polish capital, we take a small plane to Krakow and from there we have an hour's drive to Auschwitz.

Nothing describes adequately such a visit – it is harrowing, emotionally emptying, beyond comprehension. It shows the worst of humanity, alongside the best of humanity in the courage and defiance of the inmates. We have a remarkable young guide, a woman from Krakow University, who helps show visitors round and tells the history of how the Jews and other vulnerable groups were systematically mistreated and murdered by their Nazi captors.

We drive on to visit Birkenau, the bigger camp, and the scale of it is devastating. Our visit lasts two hours and we are fully immersed in the agonies inflicted by humankind on itself. It is one of the most intense experiences of my life.

We are silent for much of the journey to Krakow airport. When we get back to London, my first instinct is to go upstairs and look at my boys, safely asleep in their beds.

Wednesday 29th April

The impact of yesterday's visit is still with me as I attend a service for a friend and former colleague, Ewen Balfour, at St Martin-in-the-Fields church. Everything feels magnified as I gather with family and friends to celebrate the passing of a life that was really well lived. We listen to exquisite music and traditional hymns, and Alan Parker, head of Brunswick PR, where we had all worked, gives a soaring appreciation that makes everyone laugh a lot.

Thursday 30th April

The House is voting on MPs' expenses reform today. It is really down to Nick Brown and the Whips to deliver this for the government.

I always walk around feeling a bit nervous on Big Vote days but, like PMQs, there is nothing I can do. Maggie Darling says she always feels the same, but this time is sure it will be okay. I am told that the newspaper reports are pretty awful today but this I can do something about – I don't read them.

I head with Gil over to PiggyBankKids for our Trustees meeting which is to be chaired by Mary Goudie today, as Swraj is away in India visiting his unwell brother. We are also fortunate to have David Boutcher as our secretary of the charity who is the corporate partner of the big legal firm, Reed Smith. They have recently moved to fantastic new offices as the result of a merger with their US counterpart, so PiggyBankKids now occupies a glass cubicle of its own, free of charge, overlooking the panorama of East London. For our board meetings we can borrow one of the meeting rooms, and avail ourselves of the fabulous lattes and flapjacks from the in-house cafeteria. I do like being able to say we are based at PiggyBankKids Towers, without explaining that this really only consists of three desks and a row of brightly coloured piggy banks.

The House of Commons vote comes in online and it is neck and neck until the last six votes. Thankfully one by one, the Government wins them all. It is win or lose in the Houses of Parliament. And all you have to do is win.

Wednesday 6th May

The new President of Ghana, John Atta Mills, comes in with his wife, Ernestina, to visit Downing Street. Mrs Mills is the first visiting First Lady to admit to me that having watched the famous scenes of visiting leaders on the Number 10 doorstep on TV, she has to pinch herself now to believe it is a real moment for her. I tell her that I still have those moments, and think everyone does, too; I just don't think everyone else wants to say so out loud. It immediately says something positive about people when they are able to express their real thoughts that way.

I am having quite a week of meetings linked to the White Ribbon Alliance so of course talk to Mrs Mills about maternal mortality in Ghana. We are very proud that with Department for International Development support, Ghana is now able to offer free maternity care and deliveries for all pregnant women in Ghana.

Thursday 7th May

One final act for the maternal mortality campaign pays huge dividends for my Twitter link. I have been talking to Malaria Envoy Ray Chambers about getting the malaria campaign messages out via social media. He has found a brilliant agency, Katalyst, headed by a dynamic social media expert, Sarah Ross, who is driving malaria tweets around the world. She has been working on top tweeter, Ashton Kutcher, who has been getting international coverage from his race to become the first person to get over one million followers (in a tight race with US network CNN). Thanks to Sarah, I get a tweet from Ashton for the maternal mortality campaign and my own follower numbers shoot up a fair bit.

CHAPTER 22

Records and Receipts

Thursday 7th May (cont.)

Joe Irvin, head of the political office, contacts me to ask if he can get some quick answers to a number of questions about Gordon's MP expenses that have been submitted by the *Telegraph* newspaper.

The first question is about why Gordon has paid money via his brother Andrew for cleaning services some years before. I can answer him there and then. The reason why Andrew paid the cleaner is that we only paid for the hours where she cleans Gordon's London flat (our own flat in London before the move to Downing Street rather than our own home in Scotland where we cover our own costs). Andrew and Gordon agreed to use the same cleaner so that her total salary would entitle her to National Insurance benefit and give her some security. She has a proper employment contract and the exact number of weekly hours that she did in our London flat is what was a) reimbursed to Andrew and b) submitted on past House of Commons quarterly expenses claims for costs incurred twice by MPs who need to live and work in two different places like us. I assume that once explained, the journalist will understand this should not be a media story.

There is one other cost that Joe Irvin asks me about and I check the files immediately. I discover that we have made a mistake and double-charged a £153 bill. I feel terrible about this as I did the claim personally, and I arrange for a cheque to be sent over straight away. I know that there are numerous costs incurred over the years that don't get claimed at all, so the expenses system will not be out of pocket overall from us, but the rules exist for us to work within them, and this is definitely my mistake.

Gordon had hoped for a clean slate on his expenses as the Prime Minister and, like me, wants the genuine mistake rectified immediately. I can see that the timing of the mistake is when I was on maternity leave, but despite that, I worry how this might be handled by the newspaper. I am so anxious about this that I even call the Chief Executive of the Telegraph Group, and eventually reach him (after the newspaper's print deadline). I make it very clear that I am reporting on my mistake, that it has been corrected and that the newspaper's attack on Gordon is pretty reprehensible and vindictive. Although I feel better for saying it out loud, I sense it will not make much difference.

Friday 8th May

The next day the papers are worse than I, or anyone, could have imagined. Despite my answering the journalist's questions, the *Telegraph* front page is all about the payment to the cleaners, even though no rules were broken. Anyone who knows Gordon or his brothers would know that they are not the kind of people who would do anything with an expenses claim. Quite the reverse. In fact, everything was done to ensure that the cleaner was paid properly and that any claims were made appropriately. The accusation is that somehow we were making money out of the situation and, worse still, that we were actually paying Gordon's brother in a way that he profited personally.

Gordon is out early to visit Sheffield and Bradford and to attend the memorial service for murdered policewoman Sharon Beshenivsky, a very sad occasion with her family that he wants to give his due focus.

I am ill this morning and don't know if it is as a result of the anxiety and distress combined with lack of sleep and overwork, or if I have just caught some awful bug. Once everyone else is out of the flat, I retreat back to bed. I am still very shaky and fluey come the evening, so Mela only heads off for the weekend once Gordon is available to look after the boys.

Discussions have been held with the *Telegraph* and we hear that they will be publishing a further article to clarify that there are no accusations of any wrongdoing by Gordon or his brother. The text reads fine, but of course the worst possible photograph accompanies it. That is pretty much to be expected.

It is clear that, fairly or unfairly, the newspapers have unleashed an attack on MPs and their expenses. However, from the PM down, there has been a concerted effort to improve a complicated and outmoded expenses system for some time, but it has not been sorted out quickly enough by Parliament.

It has been a long and wretched day for us – and one where I do feel indignant and badly treated as, I suspect, do many other MPs' spouses, having had their expenses published in detail. I speak to my sister-in-law, Clare, about her day, which began with TV crews banging on her front door to try to film Andrew. The impact on them has been terrible, right down to their children being bullied by other children.

Monday 11th May

I leave with Gordon at 5.30 a.m. to travel by train to Leeds and on to Harrogate to hear him give his speech to the Annual Conference of the Royal College of Nursing. He is on the train working on his speech with Kirsty McNeill and health adviser Greg Beales. Health Minister Ann Keen also travels with us and reports from her nursing contacts already at the conference how it is going.

Gordon gets a very warm welcome as we arrive at the conference centre. He speaks without notes and just presents a straightforward, sensible speech that connects with everyone in the room by getting to the heart of the issues that matter to the nursing profession. He also finds a way to issue an apology for the problems with MPs' expenses. Despite addressing such a sensitive issue, the delegates give him a standing ovation.

Tuesday 12th May

I am meeting Ffion Hague today, wife of William Hague MP, the Shadow Foreign Secretary. She is a successful recruitment consultant, and has written a wonderful book about the women in former Prime Minister David Lloyd George's life: his wife, Margaret, who was obviously a former resident of Number 10; and his mistress, and later second wife, Frances, who worked there. Ffion is making a TV documentary to accompany the book for the Welsh channel S4C and had written asking to film some clips at Downing Street.

I have met Ffion on a number of occasions and found her very personable. I joined her at her book launch some months back and remember asking her, 'Who would you like me to say hello to?' She had scanned the room full of well-known Conservative Party faces, smiled and said, 'Sarah, I would love you to come and meet my parents. They've travelled all the way from Wales for today.'

Neither Ffion nor I have much documentary-making experience, but we are willing to follow the producer's instructions to walk 'naturally' around the state rooms, talking about Margaret and Frances. During Margaret Lloyd George's time, she would actually have used the grand state rooms as her own living quarters, and we guess that the pretty little White Room where I hold most of my meetings would have been her private sitting room. We find Lloyd George's portrait on the famous Number 10 staircase and spend a bit of time walking up the stairs 'rediscovering' it on each ascent until the programme makers have the shot they want.

The press reveals details of the Opposition MPs' expenses. I think the charge by one MP for cleaning his moat says it all.

Saturday 16th May

David Chaytor MP has been named as an MP with a terrible record on his expenses and suspended today. Gordon is so disappointed by the names surfacing on our side with serious expenses issues. The press is attacking everyone and it is very feverish, but there are some real problems, too, it seems.

Tuesday 19th May

I have been invited by Dr Margaret Chan to speak at the World Health Organization's general assembly, which will be the first time that maternal health has been given such a high profile at WHO. I am really honoured to be chosen as one of two keynote speakers (the other is UN Secretary-General Ban Ki-moon who has to address the issue of H1N1 – swine flu – and how we hope to avoid a pandemic). I am pretty certain that when I enter the great auditorium at the WHO HQ, I am likely to be the only medically unqualified person in the room.

I am up early with the boys and Gordon, who is giving me lots of support for this one. He knows how anxious I can get about public speaking, and this is the biggest thing I have ever done. Lots of hugs and kisses later, I am out of the door and off to Geneva.

My speech is to be issued to the press, so I am to give it exactly as written on the autocue. Even as I stand at the lectern and speak, I make the fateful decision in my head to decide that it is actually going well. Famous last thoughts. About two-thirds of the way through, the autocue screen goes blank. I have no back-up, and am essentially forbidden to ad lib, so I stop talking and explain what has happened.

This is the kind of moment you have bad dreams about. Except it is an agonisingly l-o-n-g moment. Finally, a quick-thinking assistant appears at my side with a hard copy of the speech, pointing her finger to the place where I need to start again.

Afterwards, everyone apologises like crazy and insists they like the speech, but I am just counting the hours until I can get home. At least I can congratulate myself on keeping going – my speech-making-self of a year ago would not have managed that.

Before going home, I join a follow-up session chaired by our UK Minister, Ivan Lewis, where we hear first-hand from the health ministers of Ethiopia, Uganda and Pakistan who put our campaign ideas into action at the country level. All the talking in the world means nothing if we can't save lives.

Thursday 21st May

Gordon meets actress and Gurkha campaigner Joanna Lumley and a group of the Gurkhas to look for a resolution to the issue of the equal rights of Gurkha veterans to settle in the United Kingdom, following the loss of a crucial vote against the government in the House of Commons. An agreement has been reached and all sides seem to be quite happy, so much so that an invitation is issued – on a beautiful summer's day – for the campaigners and their families to come for afternoon tea in the garden.

I am meeting the winners of *The Sun*'s Wondermum Awards: wonderful, sweet women who give their all for family and community, often against the odds. We can hear the cheers of the Gurkhas coming through the windows, and we are all peeking out at the sight of everyone draped in their distinctive yellow silk scarves and Jo Lumley cutting a glamorous dash through the centre of the crowd. The garden is suddenly teeming as twice as many people turn up as were expected. When I walk outside with Gordon, he gets three cheers and we are both festooned with the honour of their yellow silk scarves. Gordon makes a lovely, moving speech and we meet the oldest soldiers, some of whom served in the Second World War, and their families.

Jo Lumley is warm and full of praise for Gordon, having been a figurehead for the Gurkhas' campaign and kept a fastidiously political neutral stance. Gordon had first got involved when presented with three options, and opted for the most generous of the three, but it was only at the point of losing the vote that he understood that none of the options offered would be sufficient for what the Gurkhas were seeking for themselves and their families. Thankfully, today we can look on happy faces and see that the problem has been resolved.

The top expenses stories today are as wretched as ever, but another story does reflect better on Labour. Laura Moffatt, our MP in Croydon, is pictured on the camp bed she uses in her office, next to a quote by a Conservative MP who says voters are just jealous of his big houses.

Gordon is off for a private meeting with Tony Blair, who keeps in fairly regular contact and is expected to ask for Gordon's support for his bid to become President of the European Union. The Iraq Inquiry is coming up too, so we don't know what discussion they will have about that. One thing is for sure: Gordon will let the inquiry do what it has to do.

The press pick up that Tony Blair is visiting and draw a conclusion that Gordon is asking the former PM's advice on an election – a fairly laughable suggestion, at the moment.

Sunday 24th May

We are up in Scotland over the mid-term parliamentary recess (and school half-term holiday). Just to be on the safe side, I pack up our lever arch files of House of Commons records and receipts from over the years to have them to hand.

Mid afternoon we get a call from the press office with expenses questions relating to Gordon's office. As I have the files at the ready we are able to go through and answer everything. The final issue seems to be a £30 charge for a piper to play at a constituency event to honour war heroes. As Gordon says, he would have happily paid for that personally but as his office had booked it, they had properly put this through as a constituency expense.

It is moments like this that I realise just how far the hunt for expenses wrongdoing has gone. It takes hours to resolve everything and I know that this is also true for the many decent, hard-working MPs from all parties who have also been frightened by the hunt, and spent many hours answering queries to a cynical media on behalf of an increasingly sceptical public. We have the small minority of MPs who have abused the system to thank for this.

Tuesday 26th May

It is the sixty-fourth birthday of Burma's democratically elected leader Aung San Suu Kyi, held under house arrest by the military dictatorship since her election in 1990. The Free Burma campaign is keen to embrace social media to ensure this brave woman's graceful struggle is not forgotten. I agree to gather up people with large Twitter followings to tweet out a message of support.

I call people I have met who fit the bill: Kevin Spacey takes my call while filming in Washington DC, Stephen Fry calls me back, as does Eddie Izzard and Jimmy Carr. Together we reach over one million people.

Wednesday 3rd June

There is much talk of a new ministerial reshuffle with speculation about whether Ed Balls might replace Alistair Darling. Ed was a former adviser to Gordon at the Treasury, and a minister there once he became an MP, so everyone knows he has the economic competence and treasury experience to take it on. The question of course is simply what the PM chooses. There is some confusion when Hazel Blears appears to resign over the issues relating to her own expenses claims, but then announces that she is stepping down from the Cabinet at the time of the reshuffle and not immediately. Gordon does an amazing PMQs and everyone is buoyed up by that, but the press onslaught about his leadership is ferocious.

The *Guardian* newspaper is set on a course to support the Liberal Democrats (having supported Labour for many years) but with the current editorial leadership I can see that the Liberals outnumber the Labour supporters there so it doesn't come as much of a surprise. Losing the *Guardian*'s support will be seen as a blow at the next election though as we don't have the problem of the Iraq War that pushed many of our voters to the Liberal Democrats in 2005.

Richard Wallace, the editor of the *Daily Mirror*, comes in today to see Gordon for a drink and is reassuringly solid with his support for both Gordon and the Labour government.

Thursday 4th June

After lunch a new fax arrives from the *Telegraph* with more questions on the detail of MPs' expenses for Gordon. As I have prepared the personal ones, and kept the files from his constituency office, so I have the whole nightmare start again. We are locked into a cycle of looking up the answers within the files of receipts going back years. It is such an overwhelming and upsetting attack on our integrity; we have never profited from Gordon's time in politics, nor intended at any point to do more than reimburse costs incurred within the rules. There are many costs associated with this job that are never reimbursed, but I understand that this is not the point.

In the evening I wander down to Gordon's open-plan office. It is the local elections today and there are many people still working, even at 10 p.m., as the polling stations close. Gordon is talking to Peter Mandelson in his office with the door shut, presumably about Monday's Cabinet reshuffle. Everyone anticipates terrible election results but the *Telegraph* has confirmed that it is not running any story linked to today's expenses questions – I assume that means we have answered them properly.

As I walk past Sue Nye's desk she is on the phone listening in to a call and signals to me that all is not well. She whispers to me that James Purnell, the Work and Pensions Secretary and former adviser to Tony Blair, is resigning. Looking across at the TV news, I can see that the story is already breaking. It becomes quickly apparent that he has briefed three newspapers, *The Sun*, *The Times* and the *Guardian* and given them a copy of his resignation letter, before actually delivering it to the Prime Minister. Gordon speaks to him, and then suggests that he hand the phone over to Peter Mandelson, who knows James rather better. Peter comes out after the call to explain that he has said he is furious and explained why James is wrong in his actions, but it is too late. The job is done.

I see Gordon again upstairs a bit later; he looks tired but is his usual steady and resolute self. No one can quite predict how tomorrow will go, but Gordon is certainly not giving up.

(Overnight!)

This is also the time of year for the final rehearsals for Beating Retreat and Trooping the Colour. The military marching bands do this in Horse Guards Parade at around 3 a.m. when it is nice and quiet and private – except for us few local residents. We spend the night wide awake, listening to the (admittedly impeccable) strains of brass band and drums.

Friday 5th June

The next morning Gordon is off before I even wake up. As the morning progresses I hear that Alistair Darling is to stay as Chancellor.

I am working in my office, but pop down to see Gordon just to see how he is getting on. He is with Number 10's Permanent Secretary, Jeremy Heywood, in the Cabinet Room. Jeremy has an unbelievably calm presence and is reassuringly well organised, so that everything just keeps running smoothly, even in turbulent political times.

Once on my own with Gordon, I give him a big hug. He tells me he is just sorting the finer details on job titles for Peter and other Cabinet Ministers. Harriet Harman is waiting to see him so I make myself scarce and leave them all to get on with it.

Later, Gordon's press conference announcing the reshuffle goes well and he comes up to see the boys in the flat afterwards. I ask him how he thought it has gone. 'It was much easier than I thought it would be,' is the reply. That's good then! There appear to be about three rebels left, but everyone else is back to business.

Saturday 6th June

I fly out with Gordon and his team to France for the sixtieth anniversary of the D-Day landings. Our first stop is at the beautiful Bayeux Cathedral to attend the service for British veterans. We are joined by French Prime Minister François Fillon and his wife, Penelope. Also present are a host of young cadets, school children and a great group of Normandy veterans who have made their way over from Britain for this special occasion. There is a funny moment as the vicar taking the service, all mic-ed up for maximum volume, sings from his own hymn book an entirely different version to the rest of the congregation. There is that marvellous British awkwardness where no one wants to nudge him and let him know, so we all sing a bit quieter and glance at each other.

We are taken by car to a local hotel where we are able to spend a lot of time talking to all the veterans as they have their lunch. We are all outdoors in the hotel grounds as it is a marvellous sunny day.

Everyone is so proud to be there, and crowd around Gordon for photos. The Prince of Wales also joins the lunch and is tremendously popular with all the veterans.

After lunch, we travel to Colleville-sur-Mer, where there is a big American cemetery and memorial to the Normandy dead, and is where the main speeches are due to take place. There is a large impressive arena set out with hundreds of chairs around a central stage. We are taken to a small holding room to talk through the arrangements and meet up with President Obama and Michelle, as well as Prime Minister Stephen Harper of Canada. President Sarkozy and Carla are the last to arrive. Everyone greets everyone else warmly and we all get our instructions for where to walk, sit and speak.

Carla and Michelle are warm and friendly to me, and both look terrific. I know that I have to hold my own with these two powerful and attractive women, and although I don't project my own personality as forcefully nor have the same profile, I don't feel unconfident with them. I have developed my own voice for the campaigns that I support and fight for, plus I have a great dress from Britt Lintner. We are accompanied to our seats by three US Normandy veterans who laugh and joke with us. The sunshine is really beating down now, so we are all going to be pretty scorched in the glare with no shade.

President Sarkozy addresses the audience – and live television cameras – as the host for today's event. He is followed by Canadian PM Harper, who cleverly delivers his speech half in English and half in French, which adds a nice touch.

Gordon gives a soaring speech that lifts everyone, and both Carla and Michelle nudge me to say how good it is. At one point, he mentions Omaha Beach and it sounds as though he has said Obama Beach – bound to be a comment or two on that in the media tomorrow.

President Obama delivers the final speech and is very eloquent, giving nice, personal touches as he refers to his own great-uncle who served in the Normandy landings and who is sitting with us today in the audience.

The speeches finish with a fly-past overhead, and the spouses are taken to meet the veterans who have today received the prestigious Légion d'honneur award. Our UK veteran, Jack Wood, is a real sweetie.

Then it is on to Arromanches Beach, where the British troops landed. The glorious sunshine turns into drizzle, as though the weather knows we are British and heading to the seaside. I remember being here with my brothers Sean and Bruce more than 30 years ago on a camping holiday, and feel a strong sense of familiarity as we pass the streets with their Anglo–French signs, and the British pubs along the sea front next to the crêperie. The streets are crowded with well-wishers waving their Union Jacks, holding umbrellas aloft and sharing Thermoses of tea, and Marmite sandwiches. It is as moving a sight to me, perhaps more so, than the ceremonial grandeur of Colleville.

While we wait for PM Fillon to arrive, the crowd kicks off a good-natured 'Why Are We Waiting?' and it is tempting to join in. The soggy but stalwart cadets keep the veterans dry with their big umbrellas during the speeches. Gordon speaks simply and from the heart, keeping it short as the rain is coming. PM Fillon touches everyone when he speaks in a wonderful thick French accent in English. He explains that he is embarrassed by his English, but I tell him afterwards it was better than my French would have been. We finish with 'Land of Hope and Glory' and the Last Post before the skies break with a great torrent of rain, and everyone runs for cover. I imagine both the pub and the crêperie did good business today.

Monday 8th June

I notice my Twitter followers have risen to 137,000 suddenly and discover that the editor of the *Daily Beast* website, Tina Brown, has mentioned me and Twitter on breakfast television. We had just seen each other at the Hampton Court dinner for the Raisa Gorbachev Foundation.

I have a private visit today from Michelle Obama with her daughters, her mother and a close friend. They are enjoying a few days in London seeing the sights and have called in to say hello. We have the shared connection of a Fraser in the family, as Michelle's beloved late father was one too: Fraser Robinson. I still can't explain why we have a Fraser; the name was chosen by John and spread around the family and stuck before I had much time to think about it.

We show them our small gardening patch where we are growing our vegetables quite successfully. Michelle has really raised the profile of healthy eating and has a great vegetable garden in the White House grounds. Ours is much more modest, but I want to show what is possible in an inner-city garden. Before Michelle leaves, she does me a great service by signing a huge pink piggy bank for me to use in our up-coming auction for PiggyBankKids.

Thursday 18th June

The MPs' full expenses are finally published officially by the House of Commons. The problem is that each claim has huge black lines all over them (called redactions), which just make things worse as they look like there is something to hide.

Gordon's response at the news conference when asked about specific details of his expenses is to say: 'I didn't choose to redact that and I don't quite understand all the rules that have been applied by the House of Commons itself who have been doing so. My principle in this is the maximum transparency – it's got to be consistent of course with security but I think people have got to be as transparent as possible.' What is astonishing is that the 'redacted' black lines are so extensive that they obscure much of the information that tells the real story of each MP's expenses.

I have to admit that the media, led by the *Telegraph*, while aggressive, has uncovered wrong-doing by a small number of MPs, that might otherwise not have come to light. However indignant I, and others, might feel about the way we are all being treated as villains by the media, they have uncovered a genuine scandal. None of this feels very good.

Friday 26th June

I am to visit Glastonbury Festival today to promote the White Ribbon Alliance, and discover that I am taking police protection with me. I can't believe this will make me the most popular person at a music festival.

We drive down to Somerset, where I put on my Water Aid Hunter wellies and quickly find the WRA 'tattoo parlour' tent. The 'Mum', temporary heart-shaped tattoos – devised for us by the Karmarama advertising agency – are visible on arms, necks and cheeks everywhere. The charity has hit on a great idea and I suspect there will be lots of competition next year.

Despite Naomi's reputation for terrible lateness, I have always found her pretty punctual, and she rocks up today on time, clad in a mini-skirt and designer wellies. We cut an unlikely pair doing our photographs by the iconic Glastonbury water tower.

We are totally relying on the novelty of our being here to get us a bit of coverage for the White Ribbon Alliance campaign. Judging by the number of photographers, this looks like the right assumption.

After the photos, Naomi leaves as she is very shocked and saddened by the sudden news of the death of singer, Michael Jackson, as is everyone today. We listen to the bands on stage that afternoon, but then I do have to drag myself away and, notwithstanding the stop-off at a Little Chef for much-needed food with the Met detectives, we get home in good time. I am very impressed that even Little Chef has marked its fish and chips on the menu as sustainably sourced, having recently watched the *End of the Line* documentary film with its scary news about overfishing in the world's oceans.

*

Once back, I tweet my Glastonbury pics, including a photograph of the Mums Tattoo for my Twitter followers to see. I can see that I have now passed the 250,000 mark for followers.

Saturday 27th June

We mark the second anniversary of Gordon's time as Prime Minister with a visit to the Armed Forces Day at the Royal Naval Dockyard in Chatham, Kent. It is a family day so we take the boys but keep them well away from the cameras. There are lots of parades and receptions with lots of people to meet. This is a new government initiative to celebrate those in military service with an annual Armed Forces Day, and so far it looks like it will be a success.

Friday 3rd July

After a morning at Millbank Primary School's sports day watching John and his friends, I walk back to Downing Street in time to meet Mrs Janis Sharp, the mother of the charged computer hacker diagnosed with Asperger's Syndrome, Gary McKinnon. Trudie Styler had written to me, asking if I would meet Janis. I had explained that I am not able to take up the issue formally, but I would be happy to meet her as a mother.

We meet privately in the White Room and I hear her concerns as Gary is charged in the US with hacking into confidential government computers, including the Pentagon's, which represents a considerable jail sentence far from home if he is found guilty. Janis is very concerned that more understanding is needed for his Asperger's diagnosis. I suspect that she will get a lot of personal sympathy and perhaps even political support from other parties, but it is a complicated case.

Saturday 4th July

My Pilates teacher, Sian Williams, comes in to do a session with Gordon. Having become quite taken with Pilates over the summer with his holiday trainer, it seems worth keeping it up. He has always gone for big runs and great aerobic activities, but with the non-stop nature of life here, some strengthening and stretching exercises add a bit of balance to the frenetic pace.

I am joining the Pride March in London today, along with a group of LGBT friends and about four protection officers. We had enquired about Gordon joining the march, but the police wouldn't countenance the added security risk of joining a demonstration for even a moment. I am thrilled that I have the chance to go and show my support for a hard-won human freedom that is still threatened in so many parts of the world, and for a community who still face violence and insult in the face of prejudice in Britain.

I join my great friends, John Roberts and Tom Thorpe, as well as Labour MEP Michael Cashman and his partner, Paul Cottingham, comedienne Rhona Cameron and novelist Sarah Waters in the garden at Number 10 for a small drinks reception for the march organisers. We have a lovely, relaxed weekend feeling, even in the presence of some of the usually spiky gay news press represented there. I chat to the organisers, who seem appropriately daunted at the idea of herding one million people calmly through the streets of London; but they definitely are excited all the same.

I decide not to march right at the very front as that seems the spot for the real LGBT VIPs. I know that I am a visitor today and so I tuck myself next to the drag queens dressed in 'Union Jack' ball gowns – very striking. I am the first wife of a British Prime Minister to walk in the Pride March and the day could not have come soon enough. I get lots of cheers and whistles and a few hugs as I walk, and could not feel more welcome anywhere.

Tuesday 7th July

Gordon and I attend the 7/7 memorial unveiling in Hyde Park. HRH the Prince of Wales and HRH the Duchess of Cornwall are the guests of honour. Tessa Jowell is the government's Minister for London and has worked over the years with the victims' families to find the right memorial. She was Culture Secretary on the day of the bombing and has been involved in the details from day one. As a result, she knows many of them personally and was able to introduce us to many people that day.

The memorial is designed as 52 single posts representing each life lost that day, and has a simple and dignified presence on the edge of Hyde Park, visible to all the cars passing on Park Lane. We talk inside a marquee to the families who lost their loved ones, and despite the awful drizzle outside we gather around the posts for a short service. It is a poignant reminder of the lasting impact that such a tragedy has on so many people, and a time for reflection on the great work of our police and security services as they continue to combat the ongoing terrorist threat to our British cities today.

CHAPTER 23

Italian Hospitality

Wednesday 8th July

We leave so ridiculously early for the G8 Summit in Italy that I can't work out what to be wearing on arrival (I take my clothes onboard to sort it out once we are up in the air). I can't wake my boys so just give them sleepy hugs they won't remember.

This G8 is another important time for me. I managed to get so much out of the last one in Japan last year for the campaign I am supporting for mothers and infants, and this year I want more. I know that it is not yet top of the agenda, but I will keep working on it. I am, of course, not there as an official agitator, but have an invitation to join the spouse programme in Rome.

G8 host, Prime Minister Berlusconi, had originally planned to hold this summit on the island of La Maddalena. This would have suited the high security needs of the summit, but also allowed the flamboyant Italian PM to offer a very luxurious stay for all the leaders. However, amid a global recession, this does not feel entirely appropriate, so the resourceful PM has relocated the summit to his country's earthquake-hit region to help support the redevelopment of the shattered towns. This was a very smart, last-minute switch, even if all the official briefing information still has the blue turtle logo representing the island theme of La Maddalena.

Tea with the Number 10 team: Clockwise from bottom left: *Sue Nye, Barbara Burke, Helen Etheridge, Beth Dupuy, Leeanne Johnston, Christianne Cavaliere and Gil McNeil*

A visit by Lady Thatcher to see Chequers again, talking to Number 10 adviser Wilf Stevenson and Gordon, 13th September 2008

My first speech at Labour Party Conference, 23rd September 2008

Walking to the State Opening of Parliament wearing my purple beret from New Look, 3rd December 2008

A visit to the Vatican, 18th February 2009

At the Maggie's Centre with US First Lady Michelle Obama, 1st April 2009

In the garden at Number 10 with Michelle Obama, 8th June 2009

The G20 spouses photographed on the stage of the Royal Opera House, London, 2nd April 2009

SECRETARY GENERAL
UNITED NATIONS

World Health
Organization

Addressing the World Health Organization's General Assembly, 19th May 2009
(with UN Secretary General Ban Ki-moon)

At Colleville-sur-Mer, France for the D-Day 60th anniversary commemorations
with Carla Bruni-Sarkozy and Michelle Obama, 6th June 2009

*At Glastonbury Music
Festival with Naomi
Campbell, 26th June 2009*

*On the Pride March,
London (with Paul
Cottingham and
Michael Cashman
MEP), 4th July 2009*

*London Fashion
Week Party
outside Number
10 with Maggie
Darling (in green)
and a host of
British creative
talent, 18th
September 2009*

With Gordon on stage after both our speeches, Labour Party Conference, 19th September 2009

Wearing the beautiful Catherine Deane dress that showed rather more than I intended after I stepped on the hem, 11th November 2009

At the G20 Summit in Pittsburgh, where President Barack Obama held my hand. 'Anything you want to tell me?' texted Piers Morgan. 24th September 2009

With Biz Stone, co-founder of Twitter, in the White Room of 10 Downing Street, 21st November 2009

International Women's Day march with Annie Lennox (left) and Cherie Lunghi (right), 8th March 2010

WOMEN FOR WOMEN INTERNATIONAL

The photograph I took of Gordon announcing the start of the General Election in Downing Street, 6th April 2010

KONRAD CAULKETT

Saying goodbye in Gordon's private office to all who had helped us (Justin Forsyth is at the back), 11th May 2010

STEPHEN SIMPSON / REX FEATURES

Leaving Number 10

GEORGE MCLUSKIE

At home in Fife, 17th August 2010

*

When we arrive in Rome, Gordon is whisked off in a small plane directly to the summit meetings. I am driven to the Vatican where I join a number of the spouses for an audience with His Holiness the Pope. Here I meet my friends Margarita de Calderón of Mexico, Margarida Barroso of the EU and Gursharan Kaur of India. Also for the first time I meet Filippa Reinfeldt, First Lady of Sweden, who is herself a regional head of public health.

Having had the privilege of meeting the Pope already this year, and mindful that a number of my fellow spouses are practising Catholics, I hold back to allow them their moment. We are all photographed together and treated to a drive through the gardens of the Vatican.

Lunch at the Piazza del Campidoglio with its panaromic views of Rome is hosted by Isabella Rauti, the wife of the Mayor of Rome, and an emerging politician in her own right. We start in a room with gorgeous Caravaggios on the wall, and move to an open-air lunch with a spectacular panoramic view. I am sitting with Laureen Harper, the Canadian PM's wife, who tells me that she has, for the second year running, won her celebrity cow-milking competition back home. (It turns out she grew up on a farm.)

Michelle Obama is juggling a complicated trip with her two daughters in tow. They are in between a visit to Russia and a visit to Africa, which is a big deal for the first-ever black US President and his family. We get some time to talk at the lunch but we hope to reconnect the next day when we visit the earthquake zone in L'Aquila.

The official accommodation is reported to be a refurbished police barracks. Each block bears a country flag to tell you where you are staying. Our room is piled high with official gifts that the events team duly take off to log. PM Berlusconi has been generous to the point of embarrassment. The La Perla boxes attract a great deal of amusement until the contents are discovered to be pyjamas rather than luxurious underwear. My attention is drawn to the biggest jar of Nutella chocolate spread I have ever seen – it dwarfs the large coffee pot next to it. I wonder how much they think two people eat in two days.

The great news from the first day's summit is that an agreement on maternal health has been included in the all-important communiqué (the golden rule: if it's not in the communiqué, it won't be happening). A new taskforce is to be created to raise funding for health workers, and then make a progress report next year at the G8 in Canada.

What pleases me enormously is that people no longer feel this an unnatural subject for discussion at a G8. Just one year ago, President Bush had to use all his experience and canny judgement to force it on to the agenda for the first time; now it is being considered for pole position. I am just delighted that my issue is in the spotlight, but am realistic that as things progress we need some firm commitments and funding too!

Thursday 9th July

Gordon goes off early as today's meetings have a special focus on climate change.

The spouses, meanwhile, are assigned to buses for our journey to the worst-hit areas of the April earthquake. I am paired up with my friend Margarita from Mexico, who remembers her country's own earthquake tragedy back in 1985.

We travel to the town of L'Aquila where the beautiful old square has been particularly devastated. Michelle Obama joins us separately in her cavalcade of protection officers and vehicles. She and I are taken to meet the brave emergency service units who are now securing the area for the restoration teams. It is clear that their work will continue for months, if not years. The town has a very empty, eerie feeling since its residents have all moved out to temporary accommodation, some even in refugee camp-style tents some miles away. Michelle and I chat as we walk, stepping around piles of rubble, but there are crowds of photographers jostling for her photograph and it all gets too unruly. We head back to our buses and wave goodbye to Michelle, wishing her well on her historic trip to Ghana.

The Nobel Peace Prize winner Betty Williams is hosting an event with actors George Clooney and Bill Murray at the San Demetrius camp for the earthquake survivors. George Clooney is flying down from his home in north Italy to provide a film screening to the residents that includes an exclusive peek at the new film cartoon *Fantastic Mr Fox*, which both he and Bill voiced. I have been invited too, and see first-hand the tents that the homeless earthquake victims are living in. I fear for these people in the winter months ahead, and hope some of the rebuilding happens quickly.

Having met George before in Downing Street, I can impress Margarida Barroso by introducing her. George is funny, jokey, and as good as ever at being a famous person. He really has the knack of conveying to everyone whose lives have been pretty rotten for months, that he is there for them.

We hear some terrific speeches: ex-Mayor of Rome Walter Veltoni says, 'To love people is to connect with people,' and gets a big clap. George Clooney says, 'We are here to remind you that you are not forgotten,' and gets a big clap. Bill Murray says, 'I will be back and next time I will bring wine,' and gets a HUGE cheer (the drinking of alcohol is forbidden in the camp).

I do not let George and Bill get away without signing some PBK charity piggybanks, which I always keep with me now, just in case.

Friday 10th July

On this, the last day of the summit, the G8 leaders are to focus on food security and announce up to $20 billion of funding to address some serious famine issues in the world.

Our spouses' group is back in Rome at an event hosted by Josette Sheeran, director of the World Food Programme. Many countries are represented here today, including Nigeria, South Africa and South Korea. She greets us all with the gift of a red plastic feeding cup; this is the cup that gets filled with food on their emergency feeding programmes at the cost of just over £1 a week. We hear from experts and from children about how it works, about the links to local agriculture and building up community sustainability. It is sobering to take on board that every day one in six people wakes up not knowing if they will eat that day. I make a note for my blog to say it must be possible – indeed it is necessary – to right this wrong in our generation.

The spouses are invited to contribute as speakers today at this event. I start off with an outline of the maternal mortality campaign and am followed by Laureen Harper, whose husband will host the 2010 G8, who gives a powerful short speech about the impact of world leaders' decisions to help each other. We also hear from Gursharan Kaur of India, Mrs Zuma from South Africa and Margarida Barroso from the EU. Everyone contributes uniquely from their own perspective and country experience, and it is fascinating. I am very proud to be part of an event that has some real substance to it.

At the end it is time for me to say goodbye to the hosts and all the First Ladies and Prime Ministers' wives.

Before we return home, Gordon and I travel to the small village of Onna, which lost 40 lives on the night of the earthquake. Here we are welcomed by a British resident, Joanna Griffith-Jones, who is keen to share her story and explain how everyone is coping. She is a violinist with the local Abruzzo Symphony Orchestra (which Italian tenor Andrea Bocelli sings with). Joanna shares with us the moment she and her husband woke to the tremors and made their escape in the dark using bed sheets as both the stairs and the electricity were gone.

Today, they are all living on the village outskirts in a caravan park until the village is rebuilt and they can at last move back. The resilient villagers exude a great camaraderie about their shared experiences and feelings. As we leave to return home, Gordon and I both agree that we share nothing but admiration for the stoicism of the Onna community and their love for their village and belief in its future.

CHAPTER 24

Making a Difference

Friday 10th July (afternoon)

We board our flight in Rome heading to London, and Gordon is notified of the deaths of eight soldiers in Afghanistan. When we land, we are driven directly to a military headquarters where defence advisers have gathered to receive a confidential military briefing. I am swept up by the speed to reach the meeting, and then by the focus Gordon and the others bring to the discussion with the impressive military officers.

I am honoured to have witnessed this, and to understand better, at first hand, what we are facing. My thoughts go to the families of those eight soldiers who learn today of the ultimate sacrifice that their loved ones have made.

At this point, all Gordon can do, as he does for each casualty, is wait to receive all the details, and write to the family. (The military handles the notifications to families and arrangements for funerals, and a statement to the media.) He writes individually to the wife, husband, or partner, and to the parents. Families can be complicated, with different family members in different places, so this can mean up to four letters. He writes them fairly privately, sometimes with me, other times alone and always hand-written.

Saturday 11th July

It is upsetting to read today in the newspapers that the head of the army, General Sir Richard Dannatt, whom we last saw with his wife, Pippa, just weeks ago and on very civil terms in Arromanches, is making a personal, and surprisingly political, attack on Gordon. The accusation is that Gordon is personally responsible for the death of the eight soldiers, due to the lack of investment in the armed forces. This is an unconscionable attack and presumably designed to be professionally damaging and personally wounding. It is not true and not fair. He is due to retire from his position soon, so it seems odd to be speaking up like this, presumably as a way to get more money for the army.

Thursday 16th July

I am invited to attend a Police Bravery Awards dinner. As in previous years, the winning policemen and women come to Number 10 in their uniforms with their partners. Last year, one of the young policemen took the opportunity to propose to his girlfriend during the visit – the first engagement I can think of at Number 10.

Today, the sunshine is so glorious that Gordon and Home Secretary Alan Johnson host the event out in the Downing Street garden. The queue of heroic policemen and women who are nominated for awards stretches all round the garden as they each meet Gordon and Alan as *Sun* photographer Arthur Edwards takes lots of photographs.

In the evening I join all the police officers and their partners for a glamorous award ceremony at the Dorchester Hotel. I am seated with the new Metropolitan Police Chief, Paul Stephenson, and Paul McKeever, the head of the Police Federation.

The event is well organised with a moving film about police bravery, and although I leave when the awards themselves finish, I do hear the announcement about the free bar staying open goes down very well.

Friday 17th July

It is Fraser's birthday and, of course, Nelson Mandela's the next day. Gordon has put through a call to wish the great man a happy ninety-first, which is connected just as he is picking up John from school. Caught between the two activities, he passes on his celebratory wishes to Madiba, then holds out his phone so that the whole class can shout 'Happy birthday', too.

Saturday 18th July

Mr Marvel the magician takes over Chequers for Fraser's celebrations with lots of little friends having a 'sports day' on the big lawn, and then bopping around to Mr Marvel's famous junior disco. It is a very happy day, and the four of us collapse in the evening when everyone else has gone home.

Sunday 19th July

We have a number of people to Sunday lunch, including General and Lady Dannatt. All is surprisingly civil given the recent hostilities, and Tessa Jowell is very chatty with the general (Tessa is just brilliant at getting along with everybody and is the perfect guest to have here today). I have no difficulty at all talking to Pippa Dannatt, who had sent an invitation to Fraser to see the horses in Whitehall recently. I do wonder about the MOD, though, when I hear that she didn't receive my thank-you note for the visit.

Today, the Olympic flame comes to Downing Street, as does Major Phil Packer, the soldier who sustained a serious spinal cord injury in Afghanistan and who did the London Marathon in 14 days on crutches. He is now looking to set up a new organisation to support disabled people getting back into work and activity. He is a brave and resourceful man whose very determination to succeed will see him a long way. However, he is smart enough to recruit partners and backers to support his efforts, and that includes talking to Gordon.

The Number 10 Twitter stream @DowningStreet passes the one million-followers mark today. Fittingly, the day's tweet is to mark the passing of WWI veteran, Henry Allingham – one of the very last of his generation.

The House of Commons has a new Speaker, Conservative MP John Bercow. I invite his wife, Sally – who is moving her young family into the Speaker's residence right underneath Big Ben in the House of Commons – to come on a play date with her three kids.

Saturday 25th July

On our way home to Scotland for the holidays, we go via Leicester, where thousands have flocked to the football stadium to enjoy the Special Olympics 2009 opening ceremony. SO International chair, Tim Shriver, has flown over with his wife, Linda, and our whole family joins them to watch the teams march around the stadium with great joy. It is the long way round for us to get home by car up to Scotland, but well worth it to witness this uplifting occasion.

When I get home to Fife, the receptionist at my local health centre tells me her daughter was one of the participants and returned home with two gold medals. She says it was the most memorable thing of her life and added hugely to her confidence.

It's only one person's story, but it shines a light on the amazing impact this organisation can have, and how important it was for us to show our support.

Monday 3rd August

It's our ninth wedding anniversary and Gordon and I go out for dinner at the wonderful Beveridge Park Hotel in Kirkcaldy (run by friends Bobby and Gina Kumar, and the only place I know that serves a dual Indian and European menu so one person can have a lamb bhuna while the other has Scottish salmon!) We have a delicious meal, and even manage to get a table not too close to the close protection!

It is fun just to have the time together in a restaurant and as it is full of local Fife people, they just say hello and leave us to our meal and conversation. At home, we are so immersed in life with our kids that we don't get much opportunity to eat without discussing Bionicles (Lego action figures), Gormitis (more action figures: strangely popular, the figures come out of a volcanic mountain to battle with yet more action figures, who are the people of the earth, forest, the sea and the air), and Ben 10 and the Moshi Monsters, in rapid succession. Here we can talk about our summer plans, Gordon's interest in a volunteering project this summer, and which family and friends we will see during the holiday weeks. We both know we have some big months coming up after that, but there is no need to talk about anything like that tonight.

Monday 10th August

We pack up and head off to the Lake District for a week's holiday. We stay in a wonderful country house hotel on the edge of Bassenthwaite Lake and use this as a base to explore the area, with great walks around Lake Buttermere, trips to castles and aquariums, and a boat ride on Derwentwater past Beatrix Potter's old house. The hotel is large enough that we can be tucked at one end quite privately, but we are still able to use the hotel's main breakfast room and make use of the gym and grounds for the lakeside walks.

There are lots more things that we could visit, but we also just need a rest as well. So we enjoy a bit of peace and quiet at the hotel, eat dinner on a little terrace outside our room and work out the quietest times to go the gym and swimming pool.

As ever, the Number 10 operation is set up in the hotel, having taken over a couple of extra rooms so that Gordon can respond when needed. Sad news comes through from the office of the 200th military death in Afghanistan, as a young soldier loses his life from his injuries.

I also keep up with my emails and Twitter even though it is the holidays, and quickly spot the online comments in defence of our National Health Service when Conservative MEP Daniel Hannan makes negative comments while in the USA. Both Gordon and I choose to add our voices using the hashtag #welovethenhs started by TV writer Graham Linehan who tweets as @glinner. Gordon tweets via the Downing Street Twitter, 'GB: NHS often makes the difference between pain and comfort, despair and hope, life and death. Thanks for always being there.' I just put '#welovetheNHS – more than words can say'. Health Secretary Andy Burnham movingly posts, 'Over the moon about strong support for NHS – an institution I will defend to my dying day.' This is a big Twitter trend this summer with literally millions of tweets similarly in support.

Monday 17th August

Back home to Fife; Gordon and I have signed up to do volunteering in the Victoria Hospice in Kirkcaldy.

When Gordon comes across an important issue that needs a lot of understanding, he always does two things: he reads everything he can get his hands on about it, and, if relevant, he looks for ways to experience first-hand what ordinary people face day to day, by visiting homes, factories, offices, children's centres, schools and hospitals. This summer, he wanted to know more about hospice care, so we chose to spend several days at the hospice in his constituency (where everyone calls him Gordon, not PM or Mr Brown, which is lovely).

We are met by Anne Cargill, the senior nurse, and I realise we have met before when I visited the wonderful Marie Curie hospice in Edinburgh, some years before.

We spent our first hours in an induction meeting with patients and visitors. Hospices are very contradictory places: there is near daily loss and heart-wrenching sadness, combined with laughter and constant good humour. We then joined in serving lunches and playing games with some of the day patients (who have terminal illnesses, but return home at night).

Gordon is most useful when sitting and talking to people, both patients and their families, as they struggle to get through the pain and shock. I know that he will always remember the 6ft 3in policeman dying of cancer who admits to him of pre-wedding nerves (he married his long-term girlfriend in the hospice only days before he passed away). Gordon also talked to two teenage girls whose 41-year-old mum had just died of lung cancer – she had given them sealed envelopes to open on their wedding days.

I spend my time joining the craft sessions on the ladies' visiting day, and then the quiz time with the men's day group (everyone laughing when the question comes up to name the local MP).

Wednesday 19th August

On our final volunteering day, I ask Anne if she can think of one thing that would be useful for her that we can do with our volunteering time. Half joking, she replies that she has a big store cupboard that needs a good clear-out.

Only I am entirely aware of the irony of asking Gordon to tidy up. When his flat was burgled as a student, the police braced him for the worst, saying the place had been 'totally ransacked', only to discover they were looking at Gordon's messy study, which hadn't even been touched.

Gordon and I put on the Marigold gloves to clear out all the storage boxes and give the cupboard a good scrub down. I don't think he will do anything like that again in his lifetime, but it was satisfying to see the faces of the staff when they saw the fruits of our labours.

Thursday 20th August

I accompany Gordon to the memorial service for the head of the Scottish Miners, Lawrence Daly, at Dunfermline Abbey just a few miles away from our home. The Reverend Hugh Ormiston takes the service, Rannoch Daly speaks about his dad, and Gordon gives an oration about the impact of Lawrence Daly's life on the working people of Fife, who had relied on the mines for their livelihoods for many years and suffered greatly when they closed. He told writer Tariq Ali's great story about Lawrence travelling out to show solidarity with the miners of Vietnam, and taking a gift of Glenfiddich whisky for Ho Chi Minh. However, it arrived empty, its contents drunk in transit.

The abbey is filled with the soaring sounds of the Croy Miners Choir accompanied by the wonderful Cathy Peattie MSP singing 'The Road to the Isles', 'Ae Fond Kiss' and 'Corrie Doon'. Seriously, not a dry eye in the house – these songs are so evocative of a time gone by when every song is about leaving home to find work elsewhere and leaving loved ones behind.

Friday 21st August

Gordon meets Rose Gentle, the mother of Fusilier Gordon Gentle, the 19-year-old soldier who lost his life due to a roadside bomb explosion in Basra, Iraq, in June 2004. I think it might be a difficult meeting, but he returns very impressed by her intelligence and reasonableness to pursue what she thinks is right. Mrs Gentle has long been an outspoken critic of the government's handling of the Iraq War, so I am pleased to hear that they have both been able to exchange their respective views.

In the afternoon we also have a visit from the US Army General David Petraeus. He arrives in our Fife back garden with the new US Ambassador, Louis Susman, while Gordon is joined by his Number 10 defence advisers, Matt Cavanagh and Nick Catsaras, both wise and calm heads to have around. They have a private meeting with Gordon to cover the issues they need to, but it is quite strange to see General Petraeus sitting drinking coffee in my back garden! I do tell Fraser that he must not ask the general to show him his marching again, and today he listens.

Monday 24th August

Although we live so close to Edinburgh – just a short ride over the famous Forth rail and road bridges – we don't actually go there very much, or at least not this summer. We do head over one day, though, for a lunch with Maggie and Alistair Darling in their home there.

While we are neighbours in London, it is rare that we get the chance to socialise much these days. Today, we get to actually sit down and have a meal together prepared by Maggie; she has prepared chicken broccoli bake which she knows is a favourite of mine, but it is one of those recipes that just does not taste the same when I make it, and actually tastes best of all in her kitchen, don't ask me why.

Both Gordon and Alistair look transformed by their break – more relaxed after a tough year taking big decisions over the fragile economy and tackling all the banking problems. They do take some time to talk over the months ahead. The important thing has been to protect people's jobs and on that they both strongly agree.

Wednesday 26th August

Our day starts very sadly with news of the death of Senator Edward Kennedy. Gordon hears the news from Bob Shrum, who calls early. It is the passing of a great man, summed up for me rather well by my small son: Fraser was snoozing beside me in bed when the phone rang. After Gordon went to his study to write an obituary for the *Boston Globe*, I heard a small voice say, 'Ted Kennedy? He was a goodie, wasn't he?' (Fraser sees many things in terms of goodies and baddies thanks to Power Rangers and *Star Wars*.)

'Yes, he was,' I replied, simply.

Friday 28th August

Gordon is travelling to Afghanistan and will not be able to attend Senator Kennedy's funeral, so he has asked me to go to Boston as his official representative, and Downing Street agrees. I think this is a good reflection of our personal relationship with the Senator and his family, but also a signal of our administration's sadness at his passing as he showed such leadership on issues like healthcare and education.

The memorial service is being held in the John F Kennedy Presidential Library and Museum in Boston and the rain is coming down in sheets. The British contingent and I arrive under umbrellas, but the building looks just as magnificent on the water's edge as it did on that bright, sunny day when I came with Gordon the last time we saw the Senator.

Inside, the auditorium has an air of gentle pandemonium due to the arrival of so many VIPs. We greet endless Kennedy family members, US senators, Congressional representatives, and senior figures from Northern Ireland. I find Bob and Marylouise and just give them both a big hug, as I don't think there are words for how deeply they will feel this loss. I also see Teddy Kennedy Jr, the Senator's oldest son, here with his wife, Kiki, who were so kind to me in Cape Cod the summer after we lost our Jennifer – more hugs as I just don't have the words for this one.

As we take our seats, I realise the length of the programme and gulp, but I don't notice the time passing. Everyone has a different story of Ted Kennedy's kindness, hard work, dedication to public service and willingness to go the extra mile, and his great love of sailing. After the service I see Tim Shriver and Linda Potter, Maria Shriver with Katherine Schwarzenegger and others from the Kennedy world I have met over the years. I share with them my and Gordon's condolences; Tim and Maria have only recently lost their mother, Eunice, Ted Kennedy's sister.

I also walk over to say hello to Ted's widow, Vicki. I see her recognise me and turn to her left to say something, and then start when no one is there. She turns back with tears in her eyes. I know exactly what has happened: she automatically turned to Ted to say, 'Look, Sarah Brown is here,' forgetting for a moment that he is no longer here. I can't imagine what she is feeling as she has truly lost the love of her life. Her family will not be the same again.

Saturday 29th August

The following morning the funeral service for Senator Kennedy takes place at the Basilica of Our Lady of Perpetual Help in Roxbury. Despite the continuing rain, people are lining the streets bearing placards that say things like: 'Thanks, Teddy.' The church is full with people clearly having waited for hours for the service to start. I meet Diana Taylor from New York and Ambassador Louis Susman, before being directed to my seat next to the Irish Taoiseach, Brian Cowen, just behind all the elected representatives from Washington DC. I say hello to ex-President Bush and Laura Bush as they come past me. Beth comes to tell me that Michelle Obama would like to say hello, but we can't work out how to achieve this as I am not sure I should leave my seat before the service.

The service is lovely. Ted Kennedy Jr gives the main eulogy, and I am very touched that he goes out of his way to acknowledge that both I and the Taoiseach are here. The Senator's daughter, Kara, and son, Congressman Patrick Kennedy, both speak, as do his stepchildren, Caroline and Curran, and each of the grandchildren and younger representatives for his brothers and sisters. All these young voices demonstrate how great a family man he was, but also how his work was designed always to be an investment in their future. The performances from tenor Placido Domingo with cellist Yo Yo Ma and soprano Susan Graham testify to just what a great reach this man had, to attract some of the finest artists in the world.

As the service finishes, I wait for the high-security VIPs to leave, and then leave by the side door. Today was not the day to catch up with Michelle Obama but I will see her soon enough at the Pittsburgh G20.

I have time for lunch with Marylouise and then the plane ride home tonight.

Sunday 30th August

On landing I go to find Gordon in the airport lounge at Heathrow to get on the same connecting flight back to Scotland; he is just back from Afghanistan and our return flights have coincided with each other. His trip has been more gruelling than mine, and the media reports are very aggressive about him. He seems to be blamed for everything including the prison release of Lockerbie bomber, Abdelbaset al-Megrahi, a decision from the Scottish Executive over which he has no jurisdiction. I just give him a huge hug when I see him, realising I have had a pretty emotional trip, too, and am hugely pleased to see him again.

It is good to get back home and see the boys, who have had a great time with Grandma. When the phone rings, we look at each other, wondering what to expect, and assume it relates to Gordon's work. Instead, it is Mela's dad, who tells us that Mela has been taken into hospital with terrible stomach pains. We are very worried, and await further news.

Tuesday 1st September

We head back down to London. As Mela is not here to take the boys, Maggie Darling helps me out while I attend a big gathering of the maternal mortality campaigners. Sia Koroma, the First Lady of Sierra Leone, has joined us as she has been looking closely at tackling the problem in her own country.

We are delighted also to have with us Ann Starrs, who chairs the Partnership for Maternal Newborn and Child Health and who has waved the flag for many years on this issue. Everyone contributes and our speakers cover leadership, campaigning and 'operationalisation' – a new word for me, which I discover means getting the job done. It sounds like the right approach to me, however the word is pronounced.

Thursday 3rd September

We get news that Mela has to have an operation and will be off work for several weeks. I am sitting around a table judging *Red*'s Hot

Women Awards with a group of highly successful women like Jane Shepherdson, who runs Whistles, and Laura Wade-Gery, who runs Tesco.com, when I get the call. I leave the room to talk to Mela and reassure her that although she will be missed, she must not think about us at all; she must just focus on herself for the moment. But I have not a clue how we will manage without her!

When I return I tell the group what has happened. If you can't share with other women your worries about another woman facing an op, and the matter of having no childcare for weeks, then when can you? Everyone is reassuringly sympathetic.

Meanwhile, another member of my team has a memorable day. Christianne, who is marrying her fiancé, Cele, in Italy later this month, slips out for her civil ceremony at Chelsea Registry Office. We invite all her family back to Downing Street where Maggie and I have a big plate of little salmon sandwiches (Maggie's hard work) and a beautiful white chocolate cake (my purchasing hard work at Patisserie Valerie in Soho). We drink a glass of champagne together to wish the happy couple everything they wish for the future.

Wednesday 9th September

I wake up extremely early to a terrible smell in the flat. I'm feeling awful, having worked far too late after the boys were in bed. I suddenly remember I put some of Fraser's bottles and things on the stove to sterilise in hot water when I couldn't find the electric steam steriliser (with no Mela around to ask, I had improvised). Of course, I went to bed with the boiling pan still on the hot stove. The water has all boiled away and the plastic contents have melted down to a pungent grey glue.

I rush around opening windows to air the flat but I'm soon told that, for security reasons, the heavy explosive-resistant curtains cannot stay down for long. Nearly burning down the historic building – not a good start to the day. I vow to calm down a little, breathe more and go through my 'to do' list at a steadier pace.

CHAPTER 25

London Fashion Week at Downing Street

Thursday 10th September

Ahead of this September's London Fashion Week, Alexandra Shulman has invited me to British *Vogue*'s answer to the economic downturn – a shopping night across London including a party at the huge Burberry store, which spans a whole block and has entrances on both Regent Street and New Bond Street.

I actually have to start my partying a little early today with a tea for the launch of a new PiggyBankKids charity book. Having edited books about mums and dads, the new edition is about grandparents, with contributions from so many wonderful writers and well-known people.

Gail Rebuck has come from publishers Random House to thank everyone and there is a lot of cake on display, which seems appropriate for an afternoon tea.

I already have on a fabulous navy Eley Kishimoto dress with great military-style brass buttons and velvet-edged pockets and cuffs. I pick a pair of big earrings from jewellers Astley Clarke and feeling suitably BritFash, I am on my way to *Vogue*'s Fashion Night Out. I take Nicola Burdett with me, who is usually steering the broadcast media but is unquestionably the most fashionable person in Downing Street.

Of course, walking into Burberry in front of hordes of cameras to meet their CEO, Angela Ahrendts, and designer wonder-guy, Christopher Bailey, is a bit daunting, but I suppose they also say to themselves: 'Okay, here is Sarah Brown from Downing Street, and she is outside our usual world so we had better be nice and polite,' or something like that, as they are charming. I don't think they have time to go, 'Mmm, not sure I would have worn those shoes with those tights,' even if I have to face the fashion critics later, who might. I have had critical comment from the great fashion writers like Hilary Alexander and Lisa Armstrong, and I have had the occasional bit of praise, which is just enough to keep me going. And, so far, no toilet paper stuck to my shoe as I cross a crowded room.

I find myself in my usual position standing next to supermodels; this time German model, Claudia Schiffer (who I thank for writing to Chancellor Merkel about the maternal mortality campaign) and Erin O'Connor (I will be supporting her All Walks Beyond the Catwalk event at London Fashion Week). M&S chief Sir Stuart Rose is there also (and somehow also in all the photographs). Stuart is faced with questions from the diarists as to whether he would consider me to promote M&S as I wear so many of their clothes – he can hardly say 'No' standing next to me!

My new friend, super-photographer Mario Testino is there and adds a bit of levity by telling people that my nickname for him at the G20 spouse event was 'the first lady of Peru' (his home country). Well, he did blend in with the spouses very well.

Given that I am wearing such an excellent dress this evening, I am delighted that I have another event for it later on. I nip back to Downing Street and collect Gordon who has agreed to pop out and support the Women's Aid dinner again by attending the reception. This year we are in Claridges' Ballroom and it has been made even more exquisite than usual with probably the most beautiful event flowers I have ever seen, by Rob Van Helden. As ever, the evening has been supported by Gordon and Tana Ramsay, with a delicious meal.

Along with the glamour of the occasion, the purpose is, of course, to raise funds for the charity's work on domestic violence. I am joined at my table by Detective Sergeant Steve Francis from the Coventry police force and his colleague, Family Liaison Officer Deb McCord. When it is my turn to speak, I give a speech I have been working on closely with DS Francis and Deb.

I tell the truly tragic story of 21-year-old Sarah Brown from Coventry, who was murdered by her partner and the father of her two children in 2004. DS Francis was the investigating officer and it broke my heart when he told me that he saw probably the saddest sight of his career when he saw Sarah's body. Her coat was on as she was trying to get out of her own front door, and he could see the boot marks left by her partner on her face. As we shared the same name, I was moved to tell Sarah's story – with the permission of her father, David Brown – to get across the message that two women are killed every week in Britain, by a partner or former partner.

I can hear the silence in the room after I have finished talking, and know that a photograph of Sarah is now being projected behind me for everyone to see. I hope her story persuades people to lend their support and perhaps save future lives.

Friday 11th September

As we remember the terror attacks of 9/11 in 2001, we have hit a low, I think, with the onslaught of unfair attacks on us by the media, on the supposed lack of support being given to our troops. It can't help but affect public opinion and, more importantly, troop morale, to think such rows are going on.

Thursday 17th September

I dash up the road to the National Portrait Gallery to attend Twiggy's sixtieth birthday party. What a privilege to celebrate with such an icon; the glory of all her photographs by extraordinary photographers grace the walls. Twiggy is there with husband Leigh Lawson; such a charming couple. She takes me round the exhibition reminding herself of the different photographers and photo shoots of the past. I am very struck by a photo of her by celebrity rock photographer Brian Aris, about whom she speaks very warmly. I hope, one day, to have my picture taken by him as he has a very kind camera eye.

Friday 18th September

Following the success of the first London Fashion Week party at Number 10 last year, we have agreed to host another one to kick off this year's bigger event. The British Fashion Council is celebrating its twenty-fifth anniversary this year, and we have all worked hard to make sure that this year's activities will be rather special.

I met BFC chair, Harold Tillman; the chief executive, Caroline Rush; and PR supremo, Jane Boardman, back in June to make plans. Harold had already secured the return to the London catwalk of Jonathan Saunders, Burberry with Christopher Bailey, and Matthew Williamson.

The Mayor of London, Boris Johnson, has cut the official ribbon at Somerset House – this year's glamorous new home for London Fashion Week – and the Duke of York will host a special reception later in the year before the British Fashion Awards.

The Number 10 reception tonight kicks off the week in style. Our party will focus on emerging new talent, but the list of invitees has grown to reflect how much talent there is. So I have recruited my neighbours, Alistair and Maggie Darling, and they have agreed that we will have a joint event.

Early evening, I am supporting the All Walks Beyond the Catwalk event at Somerset House with Caryn Franklin, Debra Bourne and Erin O'Connor. The movement is all about celebrating a much wider range of colour, age and size diversity than we ordinarily see in fashion images, as beautiful and relevant to fashion.

Once I have given my speech, I pelt back to Downing Street to find that many of our guests are already there. Maggie D looks great in an emerald green Betty Jackson jacket, and I have a new Erdem dress with wonderful embroidery on the skirt that has been done in Brighton. Ozwald Boateng spots Gordon wearing one of his ties and can't resist adjusting it, which gets caught on camera. Alistair pops by and meets some of the key people, and ministers Peter Mandelson, Mervyn Davies, Margaret Hodge and Barbara Follett all stay for the evening. It is great to have the government so well represented. There are lots of photographs taken of the new designers on the Number 10 doorstep, herded there by fashion writer Hilary Alexander, who is determined to get a historic picture out of the occasion. We keep the speeches short and the drinks long, and I think it is a great party.

Monday 21st September

I keep my commitment to attend the exhibitions at Somerset House, and also attend Graeme Black's show, and host a meeting with Glenda Bailey and some of our top designers, including Clare Waight Keller (Pringle) and Emma Hill (Mulberry) with US buyers there, and that is me done for another season.

Gordon is already hard at work on the preparations for the G20 summit coming up in Pittsburgh, which will continue the work on the financial recovery. It is pretty clear to me that Gordon is the one man with the experience, intelligence and political will to steer Britain (and the world) through the global recession. I don't think this work will be completed by the time of the election but, alongside tackling national security issues, there is nothing more important to do. I see every day just how critical the detailed preparations for the global meetings are, how vital it is that countries work together to find the solution, and how necessary it is to have the right people to do this.

As Gordon is so immersed in preparations, we have to leave him behind when John, Fraser and I drive to Oxfordshire for the gorgeous outdoor wedding of our friends Paul Greengrass and Jo Kaye. It is a nice escape for me as I meet lots of old friends and just go 'off duty' for a few hours. The boys find their friend Spike Curtis and disappear off to play, and I stay for dinner, chatting away, and listening to perfectly pitched speeches before tipping the boys back in the car long past their bedtime.

I am lucky that I have been able to go, but it is gatherings like this that sometimes bring home just how many things we miss because of our Downing Street life.

One event Gordon does not miss is taking Fraser in to his first day at nursery school this morning. It is a wonderful moment as Fraser strides in confidently, and then we are packed and ready to travel to New York again.

CHAPTER 26

Taking the Chair at the United Nations

Tuesday 22nd September

After the huge impact of the London G20 Summit, a follow-up was agreed by all the nations present to be hosted by the US President, Barack Obama.

As ever, I am accompanying Gordon to join in on the spouses' programme at the G20 in Pittsburgh, but first we stop on the way in New York where I have my own events to attend for the maternal mortality campaign while Gordon attends the United Nations General Assembly meetings there.

Once we hit the tarmac at the other end, Gordon and I go off in separate cars. I won't see him until very late today as he is out in the evening to be presented with a humanitarian award, along with Mayor Michael Bloomberg and Bono.

After a meeting with the vibrant Girl Effect project, which seeks to improve the lives of teenage girls, I go and speak at the Clinton Global Initiative dinner, focusing again on the importance of girls to the future of undeveloped economies.

From the moment of landing, my schedule has been so busy and the meetings so engaging, that I have completely forgotten to get nervous about another big speech. I speak about the maternal mortality campaign, which matters so much for teenage girls when so many marry and have their children so young around the world. I talk to everyone from Secretary Clinton's Ambassador for Women, Melanne Verveer, to Sinn Fein's Gerry Adams, who are both guests. I even get to eat a bit of my dinner, which is unusual at events like this where you are always bobbing up and down to say hello.

As I am leaving, I recognise a very famous face sitting near the back quietly listening to all the speeches: Barbra Streisand, with her husband, James Brolin. I'm glad I didn't spot her before I gave my speech. I have met quite a few famous faces, but every now and then there is someone that just brings a bit of extra awe for no easily identifiable reason. I remember gibbering when I spoke to Sir Alex Ferguson for the first time when he called my office to offer support for an event I was organising for the Labour Party years ago, and Sir Terence Conran was another person whom I had admired so much, for the impact on style he brought to Britain, that I just went silent when I met him at a lunch at Chequers. Now Barbra! It is not that I am a particularly avid *The Way We Were* person or anything, though I do vividly remember going with my family to see *A Star is Born* when it came out. It is more that she is Classic Hollywood – the last great star to emerge from the golden age of the studio system. I can't explain my star-struck moment even to myself, but I am too shy to go and say hello. Always good to have these grounding moments, even if it does not feel like that at the time!

Wednesday 23rd September

I start my morning with a meeting with Bience Gawanas, the Social Affairs Commissioner for the African Union, and my co-chair on the Leadership Group for Maternal and Infant Mortality. She is based in Ethiopia so this is a great opportunity for us to meet face to face. We also go to meet the new US administration's global health people and have some time with *New York Times* journalist and Pulitzer Prize winner Nicholas Kristof, and Sheryl WuDunn, who together have just published *Half the Sky*. Their extraordinary book makes the arguments convincingly about how to improve women's lives around the world, and Oprah is to run it on her widely watched TV show all next month.

My formal programme starts with a lunch at the United Nations hosted by Ban Soon-taek, as Ban Ki-moon is presiding over the New York meetings this week. I am honoured to speak to the guests alongside Mrs Ban and Michelle Obama, and we also hear from some young speakers who are taking part this week.

I am chatting happily with the First Ladies of Zambia and the Dominican Republic when Christianne comes to get me to say we have to run to our next event. We are due to watch the big session on global health, where first the Secretary-General is the Chair, and then Gordon will take over.

The room is full and well attended by country leaders and all their ministers. Gordon speaks first and announces $5.3 billion of new funding. Ten countries have declared that they will be dropping medical charges to pregnant women so that they can receive free essential healthcare around the time of childbirth, and each country leader will speak to make their announcement. This is all very exciting.

However, it turns out that elsewhere in the UN building, Colonel Gaddafi has made a 90-minute speech (instead of his allotted nine minutes!), so everyone else's speeches in the main UN chamber are out of sequence. A note comes up to the stage asking Gordon to go to the main chamber and give his main UN address. There are a few huddles and whispers on the stage to resolve the problem and then an aide comes and taps me on the shoulder and asks me to come and fill the seat. I pass Gordon on the stairs as he is heading down and he (only half-joking) whispers that I am not to make any new financial commitments.

After Gordon has gone, and I am safely seated in the ACTUAL CHAIR leading a UNITED NATIONS MEETING on MY

TOPIC, I have a sudden realisation of what I am doing; and I really love the moment. Here I am, sitting on the stage chairing my first ever UN meeting (and almost certainly my last) alongside Bob Zoellick, the head of the World Bank; Prime Minster Jens Stoltenberg of Norway; and President Jakaya Kikwete of Tanzania; three great champions of maternal and child health. Bob Zoellick passes me a really sweet note saying how much he admires the campaign, which is a big boost. I feel massive pride for my country, my government and – at that moment – for myself, as I have put my all into this campaign and have contributed to making a difference alongside the many experts and long-time advocates. I have no intention of patting myself on the back for too long but this is a nice moment. My only real job is to confirm to Dr Margaret Chan of the World Health Organization that the figure that has been confirmed today is \$5.3 billion (I don't increase it, tempting as it is).

I see our UK Health Minister, Ivan Lewis, in the front giving me a grin and thumbs up – and I realise that, as a team, we have done so well on development that you can put me in the chair as a 'mere spouse' and no one is going to bat an eyelid or think that their more senior 'protocol' status has been undermined in any way. I am very proud of all of us.

We show the moving films that models and campaigners Christy Turlington Burns and Liya Kebede have made visiting Tanzania and Ethiopia respectively, and a succession of prime ministers take the microphone to announce the improvements to maternal health funding each are making in their own countries.

Once the meeting is over, I dash to another room in the same building to join the last part of the Global Fund's session on HIV/AIDS and how to prevent it being transmitted from mothers to infants during pregnancy. Carla Bruni-Sarkozy is speaking there in her role as Global Fund Ambassador. There really is no end to the push that the spouses are giving these important issues today.

In the evening is the fourth Important Dinner for Women that has become such a regular fixture at these global meetings. It is hosted tonight by HM Queen Rania, Indra Nooyi and Wendi Murdoch and has been relocated to a bigger space in the Cipriani on 42nd Street.

As I walk in, I am blinded by flashbulbs, and there is a terrifying photo-call moment when I find myself slinking to the back of a group, only to find model Liya Kebede and actress Nicole Kidman there. Even my friends from London, Nicola Mendelsohn and Lucy Doughty, are looking impossibly glamorous. Sometimes what I do is not even funny.

My job, when I speak, is to make sure every woman there is moved enough and motivated enough to engage with our campaign and make a contribution. I talk to them about all the campaigning actions taken so far – some by women in the room tonight who I single out and mention – and I talk about the actions taken by international leaders so far, and what more is needed now. I talk about how we have signed to the Millennium Development Goals as reasonable targets and I conclude by saying: 'We must not allow ourselves to fail in this task. What humanity do we have if we set ourselves targets we say we can meet to save lives and then fail to meet them? If we can save the lives of those mothers, they will thank us by working to meet the rest of the Millennium Development Goals in their own neighbourhoods throughout the developing world. We, in the end, will thank them when we find our path back to a more prosperous and fairer world.'

I know I have achieved getting my message across because they all stand up and clap like crazy when I finish. I have come a long way since I mumbled over a written piece of paper in Davos just 18 months earlier. Afterwards, when asked by a TV crew for a short quote on why I think the dinner will make a difference, I say, 'When a mother survives, a lot survives with her, and when women come together they are an unstoppable force for change.'

At the after-party, I run into the Mayor of Newark, New Jersey, whom I have never met before but recognise from his popular Twitter feed (we have about the same number of followers; over half a million and rising). Before I can stop myself I say, 'Hello @CoryBooker' (using his Twitter name), to which he looks at me, laughs and replies, 'Hello @SarahBrown10.'

Mayor Booker has a great Twitter feed that combines evenings out with the Newark Night Patrol, a passion for good coffee and great quotations like, 'Those who say it can't be done are usually interrupted by others doing it.'

I'm out far too late for someone with jet-lag. I have never been a great late-night groover, but it is fun every now and then. When I get back to the hotel I find Gordon fast asleep. He is always much wiser about getting a good night's sleep than I am.

Thursday 24th September

Gordon is being pummelled right, left and centre by the British media for an alleged snub from President Obama for not yet diarising a one-to-one meeting. There seems to be no stopping the media on this one, though the view firmly from Gordon's team is that there was no snub. It would appear the White House team is also saying there is no snub.

We move on to Pittsburgh for the G20 Summit, and the Omni William Penn Hotel, which we share with the US, Russian and Indian delegations. With all the security we pretty much get a whole hotel floor each.

Pittsburgh is the first city I ever visited in the United States, when I was 18 years old and on a trip with my grandfather to stay with my Aunt Doreen and Uncle Warne, one very cold Christmas time. While my uncle passed away some years ago, my aunt still lives here and it was she and my cousins, Trevor and Caroline, who travelled to Washington to hear Gordon address the joint Houses there, back in March. It is a transformed city since its industrial past a century ago, but much as I remembered it with the distinctive stadium of the Pittsburgh Steelers football team situated at the point where three big rivers meet in the centre.

*

Gordon and I are driven out to the Phipps Conservatory and botanical gardens for the reception to open the G20 summit. We arrive in our pre-assigned protocol order and walk up a long pathway to greet the Obamas in front of the mass of cameras. Michelle greets us both with her customary big hug, and President Obama is demonstrably warm when he meets Gordon, perhaps to signal to our media that the two men have a good working relationship. As we arrange ourselves in the photo, President Obama holds my hand. I stand next to him very aware that the President is clutching my hand, and wonder what on earth anyone watching this will be thinking. But I find I don't really mind at all. It just feels really friendly and nice, but we *are* in front of the world's media! Sure enough I get a text from Mariella Frostrup saying: 'Well done on pulling the Pres!', and one from Piers Morgan: 'Holding hands with Obama? Anything you want to tell me?'

The Phipps Conservatory is a lovely choice for a reception, with its exotic plants and glass sculptures. We greet the new Japanese Prime Minister Hatoyama and his wife. She has been getting all sorts of coverage for her unusual views (that she believes in aliens is one report), and I wonder if some of this may have been exaggerated. While we are talking, she speaks to me about the farm that we spouses will visit for dinner, and the importance of eating fresh fruit and vegetables. Of course I agree, but am more mystified when Mrs Hatoyama explains that eating fruit is a way of eating the sun's rays, and a better way to do this is to reach out to the morning sky and just grab handfuls of sunlight directly. I think I know what she means, but I don't ask about the aliens.

We leave the reception and are driven to the stunning location of Rosemount Farm, a family farm owned by Teresa Heinz who is hosting a dinner there for the First Lady. We enjoy drinks standing by the outdoor pool and eat dinner under an open-sided canopy with a meal made from the farm produce. This includes a goat's cheese and beetroot starter, lamb or fish with fabulous vegetables, and an apple tarte tatin.

I talk with the friends I had already made at the G8 and G20 meetings, and am delighted to see Azeb Mesfin, the First Lady of Ethiopia, whose husband is joining the meetings for the first time. She is a powerful woman in her own right and quite forthright about development and global health, so we agree that we can work together in the future. Carla is here and it is fun to see her again. I find it so easy to pick up chatting with her each time we encounter each other, perhaps because we worked so closely together preparing for our first encounter on her State Visit to London. As ever, she has her mobile phone with her and texts her husband, even during dinner. This turns out to be handy as she lets everyone know immediately when the Leaders' dinner has broken up, and we can head back to our hotels with perfect timing.

Friday 25th September

While the G20 leaders meet to discuss a global growth plan and hope to get new agreements on international cooperation for the global economy, I join the second part of the spouses' programme. We visit the CAPA Performing Arts School and hear from talented students as well as cellist Yo Yo Ma, singer–songwriter Sara Bareilles and country singer Tricia Yearwood, which thrills me no end as a fan of them all.

We chat to many of the students who seem to be enjoying the invasion of everyone and the visit from their First Lady.

Our lunch is held at the Andy Warhol Museum. The pop-culture artist was born here in Pittsburgh in 1928, and the museum houses some of his most well-loved and iconic works. I am sure all major fans find their way here. We see the Marilyn Monroe and Elvis screen prints, and then have a go at screen-printing a bag each. I am wearing a white skirt and playing with poster paint, but I don't panic, and I soon have a very nice multi-coloured bag to take home. I chat with the First Ladies from South

Africa, Indonesia, Turkey and Canada as we all work away on our individual prints.

Over lunch I have the honour of sitting next to Yo Yo Ma, who is as charming as he is proficient on the cello. He has a passion for music education all over the world, and in between his great concerts he is travelling and reaching out to children. We talk, too, of the late Senator Kennedy as I last saw his performance at the service in Boston in August.

We all go our separate ways at the end of lunch but not before I get one of Michelle's famous hugs and she tells me that she knows that our husbands have been able to book time together for their one-on-one meeting.

Before I leave Pittsburgh, I have one final visit I want to make. Teresa Heinz has kindly arranged for me to visit one of the most respected medical research centres studying pregnancy and neonatal problems. The Magee-Womens Research Institute and Foundation is a world-class centre and I am able to meet the key scientists there and hear about their work. This is of specific interest to me to take back to the Jennifer Brown Research Laboratory in Edinburgh, and I hope that we can forge future links, as discussions between scientists are almost as important as their individual work.

I also get the added treat that my aunt, Doreen – known here as Dr Doreen E Boyce as she is well known in the academic community – is able to join this visit, and at the reception I meet many of her friends.

It is time to pack up at the hotel and take the overnight flight back to London. Next on the agenda: the Labour Party Conference in Brighton.

CHAPTER 27

Speaking Up

Saturday 26th September

We arrive back in London in the early hours and in the same afternoon we are all on our way to Brighton for the annual Labour Party Conference.

The schedule is tough going, but it makes the greatest difference to how much I can pack into my day when there is someone on hand to handle luggage and passport control, and I can just step off the plane to join Gordon in a waiting car on the tarmac outside. This only happens to me on official visits, but those are the times when it is most welcome as there is no let-up in the diary then.

I head back to find our little boys and take them with us for the weekend in the conference hotel, so we can see them as much as possible. Mela is still off work for a few more weeks although I talk to her regularly on the phone as everyone misses her so much. We take Tess Dunning, who often helps us with weekend babysitting. We found Tess as she lives next door to Gordon's brother Andrew and family. She is a trainee midwife due to qualify next year, and she has been great at stepping into the breach when Mela is not around. It means that we don't have to be apart from the boys for any longer than necessary, but are still able to attend all the receptions at the conference. As far as the boys are concerned, it is a weekend at the seaside visiting the beach, buying bright pink rock, and visiting the aquarium, with rides on the carousel.

*

We start the conference in Brighton with a pretty negative round of press coverage even from the Cabinet Ministers, who have all done interviews. Peter Mandelson seems to have attracted photographs of himself with his dog, and a newspaper headline saying he would happily work with the Opposition party.

I get a lot of coverage for having a high profile on Twitter. I don't mind as it is just another way to open up about what we really do every day, but I don't suppose I will ever understand the nature of the media character attacks on Gordon: even in quite serious news programmes there is little room for discussion about policy or steering the economy. I often hear the argument that it is the public who are interested in all the personality focus, but that never resonates with my personal experience. When Gordon and I meet people they show an interest in our family life, but what they really spend time on is questions about their families, homes, jobs and the wider world.

I know I must learn to be thicker skinned, but I do feel a strong sense of frustration that people just don't get to see the real Gordon I know, and how much he devotes his combined intelligence and compassion to genuinely helping people.

Monday 28th September

After a first night of 12 receptions, and an early-morning walk along the seafront with Gordon, I return to London for the day to sort the boys out for school. Gordon's big speech to the conference is tomorrow.

When I get back to Brighton, everything is going smoothly but everyone is working feverishly away.

I have been talking to Gordon about whether I should introduce him at the conference again. There has been much external speculation about whether I will do it, and even whether it is a good idea. It does not seem such a big deal now, unlike last year. In going around the receptions the night before, everyone was urging Gordon to encourage me to do it. Today, Gordon is pretty relaxed about it and says it would be great if I want to do it. So I sit down and draft what I want to say. It only takes a few minutes to write my short speech, and then I show it to Kirsty McNeill who adds in the line, 'my husband, my hero'. When I see the words on the page, I instantly know they match exactly what I want to communicate. I show it to Sue, David Muir, Justin, Gil and Konrad, and then leave it as done. I don't show it to Gordon as I think he will be quite happy with what I have to say.

Tuesday 29th September

Gordon and I walk over early in the morning to the conference centre to see the staging and understand how we will get on and off the set. There are always so many cables to avoid, and photographers everywhere, that it would be easy to just go flying over. Come the actual moment, when the auditorium is full of people, and the strong lighting changes the atmosphere, it is much harder to work out the right way to go, so it is wise to get this sorted out in advance.

When we walk back later for the conference itself, there are people everywhere, cheering Gordon on his way. I leave him to gather his thoughts in the green room and go for a little wander backstage. I have learned from last year that the trick for me is to keep moving.

Our conference chair, Cath Speight, introduces me as 'back by popular demand' and I walk on to the stage to give her a big hug. Everyone in the hall is up on their feet, clapping like crazy, and I like to think the warmth I feel coming towards me is not just the hot lights. I can see my mum and Patrick, Andrew and Clare, Neil and Glenys Kinnock, Nicola Mendelsohn, and MT Rainey in the front row. Even a peek at the Cabinet shows me that they are all smiling.

I just speak sincerely and confidently to the room: 'I don't know as much about economics as a guru like Joseph Stiglitz, and I don't know as much about the environment as an expert like Sir Nicholas Stern, but I do know a lot about my husband.

'The first time I met him I was struck that someone so intense and so intelligent could be so gentle, could ask so many questions, could really care. He will always make the time for people, our family, for his friends and anyone who needs him – that's part of the reason I love him as much as I do.'

I get the biggest applause when I say, 'That is what makes him the man for Britain too. Gordon has got a tough job and I wouldn't want it for the world but each time I am thankful that he's the one who has it; that he's the one choosing the policies and making the calls.'

The short film *Against the Odds* I introduce at the end of my speech reminds people of all those things that people said could not be done: votes for women, the end of apartheid, the introduction of the NHS, a minimum wage, civil partnerships, and much more. It is a call to action to all of us that while many say a fourth term for a Labour government can't be done, we should all strive hard to achieve it. It also has a number of testimonies from Joseph Stiglitz, Sir Nicholas Stern, former UN chief Kofi Annan, rock star activist Bono and others, reminding people why Gordon is such an amazing man – so no one need just take my word for it. After it, there is a giant wall of applause that greets Gordon when he comes up on to the stage to take his place at the lectern. I get very choked up hearing it.

I take my seat and listen to what I think is probably the best speech Gordon has given in his life. He starts with a list of the Labour government's achievements in the last decade; as Chancellor, he was closely involved with each one. It is so smart and so clear about what Britain now needs to do. I can only hope people hear his words for themselves and understand what he can do for Britain and for global cooperation. The applause at the end just doesn't stop. I feel very, very proud.

Later in the evening, when we are due to call in to a final reception, Gordon is told that someone from News International is trying to reach him with the news that *The Sun* is to announce its support for the Conservative Party. This news strikes no one as surprising. What is astonishing is the paper's ruthless determination to overshadow today's brilliant speech with its own 'gloves off' announcement. Gordon had called all the newspaper editors as a courtesy this afternoon after his speech, and had even spoken to *The Sun*'s editor at 5 p.m. The editor had taken the call, but did not have the courage or courtesy to mention his newspaper's own plans at that stage. It is a measure of the hostility that we have already known, but a definite signal there is more to come.

We attend the final reception, for ONE, about global poverty, where Gordon gives a short speech about the decision to keep Britain's commitment of 0.7 per cent of GNP to international development. We also pop into the Arab Ambassadors' reception, and the Labour Friends of Israel reception. The only event I do miss is the Cooperative Party's reception for PiggyBankKids, which by all accounts is a great party still celebrating Gordon's speech.

Saturday 3rd October

Gordon and I travel to Sheffield to attend David Blunkett's wedding to the GP Margaret Williams in a lovely service at his favourite Methodist church. His sons and her daughters make a fabulous flanking guard as the ushers and bridesmaids. Even his guide dog, Sadie, is wearing a wedding 'buttonhole' of flowers on her collar. There are lots of other ministers and Labour friends there, and in the reception Gordon is hugged and squeezed and photographed all around the room.

We can't stay all the way to the dinner, which David is very understanding about, as we need to get back to spend time with our family. The train ride with Gordon is very enjoyable as it's just good to have time to spend together. We have a glass of wine together on the train, and chat about various family members: what everyone is up to, and the plan for John's sixth birthday, which is coming up in a fortnight. We get back to find our boys already in pyjamas after a day of climbing trees.

Sunday 4th October

After lunch at Chequers, the chef Alan Lavender tells me quietly that he is preparing for his retirement and wants to make sure that everything involving finding his replacement happens smoothly so that we are well looked after as a family. He and his wife, Diane, have been great friends to us, and his service to four prime ministers is a wonderful achievement. I am so pleased that we were able to bring Baroness Thatcher back while he was still here.

Monday 5th October

Gordon is off to Northern Ireland this morning having been on the phone to Irish Taoiseach Brian Cowen much of the weekend. The news today is dominated by the Irish Referendum win and speculation whether Tony Blair will run for the new office of European President. No one can quite understand why Tony would want to do this, but Gordon has said that he would back him entirely if he does want to go for it.

I start the day meeting two young Masai girls who are visiting from Tanzania to talk about their life. They are here with the former Tanzanian Ambassador's wife, Kasia Parham (now transferred to New York), whom I stayed with two years ago. I realise what a big journey these two young women are on with their first trip away from their own country, and yet they have already been on the radio this morning, chatting away. One thing they do comment on is the weather; for them our autumnal October day is absolutely freezing.

In the evening, I attend the annual Pride of Britain awards and, having been a judge again this year, I know that this is yet another group of extraordinary people being honoured tonight. Gordon and I are greeted by *Daily Mirror* editor, Richard Wallace, and I breathe a sigh of relief when I realise that we are among political friends this evening: I don't have that terrible effort to make with people who you just know are against you, no matter what you do or say.

Richard has been very consistent in his support for Gordon and always takes time to hear what is really happening at Number 10.

Gordon spends the evening chatting to Joanna Lumley, there to receive an award for fronting the remarkable Gurkha campaign, and I am seated with Fiona Phillips and Naomi Campbell.

We meet all kinds of people from the winners, who will come to visit Downing Street tomorrow, to the regional Feelgood Factor winners. We say hello to Cheryl Cole, who is a good Labour supporter, and to Simon Cowell, who came to supper with us not long ago.

'I read you are supporting the other side,' says Simon, meaning that he is somehow convinced that Gordon watches *Strictly Come Dancing* instead of *The X Factor*.

Gordon laughs and responds, 'You of all people should know not to believe all that you read,' but Simon insists that we really do prefer *Strictly*.

'Not at all,' says Gordon, citing his favourites from last night's *X Factor*. 'I leave it to Peter Mandelson to watch *Strictly*.'

We are there to present the Lifetime Achievement Award to Nobel Prize-winning British scientist Sir Peter Mansfield, who invented the MRI scanner, which has transformed diagnostics in hospitals. Gordon says in his introduction, 'There is not much better than a Nobel Prize – except perhaps a Pride of Britain award.'

Tuesday 6th October

We have on a number of charity receptions at the moment, and there seems to be something nearly every day. These range from breast cancer awareness or Fairtrade's fifteenth anniversary celebrations, to acknowledging the Black Power list; the Family and Parenting Institute; Britain's Kindest Kids with Channel 5; and a tea for marking Diwali. Any available slots where the big function rooms are not being used by government I try and make available for a charity event.

*

One last-minute slot comes up when a reception is rescheduled. I am sitting in the office with Konrad looking at a surprise free evening in the diary when an email message arrives from one of my Twitter followers. It is John Hibbs, a football scout from Staffordshire, asking me for help with a reception for the Lupus UK charity. His sister suffers from lupus and he is passionate about raising funds and awareness. Something about his note makes Konrad suggest the late slot, even though it is only days away. Okay, I say, and call John Hibbs to see if he can make use of the time at such short notice. John jumps at the chance and immediately starts inviting his guests. So Lupus UK became the first charity to book a reception at Downing Street via Twitter.

Thursday 8th October

The news comes that former head of the Army, General Sir Richard Dannatt, who recently attacked the Labour government, has been announced as joining the Conservative Party, with a view to becoming a defence minister should they form a future government. Totally predictable and witheringly disappointing at the same time. It seems very undignified to be engaged in something so political ahead of his official retirement from the Army in November.

Friday 9th October

We attend a service of remembrance to honour everyone who served in the Iraq war, at St Paul's Cathedral. I am seated by the Iraqi Prime Minister, and we are greeted by our own military chiefs, headed by Sir Jock Stirrup. A candle is lit by Tracey Hazel, the mother of Corporal Ben Leaning who lost his life when his armoured vehicle hit a roadside bomb in April 2007. She does it with such quiet dignity that every mother watching must feel her deep loss and immense pride in her brave son.

*

We return to the office and two things happen at once that make for a slightly extraordinary day. First, we hear the news that President Obama has been awarded the Nobel Peace Prize. While this may turn out to be both a blessing and a curse for him, adding greater expectation to his already laden shoulders, it shows that there is faith in serving politicians to have the power to do good.

As we are digesting this news, Gordon and I are told that Sir Thomas Legg, the man doing the review of MPs' expenses, has decided to change the rules that everyone thought they were operating within. As a result of this change, we are to be asked to repay £12,000 and about 500 other MPs will also be asked to return money. Sir Thomas states there is no question of asserting any wrongdoing but he has the right under his remit to arbitrarily alter the claims rules and reduce the limits on specific claim items. I don't greet this news very happily, partly because it is a lot of money to be arbitrarily asked to repay, but also because I don't believe this does any good for the reputation of MPs, in whom the public have lost enough confidence as it is.

Saturday 10th October

We are really being put through it at the moment. A Sunday newspaper is accusing Gordon of lying about his eyesight. This is incorrect. After a youthful rugby injury that cost Gordon the sight in one eye, he has regular checks on his other eye. It seems that one of these upcoming checks has come to the attention of the newspaper who assumes we have something to hide. Gordon has to go and prepare a statement about the health of his eyes, why he has checks and assure people he is fit to work. The inaccuracy combined with the thoughtless disregard in the reporting of a personal injury, for which Gordon should only be praised for overcoming, makes me very cross. The frustration is that there is no reasonable right of reply at these moments and having spoken over the years to so many people who have suffered the indignity of unjustified media attacks I do know that we are not alone. It is grin and bear it time again.

Sunday 11th October

US Secretary of State, Hillary Clinton, comes to visit Gordon at Chequers. She and Gordon do their photographs and filming in the usual 'Winston Churchill' spot in the Hawtrey Room. I pop my head round the door to say hello, but leave them to their filming and their meeting.

I go back into the other room, where I have left my two boys and their friend, Charlie Fletcher, romping around, and I notice that the BBC clip of the Clinton–Brown meeting has a very audible sound of noisy boys in the background, so much so that the Secretary of State stops to comment on the sound, thankfully with a big smile on her face!

Wednesday 14th October

I sign myself up with Jane Johnson from the *News of the World*'s colour supplement *Fabulous* to guest-edit a second issue of the magazine. Our Jools Oliver edition in January was such a success, raising lots of funds for the Wellbeing of Women charity, that we will try one more. I had enjoyed the experience, especially the treat of having a sizeable team to work with.

I then join Sir Victor Blank for lunch at his favourite restaurant, Wilton's in Jermyn Street. We are there to talk about *Fabulous* and other plans coming up for Wellbeing of Women, as he is the Chair of Trustees. This restaurant is famous for being a big Tory hangout and, sure enough, we are only there moments before former PM Sir John Major and former Tory Chancellor Lord Lamont come to say hello to Victor.

I have a nice chat to John Major who is always very sympathetic about the personal pressures of life inside Downing Street and was kind enough to contribute to the PiggyBankKids anthology I edited about grandparents. I don't know Lord Lamont but he is very courteous to me after he has had his brief chat with Sir Victor.

Friday 16th October

Both Gordon and I have been feeling as though we have not been giving the children enough of our time recently. The boys are robust enough, and surrounded by other adults who adore them, but parental guilt is a familiar thing to all mums and dads, I suppose. We do try to make sure that, apart from when we are away on trips, at least one or other of us is with them at breakfast time, and around for catching up after school, and at bedtime. But just recently we have been fitting in so much that we worry we have got out of touch, especially while Mela is away (we have a temporary nanny, Amelia Sales, who is doing a great job, thank goodness, and of course Tess Dunning is on hand to fill in with extra babysitting where more help is needed).

Saturday 17th October

John's birthday is today and he is six. I know the cliché about not knowing where time goes but I am feeling it today. Mums all know that moment when you think back to the tiny little bundle you first held, and then you look at them now, all tall and leggy and full of opinions. My other favourite motherhood cliché is when you are told, 'It just gets better and better.' When you see your little baby and feel all that love brimming over, it is impossible to understand how it could get any better – and then it does.

John has all his best friends over – a mixture of school and non-school – so there is lots of running around. I am very proud of my chocolate volcano cake with spewing white chocolate lava covered in Gormiti volcano action figures. I light the sparklers on the cake and turn off the lights for added eruption effect.

Saturday 24th October

We head up to the constituency this weekend with the boys to spend some time with them. Today though they're off on a long-promised trip to the Science Museum in Glasgow with a friend, while I head out to the Glasgow North East by-election to join the candidate, William Bain, and his organiser, Kate Watson, for a day of knocking on doors.

I start off meeting everyone at the HQ and have a terrific mug of tea (it is a pretty soggy day so the hot tea is welcome) and then we are out to follow Kate's route around the streets.

I don't find a single person who is not a big fan of Gordon's up here, and they all believe that Labour have fielded a good local guy as the candidate. I am pretty sure that the solid Labour support we find on the doorstep will hold up on polling day.

Sunday 25th October

A welcome day, as it is mostly just family time. Gordon has to nip down to London so that he can attend the St Paul's service to honour the Normandy veterans. While John is out on a play-date, I take Fraser along to nearby HMS *Caledonia* in Rosyth to present the long-service medals. In Fife, it is easy to take the boys along to events as most people know them here, and the photographers are always happy to make sure they don't appear in the press photographs. I imagine that most MPs' children have memories of visits to all kinds of local events as they grow up.

Monday 26th October

Mela is back at work and we are all thrilled to see her again, looking fit and well. She and the boys head straight out to catch up with friends they have missed seeing for weeks.

President Patil of India is visiting London to stay with the Queen, and we are due at the State Banquet at Windsor Castle in the evening.

We arrive to join a very friendly crowd including Leader of the Lords Jan Royall and her husband Stuart Hercock, and Jo Rowling and Neil Murray. Stuart talks to me about the Maggie's Centres as he has been undergoing cancer treatment and is very admiring of their work. I discover I am sitting next to Neil at dinner so I am guaranteed a good evening. I also chat to Peter Sands from Standard Chartered Bank as we proceed to coffee. He has been such a central player in the fight against malaria by using his corporate weight to help. I am a great admirer of his and leap at the opportunity to say hello. The banquet is, of course, as glittering as ever, and I hope that President Patil feels that she has been treated well on her stay in Britain.

Friday 30th October

After the boys are in bed, I slip out the back of Number 10 with Kirsty, Konrad and Stewart Wood and meet LGBT Labour people like Richard Angell, to join a vigil in Trafalgar Square. We are here to protest the homophobic murder of 62-year-old Ian Baynham. Many thousands of people are gathered quietly at the well-organised event. Hundreds of candles on the ground spell out 'NO TO HATE'. Sandi Toksvig introduces speakers, including our own LGBT ministers, Chris Bryant and Maria Eagle. Maria reads out a statement from Gordon, too. I spend over an hour there, standing in support and talking to people. I have brought a candle that says '10 Downing Street' on the side with the crest, and I light this to join the others flickering in the dark.

Saturday 31st October

My forty-sixth birthday seems to have crept up on me rather suddenly. Gordon and the boys wake me with breakfast in bed and shower me with gifts: a sweater, scarves, perfume and chocolate – my lovely family know exactly what I like. Gordon then takes the boys off to the garden to roar around, and I get a fantastic lie in. Blissful.

*

I now have 910,000 followers on Twitter and wonder if I can pass the million mark before Christmas. I would love to do something to celebrate that point, and am already mulling over some ideas.

Gordon and I have dinner on our own, treating ourselves to a leg of lamb and roast vegetables, while the boys are out Trick or Treating with Auntie Clare and their cousins.

While we are in London, the boys can do normal things like that with Clare, but Gordon and I are too visible. In Scotland, at least, we are still able to do these things as long as no one minds Gordon's protection officers tagging along.

Part of my birthday always has a bit of sadness in it as I miss Jennifer as much this day as I do on her own birthday. Most other days I can just cherish her life, short as it was, but every now and then I feel her loss very deeply and regret so much that she is not able to be with us now.

Tuesday 3rd November

UN Secretary-General Ban Ki-moon is in London to meet Gordon. We meet him and Ban Soon-taek on the doorstep for photographs outside Number 10. I take Mrs Ban off for breakfast with me and Sheila Lyall Grant, the wife of our new New York Head of Mission (the person at the Foreign Office who deals with the United Nations). For the first time in ages, we have a terrible breakfast where everything tastes a bit defrosted and microwaved. I have always paid much attention to the detail of how we entertain at Downing Street, so I am a bit thrown by my rubber croissant (and will sort out how to improve this once the guests have departed).

It is good all the same to catch up with Mrs Ban, who is here to speak at an interfaith conference in Windsor about the United Nations' work. We work out that since she joined her husband in his post three years ago, she has visited a total of 59 countries, some more than once. I think I travel a lot, but this is nothing compared to her.

CHAPTER 28

Our Changing World

Saturday 7th November

The state of the global economy is still the overriding issue whenever the international leaders are in contact with each other. In Britain it feels as though we have escaped the worst of the financial crisis and that many of the great fears for lost savings and lost jobs have not happened as decisive action was taken. Even so, there is a serious mood in the country with concerns for what happens next.

Gordon goes to speak to the G20 Finance Ministers who are meeting in St Andrews up in Fife. Alistair Darling is hosting the meetings there, and Maggie has organised a wonderful spouse programme, showcasing some of Scotland's finest products. Gordon gives his speech, which seems to be basically about the global recession and how to get through it. With agreement from the other European leaders from across the political spectrum, Gordon is also looking at ways to get the banks to play a more socially responsible role.

The US Treasury Secretary Tim Geithner is there. The two men get on very well but they are both pushing new boundaries for what needs to happen so there is a healthy intellectual tussle going on. What matters most, though, is that everyone keeps talking to work it out.

The news reports are still very much focused on the former general's criticising the government on its funding of the war effort in Afghanistan. What really does cheese me off is using Gordon as the alternative target for criticism to deflect attention from their own actions, not to mention seeing it come from a not-yet-retired general who has already signed up as an adviser to the Conservative Party.

The Sun is again using the opportunity to be very personally offensive about Gordon. No one believes any more that this is a fair line of news reporting; rather it is the propaganda arising from their announcement to back the political party that is not in government.

Our boys are oblivious, of course, to all the news of the economy and the generals, and when Gordon gets back from his office, he gets a huge welcome from them. Adorably Fraser says he is pleased to have his family all together and hugs Gordon, saying how much he loves him. It is very sweet to watch the boys clambering all over their dad with such confidence after such a tough day. Gordon always manages to relax with a combination of John and Fraser time, exercise and watching football – simple pleasures that do the job every time.

In the evening, Gordon and I change to attend the Festival of Remembrance at the Royal Albert Hall. We are seated with Defence Chief of Staff Sir Jock Stirrup and his wife, Lady Stirrup, and the charming Head of the Royal British Legion, Sir John Kiszely, and his wife, Lady Kiszely, in one of the boxes for the moving service.

I start to get signs of the vertigo I occasionally suffer when I make the mistake of looking over the edge of the box, so push my chair right back to stop myself getting completely whirly in my head. At the end of the service I realise that I had my chair so far back I had left no legroom at all for Ian Luder, the Lord Mayor of London, who was sitting behind me. I am mortified and try to explain, but he is entirely gracious and pretends he has not been uncomfortable at all.

*

We get home to find that there are still calls to make: Gordon is having quite a robust negotiation with Tim Geithner over their attempt to have some good come out of the banking crisis. This discussion will have to go on another day.

Sunday 8th November

In the morning Gordon and I attend the service at the Cenotaph. The service runs as smoothly as ever, and I always feel that great sense of British pride watching the march-past of our service veterans.

In the evening, it feels like Groundhog Day with *The Sun* who, this year, want to run a story reporting the Cenotaph service with criticism that Gordon's head was less bowed than the other politicians standing near him. This is getting ridiculous. Someone in the private office even watches a tape from the televised service to double-check that this is nonsense. It is obvious that the Editor's intention is to harm Gordon's reputation, but the shocking thing is that he will do so even when a story is untrue, and more so, when the side-effect can only be to upset those in service and their loved ones.

Almost immediately on hearing this, it gets worse. *The Sun* newspaper is to publish one of the handwritten letters of condolence that Gordon has sent to a grieving mother whose son has died in combat. The incorrect accusation is that Gordon had written a thoughtless letter to Mrs Jacqui Janes to extend his sincere condolences on the death of her son Guardsman Jamie Janes, who lost his life in Afghanistan. Gordon shows me a photocopy of the letter that has been kept by Downing Street (they keep a copy of each one written). I look at it carefully and read it through. I know Gordon's writing really well – it is not tidy, nor is it ever always entirely legible – but this letter is written sincerely and I can see that there is not one spelling mistake in the letter. The irony is that his elder brother John was given an italic writing class and has the most beautiful script I have ever seen. Gordon never did that class and does have the kind of scrawly writing many of us have. It is also true that with Gordon's eyesight, he uses fat black pens that don't help the legibility at all.

There is to be no stopping *The Sun*, who are to publish this private letter on their front page tomorrow.

Monday 9th November

I look at *The Sun* today and all I can see is a very personal attack on Gordon that must surely only be intended to assault his integrity. I am actually quite sickened by it, especially when I think of the people who must have taken the decision to do this at the newspaper; people we know and have always been friendly with. I also think of the time that Gordon takes to write each of these letters, and how personally affected he is when he writes them, caring so much about the sacrifice of these young brave lives. I hope that no other family has received his letter without understanding that it is sincerely written and honourably meant, to show how much we do care.

Fraser comes to see Gordon and me off at the back door of Downing Street and wave us goodbye. We are heading out to Berlin to join German Chancellor Angela Merkel for Germany's celebrations of the twentieth anniversary of the fall of the Berlin Wall.

On the plane, Gordon is sitting with Tom Fletcher and Stewart Wood. He is keen to talk about the impact of today's *Sun* as he has found the accusations very distressing, and is concerned that other media including the BBC have chosen to make this their top news story. He has already spoken to Mrs Janes in a private call. Stewart is the one with the really clear head today, and talks Gordon through the various implications and likely next steps for all the different media. Certainly everyone is shocked by the personal and vindictive nature of the coverage, and the rest of the media's willingness to leap on the story. Gordon remains very hurt at the accusations.

When we land in Berlin, I can see US Secretary of State Hillary Clinton's plane is already on the runway next to ours. We are met by our British Ambassador, Sir Michael Arthur, and drive in the cold drizzle to the Embassy. I know that we British talk a lot about the weather, but we are all mindful that we have an outdoor event to attend.

We have a little time to wait in the Ambassador's office with foreign policy adviser Simon MacDonald, who is soon to take up the Ambassador's post here in Berlin. Everyone is a bit anxious about the schedule for the day, and there is talk of fog later, which might affect the return flight. The Embassy chef makes us the most delicious bowl of hot soup that goes down well, especially as it is not clear when the next meal will be. We are invited to join the celebration dinner with Chancellor Merkel this evening but the threat of fog looks certain to deprive us of the chance to stay that late.

I join Gordon at the reception where everyone gathers first, and I can see that Presidents Sarkozy and Medvedev, and Secretary of State Clinton, are all using the time with Gordon to talk about the UN Climate Change Conference in Copenhagen in December, and any other pressing business.

We travel to the Brandenburg Gate on buses and are ushered to a heated, covered stand with allocated seats. Gordon sits with Merkel and Sarkozy, of course, and I am the other side of Gordon next to ex-President Gorbachev. I am so interested to talk to him as he was the 'glasnost' President of the USSR who first brought the sign of the thawing of the Cold War to Margaret Thatcher and Ronald Reagan. Alas, his interpreter has been whisked away, leaving President Gorbachev unable to communicate with anyone who does not speak Russian. I only know about three phrases, of which only two are usable right now (the third would be, 'Let me order vodka'). So we just smile, do thumbs ups and say 'Okay' a lot to each other.

We listen to a beautiful short Beethoven and Wagner concert led by the great conductor, Daniel Barenboim; the Arnold Schoenberg piece on the Warsaw Ghetto is read by that magnificent German actor, Klaus Maria Brandauer; and then Placido Domingo comes on for the finale of German songs. It is a pretty wonderful half-hour.

The government leaders are then taken off to walk side by side through the archway of the Brandenburg Gate, from the West side through to the East side, which used to be closed off in the days when the wall was there. The weather has worsened and it is now chucking it down from the skies. The spouses and others make their way through the archway by walking down the side away from the cameras and I am chatting to a former German Foreign Minister when I realise no one is looking at us at all. I have in my pocket one of my mum's hand-knitted little beanie hats and pop it on my head to stop myself getting completely soaked until I reach the identical seating the other side of the wall. We all sit again (beanie hat safely back in my pocket) and I realise that this new stand does not have the posh under-seat heating that the last one had, and that it is starting to get quite chilly. But we cannot complain as there are thousands of people out lining the streets, regardless of the weather, huddled under a sea of umbrellas.

We all listen to a performance from rock group Bon Jovi; interviews with Polish politician Lech Walesa, and President Gorbachev (with translation headphones); and speeches from Sarkozy, Medvedev, Gordon, and Secretary Clinton (with Obama on the screen); and finally Angela Merkel. Gordon has a lovely speech that is very forward looking; Clinton has a strong but quite poetic speech. Angela Merkel tells her own story. She lived in West Berlin but happened to be staying in the East when the wall was first erected; it was many years before she saw the other side of the city again. It is good to know that the wall has gone and I can't quite believe it is already 20 years since it came down.

At the end of the event, a great run of giant dominoes, painted by different artists to represent the pieces of the wall, are toppled over in a huge and impressive cascade running around the city centre, and as fireworks go off we all come out of the stands to mingle and chat. I am thrilled to find myself talking to Placido Domingo and then turn to find Gordon greeting Jon Bon Jovi warmly. It turns out they already know each other (from a big music event years ago, when Gordon was there to honour Beatles producer, George Martin, I think) – who knew my husband had been hanging out with rockers?

It is now officially freezing cold but the fireworks finale is quite spectacular. Our buses take us on to the place where dinner will be hosted, but we have bad news about the weather so Gordon and I will only stay for the reception and leave as everyone else sits down to their meal. Thank goodness for the soup we had earlier.

Once we arrive at the reception I can see that conversation between all the leaders is fast and furious. There is much focus about the environment, with concerns for what agreement can be reached by Copenhagen next month, where expectations from the public are high. The other dominant theme that Gordon wants to raise with some of the leaders is the choice of EU President. Tony Blair has asked Gordon to help him as a candidate for this new post and Gordon has been working very hard to gather as much support for it as he can. There are a number of big European positions coming up and we want to make sure that Britain gets one of them. Gordon has thought it likely that Britain would get the financial post, which is one of the top three, but has agreed to first push for the top job for Tony Blair.

There had also been speculation about another job, that of High Representative (the equivalent of a Europe-wide Foreign Secretary), and Gordon had asked David Miliband early on if he wanted to be considered at the urging of others (he did not). Someone had also told Gordon that Peter Mandelson might be interested in that post, too, but it was clear that he would not get the support so no one took that any further.

Gordon thinks that he could get support for Tony Blair from

Angela Merkel and the Spanish Prime Minister, José Luis Zapatero, and as Blair already knows Sarkozy he would presumably sort out his support, too. Gordon wanted to speak to Zapatero at the reception this evening but he is nowhere to be seen, so he heads across the reception to chat to José Manuel Barroso, head of the European Commission instead.

I talk to Joachim Sauer, Chancellor Merkel's husband, who enjoyed the concerts as much as I have. He points out to me a group in the corner in a huddle – Merkel, Sarkozy and Berlusconi – who are all there chatting, he tells me, about who they want to back for EU President. Then he laughs, which I don't quite understand.

He tells me that the only person they can all agree on is Gordon and they are trying to figure out how to persuade him. I say that I am pretty sure that Gordon is not a candidate as he has a responsibility not to quit as Prime Minister this close to an election.

Whatever troubles we have with our own rebels in government, it is clear that there is currently no one able to take over the Labour leadership.

I see Zapatero in the queue for dinner and explain to him that Gordon is leaving soon, but wants to speak to him this evening. They are good friends and when Gordon joins him he talks to him, requesting his support for Tony Blair. Zapatero tells Gordon that he will withhold saying anything until it is clear who he can choose.

We are running out of time for our flight take-off, so we have a final chat with Secretary of State Clinton, but then alarmingly Gordon disappears into the dining room where the dinner is just starting, which has the protection team looking anxiously at their watches. It turns out that he is just thanking Angela Merkel for her hospitality, and then we are on our way.

We manage to take off but we hit the fog ten minutes before landing and divert to Heathrow airport. We have a bit of a wait at the other end as the car has to drive over from Northolt to come and get us. We finally get home around 1 a.m. after a long but fascinating day.

Sadly, it is marred even at this late hour by the news that *The Sun* is to run a transcript on their front page, together with commentary, of the apparently taped private conversation that Gordon had with Mrs Janes this morning. Gordon had no idea that it was being taped, and there is concern about how this happened, which is never quite answered.

Tuesday 10th November

We all look at *The Sun* today.

I have probably read the paper more this past week than I have ever done before. I have always happily contributed articles on occasion, and have thoroughly enjoyed being a judge of *The Sun* Wondermum Awards. Today, I am reading things like, 'Gordon says sorry 18 times but never apologised once.' I don't even know what that means as I have always understood the word 'sorry' to be an apology. It is a vicious, cynical attack where there is no underlying wrongdoing.

Gordon starts the day meeting with the Cabinet at 8 a.m., followed by a press conference at 10 a.m. Today is the day that the coffins of six soldiers are arriving back at RAF Lyneham to travel through the town of Wootton Bassett. Everyone wants a day of dignity and respect, to be appropriate for the sacrifice these men have made.

Wednesday 11th November

We have another moment of remembrance as we take our seats in Westminster Abbey for the Passing of the World War I Generation service. The very last WWI veteran, Harry Patch, has passed away just recently, not long after Henry Allingham. Gordon had met both men on several occasions and it truly feels like the end of an era.

He joins a procession with the Queen as she lays a wreath on the tomb of the Unknown Soldier. The wreath is carried by two holders of the Victoria Cross: an Australian, Trooper Mark Donaldson; and the young English soldier, Johnson Beharry. It is a gentle service with a specially commissioned, haunting piece of music from Sir John Tavener, and a really discomforting but thoughtful poem by the Poet Laureate, Carol Ann Duffy. Whoever organised this service put a huge amount of thought into it and was not afraid to have something thought-provoking and challenging about the realities of war. It is a special day to remember the last surviving veterans who shared so much of their experiences with the generations that followed. Afterwards Gordon and I walk through the field of remembrance outside the Abbey with all its poppies, and talk to the families of veterans who are here today.

There is a huge outpouring of correspondence and emails coming into Number 10 in defence of Gordon following *The Sun*'s attack. I am receiving many letters and messages, too. One typical message from a friend reads: 'Sarah, please tell GB how furious we are about all of today's nonsense and that we send our sympathy to you both. Anyone who knows him will know that he wrote from the heart and it is outrageous that a paper should exploit this! I have heard nothing but support for GB.'

I also received a text from Stewart Wood that just makes me cry: 'Hi Sarah, can you pls tell Gordon I have never felt so proud to be a part of the team around him as I am today. I saw him tell Fraser today that he loved him and I immediately knew he knew how all parents feel when we see the coffins from Wootton Bassett. X'

It has been an emotional time, but my diary, long planned in advance, does not take into account the 'unknowable' events of any given day. So this evening I find myself all dressed up in a long green Catherine Deane evening gown, ready to join Gordon at the annual reception at Buckingham Palace for the Diplomatic Corps.

Just before we leave, I fit in one other engagement just over the road. I walk out of the front door and across Whitehall to pop into the *Cosmopolitan* Ultimate Woman of the Year Awards at the Banqueting House.

On the red carpet, however, my heel catches on the back of my long dress. I predict a pretty awful photo if I bend over to release the hem so I stand tall and then half-hop my way inside where I can untangle myself. Konrad texts me later to suggest I look at my photos, which are up online. The captured dress on my shoe means that the neckline I am sporting reveals rather more décolletage than I am used to. Amazing to report, but the low-cut photo appears in pretty much all the tabloids, thankfully with favourable comments.

Thursday 12th November

It is polling day at last in the Glasgow North East by-election. I go to the Labour Party headquarters in London to do some phone calls to encourage our supporters to go out and vote. I meet Barbara Roche there, who used to be the MP in Hornsey and Wood Green in North London, and a former Treasury minister. It is terrific that she has taken the time to come out and work for this by-election. She and I both get the feeling that those voters who were undecided last time are now moving in favour of voting Labour, as they come to make up their minds.

I hear that the result will be declared not long after midnight so I stay up to hear it come in. Of course, the count takes longer and the TV commentators keep saying it will be any moment. The bad news for me is that the result is not declared until 2 a.m., which means I am going to be very tired tomorrow, but the good news is that Labour won by a whopping 8,111 votes on a 33 per cent turnout (not so bad when you consider that the by-election after the previous Speaker Betty Boothroyd retired was only a 28 per cent turnout). There is a swing from the Scottish Nationalists to Labour of 2 per cent, which is also good news. I am especially pleased to see the terrible, racist British National Party is knocked back to fourth place, and will lose their election deposit.

Monday 16th November

At the Lord Mayor's Banquet, we are there again in white tie and long gowns. I have my regular seat next to Justice Secretary Jack Straw in his robe and tights, but a new ambassador on my left. Gordon's foreign policy speech covers from the start why our troops are in Afghanistan. Given the events of recent weeks it seems wise to explain this all again. He also sets out how we can start to approach leaving Afghanistan, remembering that this has already been achieved in Iraq since he became Prime Minister. Although this event has become almost routine in the yearly calendar, I find I enjoy it more each time. I look forward to my social chat with Jack Straw, my place at the table that gives me a great vantage point of the 1,000 guests in their finery (I love looking at the dresses and jewellery), and the speeches that all cover interesting topics, this year more than ever.

Wednesday 18th November

I join Maggie Darling and Martin Hayman, husband of the Lords' Speaker, Baroness Hayman, in the gallery of the House of Lords today to listen to the Queen's Speech. It only lasts seven minutes this year, but the 13 bills presented all make me very proud of our government, from tackling child poverty and enhancing the role of carers to green energy and the digital economy.

Gordon speaks in the debate that follows, and it is clear that we now have the dividing lines for the election set out. There is a great bit in the debate where Gordon attacks the Tories' proposed inheritance tax: 'This must be the only tax change in history when the people proposing it – the Opposition leader and the Shadow Chancellor – will know by name almost all of the potential beneficiaries. Is this what the Conservatives mean when they say: "We're all in this together"?'

Thursday 19th November

Gordon is in Brussels for the final decisions on the new EU President and the High Representative. In the end the Belgian PM gets the Presidency and the British get the High Representative post. A consensus forms around Cathy Ashton, an experienced political figure as a former Leader of the House of Lords, and most recently our European Trade Commissioner. She may not be as well known as any of the other names that were floated for the job, but she has been loyal in Gordon's government and effective in Brussels.

Saturday 21st November

We are in London while Gordon visits Cumbria to see the flood damage that has been incurred there from all the terrible weather recently. I have heard that Twitter co-founder, Biz Stone, is in town, over from Twitter's HQ in California, so I invite him to come to Downing Street in between his various speeches and university debates. He is smart about the fledgling business he and his partners are running and I learn a lot from him in a short space of time about things to do on Twitter. I am still keeping my fingers crossed for more than a million followers by Christmas. I am planning a big Twitter party for the moment I get there, and it is a shame that Biz has arrived in London just a little too soon.

Monday 23rd November

Baroness Thatcher is here to see her new portrait by Richard Stone, which is to be hung in Downing Street. I join Gordon to greet her at the door and walk with her to the reception. Many of her old colleagues have been invited to join her at the unveiling today so the building is full of unfamiliar characters. Gordon had promised that he would organise her portrait when they spoke on her first visit so it does seem to have all happened very quickly.

*

A new poll narrows the gap to only six points' difference between Labour and the Conservatives.

Tuesday 24th November

Callum Fairhurst comes to visit with his mum, Sarah, and dad, Mark. His brother, Liam, passed away in June after a heroic fight against his cancer. He had a great spirit and a life well lived in his short years. Callum is here to collect a Diana Gold Award on behalf of Liam at a ceremony at Number 11, but we have a chat all the same and promise to keep in touch, helping each other with our charity activities. Callum follows me on Twitter and already runs a charity fundraising sweet shop from his back garden @black-pigsweets. As my charity is PiggyBankKids I think we have a connection if only in our sense of humour.

Wednesday 25th November

A few months ago, we launched an art competition at Number 10 to attract original works of art by children around Britain to grace the walls of the waiting room. I had noticed that the walls looked rather stark and it seemed a good space to use, and one that would not step on the toes of English Heritage, who look after the building and its interiors. Mike Porter, who handles all the autocue and in-house filming, had made a great little film for the Number 10 website to encourage schools to submit their entries, and the response has been great.

Our first young winners came in to visit today with their parents. The competition is to be run regularly so the artwork can change or be added to. We took lots of photos of the winners with their pictures, to display on the website. There is such huge potential to engage with schools via website projects if we can fit in with the curriculum. It is an encouraging start.

Thursday 26th November

I join Gordon for a very sad meeting with a very dignified and brave mum today. Sarah Adams and her family come in to see Gordon in response to his invitation. Mrs Adams' son, Private James Prosser, was killed in Afghanistan on 27th September 2009, just two months ago. She speaks about her campaign for better pay and insurance for young privates, and her deep wish to visit Afghanistan and the place where her son was killed. Of course, she knows that the Ministry of Defence will not make this visit possible for her while there is still fighting but I hope she gets her wish one day. Her grief must still be so raw, but she and her family present themselves with real grace and put forward their views firmly but without anger. Their MP, Paul Murphy, the former Welsh Secretary, is with them and I know will follow up on any conversations between Mrs Adams and Gordon.

From there, Gordon and I go directly to the state room to meet some young Londoners who would be about the same age as Private Prosser. They are all nominated for the Spirit of London Awards, awarded to inspirational young people and organised by the Damilola Taylor Trust. The 21 shortlisted winners all take a huge interest in meeting Gordon and bombard him with lots of questions and news of their various activities. I move along the row of people with Gordon joining in the conversations. One guy asks me who I am and I explain I'm married to Gordon. 'Well cool,' is the reply.

Friday 27th November

I speak at the Royal College of Midwives conference in Manchester about the international maternal mortality campaign. I travel up with Health Minister Ann Keen MP and she is terrific at briefing me on all the current issues affecting midwives. Having chaired the new Nursing Commission, she is very highly regarded by the medical profession and politicians alike, and I am fortunate to have her by my side today. I'm looking forward to this, as it is one thing to campaign on the maternal health issue to those who have not considered it before, but I am truly talking to the experts today.

Ann and I have both given ourselves a punishing schedule for the next two days, fitting in as much as we can while up in the North. Ann is visiting a hospital in the North West, and I head across to the North East to visit the wonderful Seven Stories centre in Byker, Newcastle, that is a museum, gallery, shop and activity space for children's reading. I realise when I am there that I have found just the place to lodge the original artwork from our Shirley Hughes' Christmas card from a couple of years ago, which is rather precious. I have a great time seeing the Judith Kerr exhibition with her original illustrations for *The Tiger Who Came to Tea*, a book I remember my mum doing a special teaching project on in her school, many years ago.

In the evening, Ann and I both attend a party event for Chief Whip Nick Brown MP, who has a big contest on at the general election to hold his seat following some boundary changes. Nick tells one of my very favourite stories about a veteran Labour MP, who got a call on his mobile phone while sitting having a drink with colleagues. All anyone could hear from the MP's side of the call was: 'Hello…..yes…..yes…..no…….no. ….NO………I don't think so…..WHAT?…….you have the wrong number!' The MP rang off to find everyone looking at him expectantly. Finally, some one asked, 'What did that caller want?'

'Crack cocaine,' he replied, to everyone's astonishment. I know it is awful, but it is pretty funny all the same.

Saturday 28th November

Gordon has asked me to visit the areas affected by devastating recent floods in Cumbria, and to report back to him how everyone is getting on. On his visit, he identified that the collapsed bridge there needed rebuilding most urgently.

When I arrive with Ann Keen to meet local MP Jim Cunningham, we can see that this work is not yet complete, but in the Workington area, also cut off by the disaster, we can see how the community have come together to arrange temporary schooling, nursing care and food distribution until they are back to normal. A great triumph of community spirit.

Tuesday 1st December

Dr Mitch Besser, Robin Smalley and Steven Guy from the Mothers2Mothers charity, who work so effectively to prevent HIV transmission between mother and child in South Africa, are visiting London today and come in to see me. We light a candle to mark World AIDS Day. Konrad has also arranged for the African Children's Choir to come in and sing to staff and some invited guests. We have wonderful guests including representatives from the Terrence Higgins Trust as well as *X Factor* choreographer Brian Friedman, who comes with his mum and dad on a visit from the US, and our own treasured British actor, Kwame Kwei-Armah. We are all pretty sobered by the fact that one in four people with HIV in Britain are untested and don't know they have it.

After the meeting, Christianne pulls me to one side to say there is a stream of gobbledegook on my Twitter stream, and someone has contacted the IT department to ask if it has been hacked. As soon as I look at the messages, I can guess the culprit. My little chap Fraser has managed to randomly type a whole sequence of letters into my keyboard and somehow press the send button. My Twitter followers are posting messages asking if it is a kid, the cat or Gordon. I would normally just call John Woodcock in the press office and explain in case there are any enquiries, but he has not long ago been selected as a Labour candidate and is away from the office. So I take my own direct action and quickly type in a new message pledging to avoid 'junior tweet interference'. Astonishingly, this makes the BBC as a story online, and the press office tell me it is the third most popular story of the day. At least it attracts more interest to my World AIDS Day postings.

Ahead of me, this evening, is the thrill of 'The Morgans', an awards dinner hosted by Piers Morgan. But first, I host an event for the British Stammering Association with the Children's Secretary, Ed Balls, and then go with Gordon to attend the huge Muslims for Labour dinner. As Gordon goes around the room I am flattened to the side by people wanting to speak to him. There is also a great reception for Sadiq Khan MP who, newly promoted by Gordon, is the first Muslim to attend Cabinet meetings, and the first minister in the Western World to perform Haj, the pilgrimage to Mecca.

I arrive at the Mandarin Oriental Hotel in Knightsbridge for The Morgans, knowing I am set for an evening of celebrity, glamour and Piers making himself the centre of attention. I had rejected Piers's initial offer that I accept an award for being 'a good egg', and agreed instead to present a Lifetime Achievement Award to Simon Cowell. On the way up the stairs I surprise Lily Allen, and oddly she shakes my hand and curtseys. She is a great Labour supporter and I like her all the more for that.

I join Piers and Celia on their table with cricketer Andrew Flintoff and his wife, Rachael; the great Lord and Lady Sugar; Piers's fellow *Britain's Got Talent* judge Amanda Holden; and, of course, Simon Cowell. Katie Price is also there and I walk over to greet her, never having met her before. Very sweetly she thanked me for saying hello, saying she did not think that 'people like me' would say hello to 'girls like her'. Well, I am glad I proved her wrong on that count.

Piers gets up on stage and indulges in a very fun ceremony handing out plastic Morgan Awards to many of his celeb chums. My favourites are for Amanda Holden, who responds by handing out business cards with Piers's mobile phone number on them, and for Ronnie Corbett, who wins the prize for best-dressed gentleman – quite right. Andrew Flintoff and Cilla Black are also called up to be saluted as National Treasures.

Towards the end, I am all set to pop up and present Simon Cowell with his large lump of clear plastic, but then Piers does what he promised not to do – he announces that one of these great awards will be mine and will present it to me himself. At least he has the decency to tell his assembled crowd that I will not be happy about it. He is actually very sentimental about explaining why I get my award for 'being an all-round good egg' – almost as much as when praising the cricketing prowess of Freddie Flintoff. I am much more comfortable bouncing up two minutes later to present Simon Cowell with his award.

Having been the last to arrive, I think I am the first to leave, heading in the opposite direction to Lily, Katie, Celia and Tracey Emin as they head straight for the late bar.

Friday 4th December

The Nobel Prize-winning environmentalist and head of the Million Trees Movement, Wangari Maathai, is in London on her way to the climate change summit in Copenhagen. The architect John McAslan is hosting an event for her in his North London studio and I jump at the chance to see her again. She and Gordon have a very special bond between them, doubtless from the time when Gordon helped behind the scenes to get her out of prison when unfairly charged. I get there in time to chat to them both before the event starts, and Wangari truly touches me when she describes my husband as the 'Man with a Golden Heart'. I give a short address at the start, reminding everyone of her courage and fight for women, as well as for the environment.

I have the job of turning on the Downing Street Christmas tree lights this year with the local Safer Neighbourhood police team and their families.

With the tree lit, tonight is the night of the long-planned 'Downing Tweet Party'. This is a personal event so it is, in my usual way, a pretty DIY number with all hands on deck from my small team. This means that I have ordered wine and cava (the official Twitter drink thanks to recent hilarious tweets on the subject by writer @caitlinmoran) and beer, while someone has rustled up some glasses from somewhere. Foodwise we have the usual party nibbles, but I have also arranged via the Chequers chef to get some tiny little festive mince pies, each decorated with a Twitter pastry bird. I am holding the party for the Million Mums campaign as I have used Twitter so much to promote its messages, and can celebrate passing the million mark, too, for Twitter followers. I booked the party a few weeks ago aiming for the 'million moment' and have hit it pretty much spot on.

The guest list includes some tech and social media people who have embraced Twitter; and some of the charity campaigners, many of whom tweet themselves like @emmafreud and @claudiawinkle. I have also invited over 100 people whom I connected with early into my tweeting days and who have really made the most of what you can do with Twitter. I even have Gretel Truong from Haddad Media flying in from the States – she has been a great social media person for the maternal mortality campaign and has decided to jump on a flight and come with her video camera.

Singer Beverley Knight has agreed to sing live for us tonight, and we set up the Million Mums tattoo parlour offering transfer tattoos with the 'Mum' logo, which were so popular in the summer festivals.

It is one of my favourite evenings at Downing Street.

It is not a typical night but it does bring in all kinds of people who just appreciate being there, and many who are invited to Downing Street for the first time. I really enjoy meeting people for the first time who I feel I know a little from our online dialogues. The mix of people works very well from *Thick of It* actress @RebeccaFront to comedian Peter @serafinowicz; from *Guardian* editor @arusbridger to radio DJ and supertweeter @richardbacon to trainee nurse @nurseju_; from super political bloggers @willstraw and Alex Smith of @labourlist to my regular tweet buddies @nigs and @yummybum50 who were mentioned in the

Telegraph in a report on my tweeting. One of my best moments of the night was seeing the three journalists, @indiaknight, @caitlin-moran and @krishgm (Krishnan Guru-Murthy from Channel 4), all disappearing into the night covered in 'Mum' tattoos. No one was quite sure if Krishnan would be reading the news on TV the next day with a tattoo still on his cheek.

Tuesday 8th December

Gordon has invited the Shave family to visit Downing Street after a letter he received from parents, Martin and Hayley, praising the NHS treatment that their toddler daughter, Camille, is receiving for a serious brain tumour. Martin and Hayley came with two-year-old Camille and her big sister, Lucia, and I join them to say hello. They have a long haul ahead for them as she undergoes all her treatment and I admire their bravery, but can also feel their pain.

After I leave them, I go back to the flat and just cry. I know why I do as I can feel Jennifer near me, but I wish them well with their fight. As they battle on, they are also starting a charity called Camille's Appeal, and looking for every way to get some good out of their experience.

Wednesday 9th December

Today is Pre-Budget Report day, which means the whole building is busy. I get out early to join one of the Maggie's Centres board meetings. As the Patron of their Joy of Living appeal, I try to attend at least some of the organisational meetings. I must be tired as I take board member Annita Bennett to entirely the wrong place before we double back to find the right venue.

It is also the night of the British Fashion Awards and I have promised Harold Tillman that I will do the opening introduction at the start of the event, but first, the Duke of York is hosting a reception at St James's Palace.

On a night with the fashionistas, I just stick with my favourites and play safe with a black Graeme Black dress, La Diosa jewellery and black high heels that make me feel very tall.

I enjoy the reception at St James's Palace even when I get told off by the great Katharine Hamnett for government policy on cyclists, smokers and beer drinkers, and also have Stuart Rose introduce me to another retailer who gives me a lecture on how to run the economy. Stuart proclaims that he is politically neutral as the M&S chief, but I am beginning to have my doubts.

Later, at the British Fashion Awards held at the Royal Courts of Justice this year, I step out of the car, into blinding flashes and the biggest, loudest scrum of red-carpet photographers that I have ever experienced. I get in as fast as I can in my high heels.

The room is set out for 1,300 guests and is quite beautiful – though remembering last year, I don't think anyone will fuss about what they get to eat. The stage this year is very high and all blacked out, overlooking the vast audience. I pass model Laura Bailey climbing down from a run-through on the stage and she warns me it is rather treacherous up there.

I have a little walkabout backstage before my speech. I take some deep breaths and try not to look too closely at the stagehands scoffing plates of lasagne. When it is show time, I climb the stairs and admit to myself that I feel pretty frightened, but am very determined that I can manage a two-minute speech. A few moments later I am on, after Harold Tillman's elegant introduction, and all too soon am bouncing back down the stairs relieved that I did not make a giant fool of myself in front of fashionable London!

Thursday 10th December

We have representatives from 40 autism charities coming in today for a meeting with me and Health Minister Phil Hope MP, and Angela Smith MP from the Cabinet Office, who is responsible for the voluntary sector.

Some months ago, Polly Tommey, an autism campaigner and mum of a son with autism, came to meet Gordon. She had run an effective and high-profile advertising campaign that had caught everyone's attention. Phil and I had offered to bring together the many autism charities to explore ways for them to work together and be more effective in communicating with government.

It feels like an amazingly productive morning given that we are starting with a broad group, a big task and not much time. The question now is how to follow this up.

Another sign that Christmas is on its way as it is time for the turkey photo again! This year I meet the farmer from Gressingham Turkeys. He generously offers to send all the turkeys needed for the Christmas lunch at the Workington Community Centre, which I have visited in Cumbria just recently following the floods there.

I am well ahead of Christmas planning this year as I have ordered a specially designed Christmas Bombki tree decoration. It is a little Number 10 door, with a wrapped parcel on the doorstep. I have ordered one for every member of the Downing Street and Chequers staff in a special presentation box as a personal gift from our family. We have also had the Christmas ornament photographed hanging on a sprig of British holly at Kew Gardens by a young, award-winning environmental photographer for this year's 10 Downing Street Christmas card. This continues the theme of the last three years, to find an image inspired by the famous front door.

Sunday 13th December

The *Mail on Sunday* has run a story about our phone records, which are held by the House of Commons. There appear to have been some very long phone calls to a number in Canterbury, which Gordon does not recognise. One look and I know that they are me talking to Gil McNeil, covering a lot of work matters. I make most calls to her on my own mobile phone, which I pay for myself, but of course there are calls on the landline at home, too. I think the journalists all have a lot of fun speculating what the calls might be and may even be slightly disappointed that the answer is so mundane. Amusingly, one of the calls took place late on Christmas Eve, which does look like an odd time to sit on the phone to someone. However, I think most mums will understand how long the wait is when you are hoping your children will go to sleep in order for Santa to come.

Gil gets a taste of what being in the media spotlight is like as various reporters ring her bell, so she and her son decamp from her house until they go away.

Monday 14th December

Gordon arrives back around 2.30 a.m. from his pre-Christmas trip to visit troops in Afghanistan. He seems to have slept well on the trip despite reports that he has spent the night in a tin hut somewhere on the front line. It is being reported that this is the first time a British prime minister has stayed overnight in a combat zone since Winston Churchill. Gordon says that he was warm and comfortable, and found the time speaking to the soldiers of great interest. It sounds like it was really worth doing as the experience has brought him even better understanding.

Friday 18th December

Gordon returns from the environmental summit in Copenhagen having given as much time as he could, but is disappointed with the outcome, as are many country leaders and people around the world. The Copenhagen Accord is published today signed by 73 nations, but nothing in it is binding; it is all just wishful thinking.

Closer to home, I made an upsetting discovery today that Chequers is in fact partly paid for by the taxpayer and at a rather high rate. I had always understood, and believe I was told, that

Chequers was funded by the Chequers Trust, endowed by Lord and Lady Lee, and by rental income from the land. I know that it is important that the Prime Minister has a way to relax but I discover – rather by accident on a forwarded email after a Trustees' meeting – that in fact there is a very high annual charge.

My immediate thought is that a far cheaper way could have been found to make sure the PM had some leisure time. Then I realise that it is also about funding a listed building of historic interest (but one to which the public has no access, presumably because of the security needs to protect the PM).

There are so many flaws to the argument I don't know where to start. What I feel strongly is that the taxpayer is not getting value for money. I think that this needs more thought to work out, but it seems to be that at around £800,000 per year, the public deserves to get some access to this historic building, or the Trust needs to raise some money from elsewhere.

I talk to the right people at Downing Street about this and in theory this thinking will happen. I talk to Gordon as well, and we agree that as we now know this, we should not use Chequers until it is resolved (I get assurances that no one's employment will be threatened by our absence). We decide we will just stop going, except for events already booked for government use.

Tuesday 22nd December

It is the end of the year and we have Christmas coming, with time for a family break. We have ended the year on a flat note, but have to build up our energies for the New Year and a very busy break.

We go out together for the first time in a while as a family to the local cinema in Fife to see the British film, *Nativity*. It is the perfect choice for all of us. Christmas comes with lots of snow and we all indulge in a lot of snowman building.

Monday 28th December

Gordon and I spend today, Jennifer's eighth birthday, doing what we always do: visiting her grave, spending a quiet time together and going for a walk. The boys are with us for some of the day, but a friend takes them off for part of the time, too, for a big run around on the beach, dressed up warmly in the bitterly cold weather.

Thursday 31st December

The year ends with uplifting news that one of the Iraq hostages, Peter Moore, is to be released after a long period in captivity.

We spend today at home in Fife with a big meal with Gordon's brother, John, and his wife, Angela, and our friends Murray Elder, Alex Rowley and Pete and Marilyn Livingstone. When it gets to midnight we can hear the noise of the fireworks across in Edinburgh clearly coming over the water.

Celia Walden asked me for a quote for her article in the *Telegraph* about New Year's Resolutions. I am happy to send her mine: 'Work Hard. Have Fun. Stay True.'

CHAPTER 29

Opening Up

2010

Friday 1st January

A New Year and a new decade. Ten years ago today Gordon took me for a walk on Silver Sands beach and asked me to marry him. Looking back, we have had some of the toughest times together and some of the best. I have no regrets, and only one real sadness.

I feel open to what this decade has to offer and ready to face the future, whatever it holds. Gordon is calm, rested and resolved. He wants to win the next election for the Labour Party but I think for himself he will be fine whatever happens. Given all we are up against, we can only do our best. The four of us go back to Silver Sands today and we take great delight in telling the boys about the day we decided to get married, long before they were born.

Sunday 3rd January

Gordon kicks off the year with a round of television and radio interviews. Fiona Phillips comes to the flat to do an interview for *Tesco* magazine, now that she has left the *GMTV* sofa. I have always admired Fiona in the way that she has combined a career on her terms, a great relationship with her producer husband Martin, and raising her two boys – a little older than my two – sticking with good state schools, and looking after her unwell mother, too. She is certainly someone that many women can relate to.

I join them as they look at some of our family photographs, and Fiona is fascinated by Gordon's mother: a strong woman who raised her three boys in the manse in Kirkcaldy. I was lucky to know her for several years before she passed away in 2004; a strong, forthright woman who liked me more than I thought she might.

Monday 4th January

There are various rumours being relayed to us of some disloyalty to the Labour leadership again. It seems a strange choice to challenge the leadership after it has become so clear in the last year that there is no other person ready to deliver a better election result than predicted. Perhaps it is just talk about former minister Charles Clarke, who has issued his New Year message suggesting a new leader, and pretty much suggesting himself as the alternative.

The Chief Whip, Nick Brown, comes in to see Gordon at lunchtime and they eat my turkey soup in the flat, as they talk through what is coming up in the House of Commons this year, with the parliamentary bills from the Queen's Speech.

In the evening a fair number of the Cabinet come to the flat for a curry supper, and there is lots of talk about sticking together to meet the challenges of the year.

Tuesday 5th January

I've got back into our usual family routine quickly. The evening arrives with a reception for the Black and Minority Ethnic media and I hear brilliant, ringing endorsements for Gordon and the government from two heroines of mine: film director Gurinder (*Bend It Like Beckham*) Chadha and singer–songwriter Joan Armatrading.

Wednesday 6th January

Two former Cabinet Ministers, Geoff Hoon and Patricia Hewitt, have sent a letter to Labour MPs asking for support for a secret ballot to initiate a Leadership election. Turns out the swirling rumours did have some foundation after all.

It is an astonishing thing when colleagues from the same side do something that can only undermine your own team, and goodness knows what the general public will think of it all.

I carry on with my day, which involves attending a charity reception at Number 10 for the My Way! campaign to support dyslexia and other learning needs with the children's newspaper *First News*. The guest of honour today is Henry Winkler, so loved in the UK for his role as The Fonz in *Happy Days*, but also a passionate campaigner on dyslexia as someone who suffers from it.

Ed Balls, the Children's Secretary, is there for the reception. When the media outside ask if he is visiting Number 10 for a special meeting with the Prime Minister, he takes great delight in saying that he is in fact here to meet The Fonz.

The latest poll reports come in with Labour now only trailing the Opposition by single digits, but clearly this is not enough for our rebels! Harriet Harman, Jack Straw and even Alan Johnson all take time to come and see Gordon during the course of the afternoon and it is already clear that whatever rebellion Hoon and Hewitt thought might take off is not going to happen.

Thursday 7th January

Gordon calls the previous day's events 'a storm in a tea cup', and even manages a joke in his speech at a big economic launch to say he did not know yesterday if he would be here today ... 'but thankfully, the snowy weather did not hold me back'.

*

The news stories move on fast and are now focused on whether the Opposition leader has airbrushed himself in his party's new pre-election posters.

Thursday 14th January

I join Gordon on a private visit to Headley Court in Surrey, the rehabilitation centre for soldiers with serious injuries. Many are given prosthetic limbs and Headley Court is a place for them to recover and regain mobility. It is an exceptional facility that had an extra £24 million investment announced by Defence Secretary Des Browne in 2008, as well as extraordinary additional support from the public through charities like Help for Heroes, to ensure that the facilities are first class. Our visits are private, but we both leave humbled by the bravery and sacrifice of our troops serving for their country, while the team who work at Headley Court are highly professional individuals who do a phenomenal job.

Wednesday 20th January

We are reminded again of another brave soldier lost when Gordon joins the reception at Number 10 for the Mark Evison Trust, set up in memory of the young 26-year-old Welsh Guardsman, who lost his life on 12th May 2009. Mark's mother, Margaret Evison, had met with Gordon some months earlier and he was very struck by their meeting. It became clear to me as I spoke to Mrs Evison that she too had taken something unexpected from their meeting, and they had both perhaps gained a better understanding of each other's perspectives. I know that Gordon was grateful for that gift, and had been very happy to respond to the suggestion that a reception be hosted for the charity formed in Lieutenant Evison's name. As his family, friends, and other supporters of the Trust arrived, I chatted to them, and I gained a very strong sense of this remarkable young man who had made such a positive impact on so many people during his life.

*

I have to leave to attend the National Television Awards, which are being filmed at the Excel Centre down in Docklands. My role is to say thank you to the 10 million people watching for their generosity towards the people of Haiti following the devastating earthquake at the start of the year. To date, tens of millions of pounds have been raised by the British public to contribute to food and shelter, and to rebuild a big hospital damaged by the terrible earthquake. As it is an awards ceremony I make the announcement for the Best Actor award and am delighted that this year's winner is David Tennant.

Monday 25th January

Gordon heads out to Northern Ireland to join the peace talks taking place as it is reported that there are some breakdowns in the dialogue. Northern Ireland has come so far that any setbacks are terribly frustrating and no one wants to let go in case things slide backwards. He is expected to be there all day, and perhaps overnight.

Wednesday 27th January

The Northern Ireland talks continue though the day and night. On all long-distance trips, the IT guys who travel with the PM and his team form an important and often critical role in sorting out secure communications and setting up an instant office function. In Belfast this time we hear they serve an arguably more crucial role. Michael Dugher, the tough press officer working with Gordon, reports back that the IT team have made a foray out of Stormont to get new clean undergarments for those who have not been to a hotel yet, nor have a clean change of clothes with them.

Thursday 28th January

Gordon finally returns from Northern Ireland, only to go straight into a long-planned Afghanistan and Yemen conference in London today, that has attendance from our allies from all over the world. There will be some straight-talking in it, I'm sure. Much of the media coverage is focused on David Miliband's weekend statement about wanting talks with the Taliban, which distracts from the main event, but the conference is favourably reported all day.

I am off again to fulfil my destiny of being photographed with every supermodel on the planet. Today I am interviewing Elle MacPherson for another guest-edited edition of *Fabulous* magazine. Last time the issue focused on health in pregnancy; this issue will focus on more general wellbeing and women's cancer care.

Today I am talking to Elle about, well, being Elle. I arrive at the studio to find the photographic shoot in full flow and it looks amazing. Elle is wearing a Barbarella outfit and standing on the highest heels in her already extraordinary long legs. I get hair and make-up to do their best for me, and at the end have my 'interviewer' pic taken with Elle. Ironically, I have to insist on no airbrushing for me – all political players are under inspection after the Leader of the Opposition overdid the soft-focus tones in a big poster campaign.

I have met Elle many times as we both support maternal health campaigns, and she compèred at a PiggyBankKids event at Chequers once, much to our guests' delight. She is a mum of two boys a bit older than mine, and is passionate in supporting campaigns to improve the lives of women and children everywhere so of course we have overlapped on the same causes. We have a great chat for an hour – thankfully all recorded as I am so intent on our conversation I don't take down any written notes.

I am a little bit horrified to discover that we have many of the same approaches to health and wellbeing, even sharing the same osteopath at Pilates off the Square. And the differences? Naturally, there is the near perfect 'architecture' that Elle has, but I do discover one more difference. She swears by two to three litres of water a day, and insists it is nature's way of purifying our systems. That's it; from now on I am doing it Elle's way.

Friday 29th January

The US General Stanley McChrystal, in charge of the American military operations in Afghanistan, has been in London for yesterday's conference, and so made use of his time here to come in and see Gordon at Downing Street. When booked originally, the meeting had been a courtesy visit for a private update, and I was told that Mrs McChrystal would be coming too. As it turned out, the meeting was rather more serious and Mrs McChrystal did not come. Gordon instead strongly expressed his annoyance at recent events.

General McChrystal had informed Gordon a short time ago that President Karzai had vetoed the appointment of former British Defence Secretary Des Browne as the Special Afghan Envoy. Recognising that you could not have an envoy the Afghan President did not support, the matter was closed. However, Gordon had talked to President Karzai at the conference and said he was sorry that it had not worked out. He was then surprised to learn from the Afghan President that his view had never actually been sought. I have rarely seen Gordon as cross, but he was furious to discover that he had been misinformed by the General, and for seemingly personal reasons over the choice of Des Browne. I think that a good special envoy was lost who would have done a great job on the ground.

Saturday 30th January

There is a Twitter app called Tweetclouds that gathers up your most used words in a big graphic white cloud, which I look up today. Unsurprisingly, mine are 'women', 'health' and 'love'.

Gordon and I walk over to Westminster Central Hall (admittedly surrounded by his protection team) to join our Poet Laureate Carol Ann Duffy who has organised a big event: Poetry for Haiti. An audience of about 1,000 people have gathered, all paying £10 a ticket to go to the emergency disaster appeal. Gordon opens the event, not with a poem, but by thanking the 22 poets gathered, including

Andrew Motion and Roger McGough. He also makes a very practical announcement that the government has gathered up all the UK's available corrugated iron sheets to ship out to Haiti to use as the storm shelters so urgently needed in the next few weeks there.

Sunday 31st January

Gordon has a big hour-long interview with Piers Morgan coming up. While it will be personal rather than political, Gordon always prepares for everything and this is no exception. I remember Gordon's mum telling me that he was the only one of her three boys who would do his homework as soon as he got home from school, rather than 'football first and homework squeezed in at the last possible moment'.

To prepare for Piers's programme, he gathers together Justin Forsyth, Kirsty McNeill, Nicola Burdett and David Muir from his office, and they create a mock run-through with Alastair Campbell playing the part of Piers.

They are all sitting in the first-floor study at Number 10 and are joined by Peter Mandelson.

I can't resist poking my head around the door just to see how things are going. Alastair spots me and says, 'Sarah, we were just talking about you. I was just asking Gordon why you are more popular than him.'

'Because I don't have to do the politics,' I reply. 'Alastair, you too became more popular when you stepped out of politics.'

'That's true,' he graciously replies. I hear Peter start to make his comments on how he thinks Gordon is doing, and I slip away. My guess is that Piers will be easy after a grilling from Alastair and Peter.

Tuesday 2nd February

Gordon heads off for an astonishingly packed day, even by his standards. I ask him why he is so cheerful when he has so much on his plate. He replies, 'I realise that when I took over from Tony in 2007 we were 14 points behind in the polls and on 28 per cent. Now we are 32 per cent and only 7 or 8 points behind. That is an okay place to be after a recession and an expenses scandal in Parliament.'

The poll out today is the third in a row showing only a 7 or 8 point difference. If that was a real result, the assumption would be for a hung parliament. You can hear the whispers around the corridors of Whitehall among the civil servants that this is what they might be expecting.

Gordon is still waiting on news from the Northern Ireland discussions, but there is not quite enough progress made for him to go there himself yet. He answers questions on live television for a full two-and-a-half hours in front of the Liaison Committee hearing.

Liberal Democrat MP Phil Willis asks a question at the hearing about higher-education cuts and Gordon is able to reel off all the investments and results in higher education off the top of his head. I know that the secret to Gordon is preparation, but he has a real command of detail, too. As I watch, he is also asked a question about the departed Trade Minister, Digby Jones, and the GOATs (Government of All the Talents) ministers. Gordon just laughs and says they are big personalities and they all provide useful input to government. This is certainly true from where I have been able to observe their contributions; even Digby, who left and then attacked the government.

Thursday 4th February

I meet Tina Weaver, the editor of the *Sunday Mirror*, who, together with the *Daily Mirror*, have been solid supporters of the Labour government and are unlikely to change that position when the general election is called.

As the election must take place before June this year, I had expected to talk to Tina about what we can do together during the campaign. However, Tina and her colleagues have been faced with the devastating news of their journalist, Rupert Hamer, being killed in Afghanistan while photographer Philip Coburn suffered the loss of both his legs. It has clearly been a distressing time for everyone at the *Mirror* as they find the right way to support both Rupert and Philip's families, and cope with everyone's distress. We do agree that I will write a weekly column during the election time, but leave it to another day to discuss the details.

In the evening, Gordon and I attend the LGBT Labour dinner at the Café de Paris. There is a great turn-out for the dinner, from Michael Cashman MEP to music manager John Reid and host Amy Lamé, and a cracking atmosphere. A real treat tonight is the presence of the legend that is Stanley Baxter. Kirsty McNeill is very excited and says, 'I can't believe Stanley Baxter is here.'

'Why?' I ask. 'Didn't you know he was gay?'

'No,' she replies, 'I didn't know he was Labour.'

Saturday 6th February

Today Gordon is recording his interview for *Piers Morgan's Life Stories* at the ITV studios on London's South Bank. The bulk of the audience is made up of members of the public who have no idea who they are about to see being interviewed. Given that Piers's usual subjects range from Dannii Minogue to Sharon Osbourne and Ronnie Corbett (one of my favourite interviews ever) to Richard Branson, I wonder how they will react to seeing it is Gordon today.

I leave Gordon to do his advance clip in his dressing room, which will be shown at the start of the final programme. I run into Piers as he trots through the hallway where I am chatting to Gil. Typical Piers: 'I have just been looking at your clips for the show and you look really fit.' We are all trusting Piers to do an interview that shows fairly the Gordon that I know, and not the media caricature that we live with daily.

I take my seat in the studio audience next to my mum and Patrick, and the filming finally gets going. Gordon has said to Piers that he can ask whatever he wants and to take the time he wants. Piers takes him at his word, and the interview lasts well over two hours.

It is an extraordinary interview for me to listen to, so I wonder how it will be for those who don't know Gordon as I do. I hear him talk about his childhood eye injury in a school rugby game, the endless time in hospital and operations to save his sight when he should have been in his first university year; his parents and his brothers; his role as a father today as the dad of John and Fraser; and, of course, about our short time with Jennifer before the boys were born.

We have talked together so many times of Jennifer and think of her every day. I often cry to think of her, and remember the precious time we had for ten short days. I cry now watching Gordon talk openly and honestly. I don't mind who sees as this is all part of me now. I know that some people will comment on whether Gordon should or should not have talked about Jennifer, but the truth is that there is no conversation about the kind of people we are that does not include all three of our children.

Afterwards, we are greeted by ITV's Director of Television, Peter Fincham, who has been so instrumental in commissioning this film. I appreciate that he has had to juggle a lot of push back from the other main political parties about this interview. One thing I know is that whatever else gets made, nothing will match this interview; maybe sometimes taking the politics out of things gives you a truer sense of perspective.

When we get home Gordon and I are just exhausted and emotionally quite drained. When we sleep, it is solidly and for hours.

Monday 8th February

My brother, Sean, is over to stay from Los Angeles. I accompany him to the *Evening Standard* British Film Awards, where he and director, Sacha Gervasi, are receiving an award for *Anvil! The Story of Anvil*. We are in the London Film Museum in the old County Hall building, which seems oddly familiar but I can't place it. Then I realise the last time I visited these rooms was with John as a toddler when it was an aquarium. The fish are gone and have been replaced with all kinds of eclectic film memorabilia.

Sean is over to develop his next film project – a hilarious account of world record breakers with the support of the Guinness World Records guys, Rob Molloy and editor Craig Glenday. I join Sean to meet them for tea and I laugh more than I have for ages just hearing the stories of people's efforts to be the best at something. I love the tale of their attempt to verify the world's longest kebab with the visual imagery of trying to turn it round to cook it, and the world's biggest bowl of soup, so large that it had to be served in a giant copper bowl in the village square outdoors, which inevitably meant a bird flying overhead picked that moment to poop in the soup.

I truly love the striving of people to be the most, the best, the first, but we are none of us perfect, and it is the stories of the attempts that show the best and worst of us.

Sean's stay is all too brief this time as he has to get back to his family in Los Angeles, but as children, and later when we shared a flat, he could always make me laugh! All these years later that has not changed, and I feel as though I have had intensive laughter therapy with his visit, and feel much rejuvenated.

Thursday 11th February

I start my day in my office with a call to Sir Stuart Rose at Marks and Spencer. I ask if he will sign up to Women's Aid's new 'Real Men' campaign at my friend Nicola Mendelsohn's request (she is chairing the corporate development board now). The campaign will be fronted by high-profile men from all walks of life, to make the point that 'real men' don't engage with domestic abuse or hurt women and children physically or emotionally. Thankfully, he agrees straight away, and pledges to attend the September fundraising gala night for the charity.

Today I fulfil a long overdue obligation to go to leading online social network Mumsnet, to join their Big Night In charity party at Mumsnet Towers, an unprepossessing office unit off Kentish Town Road in North London.

All the team are there and have laid on wine and plates of delicious British cheeses with biscuits and home-made cookies. Mumsnet founders Justine Roberts and Carrie Longton greet me and we take lots of snaps for all our new media outlets – I am certainly tweeting about my time here.

At 9 p.m. on the dot, I join the mumsnetters on line and the questions start coming quick and fast. The mumsnetters are a savvy lot, and know just what questions they want to put. I answer 31 questions in an hour, which is good enough, I think, to finish with a glass of wine in celebration.

Sunday 14th February

Back in Scotland for the weekend, I am rewarded on Valentine's Day with a lie-in followed by breakfast in bed. I get a plate of grilled bacon, a poached egg and a mug of tea made just as I like it: very hot, not too strong and just a dash of milk – all made by my husband.

There is something about husbands in the kitchen – or mine at least – where they never quite do anything the way you want it. I spend a great amount of time doing things myself as it seems the quickest, most efficient way to get the meal/clean up/dishwasher stacked the 'best way'. Today the opposite happens: I actually get everything done to perfection, and it is really lovely. So, too, are my lovely flowers, and a sweet Vinnie Day necklace with a circle of gold on a light chain from Astley Clarke.

*

After lunch, I arrange for the boys to go to a play centre for a really good run around, while Gordon and I make the journey to the churchyard where Jennifer rests, about 30 minutes' drive from our home. We spend a little while tending to the headstone, which needs a bit of cleaning up after the recent snow falls, and I lay most of my Valentine roses there. When we have an important day or even just some time to ourselves, it brings us great peace to visit there. The quiet moments are so important to me, and I really need the time just to rebalance myself.

Afterwards, Gordon suggests that we take a walk down to the neighbouring village, which is where his own father lived as a boy. We wander through the streets past the small stone houses as he tries to remember exactly where his father's old house was. We find it in a small cul-de-sac where the three tiny adjacent houses are now knocked together into one home. Gordon's father grew up as an only child, and saw the family move house three times as a result of his fathers' struggle to find steady employment. Gordon's dad finally achieved a scholarship to university, something that allowed him then to train as a church minister.

Once back home, with the boys tucked up in bed, Gordon and I settle down to watch the edited version of his interview with Piers Morgan. It is fascinating to see an interview that had stretched out for well over two hours, cut back to 40 minutes. Nothing actually seems to be lost from it, and the two men cover much ground about Gordon's early years, personal life and political career. The hardest part is hearing him talk about Jennifer, but I know from the letters I get every week that talking about grief and loss is important to people who have suffered their own personal tragedies. This is a rare opportunity to be open and share those personal feelings and the journey we have travelled, and I feel very proud that my husband, contrary to some people's perceptions, is truly connected to his own emotions, and able to articulate both the joy and the suffering of loving and losing a much-loved child.

I see myself crying on screen, and apart from wishing I had been smart enough to take a tissue with me, I actually think that viewers can see an honest response from me. I don't mind that this is so open. We need to allow people in closer to know us better.

Piers had sent me a text after he had seen the final edit that said: 'Just seen it. The editing is fantastic. He comes over better than I have ever seen him on TV. Funny, warm, smart, open, honest, emotional, passionate, decent. People will really like him afterwards.' Watching the programme now as it is broadcast, I don't think I could have expressed it any better myself.

CHAPTER 30

And We're Off

Monday 15th February

Gordon and I host a reception at Number 10 with the British Chinese community to celebrate the Chinese New Year. TV presenter and styling expert Gok Wan is there with his ma and poppa; really sweet people who are half his height. When we are introduced, Gordon asks him, 'Are you here to give me a makeover?' which draws peals of laughter from everyone.

'There are only so many ways to style a navy blue suit,' I say, to which Gok smartly replies, 'There's always room for a few sequins.'

Thursday 18th February

It is London Fashion Week again and I can't believe how quickly it comes around. I head to the Fashion for Relief event in aid of Haiti and the White Ribbon Alliance, which is being held at Somerset House. I meet BFC chair Harold Tillman, and we venture backstage to thank everyone who is giving their time tonight. I introduce Harold to Ronnie Corbett who is looking his usual dapper self. Quick as a flash, Ronnie quips, 'Mr Tallman' as he stretches up on his tiptoes to talk to the nearly 6ft-tall Harold.

The models look stunning in some of the best of the new season's outfits, as does Geri Halliwell, resplendent in a ruffled and feathered pink mini dress, with a tiny tiny waist.

Trudie Styler has generously broken off filming in Paris to come and compère the fashion show. While we are waiting for the start,

Naomi comes over to say hello with Kate Moss and Annabelle Neilson, the model who was Alexander McQueen's muse. They are all very affected by the recent and shocking death of McQueen, and have on his beautiful dresses.

I keep my speech short, describing the charities to be supported this evening and the scale of the challenge in Haiti for mothers and babies. I do say that I have gone as far down the catwalk as I am prepared to go – which is, of course, about two steps to the microphone. It does make me appreciate that catwalk modelling might not be as easy as it looks.

The show starts with a tribute to Alexander McQueen and there is an audible gasp as Naomi steps out, shortly followed by Kate and Annabelle. A run of famous faces follows as the show moves on with The Saturdays; Jamelia and her daughters; a very pregnant Denise van Outen; Dame Shirley Bassey; Ronnie Corbett, who skips with a cane the length of the catwalk; and David Walliams and James Corden, who share a big man-to-man kiss at the end of the runway.

At the end of the show, the lights dim and there is a rather alarming gap suddenly filled by Naomi walking out, arm-in-arm with Piers Morgan. Given that Piers was the former tabloid editor who was successfully sued by Naomi for a breach of her privacy many years ago, we can assume that they have now made it up for this very good cause.

I am sitting by Piers's fiancée, Celia, who gets a big wink from her guy as he passes.

I took Pauline Prescott with me as my guest tonight. She has always been an avid follower of fashion and an elegant dresser herself, and I knew she would enjoy the night. She has been a friend ever since I first met Gordon, and we have entertained each other over the years in our respective homes in Hull and Fife. Since John has stepped down as the Deputy Prime Minister, and deputy leader of the Labour Party, we don't see her so much in London and, of course, since her biography and recent TV appearances with John, she has become quite a sought-after celebrity in her own right.

We have had a good night and I drop her off at her flat on my way home.

I pick up a voicemail from a good friend who has been very upset by a journalist contacting him to ask if it was ever the case that Gordon had hit him. It is clearly nonsense, but he is upset and insulted for Gordon by the question. He has also been told that another newspaper is publishing book extracts by political writer Andrew Rawnsley, with similar allegations. This does sound terrible and very wrong, but I don't expect the story to go anywhere as it sounds so ludicrous.

Saturday 20th February

It is Gordon's birthday but he is out for most of the day with all the Cabinet Ministers in Warwick for a launch of Labour's long campaign, pre-general election. When he returns to do an interview with *Marie Claire* magazine, the journalist Andrea has very thoughtfully brought along a birthday cake. Good advance preparation!

We have a birthday gathering that evening with Gordon's brother, Andrew, and Gordon's nephew, Patrick. Maggie Darling has a big event next door with her family where the children are being entertained by Mr Marvel. John and Fraser pop out to see his much-loved show and think it is entirely normal for Mr Marvel to come and entertain everyone on their dad's birthday. Why wouldn't he want the same as them?

Gordon is a notoriously difficult person to buy presents for as he pretty much has everything he wants already. I have struck gold this year as I have got him one of the new Kindles for downloading books from Amazon, which I hope will be a great thing for him while travelling. He seems to like it a lot and has it out straight away to try and download a book to get going. Gordon is a voracious reader and some of our holidays have been famously reported as being accompanied by a whole suitcase of books. Most of these kinds of stories are not true, but the travelling with lots of books tale is entirely accurate. The Kindle is, I hope, one way forward to lose a suitcase.

Sunday 21st February

My guest-edited edition of *Fabulous* comes out with this Sunday's edition of the *News of the World* with the stunning picture of Elle MacPherson on the front cover, and her inspirational interview about keeping healthy, body checks, happy family life and, of course, drinking lots and lots of water.

Less wonderfully, Andrew Rawnsley has published the serialisation of his book about Gordon, and it has kicked off an almighty row. I don't know Andrew other than to meet fleetingly, so I only know him by what he writes. He is a really good writer, and was always a good TV presenter too, but there is something about the world of Westminster that enables personal accusations to spiral out of control, with no reference to the truth. Andrew's book has an unnamed source that says Gordon has been accused of bullying staff at work, and pushing them out of the way with physical violence. It is really hurtful and not accurate at all. The most alarming thing is thinking about who would want to speak to Andrew to make these accusations, as he has clearly published them in good faith, believing them to be true.

The story then spirals away beyond all reason after a woman from an anti-bullying charity in Swindon declares that she has been contacted by Downing Street. Her story starts to unravel quite quickly but, of course, with the story already reported, the damage is done. I feel really furious about it even though I know it will run out of steam in the end, as there is no truth in any of the claims. What really upsets me is knowing that this is a very deliberate attempt to smear Gordon's character and to, in some way, damage his reputation as we approach an election. It is so personal, so destructive and comes from a place of low morality.

Monday 22nd February

I take Fraser to nursery only to find I have forgotten it is an Inset Day, so we turn around and head back to the flat. Once he is settled, happily playing with Mela watching over him, I take off again for one final visit to London Fashion Week.

As I leave, I run into Piers heading out from his interview with Alistair Darling for *GQ*. He is at the wheel of his car, leaning out to tell me he has spotted my interview with Elle MacPherson when, inexplicably, he reverses his car and bumps straight into the car behind him with an awful crunch. The car is actually my little Ford Fusion runaround; a policeman with a large gun watches Piers as we both inspect the damage. It turns out to be miniscule despite the dramatic sound effects, and Piers makes all the right noises in offering to pay for any damage. I am pretty sure that this is some more newspaper column inches for Mr Morgan.

I go to Somerset House for the *Elle* UK Style awards, the end point of a successful London Fashion Week. I wear a long, dark blue Osman Yousefzada dress with dramatic gold ringed neckline. Not being one to miss an opportunity to add to my collection of my photographs with models, I meet Agyness Deyn who is just exquisite looking. Her great pal, Henry Holland, is co-presenting the awards with *Elle* editor, Lorraine Candy (looking wonderful in her peacock dress; a personal tribute to Alexander McQueen).

At the award ceremony, I speak about the White Ribbon Alliance, which has been well and truly adopted by the fashion industry. I make a presentation to Naomi Campbell to thank her for her contribution via Fashion for Relief. I do this acknowledging that with all the controversy she has attracted in the past, she might not previously have been honoured this way, but without question her work to date has raised huge and vital funds for the maternal mortality campaign.

At the end of the evening, I am asked to do a short piece to camera about the awards for *GMTV*, with their fashion reporter.

As the cameras start rolling, I can see the producer moving to block my team and I know something is up. After quick questions about the White Ribbon Alliance and British fashion, I find I am unable to move away from the camera line so the reporter swiftly moves on to the news stories about Gordon, and the daft bullying allegations that have got the media so excited.

I don't usually involve myself with comment on political stories, but as I am asked I reply: 'Gordon is the man I know and the man I love. He is a strong, hardworking, decent man. That's all there is. What you see is what you get with him.' Afterwards the producer is keen to stress that this bit won't be separated from the rest of the clip to make it look like I have been hijacked at a press award. I don't believe any of it, and it is of course to be part of the political story. I have said what I know to be true and can live with that.

Tuesday 23rd February

After the bullying allegations, it takes a few days for the press to settle down again, and resume reporting real news.

I have the ongoing run of charity events at Downing Street to attend to, and a few visits out and about. One of the most significant charity receptions held is for Breakthrough Breast Cancer's Generations Study. This is the health study being undertaken by over 100,000 women over the next 50 years. I have joined the study myself and completed my lengthy questionnaire.

I enjoy the evening's gathering with the Breakthrough Breast Cancer Chief Executive, Jeremy Hughes, and his team: a handful of his 100,000 volunteers, doctors and other medical experts and the funders. Mervyn Davies, who was head of a large bank, but who is now a government minister, had chaired the fundraising appeal raising the £12 million costs. I spot lots of familiar faces who must all have been persuaded by Mervyn to contribute: Finsbury PR chief Roland Rudd; M&S chief Sir Stuart Rose; and the Executive Director of General Merchandise for M&S, Kate Bostock. Stuart is very friendly and immediately introduces me to various guests until it is time for me to make a short speech to thank everyone for their part in making this important study possible.

Wednesday 24th February

I am investing a lot of time into the maternal mortality campaign at the moment, as there are real concerns that the momentum is fading for investment in global health in light of the world recession. I host another gathering in the State Dining Room at Number 10 with the support of Dr Margaret Chan of the World Health Organization; Ann Starrs, Ray Chambers, Mark Dybul, Bience Gawanas, Brigid McConville and Jo Cox; and two First Ladies with strong reputations for getting things done, Janet Kagame, the First Lady of Rwanda, and Azeb Mesfin, the First Lady of Ethiopia.

The two First Ladies both address the group, and we cover a lot of ground from cultural change, local community mobilisation, banning FGM (female genital mutilation), and preventing mother to child transmission of HIV/AIDS.

Dr Chan really helps me at these meetings: she sets the right tone and raises everyone's expectations to her own high standards; all with a lovely, personal manner that engages, listens and encourages everyone's contribution.

In the evening, I am amazed to see in the diary that LGBT History Month has rolled round again. I arrive at a reception in Number 10 with Gordon to find the room teeming with people, all chatting away. Everyone feels far more at home in Number 10 than I remember from last year, when it was all a bit of a novelty. What gives me a moment of great pride in our country is to see LGBT members of our armed forces here in uniform.

When Gordon speaks, he singles out one guest in particular, 21-year-old James Parkes, who I remember standing vigil for in Trafalgar Square as we gathered to remember Ian Baynham. James, a young policeman, was so badly beaten in a homophobic attack in Liverpool that no one knew if he would survive. Tonight he is here with his partner – whom he has just married, a month after he came out of his coma – and he gets a big cheer when Gordon mentions his name.

Saturday 27th February

We are having a very mixed time at the moment and I am never quite sure whether to feel optimistic or pessimistic about our chances of being returned to government the other side of the election. While I am very clear that, as with the last three years here at Number 10, I will just be putting my all into the campaign, that is a different feeling to how I think it might turn out.

After joining Maggie Darling for a doorstep photo with the Fairtrade people, who are dressed as tea ladies, to celebrate fair-trade tea, coffee and lots and lots of chocolate (from KitKats from the Ivory Coast, to chocolate buttons from Ghana), I find Gordon in his office. He seems a bit down and I realise that he is feeling disappointed about what has until now been a good relationship with the top civil servant, the Cabinet Secretary, Sir Gus O'Donnell. It was Gus who welcomed us in, and whose contribution as a civil servant to Andrew Rawnsley's book attacking Gordon seems surprising, to say the least.

The boys and I fly up to Scotland, and I go to join Gordon at the annual Scottish Labour gala dinner in Glasgow, where he gets a great laugh when he says of the current media climate: 'I think the only thing I have not been accused of this week is killing Archie Mitchell [the latest death in *EastEnders*].'

The polling gap has narrowed this weekend to five points, the smallest difference for a while.

Sunday 28th February

To Swansea for the Welsh Labour Party Conference, where we feel wonderful warmth from everyone. It was not so long ago that we were getting terrible European and local election results in Wales, but there is a palpable optimism here now. The new leader, Carwyn Jones, is settling in, while the departed First Minister, Rhodri Morgan, is so highly regarded that he is pretty much a national treasure.

I use the time in Swansea after Gordon's speech to nip out, taking the boys with me, to go and meet the team at the new site for the Maggie's South West Wales Centre, the new cancer care centre designed by the extraordinary Japanese architect, Kurokawa, which will open in the near future. The Swansea centre falls under my watch as the Patron of the Joy of Living Campaign and will give Maggie's their first centre in Wales.

As we are all due on a train to get us back to London in good time, we do miss out on a visit to the famous Joe's Ice Cream parlour. I make up for it with taking two Happy Meals on board – a real treat! Gordon does an interview with *Red* magazine on the train back. I know he thinks that women's magazines are an important way to communicate with women all over Britain.

Tuesday 2nd March

Having both made our respective appearances online on Mumsnet, Gordon and I have been invited to their tenth anniversary party to be held at the state-of-the-art (i.e. rich and nerdy at the same time) Google headquarters, which are just near Victoria Station, so not very far from Downing Street. The party is full of sophisticated, metropolitan journalists clutching their wine glasses, and ten mumsnetters who won tickets to go, who are entirely buoyant and thrilled to be there.

Founders Carrie and Justine both speak about their decade of mumsnetting as it has grown and grown, and been discovered by all the politicians, M&S and Boden. Then Gordon and I are invited to speak. Just for fun, we swap roles and Gordon goes first so that he can introduce me. He first of all calls Mumsnet a British institution, and then makes the sobering point that it has more members than all the political parties put together, and more online readers than most newspapers. Then he very sweetly calls himself Mr Sarah Brown and introduces me. He is a hard act to follow – I think I prefer to do the introductions.

Once back at the flat, I leave Gordon to check on some urgent overnight papers sent up by James Bowler, while I head off with Konrad to attend an event for our new candidate for the seat of Bethnal Green and Bow. This was the seat that the great Oona King lost to George Galloway and his newly formed Respect Party in the East End of London. Both me and my mum had campaigned for Oona, calling on the support of the wonderful Bangladeshi community there (my mum even speaks a bit of the Bangla language from the time when she and Patrick lived there for six years in the 1990s).

The woman we hope will win the seat back for Labour this time is Rushanara Ali, a young Bangladeshi Muslim woman who will blaze a trail if elected. I arrive to join MPs Ed Miliband and Frank Dobson at the Red Fort Indian restaurant in Soho, run by long-time Labour Party supporter, Amin Ali. I remember attending events here for the charity One World Action many years ago, and am really touched that Amin Ali remembers me, too.

Ed, Frank and I all make our speeches. Ed comes out with a great expression when he says that Gordon and I have 'great resilience' in fighting to win. You do need resilience in a political life.

Wednesday 3rd March

Buckingham Palace has been hosting the State Visit of President Zuma of South Africa. There has been lots of activity in Horse Guards Parade, and the flags do look truly splendid.

In the evening we have the traditional State Banquet to attend. I have a rather gorgeous long, green Issa dress that I am going to wear, with a sea-green stone earring and necklace set that Gordon bought me as a gift a couple of Christmases ago.

I have been given an immaculate briefing on my dinner guest, who I am told is the South African Sports Minister, and by the time I set out there is little I don't know about the forthcoming World Cup. I am seated at the banquet and start to chat to my guest, and realise pretty swiftly that he is neither South African nor a sports minister. All the same, I have a great chat to the very delightful High Commissioner for Malawi.

Thursday 4th March

I travel to Canary Wharf and attend an editor's conference at the *Mirror* newspaper. It is a bit like entering the lion's den to join a tabloid newspaper team as they discuss their stories of the day, but it is a fascinating experience to hear the journalists raise what they think are the most important issues, and get the editor's immediate response.

I am there to plan a special edition of the newspaper for International Women's Day when I will guest-edit a supplement to be published soon. I am writing an article about 15 inspirational women that I think will interest *Mirror* readers, and am getting lots of quotes together to feature in the issue.

On the way back I hear on the radio that my friend, Penny Smith, is to leave *GMTV* after 17 years as a successful presenter. All I know is that when I grow up I want to look like Penny Smith.

My final stop in the evening is for the White Ribbon Alliance, which has a dinner party being hosted by Yasmin Mills in the achingly trendy Sanderson Hotel. I am popping in for a few moments before everyone sits down to dinner so that I can still make it back for the boys' bedtimes.

It turns into one of those evenings when I wonder if everyone thinks that my life is all effortlessly glamorous at all times ... The first mistake is to pick the back entrance to avoid cameras or any fuss. It's very tricky to find, with a long damp car park area that is freezing cold, and a back door that is firmly locked. When

Christianne and I are finally rescued (she is a few months pregnant so I am worried about the wait in the cold), we make it to our more sophisticated destination. Then I find all the guests have followed a colour theme and are wearing white, except me – I am in grey.

I do get home in time for John, who is still reading in bed, so we chat in the dark about his important things. We have a detailed conversation about Gormitis, and I try and keep up with all the individual characters and their personal stories, but in the end it is, as ever, all about goodies versus baddies.

Friday 5th March

It is an important day today as Gordon goes to make his presentation to the Chilcot Inquiry on Iraq. He has, as always, prepared for this and seems very comfortable going off to it. This has been such an important issue over the past years that I do watch some of the television reports, and I think it is right that he allows himself to express regret over the war.

The generals are, of course, attacking him but he has done well today.

Once I get John and Fraser home from school we come back to see Gordon before he leaves for a trip to Afghanistan. He is going there in order to make announcements about new equipment directly to the soldiers.

Monday 8th March

It is International Women's Day, so my supplement in the *Mirror* is out today, and I get lots of great texts and emails from people who have spotted it.

I join the Women for Women International march over the Millennium Bridge and I walk along with Annie Lennox – wearing her HIV Positive T-shirt – and actress Cherie Lunghi, who looks just as she did when she played Vera Brittain in *Testament of Youth*. We march with nurses, midwives, mums, their children, and a host of others. It feels powerful to know women all over the world are marching over bridges today, including the bridge that connects Rwanda with the Democratic Republic of Congo, the country where it is currently officially the most dangerous place to be a woman.

From the White House, Michelle Obama sends me her responses to some questions I had sent her to help promote International Women's Day, and we post them on my page on the Downing Street website.

Wednesday 10th March

After joining Gordon's event with Oxfam in the Pillared Room to show photographer Rankin's exhibition of his journey to the Democratic Republic of Congo, I go to meet Sue Nye. I have a quick 20 minutes with her as she gives me the first heads up on the election plans so that I can start to think about how I organise myself – and my family – through what will be a really busy time. Her outline for the campaign is fairly broad, with various options that allow everyone to respond to unfolding events so nothing is fixed in stone. It does, however, enable me to make my own plans and build in contingencies around childcare and my own involvement in the campaign. All I plan to do is to accompany Gordon as much as possible, and to use the time in between to see the boys, or to join in some of the campaigning whether door knocking or making calls to voters.

Thursday 11th March

Having missed the original opening of the National Memorial Arboretum in Staffordshire when Gordon went three years ago, I can now be there with him for the rededication of the Basra memorial wall, which has now been erected there. The ceremony is to be conducted with the families who lost loved ones in service during the war in Iraq.

After the moving outdoor service, wreaths are laid by HRH the Duke of Gloucester; Gordon; the Chief of the Defence Staff, Sir Jock Stirrup; and then finally by the father of Lieutenant Tom Tanswell, on behalf of all the families.

At the end, all the family members come forward to lay their own flowers, pictures and cards. The grief on their faces is very hard to watch and everyone feels tearful as they remember these brave men and women. Gordon rises to shake hands with Mr Tanswell, and is greeted with a warm hug and some kind, supportive words. What a modest and generous man, and what humanity to be able to think of others at a time of personal loss. He and his wife walk with us to the marquee where we join everyone for a time, in order to speak to as many people as possible. I am very struck by this couple, whose love for their son speaks volumes, but whose compassion and sense of personal peace is quite breathtaking.

On the train back, Gordon is ensconced with Ginny Dougary, a journalist doing a big interview with him. I tune in at one point to hear her asking questions about 'finding his hinterland' and sounding quite excited when he mentions an interest in poetry. As we draw into Euston Station, they are both still quoting favourite bits of poems at each other. Goodness knows how the interview will end up when printed.

Friday 12th March

President Sarkozy comes to London to see Gordon, and we all bear witness to the huge hugs on the doorstep. Inside I talk to him in the stairwell, exchanging family news and best wishes from Carla. He is a man for whom loyalty in international politics is extremely important, and the two men have forged a strong friendship. As we are chatting, we turn the corner and I realise there is a huge bank of cameras ahead so I duck out of the way leaving the two of them to it all. President Sarkozy will host the G20 meetings at the start of 2011 so he will have the aftermath of the global financial crisis to deal with, however things have worked out. Actually Lauren Laverne gets to slip in to observe part of the meeting as she is covering a day in the life of Gordon for *Grazia* magazine.

Saturday 13th March

As a family we all travel out to Chequers for the retirement of Alan Lavender, the wonderful Chequers chef who has worked there for nearly 30 years. We have not been to Chequers for several months, partly as it has been a busy time, but also because of the surprise revelation that the luxury of Chequers was actually costing the taxpayer quite a sum of money every year.

It is a great treat to be going there to join Alan Lavender at his farewell tea with his family, and to take the opportunity to express our thanks to all the staff at Chequers. It is wonderful to see Pat, David, Harvey, Paul, Gemma and the rest of the team, and to see chef Jim Bob and his wife, Claire, with their new baby son.

The gardener had expressed a wish to regenerate the old orchard, so lots of good new things have been happening there, including the introduction of a new vegetable garden and, at my suggestion, beehives.

It is traditional for prime ministers to plant a tree at Chequers, and there are small signs for each PM's tree; they make a great walk around the estate. Gordon plants a wonderful new apple tree, which is a descendent of the famous apple tree Sir Isaac Newton sat under when he discovered gravity.

Sunday 14th March

Gordon and I travel up to Golders Green crematorium to attend former Labour leader Michael Foot's funeral. His family are joined by many friends from across the Labour movement, as well as his network of fellow supporters of his much-loved Plymouth Argyll football club.

Gordon joins in paying tribute during the service, and we take a moment to greet everyone outside in the spring sunshine, before heading back to Westminster.

Wednesday 24th March

It is Budget Day, and everyone in Number 10 keeps out of the way when it comes time for the Chancellor to leave for the Commons from Number 11, with his famous red despatch box. I watch out of the window as Alistair Darling and his team come out for the cameras. The Treasury ministers move off, leaving him on his own, and then the great surprise comes when Maggie comes out to join him. She looks fantastic and their body language together is so affectionate, it is really touching. When Alistair puts his arm round Maggie you can see her just melt a little bit with her head against him, and the whole crowd are with them both at that moment. She has been the greatest support to him, and a true friend to everyone in Downing Street, and it is wonderful to see her have her moment.

Today is also significant as Ada Lovelace Day, which celebrates the achievements of women in the areas of science and technology. Coincidentally, there is a huge Margaret Carpenter portrait of Ada Lovelace, who was actually the poet Byron's sister, which hangs in the Pillared Room of Number 10. She was the top mathematician of her day, which seems appropriate on a Budget Day, and probably the first computer programmer. I make sure that I have added my tweet to note this, and find a copy of the picture that I can post up on my Twitter feed.

Friday 26th March

I am doing calls with Konrad at the Labour Party HQ for Glenda Jackson to ask voters if they will be supporting her once the general election is called. Last time in 2005 I remember canvassing for Glenda and hearing a lot of disgruntlement about the Iraq War, which was such a sensitive issue at the last election. This time I hear from a number of people who are undecided, but no one is telling me that they are strongly supporting other parties now if they voted Labour last time. This does not match what the more liberal newspapers are reporting, but time will tell which version is true.

Sunday 28th March

Everyone expects the election announcement next week, and I have been sorting out clothes and make-up, computers and cameras, ready to be out on the road myself. I don't really have anything else to do other than spend time with the boys so we head out to the Coram Fields play park in the afternoon, meeting up with my step-father Patrick. He watches the boys while I do a quick shop at a nearby Waitrose to pick up some food for supper.

We all have a roast chicken supper together, and I wonder if this will be the last proper family meal for a few weeks. I am very keen on sitting down to eat as a family – it is a good way to be together and to just have conversations. All our lives are so rushed, and a shared meal makes all the difference.

Monday 29th March

Back in my office, I am drafting a speech for a mentoring event with *Marie Claire* magazine that I have coming up later in the week. I pop down to see Gordon who has endless interviews and meetings on, and he seems to have the beginning of a sore throat and a bit of a cough. I hope it does not turn out to be anything serious given the schedule we have coming up.

Overfull diary or not, I still take Gordon off to join the protection team and their spouses for a drink, as we rarely get to see them off duty.

Tuesday 30th March

I talk to David Muir who is the person who knows most about where Labour stands with the electorate. We have not improved our position through the Budget time, but we don't seem any worse off, either. I get a fair idea from David of how the campaign schedule will unfold, what part I can play, and I am certainly ready to sign up for it. Gil is in later to go through the daily details, and Konrad goes off to join the election meetings from today. It is all becoming quite real now.

Thursday 1st April

Gordon calls me to ask if I have seen the awful letter in the *Telegraph* newspaper signed by business leaders saying they would back the Shadow Chancellor's reversal of the 0.5 per cent National Insurance increase, calling it a tax on business and employers. I somehow don't believe for a second that this reversal would take place whoever wins the election, but the point is those business leaders who have signed the letter. The vast majority of names are high-profile business figures who are publicly known to be Tory supporters or donors, and so their support for the Shadow Chancellor would be expected.

What is more surprising – and will definitely have the greater impact – is the inclusion of the two big corporate figures that have sat on the Prime Minister's Business Council and attended regular meetings with Gordon. Both Sir Stuart Rose, as chairman of Marks and Spencer, and Paul Walsh, the chief executive of drinks company Diageo plc, have chosen to add their names.

I clearly remember Sir Stuart telling me when I first met him that he always thought it was inappropriate for public-listed company chairmen or chief executives to act in a political way. I think that is what hurts me the most: I placed great trust in his earlier comments about being apolitical in the corporate world, so that I was prepared to be photographed and seen in quite a high-profile way alongside him, for the British Fashion Council and beyond. I suspect the defence will be that this was an important issue for the business he represents, but it is just too obviously political and I feel wounded by his actions. The same is true of Paul Walsh, too, although I have not worked with him so much, so truthfully this hurts a bit less for me. But I imagine it might be worse for Gordon.

Gordon, meanwhile, has his eyes on rather more global matters and is talking to presidents Obama and Sarkozy and Chancellor Merkel about the ambitious prospect of advancing an agreement on a levy on banks to raise funds globally.

Friday 2nd April

Gordon emerges from a long day of meetings with Peter Mandelson, Kirsty, Justin and David. Everyone is quite aware that there is a big fight on our hands to have any chance in this election, but seem up for the challenge. One or two people outside the immediate office appear to be undermining Gordon's confidence, telling him the general election is all a disaster waiting to happen, but then those in the office fight back and off we all go again.

Monday 5th April

Over the weekend, it became clear that we don't have the strongest position in the polls, and may even have gone backwards a bit, which is not helped by the fact that the Labour Party's funding is also very tight for the election battle. This is despite a 0.4 per cent growth rate, higher than expected, and reports of good figures on declining unemployment.

It is a strange thing to have come through a global recession leading from the front, and be at a point where there is real growth in the economy, but to be so vulnerable.

I spend the weekend with my sister-in-law, Clare, who comes over with her son, Patrick, to keep John and Fraser thoroughly entertained. Clare has been such a stalwart friend and supporter, and is certainly my phone-bank chum, putting in many hours calling voters. We make calls from the Labour Party's HQ in nearby Victoria Street and the phone banks are now filling up with staff and volunteers. As the election team move in and set up their desks, we phone-bankers get ready to move to another site in North London so that the calls can continue.

I can't remember exactly when I knew that the election date was to be announced on 6th April – probably about a month ago – but in politics things change so often, I know to treat not much as a certainty. Over the weekend, though, we are all crystal clear that it is all systems go tomorrow, and it finally feels much more of a reality. So, 6th May it is.

Tuesday 6th April

Gordon heads off for an early-morning run, and then heads down to his 9 a.m. Cabinet meeting.

As soon as the Cabinet meeting is over, Gordon goes by car to Buckingham Palace to ask permission to dissolve Parliament and hold an election. The Queen has travelled in by helicopter from Windsor Castle for the meeting.

Gordon's audience with the Queen lasts about 20 minutes. On the TV, I see him leave the palace accompanied by Jeremy Heywood. They both get back into the Jaguar and the aerial footage shows their journey back to the rear entrance of Downing Street.

I am dressed and ready to go. I have put on a fairly understated navy LK Bennett skirt and a belted lilac cardigan. I don't think I am going to make the fashion headlines today, but my campaign will be more about the conversations I have than the clothes I wear.

I go downstairs to find Gordon. He is taking a couple of quiet minutes to collect his thoughts in Number 11, which is peaceful compared to the swarm of people in his open-plan office. When Sue takes him to the Number 10 door, I rush upstairs to watch him on TV. He steps out to face the media with the full Cabinet lined up with him. He speaks brilliantly, beautifully, fluently, authentically. One of his best moments ever as PM.

When Gordon comes back in, I whizz back downstairs to find him. He takes the lift to come and find me, and we have a bit of a goose-chase around the building to meet up. As I dash about, I run into lots of the Cabinet Ministers, who are all geared up and ready to go.

I finally catch up with Gordon on the way to the Pillared Room where all the staff is waiting. We catch a minute together to one side – not really to say anything, just to be together at an important moment while he thinks through his next words to the staff – and then we go and join everyone. Gordon speaks to thank everyone for their work and for their friendship to him, me, John and Fraser, and for their public service during important times. He tells everyone the story of Fraser coming back from school with Gordon in the car, and him telling his dad that when he grew up he wanted to be, 'a builder, a teacher and a dad'. Then he looked at Gordon and said, 'But you are just a dad.'

When he finishes speaking he gets a wonderful, heartfelt round of applause from everyone.

Sir Gus O'Donnell speaks. He manages to thank Gordon for his service to international development issues, and then cracks an awkward joke about not being able to say he would look forward to welcoming Gordon back (this, from an 'impartial' civil servant). To rescue the situation, Gordon jokily says, 'Gus, just stop talking.' He does and everyone claps again.

I race up to the flat to grab my bag and laptop. I join Gordon in the car at the back door and we are off.

The election time is ahead, the British people will decide, and then we will see what happens.

CHAPTER 31

Final Votes and Farewell

Tuesday 6th April (cont.)

With the starter gun pulled on the general election, Gordon and I are out on the road within the hour, heading first to the newly refurbished St Pancras station and on to a train to Kent.

Our first stop is an ASDA supermarket, meeting shoppers and staff to talk about their concerns and needs. Everyone seems excited to see Gordon, except for one woman who goes diving into one of the trolley lockers by the supermarket café. One of the team goes to find out what's wrong and discovers she's just avoiding the TV cameras: 'I pulled a sickie at work and told my boss I was ill. The last thing I thought I'd see is the Prime Minister walking in here!'

We join a Labour supporter's home meeting and talk to local residents about their community and quality of life under a Labour government.

Then it's off to a manufacturing plant to talk about jobs, apprenticeships and what makes Britain work. It is a good start with friendly well-wishers everywhere. My phone is buzzing with texts from friends and colleagues. One that stands out, but which is not atypical, reads: 'I know it will be crazy so I wanted u to pass this message to GB. Please tell him personally – it means a lot to me that he knows: I know he can do it; my blood runs cold at what could have happened if anyone else had been at the helm in the last 2 years; but unfortunately the crisis is not over so we – globally – need him at the helm just as we did for last 2 years. I'm there and helping just like thousands are because we believe in him.'

I know that the ensuing days will unfold with visits to all parts of the country, mostly using our new 'go anywhere' rail passes. Most evenings, we will go back to the flat or home to Scotland. I will campaign as much as I can without making life too disruptive for John and Fraser, who are to carry on with daily school, homework and fun.

To plan for the election I have sorted out everything from clothes (a few new things, but lots of my existing wardrobe, and the greatest essential: comfortable shoes) to childcare (Mela will bear the brunt of it through the coming weeks, with a bit of back-up from Tess and my mum), so I feel happy with things on that front.

Gordon is asked in a press conference about my role in the campaign and responds, 'She is the love of my life and we work well together. We like going around the country together and I am looking forward to the campaign.'

I could just substitute 'she' for 'he' and have said the same thing myself.

Konrad officially resigns as a political adviser from Downing Street and joins me on the campaign, while Christianne, as a civil servant, remains behind. Gil is also here with me every step of the way. We spend any spare time in London up at a call centre run by the calm and organised Paul Harrington, making calls to voters for marginal candidates like Sadiq Khan in Tooting and Karen Buck in Westminster North. I am regularly joined by various family and friends all pitching in, including Sally Bercow, the Speaker's wife, who is a Labour supporter (I am pleased that she holds her own political ambitions and is standing as a local Councillor). I am delighted to see Jo Cox too. She has taken leave of absence as the Director of the maternal mortality campaign to come and hit the phones.

*

I keep up my Twitter account (although I do take down the link from the Downing Street website), and I will keep notes in the campaign trail to write a weekly column for the *Sunday Mirror*. Throughout the campaign I will use social media as much as I can, reaching my million-plus Twitter followers, and contributing video clips and 'audioboos' to YouTube and Facebook. Instead of tackling this alone, I get help from an expert, taking up @dominiccampbell of FutureGov's offer to volunteer his time.

One of the great themes of Labour's campaign across Twitter was the use of the hashtag #changewesee, with supporters every-where recording examples of visible, positive change created in the last 13 years by the Labour government. Avid political tweeters like @wesstreeting, @BevaniteEllie and @tscholesfogg posted their versions.

From my campaign, my #changewesee moments include:

- the brand new hospital in Birmingham Edgbaston, from where Labour's electoral manifesto was launched
- the Leeds heath centre, and meeting Dr Marshall, a serious, no-nonsense GP. He had worked night and day to turn a seventies, asbestos-ridden building into a modern, airy, happy building with staff delivering over 40,000 appointments per year, covering preventative health as well as treatments
- the children's centre in Selly Oak and the Sure Start in Atherton, with their brilliant early years programmes and services for parents, too
- the Mini factory tour in Cowley, Oxford with Gordon, Ed Miliband and Peter Mandelson, seeing new cars pouring off the factory line, all gorgeous, especially the 'chilli red' ones
- great businesses like Innocent Smoothies at 'Fruit Towers' in West London, and Eddie Stobart's Trucking Group in Cumbria where the staff are all made to feel like family

- the ASDA in Bournemouth, and hearing a parent asking about educational support for children with autism, and being able to speak for the joined-up thinking across government and a new strategy for adults with autism. That made me feel very proud.

Tuesday 13th April

We return to London to visit the Polish Embassy to sign the book of condolence for President and Maria Kaczyński of Poland, who have been killed in a tragic plane accident. We had seen them so recently when we visited Warsaw.

Thursday 15th April

There is much excitement over the televised debates. They are to be held over the next three weeks in Manchester, Bristol and Birmingham.

Having watched the first, it is clear that Gordon is leagues ahead of everyone on matters of substance. As the economy debate takes place, the latest quarterly figures are published, and show that at 0.2 per cent growth, the fragile recovery that Labour claims is taking place is actually taking place.

During the campaign so far, several well-known figures have demonstrated their support: Alan Sugar, as ever, stands up for what he believes and makes a big donation; business man Nigel Doughty has become a Vice-Treasurer of the Labour Party; David Tennant voices a party broadcast; Jo Rowling publishes an article about one-parent families in *The Times*; and Eddie Izzard, Ross Kemp and Duncan Bannatyne have all joined Gordon at events to show that they believe in what the Labour government has achieved for people everywhere.

Wednesday 21st April

We attended a member's house event in Cardiff today, with local MSP Julie Morgan, Peter Hain and Carwyn Jones. It was held in a gorgeous, big house where we gathered outdoors in the summer sunshine, only to hear the neighbour (with a large Opposition poster held up) shout, 'But these are the most expensive houses in Cardiff; why is Gordon Brown here?'

Thankfully, moments like these are more than made up for by our candidates: decent, hardworking people for whom jobs and justice, decent standards of living and good opportunities for young people, all matter.

I will remember the warmth of people everywhere, from the walk down Sauchiehall Street in Glasgow where we are surrounded by a great crowd in front of Donald Dewar's statue, to being harbour-side in Weymouth greeting holidaymakers from all over the country, while Gordon sat at an outdoor café table, doing a television interview with Nick Robinson of the BBC.

While the campaign continues, ministers return every day to their government duties, and Gordon attends to papers and meetings as usual. One dominant issue is the ash cloud rising from the volcanic rupture over the Arctic, and Transport Secretary of State Andrew Adonis is dealing with it daily.

Gordon is working on a plan with his friend, Prime Minister José Luis Zapatero, for our stranded Britons in Spain to ensure their return home. There is a wonderful newspaper image of a flotilla of boats of all shapes and sizes ready to go to their rescue, headlined 'Gordon's Ark'.

Wednesday 28th April

I am not present for one moment in the campaign, which attracts a lot of attention, on the day that Gordon is recorded on a microphone in Rochdale responding to a conversation about immigration with a senior resident, Mrs Gillian Duffy. Gordon calls me while I am on a train to join him in Manchester and is mortified that he has upset her. Mrs Duffy had approached him to talk about immigration issues, and also to raise her views on higher education. Gordon seems to have thought the two issues were combined and expressed his annoyance as he got back into the car, with the news microphone still attached and recording. Having visited Mrs Duffy privately in her home, he has understood better what she was trying to say, and is very upset by any offence he may have caused her – not least having unleashed the nation's media on her, following up the story.

I was there, however, in Swindon a week earlier when Justin brought in John Doyle, a local publican in financial difficulty. He was angry and prepared to attack Gordon in front of the media. He spoke privately to Gordon and Ed Miliband for ten minutes, asking more about the government's initiative for businesses amid the recession. Mr Doyle was satisfied he had had a useful conversation with both of them. Outside again he told the media that he was considering switching his anti-vote to a Labour vote. This did not, of course, make the national media in quite the same way.

Saturday 1st May

I attend the Duckie nightclub at the Royal Vauxhall Tavern as a guest of comedienne Amy Lamé to celebrate Labour's many achievements for the LGBT community. After I speak, I get to pull out the winner of the raffle. The winning ticket is number 10 and pink. Big cheers all round.

Monday 3rd May

Gordon gives a rousing speech to a 1,000-strong audience gathered for the Citizens UK event in London, which goes up on YouTube and attracts 15,000 hits in the first 24 hours. I get more comments from friends and fellow tweeters on this, than on any other part of the campaign – even the televised debates.

Tuesday 4th May

We receive the very sad news that our great friend and Leader of the House of Lords, Jan Royall, has lost her husband. Stuart had battled bravely with cancer for a number of years and has finally succumbed just two days from Polling Day. Our hearts go out to Jan and her family, and the campaign team are really saddened by her loss.

We return to Manchester for a big rally. I watch Gordon's speech seated by our candidate, Gloria de Piero, a former *GMTV* reporter, who is battling to win Ashfield.

From Manchester, we drive to visit the famous Sheffield Forgemasters, who had negotiated a government loan that enabled this proud manufacturing and export business to return to its former glory.

Wearing our hard hats, Gordon speaks at length to the management and workers, while I look in awe at the giant, white-hot steel tube coming out of the fiery furnace.

Wednesday 5th May

On the final day before Polling Day, we start at dawn with a visit in Leeds to the Yorkshire Produce Market, and then move to the University of Bradford to witness pioneering new nanotechnologies. We continue across the North West via Skelmersdale, Blackpool and Carlisle, right up to Dumfries in Scotland.

Throughout the day, the breaking news comes that the economy in Greece is in real trouble, with riots in the streets and reports of three people dead. This is troubling news and it is difficult to interpret what impact this news will have here in Britain.

Thursday 6th May

On Polling Day, we visit our own polling station to cast our vote in North Queensferry, and then return home. Later Gordon and I go out to visit some of the polling stations in his constituency and thank the loyal Labour supporters attending each one. I leave Gordon with his political team for a while, and go out door knocking with Thomas Docherty, the neighbouring candidate for Dunfermline, a seat we dearly want to win back after a by-election loss some years earlier.

At 10 p.m., the polling stations close and it is time to count the votes. David Muir says that he believes that the BBC's exit poll prediction of Conservatives 305 seats, Labour 251 seats and Liberal Democrats 61 seats will be pretty accurate. (Labour actually goes on to win 258 seats.)

If that is the result then we will no longer have the greatest number of seats but no single party has a majority to automatically form the new government.

Friday 7th May

We leave at around midnight for the election count for Gordon's parliamentary seat of Kirkcaldy and Cowdenbeath. When his result comes through an hour or so later, we discover Gordon has increased his own majority to 23,009, the second biggest in the country (Stephen Timms, Labour MP for East Ham, gets the biggest). This is a great tribute to everyone who worked on the campaign there, led by Alex Rowley. I am hugely proud of Gordon, too, and can see that he is really touched by the overwhelming faith that the Fife people have placed in him.

After his acceptance speech, and those of the other candidates, Gordon and I go to the nearby Beveridge Park Hotel. The local Fife Labour members are all glued to the television screen for the Dunfermline and Central Fife result. There is a great cheer as we hear that Thomas Docherty has won a comfortable victory.

Soon after, we see Lindsay Roy returned as the MP for Glenrothes, a good hold after the last by-election victory. The Glasgow seat we lost to the Nationalists (the night we watched

Hamlet) also comes back to Labour. All over Scotland, the results are looking very good, as they are in Labour's heartlands across the North of England and the Midlands.

The BBC's – and David's – predictions look like they are coming true as we lose key seats in the South, even while our London results look very good. Overall, there is a 5 per cent swing to the Conservatives.

It is time for us to return to Downing Street via the Labour Party Headquarters to thank our brilliant General Secretary Ray Collins and all the staff, and to see what the coming days bring.

Saturday 8th May

We have entered a time of great uncertainty for the country, and there are intense discussions being held by the third party, the Liberal Democrats, with both the Conservatives and Labour. I am not part of those discussions, or the sideline discussions about the discussions. It will be a fascinating story to tell, of each twist and turn in the few days when power was held in the balance, but it is not my story to tell. Gordon's primary focus is on doing the right thing for the country, the government and the Labour Party – probably in that order.

I stay in the flat and take the decision that we will maintain our normal days, and I keep up my daily routines and clear some of the paperwork on my desk, including parcelling up two little Number 10 teddy bears to send to my friend, Amanda, for her newly adopted sons.

I also decide that we will not pack up one thing. While the discussions take place downstairs and elsewhere, I do not want to allow anyone to send out information that we are getting ready to leave. I am adamant that we do not inadvertently contribute to any rumour or leaked press story. These are sensitive times and the final decision will come once all the right avenues have been followed through.

Of course, since the election result, Gordon and I have talked, and we both understand that the most likely scenario will be our departure, the only question being when. I feel very calm about everything, and just very relieved that the result has been nowhere near the terrible loss that was predicted. What is interesting is that the British people did not pick anyone in the end. Whatever happens next for Gordon and me, our family will be fine, and so all the emphasis now goes on smoothing the way for whatever takes place in the office downstairs.

Monday 10th May

Following Gordon's own discussions with Liberal Democrat leader Nick Clegg and his colleagues, Gordon proposes that in the event of an agreement with Labour he will step down as Prime Minister within a matter of weeks at the latest. There is a natural expectation that the majority of Liberal Democrats would prefer this option in order to maintain a government with progressive politics and, of course, based on matters of principle over issues like Europe.

Gordon steps outside the black Number 10 door on his own to address the large media mass with a statement confirming that he would make way for his successor in September, and hopes that this opens the way for a Labour–Liberal Democrat agreement.

Throughout the building, everyone waits for the final outcome. Gordon continues his discussions throughout the day. He and I talk more about the scenario for our final departure, and agree privately that we will leave as a family. I have already talked to the boys from the start of the election about the different outcomes and, although young – John is now six, and Fraser is nearly four – they are ready to leave if we need to go. I am neither anxious nor worried about what will happen – everything now has its own momentum and I will just adapt as we go along. I know that as a family we will be together and all will be fine for us, which is my priority right now.

*

I talk from time to time with the various members of Gordon's team. They are amazingly strong and resolute, and holding out patiently during the long waits between discussions.

Tuesday 11th May

As the day progresses, Gordon holds numerous conversations on the telephone with Nick Clegg. I pop down to his office intermittently to get a mood reading; at one point he comes upstairs and tells me that we should now get ready to go although nothing is yet final.

I use that moment to gather together Jeremy Heywood, Sue Nye and Justin Forsyth in the Number 11 sitting room close to Gordon's open-plan office. I explain to them that Gordon and I will leave together, with the boys. Jeremy confirms that he will gather together the staff in the hall and along the corridors as is traditional. Sue and Justin talk through the detailed arrangements for departing Downing Street and continuing on to the Palace. It is very useful to have Justin there as he was present for the Blairs' departure three years earlier.

I change quickly into a teal green Osman dress and put on some make-up, but realise time is short and I want to thank my team before I go. I don't have any real time to say goodbye to what has been our home for the last three years, but do see Gil and Konrad who will stay behind to get a removals company organised and working quickly. This is something that we need to arrange person-ally so we have prepared a plan, but have yet to put it into action.

Mela has got the boys ready upstairs in the flat and we have a very emotional goodbye with Clare Cains, who has been our housekeeper for many years in Downing Street. The boys managed a quick goodbye to their own bedrooms and I promise them that all their toys and favourite duvet covers will be packed up fast and they will see them all again soon. We already have a small bag of much-loved action figures out in the car, ready to see them through the next few days. The boys are very calm and seem to be keeping up with all that is happening. I go downstairs to Gordon's office, and Mela follows with the boys very soon after.

Everyone in the private office seems rather stunned as events start to move very quickly. Gordon has his final conversation with Nick Clegg on the telephone. As it has become clear that no resolution is in sight from the Lib-Dem side, it is Gordon who draws the conversation to a conclusion. He simply explains, as several of the aides listen in on phone extensions, that there is no further time to wait while Clegg wrestles with his difficult decision. It is time now to move, and to let a new government start work.

With the decision taken, the boys and I join Gordon in the centre of his office with his closest team around – both political aides and the core team of hard-working loyal civil servants, too. Gordon speaks to thank everyone from the bottom of his heart for their hard work, their support and most of all their friendship to us as a family. John and Fraser stand on a desktop to see everyone gathered around in a big circle.

It is a highly charged moment, and when Gordon finishes talking and the clapping subsides, I don't dare speak to anyone for fear of my voice cracking or tears falling. I recognise entirely that it is our time to go, but I realise, too, that this sadly means we are leaving behind close colleagues, some of whom we may not see again. Some of the staff are visibly very upset and it is tough not to join in. They can all be very proud of the contribution they have made to the government in these past few years, through some historic times.

As we get ready to leave for the last time, we say our goodbyes to the team standing there and many of them walk with us out of the big private office. Gordon gives a special handshake to Jeremy Heywood and James Bowler who have been at the centre of his office, and who will now pave the way for the new administration, within a matter of hours. Sir Gus O'Donnell has joined the gathering too, and Gordon shakes his hand, thanking him for the many years they have worked together. I think Gus and I understand that I still feel some hurt over recent events and hope to have a moment to make up another day.

We walk to the hallway of Number 10 shaking hands and hugging the many staff gathered there. I can't quite cope with the level of emotion and hang back a bit behind Gordon, recognising that this is his big departure more than mine at this moment. Mela takes the boys' hands to keep them back in the hallway just a while longer, while Gordon and I step outside to the waiting cameras.

From here we will take the car to Buckingham Palace where Gordon will meet the Queen to formally resign as Prime Minister, move on to the Labour Party Headquarters to address the staff and resign the Labour Party Leadership, opening up a new contest there, and then we will board a plane home to Scotland.

On the street in front of Number 10, Gordon steps up to the microphone while I stand to one side, to watch and hear him speak. He says, 'There is a strong, progressive majority in Britain. I wish, more than I could possibly say, that I could have mobilised that majority to carry the election.' He continues, 'I wish the next Prime Minister well as he makes important choices for the future,' and adds, 'Above all, it was a privilege to serve. And yes, I loved the job.'

He ends his speech saying, 'As I leave the second most important job I could ever hold, I cherish even more the first – as a husband and father. Thank you and goodbye.'

As he finishes speaking, we both turn round. Gordon steps up into the entrance of the doorway to take the boys' hands. John comes out cautiously and holds my hand, taking in the sight of all the cameras, followed by Fraser, who skips out as he grabs his dad's hand. The two boys link hands together and as a family we bid Downing Street goodbye and set off down the road as the black door closes behind us.

We go straight into the waiting car and can see waving crowds lining the entrance to Downing Street as we pass through the black gates. Gordon looks quite relaxed but not yet smiling. He asks me if the boys are okay in the car behind, which is following us. It is time for him to attend to one last duty in meeting the Queen, and returning to me as just Gordon Brown, MP for Kirkcaldy and Cowdenbeath, and my lovely husband.

While we may not have won this election, we certainly did not bring about the doom and disaster that was predicted. There is a great array of talent in the Labour Party and I feel confident already that there is a bright future ahead in winning power for Labour again.

Whatever happens now, and whatever the future holds, we did what we promised to do. We did our utmost – and did it for the country with great effort, huge pride and tremendous love for the British people.

Epilogue

'Everyone can be great because everyone can serve.'
Martin Luther King

Entering Number 10 as the wife of the Prime Minister, I held certain expectations and had set myself goals. I think I met my goals but none of my expectations were quite as I had forecast – but, truthfully, when are they ever in life?

My goals as I walked through the door were fairly simple. I intended to keep our family life ordinary during some extraordinary times; to support Gordon politically, diplomatically and personally; and to create for myself a role that contributed to the causes that matter to me. I knew to expect the unexpected, but both the highs and the lows exceeded anything I might have imagined. I achieved a lot for those causes as well, but I am all too aware that there is so much more to do.

I set out to write this book just weeks after leaving Downing Street. I wanted to set everything down while it was fresh in my mind. In writing my story, I used my very detailed schedule, my own notes, emails, letters and the wonderfully detailed files prepared for my overseas visits by Konrad, Christianne and myself. I spent the summer after leaving Number 10 writing it all down, and then took time off with the family so I could return to it afresh for a vigorous edit. I decided not to let the benefit of hindsight enter the book – I thought it was important and more valuable to the reader to be able to hear about life as it happened, and how it felt, on a daily basis. So, of course, any errors of judgement really are my own. Not enough time has yet passed to figure out how some of my perceptions and assessments will alter, but I do look back now knowing the outcome of the election and all that has followed since.

I think for spouses at Downing Street, the role changes as the world changes. Each person can make their unique contribution and, given that it is not a paid job, is fully entitled to do as much or as little with their time there as they want. It is a tough life for a family in many ways, but in others a life of great privilege. None of us is dragged there; we all willingly volunteer.

Gordon, John, Fraser and I walked out of the front door in front of a bank of cameras and reporters. From there we made our way home to Scotland to look forward to the next phase of our life. First, the boys had to finish their term at their wonderful nursery and school in London and say goodbye to friends and teachers as the summer holidays began. Gordon had to set up a new parliamentary office as the re-elected Member of Parliament for Kirkcaldy and Cowdenbeath in Fife. Our home in Scotland really is the place we love to be, so we enjoyed the summertime there, spending a lot of time with each other and visiting family and friends. Gordon set down his perspective on the global financial crisis and published his account before the end of the year. The boys started a new school and settled into their new life seemingly effortlessly, but still keep in firm contact with their friends in London with holiday visits and sleepovers.

While neither of us has made any fast or firm decisions about our future, we both still want to remain involved with some of the varied campaigns and causes in which we believe passionately. So we have established the Office of Gordon and Sarah Brown as a base, and have a fantastic small and dedicated team who contribute so much to our overall enterprise. I remain passionately involved with PiggyBankKids, the cause so close to my heart. We will shortly be launching a new appeal to expand our successful medical research laboratory and ensure the continuity of its brilliant work. I have kept my focus on the maternal mortality campaign, increasing my role as chair of the Leadership Group on Maternal and Infant Health and working closely with the White Ribbon Alliance. I am also figuring out how best to help the UK charities of which I am Patron – focusing on women's and family health, domestic violence, cancer care and education.

Our new website www.gordonandsarahbrown.com acts as a gateway to all we are doing, and keeps a wider audience up to date with our most recent activities. We started at the end of 2010 with the Jobs and Justice Campaign. This will continue to be a feature of much activity – our work has taken us all over the world, and time and again these are the two things we hear are the most urgently needed.

The snow has come early to Scotland this year and I have just emerged from nine days of being snowed in – no car, no school, no airports and few trains. I have spent my days out sledging and building snowmen with legions of small boys, and my evenings looking over my manuscript. I am more rested than I have been for months, but truthfully I feel a bit exhausted just re-reading about my life in the past few years.

Looking back I am very unclear how I managed as much with small children, but then lots of mums can say that. I do recognise just how determined I was not to let my time at Number 10 slip by without taking part in whatever was happening politically day by day.

Right now I am able to be with our boys more and I want to keep it that way. I am honoured to have had the many experiences I have had, and hope I have made best use of the opportunity, if imperfectly.

I am aware that the challenge to meet the maternal mortality goal is pressing and still looks at this moment beyond our grasp. In my time in Number 10 I never thought anything was impossible and am not going to start now. Of course, there is a bigger picture. I see Britain and the rest of the world struggle to regain its balance after the financial crash, and recognise the great challenge ahead of us all to create millions of jobs globally. However,

I am optimistic we can learn to work together as a world, and we will together achieve a better life for everyone. I will continue to play my part.

Sarah Brown
North Queensferry
December 2010

Acknowledgements and Thanks

It goes without saying that as this book carries a very personal perspective every mistake here will be of my own doing. I take every responsibility, but know that I would not have made the journey through Downing Street, engaged with many important campaigns, visited all kinds of interesting parts of Britain, and numerous other countries around the globe, hosted many visitors and charity events at Number 10, and been able to achieve my top priority, looking after my family, without the help of others.

First of all I thank Gil McNeil for her wonderful and lasting friendship and shared commitment to our causes, not least of which is her stewardship of PiggyBankKids. I also owe all my achievements during working hours to my exceptional hardworking, loyal and inspirational Number 10 team: Konrad Caulkett, Beth Dupuy, her successor Christianne Cavaliere, and Pauline Pennington who started off the work on the in-tray. At PiggyBankKids I also thank Victoria Keene, Joe Hewitt, Hugo Tagholm and Emma Briggs. And Emma Parry for joining me to help launch the maternal mortality campaign. I also thank the long-suffering partners of my Number 10 team: Victoria Jonson, Josh Dupuy and Celedonio Moncayo, and, of course, Gil's fabulous son Joe McNeil.

In helping make everything work smoothly, my gratitude also goes to: firstly, Mela Darby, our wonderful nanny, who stayed with us through every week to help look after our boys, and her family Carol, Glyn, Steve and Claire, Tim, Vicki, Bea and Mimi for having the boys to stay for some fun weekends. Also to Clare Cains MBE for her role as our Number 10 housekeeper; to Roy Gibbons

MBE for all the driving, and his wife Monica for her patience and care; and to Maggie Betts for assistance on occasion to Clare in the flat. Also to Tessa Dunning, Amelia Sales, Nicola Mackinnon and Megan Dyce for the extra babysitting.

My gratitude to those who enabled me to continue to work with PiggyBankKids and for constant friendship: Lord Swraj Paul, his wife Aruna and their family, for a long-standing relationship with the Brown family and taking the Chair of PiggyBankKids.

David Boutcher, secretary of PiggyBankKids, and my wise counsel, adviser and friend. Greg Jordan and the Reed Smith law firm who house the charity and allow us use of great facilities. Anne-Marie Piper who keeps us right with top legal guidance. And to all the PiggyBankKids Trustees who give their time and share ideas: Baroness Mary Goudie, Jim O'Neill, Helen Scott Lidgett and Arabella Weir.

The 10 Downing Street staff is a big team and all of it fits together to make up the smooth-running machine that is the Prime Minister's office. From the private office to the press office, the garden rooms to the switchboard, the policy team to Events and Visits, facilities, IT, digital media, the cleaners, the messengers, the porters, the café staff, the custodians, the Metropolitan Police, everyone makes a difference every day in the job that they do. For my part, I am grateful to them all for their service, but there are numerous individuals I want to thank personally for their contribution to my activities and/or their support for our family as we lived above their workspace.

From the civil service: Sir Gus O'Donnell, Jeremy and Suzanne Heywood, James Bowler, the super-efficient Leeanne Johnston who managed Gordon's diary for many years, Sue Gray, Sir Jon Cunliffe, Simon Macdonald and Tom Fletcher. Simon King, Nick Catsaris, Christina Scott, Gila Sacks, Matthew Style, Michael Lea, and Kirsty O'Brien. Helen Etheridge, Barbara Burke and Charlotte Todman. Eric Hepburn, Anne Marie Lavery, David 'Heat Heat' Heaton and Mark Antoniou. And Penny Johnson at the Government Art Collection.

From the political team: Sue Nye who also has been my long-time friend, David Muir, Justin Forsyth, Gavin Kelly, Nick Pearce, Dan Corry, Greg Beales, Stewart Wood, Brendan Cox, Matt Cavanagh, Stephen Carter, Jennifer Moses, Oona King, Jo Dipple, Patrick Diamond, Theo Bertram, Stuart Hudson, Nick Butler, Anthony Vigor, Richard Lloyd, Michael Jacobs, Rachel Kinnock, Lisa Perrin. And Joe Irvin, Fiona Gordon, Jonathan Ashworth, Jill Cuthbertson, Clare Moody, Rachel Maycock, Ayesha Hazarika, Lisa Stephens and Anna Yearley. And Kirsty McNeill and Nicola Burdett for their dedication and hard work then and now.

From the Number 10 press team at various different times: Michael Ellam, Simon Lewis, Damian McBride, Michael Dugher, John Woodcock, Iain Bundred, Katie Martin and the press office team, and Balshen Izzet. From the IT and digicoms teams who put up with my tweeting, blogging and updates on the Number 10 website with enthusiasm and creative ideas aplenty: Ian Green, Mike Porter, Mark Flanagan, Catherine Wilson, and Richard Lewis for all his pictures.

And a big thanks for endless small kindnesses that made such a difference: Glen Baxter, Steve Newbound (look after the blue turtle), and the rest of the Front of House team, Michael, Ann, Pauline, Olly, Scott and Charlotte; and to Alf Smith and Jilly Hume, and everyone on Switch.

A thank you to 'those people who': For superb catering, Nicola Hayes and her Creative Cooking team who blend great service with great food, and Juliet Graham who had all the right personal – and tasty – touches. And to Alison Price for the Carla Bruni-Sarkozy lunch, Anton Mosimann for the state room dinner for President George W Bush, Jamie Oliver and his apprentices for the G20 leaders' dinner, and the Government Hospitality Service for many occasions. Each and every meal was delicious. For immaculate service, Kwame Adu-Gyamfi. For keeping the Number 10 garden so perfect and introducing vegetable and bee boxes, Paul, Jane, Guilleme and the Royal Parks Agency team. For making many children smile, Matthew Arnold (aka Mr Marvel). For helping me stay fit and able in a Pilates-like way, Sian Williams and Aud Aasbo. For making gifts and ways to entertain guests so perfectly, Mary and Philip Contini of Valvona and Crolla, Ozwald Boateng, Kelly Hoppen, Nippers of Edinburgh, Bombki, McQueens florist, Rococo chocolates, Charbonnel and Walker, and Fortnum & Mason. For great official photographs that stand the test of time, Tom Miller. For our unique Christmas cards displaying the Number 10 door: illustrator Shirley Hughes, and photographers Lottie Davies and Jordan Mary.

To everyone who contributed to the protection of the Prime Minister and the wider team, you risk yourselves in service and we appreciate all you do. Many thanks to Peter Cole, Jon Wild and Dave Gardner, Stuart Lockwood, Alan Earl, Gary Richmond, Craig Rowe, Andy Wilkinson, Ken Gambrill and Dave Gardner (and their patient families) and to those who served past and present as detectives, drivers and on those famous bikes with the woo-woos and blue flashing lights. Our gratitude also goes to Norma Graham, Chief Constable of Fife, and her team led by Inspector Gordon Penman, including Inspector Stevie Gray and Sergeant Kenny Wilson. Thank you all for what you do, whatever the weather.

Of course, I thank all the Cabinet Ministers, Ministers and Labour Members of Parliament and particularly, for me, Gordon's own Parliamentary Private Secretaries: Ann Keen, Angela Smith, Anne Snelgrove, Jon Trickett and Alison McGovern. And I thank Neil and Glenys Kinnock for political friendship across many years.

I thank my friend and Downing Street neighbour Maggie Darling, and her family, Alistair, Anna and Calum, and the late Sybil who came to stay. And I would especially like to include for very special mention, and express my appreciation for, all the other Cabinet spouses and spouses of our Members of Parliament, past and present. I know just what a public service you all provide, and what personal support you give, while running your own busy lives.

Our political team expanded when the election was called and I would like to thank our additional members of the campaign team: Victoria Mitchell, Anna Turley, Rhiannon Wilson, Wesley Ball,

Jonathan Pearce, Kenny Young, Ciaran Ward, Matthew Doyle, Tom Price and Caroline Adams who looked after me personally on the campaign trail; Sue Macmillan and Adam Dustagheer for their great work on new media throughout, and Dominic Campbell and Merici Vinton for helping me with their digital media wizardry. And Will Straw at Left Foot Forward and Alex Smith at Labour List for their work to engage more people with progressive ideas.

A huge thank you for being a great General Secretary, Ray Collins (and his partner Raphael). The Labour Party Vice-Treasurer, Nigel Doughty, and wife Lucy, whose support of the party made a positive difference. David and Susie Sainsbury whose generosity over many years has been of the greatest help to the party. And John and Pauline Prescott for tireless campaigning, support and friendship.

And all the Labour Party staff whose loyalty and hard work is second to none. Thank you to Stewart Till and Mark Lucas for the great films and to Sean Pertwee for that compelling performance in the best party political broadcast ever.

Our family enjoyed relaxing times at Chequers and we were able to entertain great Heads of State too. My thanks to all the serving Chairs of Trustees of Chequers during our time: Baroness Valerie Amos, Baroness Cathy Ashton and Baroness Jan Royall as they each served the government as the Leader of the House of Lords. All the wonderful staff and former staff at Chequers including Alan and Diane Lavender, Pat Evans, Harvey Shelton and David McCormick. And Rodney Melville and the Trustees and former Trustees of Chequers as well as the police service who protect the house and grounds.

Keeping a personal life is so important during the busiest of times, and I want to thank my 'oldest' friends who stick with me through all the years, through good times and bad times: Ailsa, Caitlin, Fiona, Sara, Jane, Suzy, Zim, Kathryn and Bethany. Heartfelt thanks to Emma Freud for staying by my side on the maternal mortality campaign from the start, and also to her and Richard Curtis, Jo Kaye and Paul Greengrass, Tracey Macleod and

Harry Ritchie, David Morrissey and Esther Freud and all their families for a memorable and very fun summer holiday in Suffolk. And other close friends and newer friends from recent times who were there at different moments to make both me and Gordon laugh and help with all my requests time and time again: Vivienne and Alan Dyce and family, Jo Rowling and Neil Murray and family, Kathy Lette and Geoff Robertson, Piers Morgan and Celia Walden, Nicola and Jon Mendelsohn, John Roberts and Tom Thorpe, Heather McGregor, Penny Smith, Mariella Frostrup, Amy Gadney, Lynn Forrester de Rothschild, Susan Boster and Anthony Simpson, Sally Ann Lasson and Simon Kelner, Trudie Styler, Lisa Aziz, Charlie Whelan and Philippa Clark, Michael Cashman and Paul Cottingham, Elsa McAlonan and Murdoch Maclennan, Barbara and Ken Follett, Angela Forrester and Larry Whitty, Jane Tewson, MT Rainey, Amanda Rayner, Victoria Chilcott, Joan Armatrading, Annie Lennox, Zainab Salbi, Gurinder Chadha and Paul Barges, Kim Cattrall, Carol Ann Duffy, Bonnie Greer, June Sarpong, Amy Lamé, Lucy Kneebone, William and Nadine Benn, Neil and Laura Ashton, Mark and Sue Pittman, John and Victoria Cadogan-Rawlinson, Sally Bercow, Davina McCall, Julia and James Ogilvy, Jenny Halpern Prince, Flic Howard-Allen, Paul and Alison Myners, Angad and Michelle Paul, Sam Taylor-Wood, Wendy Mandy, Eric Salama, Lord Waheed Alli and Charlie Parsons, Baroness Liz Symons, Alastair Campbell and Fiona Millar (with special thanks for the early advice), Gail Rebuck and Phillip Gould, Eddie Izzard, David Tennant and Georgia Moffet, Richard Wilson, Martha Lane Fox and Chris Gorrell Barnes, Trevor Beattie, Jo Brand, Lesley Garrett and Peter Christian, Darren and Sara Dein, Claudia Winkleman, Kirsty Young and Nick Jones, Clive Jones and Vicky Heywood, David and Susan Davies, Jane Zuckerman, Ed Owen, Sabrina Guinness, Beeban Kidron and Lee Hall, Antony Gormley and Vicken Parsons, Lucy Parker, Alan Parker and Louise Charlton.

My friends who are also Gordon's long-standing friends (and which is how I know them): Colin and Ann Currie, Lord Wilf

Stevenson and Ann Minogue and Iona, Tobin and Flora Stevenson (who let us have Mela), Shriti Vadera, Carolyn Choa and the late beloved Anthony Minghella, Tom and Siobhan Watson, Ian Austin and Cath Miles, Murray Elder, Nick Brown, Michael and Gaynor Watt, Jeffrey and Penny Lent, Ronnie and Julie Stevenson, Rosemary Spence, Duncan and Jo Bannatyne, James and Aisha Caan, Sir Magdi Yacoub, Sir Martin and Lady (Esther) Gilbert, Sir Ronnie and Lady (Sharon) Cohen, Mervyn and Jeanne Davies, Ara and Wendy Darzi, Alan and Rosie West, Lord and Lady Sugar and all those GOATS.

And our great friends in the USA: Marylouise Oates and Bob Shrum, John Sexton, Tammy Haddad, Ted, Rachel and David Greenberg, Ambassador Louis and Marjorie Susman, Kathy Hendricks, Andrea Mitchell and Dr Alan Greenspan, Vicki Kennedy and her beloved late husband, Senator Edward M Kennedy, Tim Shriver and Linda Potter, Maria Shriver and Katherine Schwarzenegger, David Mixner, Arianna Huffington, Connie Milstein and JC de la Hay St Hilaire, and Gretel Truong.

For my online life, I am grateful to MLF for introducing me to Twitter, Biz Stone for explaining its full potential, and all my Twitter followers for our ongoing conversation. Thanks also to Carrie Longton and Justine Roberts for creating a great forum at Mumsnet ☺

For their support of me in taking on the maternal mortality campaign in the UK: Professor Anthony Falconer, Professor Jim Dornan, Sir Sabaratnam Arulkumuran, Lord Narin Patel, Peter Carter, Cathy Warwick, Dr Nynke van der Broek and Dr Anthony Costello. I thank Carla Bruni-Sarkozy for using her voice on her visit to London to speak up for mothers' and infants' health, and for her continuing focus as Ambassador of the Global Fund to campaign for the prevention of Mother to Child Transmission of HIV/AIDS. I thank all the First Ladies and spouses of serving Presidents and Prime Ministers whom I spent time with at our international meetings. Their kindness and friendship will always be remembered and their unequivocal support for the maternal mortality campaign. The US First Lady Michelle Obama was also gracious in supporting my wider work including her memorable visit to the Maggie's London centre.

For supporting me on the international stage and encouraging me to raise my voice: Secretary-General Ban Ki-moon and Ban Soon-taek, Robert Zoellick and Ngosi Okonjo-Iweala, Dr Margaret Chan, Ambassador Ray Chambers, Ambassador Mark Dybul, Thérèse Rein, Melanne Verveer, Professor Lynn Friedman, Dr Ann Starrs, Lord Nigel Crisp, Susanna Edjang, Ann Veneman, Anita McBride, Liya Kibede, Christy Turlington Burns, Dorothy Rowe, Hamid Rushwan, Flavia Bustreo, Dr Monir Islam, Maria Eitel, Mabel van Orange, Frances Donnay, Cindy Lewis and, with great admiration, Melinda Gates.

And all of us walk humbly in the steps of the late Professor Allan Rosenfield when it comes to maternal, newborn and child health.

For joining the leadership group for Maternal and Newborn Health, I thank my co-chair, Bience Gawanas, and our group members. A special thanks is due to Prime Minister Jens Stoltenberg for backing the group, and to his wonderful adviser Tore Godal for making it happen, and for his wise counsel. The Important Dinners for Women were a central feature of the maternal mortality campaign, and I thank Matthew Freud for creating a memorable and special platform both in Davos and New York, and Freud Communications especially Kate Garvey and Hannah Cameron. The greatest thanks goes to Wendi Murdoch for conceiving the early idea, and to championing the events each year, and to Her Majesty Queen Rania Al-Abdullah and Indra Nooyi as the co-hosts. Together you created awesome occasions.

What a WPM wears is under constant scrutiny. I bear total and full responsibility for anything that did not bear up under the glare as I suspect someone somewhere gave me better advice before I dressed to go out. I did wear some wonderful dresses and coats and hats – and all credit goes to the designers and retailers. For the designers whose clothes (and hats) I wore with such pleasure: Graeme Black, Erdem Moragliu, Osman Yosefyada, Ben

De Lisi, Jasper Conran, Britt Lintner, Amanda Wakeley, Stephen Jones, Linda Bennett, Deborah Lloyd at Kate Spade, Belinda Earl and Shailina Patel at Jaeger and Misa Hirada, and for the gorgeousness of jewellers Garrard, La Diosa and Astley Clarke. And for guiding me around M&S, Tania Littlehales. My thanks to the British Fashion Council for inviting me to join them in their efforts to promote our fine creative industry, especially Harold Tillman CBE, Chair of the British Fashion Council and his CEOs, Caroline Rush and Simon Ward and their predecessors Sir Stuart Rose and Hilary Riva CBE, and thanks to Louise Carter and Jane Boardman for guiding me around each London Fashion Week. I also thank each and every supermodel who ever posed with me for a charity photograph, especially Naomi Campbell, who generously brought Fashion for Relief behind a life-saving cause. And Erin O'Connor, Caryn Franklin and Debra Bourne whose All Walks Beyond the Catwalk opens up a whole new world of beauty to appreciate. And personal thanks to Glenda Bailey MBE for her wisdom and top tips.

To the editors who let me take over their publications: Jane Johnson at *Fabulous* magazine (and to Jools Oliver and Elle MacPherson who let me interview them); to Richard Wallace and Tina Weaver at the *Mirror* and *Sunday Mirror* respectively for letting me on to their pages. And to them both for keeping the faith through the election, together with John Mullin at the *Independent on Sunday*. For the magazine and newspaper editors who invited me to take part in their awards, events and activities: Louise Court, Jo Elvin, Sam Baker, Lorraine Candy, Dawn Alford, Jane Bruton, Lucy Yeomans, Trish Halpin, Lindsay Nicholson, Nicky Cox, and at *Guardian Society*, David Brindle, and, of course, Peter Willis and the Pride of Britain team at the *Mirror*.

For the charities I have worked so closely with: Charles Jencks, Nigel Cayzer, Laura Lee, Marcia Blakenham, and the Maggie's Centre teams and the Joy of Living boards for Cheltenham, Oxford, Nottingham, Swansea and Newcastle, and everyone at Maggie's Fife. Thank you, too, to Ferzana Barclay for championing Maggie's so brilliantly. Brigid McConville, Theresa Shaver, Betsey McCallon, Maeve Shearlaw, James Cox at the White Ribbon Alliance, and Jo Cox for her directorship of the maternal mortality campaign, and Karmarama for their 'hot' advertising from tattoo parlours to 'mum's cafés'. Sir Victor Blank, Eve Pollard, Professor Lesley Regan, Liz Campbell, and the Wellbeing of Women team, especially everyone who contributed to the Patron's advisory board. Nicola Harwin and the Women's Aid team, Gordon and Tana Ramsay for initiating the annual gala dinners, Rankin for his photos for the first big Women's Aid campaign (and so many other great campaigns, too). And to Duncan Bannatyne and the Real Men who signed up to the campaign to combat domestic violence, and to Grey Advertising for the creative idea. And the Corporate Advisory Board who all work so hard to make the greatest difference to the charity every year. Stephen Shields and the SHINE Trust team led by Jim O'Neill who have opened up such great opportunities for learning for young people.

The team at the Jennifer Brown Research Laboratory: Professor Andrew Calder, Dr Ian Laing, Dr Rhona Hughes, Professor Jane Norman, Dr Henry Jabbour, and the rest of the advisory team. All our young scientists, past and present, who dedicate their working lives to saving young lives, and our champions, especially Jennifer and Iain Macfarlane. And for their leadership at the University of Edinburgh to make the laboratory possible, Professor Sir Timothy O'Shea and Professor Sir John Savill. My gratitude also goes to Dr Tahir Mahmood and the Fife teams supporting the community projects at the Forth Park, Victoria and Queen Margaret hospitals.

On international visits, many people were involved in making our trips so successful, and for enabling me to have a busy and active programme each time. I am very grateful to all the Ambassadors, High Commissioners and their spouses, and their staff who looked after us.

In London, my responsibility for hosting the G20 spouse programme was only possible with the wonderful assistance of two of our finest cultural leaders, so my eternal gratitude goes to Tony

Hall and Deborah Bull at the Royal Opera House and all the wonderful performers; I also thank Alexandra Shulman, Lucinda Chambers and Mario Testino for images to treasure; and all our brilliant guests at the G20 spouses' dinner. And the team at Maggie's London for hosting the US First Lady Michelle Obama as well as Richard and Ruthie Rogers, the late Rose Gray, Dan Pearson, and centre Patron Janet Ellis and her daughters Martha, who makes spectacular cup cakes, and Sophie who sings.

Our home and family are so important to us and I have many people I cherish very much in our lives. In Fife: Alex Rowley and family, Jim Metcalfe and Sarah Miller and baby Rosa, Marilyn and Pete Livingstone, Helen and Bob Eadie, Rhona White, Jayne Baxter, George and Liz Mcluskie, Margaret O'Sullivan, and John Rowan, everyone at North Queensferry Church, at the Victoria Hospice, and the wonderful, loyal support of our Fife friends, party members and the communities of Kirkcaldy, Cowdenbeath, Lochgelly, Kelty, Ballingry, Lochore, Crossgates, Dalgety Bay, Burntisland, Kinghorn and Aberdour, as well as Inverkeithing and North Queensferry.

Gordon's family and my own have been extraordinarily supportive through the last few years – they always are, but it cannot have been easy for them. My love and gratitude goes to: Pauline Macaulay and Patrick Vaughan; Sean, Caroline, Isabel and Honor Macaulay; Nico Vaughan, Ruth, Sam and Luke Tosh, and Megan Vaughan; Bruce, Sarah and Fergus Macaulay; Kit Vaughan and Ruth Fuller, and 'Uncle' John Vaughan; 'Auntie' Doreen Boyce and to Trevor Boyce and Caroline Boyce Neri and their families; my godmother Irene Skolnick; and to all of Patrick's family especially Mark Vaughan and Christina Shewell.

From Gordon's side: his 'big' brother John and Angela Brown, Karen, Paul and Mary Dickson; Jonathan, Helen and Finlay Brown. And 'little' brother Andrew, and Clare, Alex and Patrick Brown (Clare was there for me any time I called for help whether babysitting or accompanying me to an event – and defended us all in her magnificent article during the expenses crisis). And in

Ireland my beloved dad's family and so mine too, Elizabeth MacAulay, Patrick and Carolina, and Iain Alasdhair.

I am enormously grateful to the wonderful team at Ebury Publishing who have steered me through the writing and editing of this book with great wisdom, patience and enthusiasm: Fiona MacIntyre (who understood from the start how I should tell my story), Charlotte Cole (who has been diligent beyond the call of duty through many proofs), Rae Shirvington (for handling the rights with her usual professionalism), as well as a great sales team: Hannah Telfer, Colin Thomas, Han Ismail, Hannah Grogan and Sarah Collett; excellent marketing team, Di Riley and Louise Jones, and Katie Johnson for handling digital media; and the wonderful publicity team who have spent many hours with me: Sarah Bennie and Ed Griffiths; and for patient assistance behind the scenes, Joy Chambers and Kasi Collins. Thanks too to Belinda Jones for a top copy-editing job addressing my grammar deficiencies. And to Chris McCafferty and Gemma Dudley at Kaper for their social media work. And to Kate Thomas for producing the audio book and Tom Johnson for engineering.

My final thanks goes to the people who are at the centre of my life and whom I love so very very much: Gordon, John and Fraser.

Appendix – Charities

You can follow Sarah Brown on Twitter on @SarahBrownUK and follow her work on www.gordonandsarahbrown.com.

PiggyBankKids

www.piggybankkids.org
Twitter: @piggybankkids

PiggyBankKids is about changing children's lives. Every single child is precious and unique. At PiggyBankKids we work hard to give children the best possible chance of living a healthy and happy life, here in the UK. We want to help as many children as we can: from the vulnerable babies whose lives could be saved with the right scientific breakthroughs, to those kids and young people who have the hardest start in life.

The charity was founded in 2002 to help inspiring professionals continue their world-changing work in saving and transforming children's lives.

The Jennifer Brown Research Fund

http://piggybankkids.org/our-projects/jennifer-brown-research-fund

The researchers at the groundbreaking Jennifer Brown Research Laboratory are working to solve some of the most devastating pregnancy problems and find better ways to look after premature babies.

White Ribbon Alliance

www.whiteribbonalliance.org
Twitter: @WRAGLOBAL

The White Ribbon Alliance for Safe Motherhood is an international coalition of individuals and organisations formed to promote increased public awareness of the need to make pregnancy and childbirth safe for all women and newborns in the developing, as well as developed, countries.

The white ribbon is dedicated to the memory of all women who have died in pregnancy and childbirth. In some cultures, white symbolises mourning and in others it symbolises hope and life. The white ribbon represents this dual meaning globally. The White Ribbon Alliance not only works to sustain life and hope for all women, but also mourns and honours those women who did not survive their pregnancy or childbirth.

The White Ribbon Alliance represents an opportunity for individuals, organisations and new partnerships to work together to advance women's health and women's rights everywhere. Everyone can play their part.

Since its launch in 1999, the White Ribbon Alliance has been a leader among those holding governments and institutions to account for the tragedy of maternal mortality. With members in 148 countries, WRA is amplifying the voices of people suffering from the greatest burden of morbidity and mortality of complications due to pregnancy and childbirth.

Other related campaigns can be found at:

Maternal Mortality Campaign

www.whiteribbonalliance.org/GlobalMaternalMortality.cfm

Half the Sky

(from the book by Nicholas Kristof and Sheryl WuDunn)

www.halftheskymovement.org
Twitter: @nickkristof

Every Mother Counts (the campaign launched by Christy Turlington Burns to address maternal mortality)

www.everymothercounts.org
Twitter: @cturlington

Wellbeing of Women

www.wellbeingofwomen.org.uk
Twitter: @WellbeingofWmen

WELLBEING
OF WOMEN

Wellbeing of Women is a charity that raises money to improve women's health through research, training and education. Established in 1964, we have been raising funds ever since to invest in medical research and the development of specialist doctors and nurses working in the field of reproductive and gynaecological health.

We are the partner charity of the Royal College of Obstetricians and Gynaecologists and a member of the Association of Medical Research Charities.

Women's Aid

women's aid
until women & children are safe
www.womensaid.org.uk

www.womensaid.org.uk
Twitter: @womensaid

Women's Aid is the key national charity working to end domestic violence against women and children. We support a network of over 500 domestic and sexual violence services across the UK.

www.thehideout.org.uk

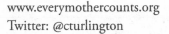

THE HIDEOUT
www.thehideout.org.uk
until children are safe

Women's Aid website for children and young people.

Maggie's Cancer Caring Centres

www.maggiescentres.org
Twitter: @Maggiescentres

A Maggie's Centre is a place to turn to for help with any of the problems, small or large, associated with cancer.

Under one roof, you can access help with information, benefits advice and psychological support, both individually and in groups, with courses and stress-reducing strategies. You don't have to make an appointment, or be referred, and everything we offer is free of charge. It is there for anybody who feels the need for help, which includes those who love and look after someone with cancer, who often feel as frightened and vulnerable as those who actually have the disease.

A Maggie's Centre will be many things to many people. It is there for anybody to use in the way they want to. There isn't a one-size-fits-all recipe for how you live with cancer. Everybody needs to find their own way. The job of the professionals at Maggie's is to listen to you, to help you find out what you want and give you the tools to help yourself.

'A community jewel.' Michelle Obama, First Lady of the United States

SHINE Trust

www.shinetrust.org.uk

SHINE: Support and Help in Education was founded in March 1999. Our mission is to support additional educational initiatives, which encourage children and young people to raise their achievement levels. We fund organisations working with underachieving 6–18 year olds from disadvantaged areas in London and Manchester.

About the Author

Sarah Brown is President of the charity PiggyBankKids and Patron of a number of charities including Women's Aid, Maggie's Cancer Caring Centres and SHINE education trust. She is also the Global Patron of the White Ribbon Alliance for Safe Motherhood, a member of the Global Campaign for Education's High-Level Panel, and an international speaker on maternal health and women's issues. She and Gordon have two boys, John and Fraser, and she tweets at www.twitter.com/SarahBrownUK.